Course   TPS1107 Theatre In Society
Department of Theatre and
Performance Studies
KENNESAW STATE UNIVERSITY

http://create.mheducation.com

ISBN-10: 1307090117   ISBN-13: 9781307090116

Contents

Credits

College of the Arts

Department of Theatre and
Performance Studies

The World's a Stage

TPS1107: Theatre in Society

*All the world's a Stage
And all the men and
women merely
players...*

William Shakespeare's
As You Like It *(1623)*

Welcome to TPS1107: Theatre in Society! This class studies the arts as vital and relevant forces in our lives, with particular focus on the art forms of theatre and performance. Through a variety of aesthetic experiences, you will examine elements of theatre and performance and investigate the ways in which they reflect our lives, express varying worldviews, foster community, and deepen our understanding of others. We have designed this custom textbook for you, using select chapters from *The Creative Spirit*, 6th edition, by Stephanie Arnold. Other required texts for the class include specific playscripts chosen by your instructor and tickets to performance events that offer you the essential *live* theatre experience.

We are thrilled that you have chosen to take this class and witness the wonder and diversity of theatre and performance on campus, in community, and in the world at large. Let the playing begin!

Margaret Baldwin, General Education Coordinator
Rick Lombardo, Department Chair
Department of Theatre and Performance Studies

CHAPTER 1

The Impulse to Perform: Origins

As dusk falls, the people gather in the ceremonial house for the Winter Dance. All the members of the community are present, from the oldest to the youngest, as well as honored guests who have arrived by boat to the island village located on a remote waterway. A fire burns in the center of the large dark lodge. Beyond the blazing logs stands a screen painted with images of sea animals, whales and otters and eagles, flickering in the firelight. The screen represents the house of the chief of the undersea kingdom.

A loud, commanding whistle sounds, filling the lodge with its notes and announcing the presence of supernatural forces. A rustling is heard from behind the screen and then a large whale swims into view. Swooping and spouting, the whale glides around the fire, bringing with it the authority of the natural world and an ancient story told many times by the community elders about their ancestor, Born-to-Be-Head-of-the-World. A young man from this village was drawn beneath the sea, where he performed feats of heroism in the undersea kingdom. When he returned, he possessed the knowledge and power of the sea.

A dancer wears the enormous whale mask that recalls one of the forms in which Born-to-Be-Head-of-the-World appeared. The mask is animated by this actor through the movement of his own body and the moving parts of the mask, which the master carver has fashioned for this fantastic creature and which the dancer controls by manipulating strings. The enormous, ferocious mouth drops open and snaps shut. The double tail with flukes, curving forward and back, can be lowered to suggest the motion of a diving whale. An eagle rides on the whale's back and even his wings flap as the whale swims on. Paint and mica make the eyes glow in the firelight and glisten as if they carry drops of water from the sea.

The whale mask shown here was collected by the anthropologist George Hunt in 1901 and would have been used to enact the story of Born-to-Be-Head-of-the-World during the nineteenth century in Hopetown, British Columbia. Made from wood, hide, and rope, this heavy piece, measuring about 7½ feet long and 2½ feet wide, would have required skill and practice to maneuver effectively. This mask is in the collection of the American Museum of Natural History in New York City.

The dancer stops and a further pull of the strings causes the entire face of the whale to give way and open to reveal another presence inside, a large bullhead fish (a sculpin), carved and painted to be both fish and man. This transforming mask and the performance itself are nothing less than a display of the supernatural powers of this community's ancestor, Born-to-Be-Head-of-the-World.[1]

This whale performance is part of the **potlatch** ceremonies of the indigenous peoples of the Pacific Northwest Coast of the United States and the Southwest Coast of Canada, and dates from the nineteenth century and perhaps earlier. It is one example of the many ways storytelling and performance function in almost all human societies. Storytelling is central to the formation of human culture. Myth and metaphor are fundamental, imaginative constructs that we employ to distill human experience. But it is not enough for us to tell our stories through words alone. We are compelled to act them out, to perform our understanding of human behavior and the forces that we believe govern our world. This impulse to perform is an essential part of human nature that appears in our daily interactions as well as in the dramas we put on the stage and on film.

Performance and Human Behavior

If we step back from organized dramas to examine individual behavior, we see that the impulse to perform is part of the way we survive. We adapt to changes in our circumstances by making adjustments in the identity we present to other people. We seek to transform ourselves or to emphasize a compelling characteristic, such as courage or humility, that will carry us safely through danger. The human mind is elastic and imaginative in the construction of identity. Part of growing up depends on observing successful role models and experimenting with identities that make us feel comfortable in the face of changing social pressures or demands. Identity is fluid rather than fixed; we may be one person with our families and quite a different person at work or in public situations. Peer pressure or social conditioning can cause people to adopt various sets of behaviors that make them a recognizable part of a group.

Sometimes we feel that we cannot know certain people until we can break through the masks that they wear to protect themselves or, perhaps, to take us in. Consider on one hand the politician who puts on a different face for every new situation or constituency. We may even doubt that such a person has a core identity at all. On the other hand, we may believe that we cannot really know someone until we

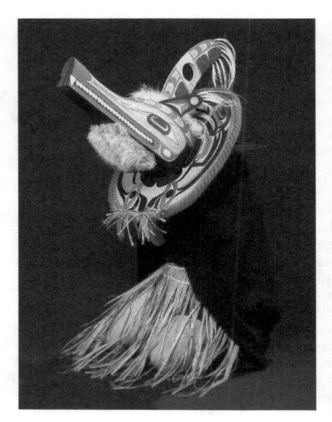 

The mask shown in these photographs represents the continuation of the ceremonial traditions of the Kwakwaka'wakw people in the present day. The artist George Hunt Jr. has resumed the carving practices that were almost lost when the cultural practices of Native peoples were suppressed. Today Hunt Jr. makes masks and costumes for the potlatch ritual, which is observed by coastal Native peoples of Southwestern Canada and Northwestern United States. At its height in the nineteenth century, the potlatch ceremony lasted for days. It was a major social occasion involving the immediate community and many invited guests, and was also an essential means of expressing changes in the social order. Rites of passage for the young, marriages, and mourning cycles were all observed through the potlatch. Dramatic performances were a highlight of these gatherings and included elaborately carved masks, spectacular costumes, and astonishing special effects. The transformation mask in these photographs changes from a wolf, in the first image, to a killer whale, in the second, when the performer pulls on strings threaded through both sides of the wolf's long face.

recognize that he or she is made up of different identities. Certainly we understand the great release in letting go of certain "expectations" of behavior and trying out a role that is "nothing like us." In the theatre, actors build on this fundamental human impulse to perform in order to describe and interpret human existence for an audience. As audience members, we take great pleasure in watching the work of actors who have made an art out of an impulse that is part of human nature.

Performance and Role Playing

We begin our study of the theatre by exploring the place of performance in human behavior. What human needs are met through performance? What are the psychological, social, and cultural conditions that motivate performance? Understanding the functions of performance in our lives provides a basis for approaching the professional performance of the actor, whose work is the essence of the theatre.

These children, living in Iraq, use dramatic play to imitate and interpret the violence that governs their lives.

If we observe children at play, we see that many of them pretend to be the adults who are prominent in their lives. Children often start taking roles by "playing house" or "playing school"—pretending to be parents or teachers. Children living in war zones play out the violence that surrounds them at a very early age. Certainly children's imitation of the behavior they observe is a way of learning about or preparing themselves for roles they expect to assume. But there is more to dramatic play than social conditioning.

Imagine a four-year-old boy going out with his mother. Before leaving the house he insists on putting on his cape and strapping on his sword. Whether he sees himself as Superman, Batman, Spiderman, or the latest incarnation of a superhero, his impersonation is a serious business. At four, he is old enough to know that the world can be a threatening place. He is aware that he is physically small and lacks the skills of older children or adults that would give him more control in a dangerous and confusing environment. So he puts on the costume or "signs" of what he recognizes as power. And through wearing the cape and bearing the sword, he takes on a role that enables him to share in the power of his hero.

We recognize in this small boy's actions a pattern of behavior that occurs in a variety of situations and at different ages. Life is difficult and full of obstacles. In certain situations, we enact roles; we make adjustments in the way we present ourselves, particularly in ways that make us feel more powerful. The small child is not concerned about being obvious as he carts around his sword. He wants threatening forces, whether real or imaginary, to be clear about his new identity. As adults we try to be more subtle as we put on the clothes and accessories of power, assume certain postures, and alter our language or vocal intonation. The actor Bill Irwin, whose work is discussed in Chapter 4, says he approaches many of his characterizations by asking himself two questions: (1) "What am I afraid of right now?" (2) "What are all the mechanisms that I'm putting into play to show that I'm not really afraid of that?"[2]

Community Performance

The story of the little boy and his superhero battle gear is one of many examples of individual role playing. But humans also engage in forms of collective dramatic expression that are fundamental to the community. Through **dramatic rituals** we reinforce community values and act out community stories that preserve a way of life. The term *ritual* refers to a ceremonial observation that is repeated in a specified way in order to confer certain benefits on the participants. Rituals are highly symbolic events with densely coded meanings. There are sacred rituals, and there are distinctly secular rituals. Indeed, some of the richest forms of ritual dramatic expression take place as part of religious observances such as the enactment of the birth of Jesus in the Christian community or the observation of the seder meal at Passover in the Jewish community. The Kwakwaka'wakw whale performance at the beginning of the chapter is part of a traditional religious ritual.

La Carpa del Ausente, the 2007 production for Día de los Muertos at the Miracle Theatre in Portland, Oregon, is shown in this photo. Directed by Philip Cuomo, the production combined vaudeville, acrobatics, and political satire enacted by various skeletal characters. The actors are Daniel Moreno, CarlosAlexis Cruz, Matt Haynes, and Jorge Arredondo.

A ritual that is becoming more prevalent in the United States takes place in communities with a Hispanic heritage. *El día de los muertos,* or the Day of the Dead, is observed at the beginning of November as a way of remembering family members who have died and celebrating their lives. The beliefs that underlie the Day of the Dead come first from Aztec worship and embrace a view in which life and death are seen as part of a continuum. Death is accepted rather than abhorred or denied. By tending to family graves and bringing to the cemetery the food and drink enjoyed by those who have died, "the way is prepared for the spirits to return." Far from being a morbid or sad occasion, the day is filled with humor, music, processions, food, and performances. At this time, comic figures of skeletons appear who are engaged in all the activities of life, bright orange marigolds decorate cemeteries, and special breads take over bakeries.

Olga Sanchez is the artistic director of the Miracle Theatre in Portland, Oregon. Each year this theatre celebrates the Day of the Dead with a musical festival or a play that builds on the more personal observations of families. Sanchez sees the Day of the Dead as a "chance to revisit with your ancestors and acknowledge the people who came before us, to hear of their stories, their sacrifices,

and their values." The connections to the past help to form more meaningful "personal and community identity."[3]

Weddings and graduations exemplify two types of well-known community rituals. In a traditional wedding, a sacred ritual, the bride, the groom, and the attendants wear elaborate and highly ceremonial clothes, and the couple enact their vows according to the custom of their religious faith. Many believe that such a ceremony strengthens the marriage and subsequently the community, whose members participate as witnesses and join in the celebration; they see the wedding ceremony as essential to the stability of the community. Although rituals tend to change slowly because their form needs to be fixed to be effective, they can also be somewhat flexible. One element of the wedding ritual currently undergoing significant change is giving away the bride. At one time this gesture symbolized shifting authority over a woman from her father to her husband. Today other family members or friends may "give the bride away," or the couple may choose to eliminate this custom altogether.

The secular ritual of the high school graduation is of great significance to towns and cities across the United States. The graduation ceremony is a formal rite of passage for the community's young people, a way for them to be accepted into adulthood. Robes and caps are worn; solemn music is played; the graduates accept their diplomas and congratulations and best wishes for the

In this late nineteenth-century photograph, a kachina ritual observation takes place in the plaza of Walpi Village. Walpi Village, on the First Mesa in Arizona, was settled in the ninth century and is the oldest continuously occupied community in the United States. It is striking to compare the dates relating to the development of medieval European theatre presented later in the chapter with the time frame in which performance rituals were evolving on the North American continent. This photo shows only a modest number of participants; other ceremonies could involve many more community members.

future from their community leaders. Most students play their parts with an unusual amount of dignity. To complement the formality of the actual graduation ceremony, many graduating classes develop their own more ecstatic, freer ritual festivities to mark the significance of this event.

Other secular rituals include sporting events, particularly college and professional football games. Sports fans wear costumes and makeup as part of their identification with the drama enacted on the playing field. Beauty pageants, too, are community rituals, as are parades, such as the gay-pride parades that occur in a number of communities and involve many dramatic elements of costume and impersonation.

Community rituals bind community members together by reinforcing their common history and shared goals. They help shape the yearly calendar and the many rites of passage in the human life cycle. Because the United States is made up of many religious faiths and cultural groups, our national rituals tend to be secular, which may be one reason sports have become so important to us. Nonetheless, some community rituals in the United States are a form of worship that interpret religious history or values and also allow for intense identification with the most sacred beliefs of the community. For some communities, dramatic religious rituals are central to community life and govern a great deal of community activity throughout the year. It is from such entrenched dramatic rituals that many of the major dramatic traditions worldwide have evolved.

We turn to the dramatic rituals of a small Native American community, the Hopi, as a source for our further examination of the impulse to perform. This community has been chosen for two primary reasons: the richness of its ceremonial performances and the fact that its rituals—as well as other Native American ceremonial dramas—represent one of the earliest dramatic forms indigenous to our continent.

Ritual Performance Among the Hopi

In an elaborate sequence of dramatic ceremonies, the Hopi Indians of the southwestern United States represent the *kachinas,* whom they view as their spiritual guardians. According to Dorothy K. Washburn, "Kachinas are the messengers and intermediaries between men and gods."[4] The concept of the kachina is associated with the clouds from which rain falls and with the dead, whom the Hopi believe become part of the clouds and return to earth as rain. The Hopi believe that the intervention of the kachinas will bring rain to the arid landscape of the high desert and ensure the success of their crops.

With their brilliant costumes and **masks** incorporating animal and plant images, the ceremonial dramas make the kachina spirits visible to the Hopi community. Because most elements of the costumes and masks have a symbolic meaning, the Hopi figuratively "wear their world" when they are in their ceremonial dress.[5] For example, different colors represent the different geographic and spiritual directions and the weather and resources represented by those directions. Tortoiseshell rattles refer to the water of the ponds and springs where the tortoises live. Eagle and turkey feathers become the flight of prayers.

Kachina Performances

The kachina ceremonies are central to the Hopi worldview and may have originated as early as

The performance of the kachina cycle binds the Hopi community together through the preservation of a belief system and a way of life. Kachina dolls like the one shown here are carved by Hopi artists as a sacred representation of the kachina ritual. The preferred Hopi word for kachina is *katsina* and, in the plural form, *katsinam.*

the twelfth or thirteenth century. There are more than 300 different kachinas, and kachina rituals are spread over much of the year. From December to July a great epic cycle of kachina performances involves all members of the community in varying responsibilities for the ongoing ritual drama. In fact, the Hopi villages are built around the plazas in which the ceremonial dances take place. The kachina performances are at the center of the community physically as well as spiritually and socially.

Soyal, the first observation of the **kachina cycle,** occurs at the winter solstice, in December, to break the darkness and prepare for the new year. *Niman*, the last ceremony, anticipating a successful harvest, occurs in July. Following this final Home Dance, the kachinas are believed to return to the San Francisco Mountains west of the Hopi villages, where they remain until they rejoin the Hopi at the winter solstice. Between the initiation of the cycle in December and the conclusion in July, the kachinas perform a series of ceremonies in which seeds are planted, children are initiated, community members are taught discipline, and, finally, crops are harvested. Rain, fertility, and maintaining social order are the underlying goals of all kachina activity. The dramatic ritual is a highly complex way of exerting control over the environment—that is, the physical, social, and spiritual world.

The kachina ceremonies are frequently serious and sometimes even frightening. But humor is also an essential part of the ritual; laughter is understood as basic to human survival. Clowns appear among the kachinas, and they offer a critique of negative behavior through **parody** by performing outrageous acts that would be unacceptable outside the ritual observation.

The Hopi Performer

The Hopi man who takes on the persona of a kachina is transformed (women do not participate as performers). He transcends his own being and becomes the kachina spirit that he embodies. He takes on the presence and the power of the kachina and therefore can act for the kachina in the ceremonies. Through the ritual dance, a transaction takes place between the human and the supernatural, a merging of the two levels of existence.

Like personal performance, community performance is very much tied to the quest for power. But in sacred community performance in particular, performers become separated from their status as mere mortal beings. They become elevated. By the nature of their special religious knowledge, their enactment of the ceremony, and their performance skills, they become "magicians" who act on behalf of the other members of the community.

Society and Aesthetic Expression

Throughout the world the impulse to perform, to interpret human existence through the presentation of characters on a stage, has evolved into an astonishing variety of theatre traditions. Just as the human capacity for speech has produced many languages, so the impulse to perform has found expression in many distinct forms. In Indonesia shadow puppets play out complicated stories of kings and battles; in

Traditional theatre throughout the East uses various forms of dance as the foundation for storytelling and dramatic expression. The Odissi style of classical dance from eastern India shown here uses elaborate symbolic costumes as well as makeup and ornaments to complement the skills of the dancer, which take many years of training to master. Isa Prieto is a student working to learn a revived form of this temple dance that has been handed down for as long as 2,000 years.

China animal gods fight with demons as actors in highly stylized makeup and costumes perform a combination of sensational gymnastics and martial arts; in India barefoot women with painted faces, hands, and feet perform eloquent dances made up of densely coded, intricate gestures. Sometimes actors speak; sometimes they dance; sometimes they sing. Actors may wear masks or elaborate symbolic costumes, or they may wear the clothes of everyday life. They may inhabit mythical regions, historical locations, or realistic, contemporary environments. They may use elevated speech and gestures or language and actions that correspond with contemporary behavior.

From culture to culture and continent to continent, the theatre responds to the unique worldviews of differing human communities and develops forms of expression that reflect specific community concerns and community aesthetics. By community concerns, we mean the ideas or subjects of theatre performances. By **community aesthetics,** we mean the actual nature of the elements that construct the performance itself, elements that have precise meaning for a particular community and that contribute to the images with which the community describes itself.

For example, the Hopi kachina performances emphasize the importance of the harvest and the place of the entire agricultural process in maintaining social order. The relationship between agriculture, the natural environment, and the social order of the community is shaped by the proper regard for a spiritual presence. This complex interaction is the subject of the ritual; it is what the dramatic cycle is about. The performances themselves are created through certain sequences of dance steps performed by celebrated characters wearing symbolic costumes and carrying iconographic props, all of which form images that express the Hopi view of the world. These characteristics of performance are part of the aesthetic expression of this particular people. Geography, the physical environment, material culture, family structure, social organization,

history, religion, and philosophy are some of the basic forces that shape artistic expression.

The Collective and Public Nature of Theatre

Sometimes the theatre retells the sacred stories of a community. Sometimes individual playwrights forge the body of work that interprets the life of the social group. Myths, legends, history, contemporary events, and personal experience filtered through the imagination of the playwright may all serve as sources for theatrical expression. Celebrated plays of individual playwrights may come to function as sacred stories, anchoring community values or providing a measure against which new experience can be tested. But whatever balance is struck between sustaining stories and the innovations of individuals, the formation and evolution of the theatre takes place in a public forum in a collective endeavor. A community of artists gathers to present a performance for a community audience.

Theatre as a Social Force

It is particularly the collective and public nature of the theatre that makes it such a potent social force. The theatre is a gathering place for the public presentation of ideas. Because ideas are expressed through characters caught in difficult or dangerous situations, the theatre creates an intensely emotional experience for the audience. And the impact of the work is then magnified by the number of people present. A collective emotional response is a force of enormous energy and can function in different ways. On one hand, theatre can evoke a collective sigh of relief, an emotional release: Sometimes when a group of people have laughed very hard together or cried together, they feel that they can more easily accept the difficulties of their daily lives or the pressures that face the entire community. On the other hand, theatre can generate and focus collective anger or outrage, which can then take form as a revolutionary force.

The relationship between theatre and society is complex because the theatre has so much potential power. Theatre can be a conservative force that contributes to stability and reinforces the status quo, or it can be part of an experimental process through which a society redefines itself. Theatre can release social tensions, or it can lead to social upheaval. Theatre can be part of social debate, part of the free exchange of ideas, or it can be used for the dissemination of propaganda. Because of its unique power as a collective, public form, theatre has always been of great interest to philosophers and governments.

Theatre and Religious Festivals

We now examine the relationship between theatre and society by studying examples of theatres from different nations and different historical periods that have been particularly influential in the development of the modern theatre. We study the subjects and ideas of the particular theatres and the aesthetics of the different styles of performance. As we move from theatre to theatre, we explore some of the issues that have arisen from the volatile relationship between theatre and society: issues of religion and politics, race and gender, social stability and revolution.

Two very different European theatres both developed in conjunction with religious festivals: the Greek theatre of Athens in the fifth century B.C.E. and the medieval mystery cycles, specifically those of England, which reached their high point between 1350 and 1550. Although both of these theatres were associated with community celebrations and ceremonies, the Greek theatre developed into a forum for highly sophisticated philosophical debate about the place of human beings in the universe, whereas the medieval theatre produced a pageant that functioned as a form of devotion, an affirmation of accepted religious beliefs.

The Greek Theatre: Athens, Fifth Century B.C.E.

By the fifth century B.C.E., Athens had become the dominant force in the group of city-states politically, culturally, and geographically linked on the peninsula and islands of Greece. The century produced a dazzling record of the Athenian genius for the arts, for learning, for government, and for the building of an empire. The Athenian theatre and literature of the fifth century B.C.E. has inspired much of the theatre and literature in later eras and throughout the world. The great **tragedies** that came from this period—*Prometheus Bound*, *Oedipus Rex*, *Antigone*, and *Medea*—were intricately bound to the religious as well as the political life of the community.

The Origin of Greek Theatre in the Worship of Dionysus

Early on in the development of theatre in Greece, plays were associated with festivals to honor the god **Dionysus**. There is much debate among theatre historians and anthropologists about whether the plays actually evolved out of ritual worship of Dionysus or whether they grew out of the more secular impulses of individual playwrights. Whatever path the evolution of Greek drama followed, the worship of Dionysus was central to the place of theatre in Greek culture.

Dionysus was the Greek god of the life force; he represented new growth for vegetation, new life for herds and flocks, and fertility for human beings. A god of nature, wine, and fertility, Dionysus was honored in the spring with festivals that celebrated regeneration and renewal. These were ecstatic celebrations in which social inhibitions were supplanted by liberated, intoxicated behavior. The worship of Dionysus supposedly began with his followers' tearing apart his body and eating it in order to absorb his power into themselves. In the spring following the dismemberment of the god, Dionysus was miraculously

IN CONTEXT

Origins of the Theatre in Greece

Date	Event
1300–1200 B.C.E.	Worship of Dionysus introduced to Greece from the Middle East
c. 800 B.C.E.	The *Iliad* and the *Odyssey* composed by Homer
534 B.C.E.	Dramatic competition established at City Dionysia
523–456 B.C.E.	Life of Aeschylus
508 B.C.E.	Athenian democracy established
496–406 B.C.E.	Life of Sophocles
490 B.C.E.	Defeat of the Persians by the Greeks at Marathon
480–406 B.C.E.	Life of Euripides
c. 460–430 B.C.E.	Rule of Pericles
458 B.C.E.	*The Oresteia*, by Aeschylus
441 B.C.E.	*Antigone*, by Sophocles
431 B.C.E.	*Medea*, by Euripides
430 B.C.E.	*Oedipus Rex*, by Sophocles
429–347 B.C.E.	Life of Plato
404 B.C.E.	Athens defeated in Peloponnesian War
384–322 B.C.E.	Life of Aristotle
c. 330 B.C.E.	*The Poetics*, by Aristotle

restored to life, resurrected. In its evolution, the worship of Dionysus at first actually involved human sacrifice; later, animals were used for the communion ritual. Stories and songs celebrating the life of Dionysus were added to the ritual observations, which grew into community festivals involving civic and religious activity. Finally, in the sixth century B.C.E., dramas were added to the various activities of the festival of Dionysus, setting the stage for the brilliant Athenian **drama** that would emerge in the fifth century B.C.E.

Although the Greek dramas that came to dominate the festival of Dionysus are profoundly different from the Hopi kachina cycle, certain remarkable similarities are apparent. For both cultures, the drama is central to community observations concerned with renewal and regeneration. The transformation of actors into characters concerned with issues of social and religious order coincides with the transformation of nature to sustain human existence once more. The suffering and rebirth of Dionysus became a model for the theatre, which explores the suffering and triumph of the human community. This transformative function for the drama would recur in the Christian drama of medieval times, when pageants celebrating the Christian history of the world were performed in conjunction with the Corpus Christi festivals held throughout Europe in the late spring to celebrate the sacraments of the church associated with the body of Christ.

Like the Hopi ritual performances, the Greek theatre was part of the soul of the community, essential to the basic fabric of the life of the city-state. Through plays, the Greeks examined the relationships necessary to sustain human existence as they understood it. Family relationships, social organization, the relationships and obligations of individuals to the larger society, and the interplay between human action and the actions of the gods dominated the dramas written by playwrights such as Aeschylus (523–456 B.C.E.), Sophocles (496–406 B.C.E.), and Euripides (480–406 B.C.E.). By raising ethical and political questions, the Greek plays helped shape the emergence of democracy in Athens.

There are, however, significant differences between the kachina cycle and the theatre of Greece. The kachina performances evolved over generations of community participation; no single playwright shaped the ideas and images. By contrast, in the Greek theatre the imagination of the individual playwright was celebrated.

The theatre at Epidaurus dates from about 300 B.C.E., which is later than the period we have been studying. However, these well-preserved ruins give a sense of the scale and setting of the theatre of Dionysus in Athens in the fifth century B.C.E. The theatre at Epidaurus seated 14,000 spectators and was known for its excellent acoustics. In spite of the vast size of the theatre, the actors could be heard by everyone present. Our knowledge of Greek theatre practice is based on fragmentary evidence and involves much speculation on the part of theatre historians. We imagine that the actors in the fifth century B.C.E. performed on a circular, unraised playing area, with a wooden building behind, which served as a place to change costumes and masks and from which actors entered and exited the stage. The wooden building might have created the sense of a palace facade. The roof of the scene building also provided a raised level for the appearance of the gods and a crane to facilitate special effects like Medea's final exit in a flying chariot.

The presentation of plays, in fact, took the form of a competition, at the festival known as the **City Dionysia,** and prizes were given each year to the outstanding playwright. Further, the kachina performances reinforce an accepted set of religious beliefs, whereas Greek theatre questioned the nature of fate and the very existence of the gods.

The Greek plays were presented each year over a period of several days. Most traditional work stopped, and 15,000 community members or more would gather on a hill outside the city where a rudimentary theatre had been constructed. From wooden benches built into the hillside, the audience would look down on an open-air playing space. At the back of this circular playing area was a plain stone building that provided for the entrances and exits of the actors and served as a place for costume changes and storage for simple stage machinery. Beyond the theatre lay the sea. The audience and the actors gathered in the middle of the geographic features that delineated the external boundaries of the Athenian world as they witnessed or acted the plays that probed the internal nature of that world. From early morning to late afternoon, the playwrights staged dramas to entertain, to illuminate, and to reflect on the concerns of the huge audience. We now examine one of the Greek dramas, *Medea*, to explore the merging of ideas and aesthetics in the Greek theatre. Accompanying our discussion of *Medea* are photos from two of the numerous recent productions of this work, which continues to be compelling for modern producers and audiences. Reviews of these productions are included in Chapter 14.

Medea, by Euripides

Medea was written by Euripides in 438 B.C.E. and is one of eighteen of his plays that have survived into our own times. Euripides is known for his concerns with the complexity of human motivation, the difficulty of negotiating love and desire, and the conflicts between men and women. Human behavior out of control is the subject of both *The Bacchae* and *Hippolytus*. Euripides has also written eloquently about the destructive nature of war in the often-produced *Trojan Women*.

With characters drawn from well-known Greek mythology, *Medea* focuses on the obsessive passion of the title character, Medea, for her husband, Jason. The play is both the intimate and the public telling of the breakdown of a marriage. As a domestic story, the plot is familiar. A married man leaves his wife, the mother of his children, for a younger woman. Euripides' rendering of this material not only portrays the shifting terms of a relationship but also presents a struggle for power and self-preservation. The younger woman Jason hopes to marry, Glauce, is the daughter of the king of Corinth. By marrying her, Jason stands to inherit a throne. Medea faces losing her husband, and as the play begins, she is threatened with banishment. Furthermore, she bears the weight of a complicated history. Early in their relationship, so devoted was Medea to Jason that she committed murder and alienated her own family in order to help him obtain and then escape with the legendary Golden Fleece. Now, she is regarded as an outsider, a barbarian, among the majority population, the Greeks. For Jason, his alliance with Medea is no longer useful. He sees her as a dangerous and disruptive force. Medea sees the man for whom she sacrificed home and family abandoning her to a life in which she will be alone with neither a country nor friends to support her. The explosive conflict between husband and wife results in the deaths of their children, an outcome that has both personal and symbolic significance. Euripides' *Medea* tells a bloody story of revenge and murder as disturbing as some of today's films. Violence in the drama and in the conduct of human affairs is not a uniquely contemporary phenomenon.

Staging Conventions

Every theatre has its own conventions, which are understood and accepted by performers and audience members alike. **Theatrical conventions** are the unique devices of dramatic construction and performance that facilitate the presentation of stories on the stage. One convention in Greek theatre was that no more than three actors appeared on the stage at any one time; another was that the actors always wore masks. Although we know some of the major conventions followed in Greek performance, many others are unrecorded or are the subject of continuing intense debate. However, using evidence from the plays themselves as well as from other writings, artwork, and archaeological investigation, we can imagine some aspects of a performance.

Male Actors

We know that women did not participate in the Greek theatre in any way. All the roles, male and female, were played by men. Therefore, the central role of Medea would have been played by a man, as would the Nurse and the chorus of Corinthian women. We also know that the Greeks used a small number of actors, two or three, to perform all the individual speaking parts in any particular play; so actors usually played more than one role. In imagining a performance of *Medea* in its own time, we must shift our contemporary perspective to envision two or three men onstage at a time, wearing masks and costumes to indicate the roles they are assuming. One of the actors would probably have played only Medea because this character is onstage throughout most of the play. All the other roles—Nurse, Tutor, Creon, Jason, and Aegeus—would have been divided between two additional actors. After an actor finished one scene or section of the play, he would exit to change his costume and mask so that he could appear as another character. *Medea* is clearly structured with two-person scenes in order to allow the third actor to exit and prepare to reenter in another role.

Mythological Background

Jason sails on the ship *Argo* to find the Golden Fleece, which is in the possession of King Aeetes of Colchis. Medea is the daughter of Aeetes and the granddaughter of the Sun. With her mixed ancestry, human and divine, she has the powers of a sorcerer. She falls deeply in love with Jason and resolves to become his partner in his quest for the Golden Fleece. To help Jason escape from her father's pursuit, she kills her brother Apsyrtus and cuts his body into pieces, forcing her father to stop to gather the scattered remains of his dead son. Medea then tricks the daughters of Pelias, king of Iolkos, into killing their father, who had promised to restore Jason's inheritance in exchange for the fleece. Medea and Jason must flee once again and travel to Corinth, where Euripides' play takes place.

Character Relationships in the Play

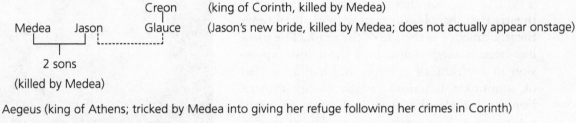

Aegeus (king of Athens; tricked by Medea into giving her refuge following her crimes in Corinth)

Members of Medea's household

Nurse

Tutor

In general, the same actor could play a man, a woman, and a god all within a few scenes. This particular staging convention reveals a great deal about Greek society. In a story about marriage and betrayal, jealousy and infanticide, the central character, who is held up as a psychological study of a woman in extreme circumstances, was written by a man to be played by a man. Furthermore, the audience would have been composed largely or completely of men.

Offstage Violence   The murders in *Medea* bring us to a particularly noteworthy convention of Greek theatre. All the violence was performed offstage. Frequently, dead bodies were wheeled onstage on a special wagon called the **ekkyklema.** The audience heard in gory detail from messengers about the violent encounters that resulted in the loss of life, and they saw the reactions of the other characters. But the Greek audience did not witness the fight scenes, the murders, and the dismemberments that played a prominent part in their dramas and that have essentially taken center stage in contemporary plays and films.

During the course of this play, Medea commits two atrocious crimes. First she sends a gift to Jason's new wife, Glauce: a beautiful dress and crown infused with poisonous chemicals that bring the girl to a fiery death when she puts them on. The poison also envelops Glauce's father, Creon, when he tries to rescue her. Following the murders of Glauce and Creon, Medea kills her own sons by Jason. In the play, as it is written by Euripides, none of this violence takes place onstage. The episode of the poisonous dress is described in graphic detail by the Messenger in a speech of over two pages which he delivers to Medea:

> Blood mingled with fire dripped from the top of her head, her flesh melted from her bones like teardrops of resin as your poisons gnawed invisibly.[6]

The cries for help of Medea's children are heard from offstage, and then their dead bodies are revealed in the chariot in which Medea makes her exit at the end of the play, pulled through the sky by dragons.

The Mask   Another convention of the Greek theatre that sharply contrasts with contemporary theatre practice is the use of the mask. The mask has been a vital element of theatrical expression in a variety of cultures and had a number of significant functions in the Greek theatre. For the Greeks the mask had practical implications as well as aesthetic ones. As our discussion of *Medea* demonstrates, masks allowed one actor to play a number of roles. The same actor may have played Creon and Jason or the Nurse and Aegeus. Masks also enabled male actors to play female roles. And masks allowed mortals to play the roles of the gods, projecting the power and authority of Olympian deities. Because the Greek plays took place in huge outdoor theatres, the mask also increased the visibility of the actor, who would have been at a considerable distance from many of those in the audience. And in the case of the Greeks, the mask put yet more emphasis on the importance of the voice in conveying the meaning of the text and holding the audience's attention.

The mask also significantly affected the nature of acting. Whereas contemporary performance is frequently dominated by the personality and appearance of the actor, the use of masks in the Greek theatre put the emphasis in performance on the character rather than on the actor. The mask allowed the character to emerge as an entity separate from the actor who wore it.

Fiona Shaw plays Medea and Jonathan Cake plays Jason in a production of *Medea* directed by Deborah Warner for the Abbey Theatre of Ireland in 2002. This production emphasizes Medea's obsession with her husband and the intensity of their sexual relationship. The play is placed in a contemporary setting and the chorus speeches are divided between individuals rather than spoken in unison. The realism of the domestic conflict takes precedence over the mythical dimensions of the story. Note the children's toys in Medea's left hand.

The mask shifted the actor's focus to his voice and gestures, although the positioning of the head would have been eloquent in the absence of changing facial expression. In the Greek theatre, the gestures and body positions would have had to be large and striking to communicate across the vast space of the amphitheatre. The most sharply drawn contrast with performance today would be to the close-up of the actor in a film

Medea, played here by April Yvette Thompson, clings to her children, played by Brian Gilbert and Laron Griffin, in the production of *Medea* staged by the Classical Theatre of Harlem in 2005. The director Alfred Preisser incorporated dance and music throughout the performance, using the movement and chanting of the chorus to provide a rhythmic underscoring and strong visual images to accompany the actions of the main characters, reinforcing the mythological background.

where the most subtle and natural expressions of the face suggest great depth of feeling. The eyes that turn inward, the mouth that trembles slightly—these can convey significant meaning. The Greek actor had to work with an entirely different apparatus and on a much larger scale to make his meaning clear.

Any actor who wears a mask experiences some degree of transcendence as he or she identifies with the spirit of the mask. For actors such as the Hopi or the Kwakwaka'wakw engaged in a religious ceremony, the mask is an essential intermediary that transports the actor into the spirit world. In more secular performances, masks can still have the effect of lifting the actors out of themselves to identify with the essence of what the masks represent. Finally, for the audience, masks transform the stage or playing space into a magical world inhabited by larger-than-life characters who prompt a shift in the audience's consciousness. The audience members feel that they are in the presence of powerful, archetypal figures who bring a cosmic drama onto the stage.

The Chorus   The **chorus,** like the mask, was another convention of the Greek theatre. Although audiences today are familiar with singing choruses of all kinds, they might find a speaking or chanting chorus on the contemporary stage somewhat strange. A group of twelve to fifteen characters dressed alike and speaking in unison would not seem to represent the world as we see it. But for the Greek audience, the chorus was an expected part of the theatre experience. The chorus first appeared in early religious festivals, when groups of fifty would sing choral hymns in honor of Dionysus. Some theatre historians believe tragedy had its beginning when one of the chorus members initiated a dialogue between himself—as a single speaker or character—and the rest of the chorus. This legendary first speaker, Thespis, is the source of the word **thespian,** meaning actor.

Sometimes the Greek chorus spoke in **dialogue** and sometimes in longer poetic passages. In the sections of dialogue, the chorus played opposite major characters, asking questions and then listening, serving as a confidant who allowed the central characters to explain themselves. The chorus in *Medea* is made up of Corinthian women who remain sympathetic to Medea throughout the play, relating the painful history of Medea and Jason's relationship and then, as the action progresses, pleading with Medea not to kill her children.

Choral passages also contained many references to other mythological situations, and these allowed the playwright to expand on the significance of the immediate dramatic conflict. He built a complex background through the choral commentary.

In addition to functioning as both a character and a storyteller, the chorus had rhythmic and visual functions. The choral sections were accompanied by music and had their own meter, which contrasted with the dialogue episodes and heightened the growing tensions. The staging of the choruses involved intricate choreography and were an important part of the visual spectacle.

In *Medea*, a tormented woman kills her enemies and kills her own children. But performed in its own time, the horror of the play was contained by the formal nature of the presentation. The masked male actor portraying Medea was surrounded by the masked members of the chorus who chanted their responses, while the violent actions took place offstage.

The Greek theatre of Athens in the fifth century B.C.E. reinforced the existing social structure and celebrated Athenian democracy. But it was also a theatre of questions. The playwrights recognized that life is full of contradictions and that the future can be neither predicted nor controlled. The dramas that have come down to us call the community to account for its actions and charge individuals with responsibility for their choices. Characters struggle toward self-knowledge, but their view is frequently distorted by arrogance and passion. Wisdom follows only from catastrophic suffering.

The Medieval Mystery Cycle

Medieval society was organized largely around the Catholic Church, and it was as part of religious observation that the theatre developed in medieval Europe. The great medieval **mystery cycles** that were staged across western Europe from the thirteenth century to the sixteenth are a fascinating example of a religious theatre tradition that depended on the same kind of broad community participation found in the Hopi kachina cycle.

Initiated by the Catholic Church in the tenth century to make Christian teachings more accessible to a largely illiterate population, the mystery cycles dramatizing the Christian history of the world grew into elaborate pageants associated with the late spring festivals of Corpus Christi. Towns in England, France, Germany, Italy, and Spain all staged similar variations of these performances, which focused on biblical events from the creation of the world to the birth and crucifixion of Jesus to the last judgment. The number of episodes presented ranged from forty to as many as one hundred. Not only did the normal work of the communities cease during the time the plays were performed—as it did during the City Dionysia in Athens and as it continues to do during the kachina cycle in Hopi communities—the entire town was responsible for the presentation of the elaborate sequence of plays.

Staging and Production: A Community Endeavor

In England, production of the plays was organized through the business community and specifically through workers' unions known as guilds. Different guilds were responsible for the production of the different plays. In fact, the work of a particular guild would sometimes relate to the subject of its assigned play: The boatwrights produced *Noah's Ark*, and the bakers were responsible for *The Last Supper*.

The individual playlets of the English cycles were staged on **pageant wagons,** or carts that were drawn through the town by horses, each wagon essentially a miniature traveling stage. In the town of York, for example, forty plays were presented beginning at the earliest morning light and continuing far into the night. Each play was performed at twelve different sites throughout

During the 2012 Cultural Olympiad presented concurrently with the London Olympic Games, the people of York, one of the most celebrated sites of the early medieval mystery cycles, staged a major revival of their city's mystery plays. The plays were originally staged in York from the 1300s to 1569 when they were suppressed during the Reformation. About 1,500 community members worked to create the production shown in this photo. Two casts of 250 actors each performed, almost 200 musicians accompanied the performance, and hundreds of local residents sewed costumes and built scenery, just as the community would have gathered to produce the plays in medieval times. The episode shown in the photo is the story of the Flood, with the wooden structure in the center representing the Ark, while the figures with umbrellas create the rolling motion of the sea. The play was staged in the ruins of St. Mary's Abbey, a monastery that was closed at the same time the mystery plays were suppressed and gradually crumbled, leaving only some of the arched stone walls. Seats for 1,400 spectators were set up around the grounds of the Abbey for the performance, which lasted three hours. The adaptation of the text was written by Mike Kenny, Ferdinand Kingsley played God and Jesus, Graeme Hawley played Satan, and the co-directors were Damian Cruden and Paul Burbridge.

the town. People would gather at the designated locations along the "parade" route, and the plays would come to them. Food and music added to the air of great festivity and celebration.

The involvement of the guilds in the production of the plays is not unlike the corporate sponsorship of contemporary entertainments, including parades. The huge nationally televised

The Los Angeles Theatre Center has created a contemporary performance honoring the Virgin of Guadalupe, entitled *La Virgen de Guadalupe: Dios Inantzin,* that draws on traditions tied to the Catholic mystery or miracle plays in combination with Aztec performance traditions that pre-date the arrival of Europeans in the Americas. Presented annually in the Cathedral of Our Lady of the Angels, a church seating 3,000 people, the play is performed in both Spanish and Nahuatl, the Aztec language, and is a Christmas celebration for Los Angeles area residents of Hispanic heritage. The Director Jose Luis Valenzuela says, "the intent of this piece has been that every year we can come together and have a performance of a play that is ours and is built by us together as a community."[7] The goal of the performance is to empower the community in addition to reinforcing culture and faith.

parades, such as the Tournament of Roses parade on New Year's Day in Pasadena, California, with its flower-covered floats, and the Macy's Thanksgiving Day parade in New York, with its gigantic balloon characters, are supported by both commercial enterprises and city and state governments.

However, perhaps closer in spirit to the community involvement in the medieval mystery cycles is the small-town parade on the Fourth of July or another day dear to the heart of a local community. The high school bands, groups of riders on horseback, veterans, civic dignitaries, Shriners, and floats sponsored by local businesses—all represent community institutions and community values. The people who line the parade route recognize their friends and neighbors in the parade, and they clearly understand the significance of the celebration.

The kind of community effort that was required to produce the medieval mystery cycles is hard for us to imagine, because most of our elaborate entertainments are put on by professionals and involve a variety of commercial considerations. Over a hundred male actors, and sometimes several hundred, were involved in the mystery plays, as were dozens of men to build scenery and arrange the stage or pageant wagons. Numerous musicians played during or between episodes. And a director and technicians in charge of special effects coordinated the many participants. The undertaking was so complex and demanding of community resources that productions took place only every few years rather than annually.

Aesthetic Expression: A Shared, Sacred Language

We have seen that the Greek theatre of the fifth century B.C.E. developed a distinct life of its own in part because of the brilliant playwrights who shaped the ideas in the plays and the conventions of performance. In fact, the Greek playwrights directed their own plays, thereby exercising virtually complete control over the material. The medieval theatre, in contrast, was guided by no such original thinking. Rather, it can be seen as one element in an overall pattern of aesthetic expression influenced by the Catholic Church. Because artwork was done for the glory of God, the artists, including visual artists, were all anonymous. We know neither the names of the playwrights nor the identity of the artisans who made the glorious stained glass windows of the great medieval cathedrals. Art was seen as a collective effort of devotion rather than as something done for personal aggrandizement. Instead of focusing on individual innovation or style, artists used the same system of signs and symbols that had evolved within the church and that functioned as a kind of sacred language or writing understood by the entire community. The theatre and the various forms of visual art all used the same subjects, the same ideas of organization, the same details of character, and the same symbols of religious significance.

Story and Symmetry We have already observed that the mystery cycles were organized in an **episodic,** or processional, manner, constituting a number of separate incidents all related to one epic story. The visual art forms of the time, such as stained glass windows and paintings, were also structured as a group of individual panels with episodes or story incidents all related to one larger theme. Within each panel the figures were organized in a symmetrical and hierarchical manner. For example, three angels at the top of a panel might be balanced by three devils at the bottom, or a certain number of virtuous characters might be depicted to the right of Jesus, with a comparable number of sinners to the left. Functioning as a background in many of these visual images was often a small building or emblematic structure that indicated the location of the scene. The same small buildings became the scenic units placed on the pageant wagons. The arrangement and spacing of the characters probably drew on the same principles of symmetry and hierarchy.

Performance and Special Effects The simplicity and order of the staging, however, did not restrict the exuberance of the performances, which were far from stiff religious exercises. The point of the performances was to give the audience a chance to identify with Christ's suffering, to feel the power of the miracles and the

degradation of the devils and those who had sinned. The central subject of the entire pageant was salvation itself. To have a powerful and useful effect on the audience, the staging had to be clever, magical, lively, and humorous.

Much effort went into the staging of special effects, such as fire, flying angels, ascensions, flowing water, and the bouncing head of St. John the Baptist. One of the most popular parts of the spectacle was the hell mouth, a gaping, monstrous structure emitting smoke and fire and discharging devils in fantastic costumes out into the audience. And the small plays themselves all had compelling details of human interest that connected the situations of the characters to the immediate hardships and joys experienced by those in the audience.

The Role of the Mystery Cycles in Medieval Society

There are several ways to view the relationship of the Christian mystery cycles to society. On one level they must be seen as a celebration that gave people a break from their routine tasks and a chance to work together to re-create primary community stories. Participants had the double satisfaction of contributing their own skills to the performances and enjoying the results of their neighbors' contributions. Although the mystery plays quickly grew beyond the walls of the church buildings themselves, they served to tie the church and community together. The plays reinforced people's faith by allowing community members to identify with Christ's suffering and triumph and to act on their devotion through the production of the plays.

At the same time, the plays served the interests of the ruling classes and the Catholic Church. They reinforced the social organization of the time, which held people in rigidly structured hierarchical positions with almost no possibility of upward mobility. The plays were full of lessons based on accepting one's position in society no matter what the degree of poverty or deprivation;

The mystery cycles were performed in a holiday atmosphere. Music, food, large crowds, and the interruption of work contributed to the audience's anticipation of the performance. Fire, smoke, and the appearance of devils who interacted with the audience all made for very lively entertainment.

the true rewards of human existence, the plays taught, were to be received in the hereafter.

The relationship of the mystery cycles to society can be seen clearly in the changes that occurred in England in the sixteenth century. In medieval times the mystery cycles benefited both church and state, but after the Protestant Reformation (beginning in 1511), the religious theatre became embroiled in the political upheavals of the day. In England, Henry VIII broke with the pope in 1534 over issues of autonomy in general and divorce in particular. His daughter, Elizabeth I, governed a nation with an expanding sense of national identity and power and a newly established Church of England, which allowed Christian worship without papal interference. Up to this time, the performance of the mystery cycles had reinforced a strong Catholic presence in England. Worried that continued performances would provide a rallying ground for supporters of the pope and Catholicism, the English government set about eliminating the mystery cycles. Manuscripts recording the plays were destroyed, regulations against religious performances onstage were enforced, and plays expressing Catholic views were not licensed. The mystery cycles, long considered a fundamental part of English society, were suppressed when they no longer served the interests of the state.

 # Summary

Performance is a vital part of human expression that may involve playing roles in daily life, participating in community rituals, or working as a professional actor. Performance is an essential human activity that relates to successful personal adaptation. Children use performance to test new roles; adults use performance to adjust to changes in their circumstances. Much of the shifting of roles in daily life relates to our attempts to become more powerful.

Through dramatic rituals, communities reach out to supernatural forces to secure control over their environment. Ceremonial performances, such as the kachina cycle of the Hopi, are central to the social and religious organization of the community. The individual who takes on a ceremonial role goes through a process of transformation.

The power of the theatre derives from its collective public nature, from the combined energies of the community of artists and the community audience. Theatre addresses issues of religion and politics, gender and race, social stability and revolution. It functions as a mirror to society, reflecting the themes and subjects that concern the people and the forms of aesthetic expression deemed appropriate and acceptable in that community.

Some theatre traditions developed in association with religious festivals. The theatre of Athens in the fifth century B.C.E. arose from festivals celebrating the transformative powers of Dionysus, god of the life force. Performed outdoors in natural amphitheatres overlooking the sea, the Greek dramas provided the occasion for thousands of Athenians to gather for a few days every year to experience community myths and legends in the form of drama. Greek theatre employed certain well-understood conventions of performance, including the mask and the chorus. Through drama, the Greeks explored difficult questions about human existence. *Medea*, by Euripides, explores troubled relationships between individuals and the chaos generated by unchecked passion and relentless ambition.

Like Greek theatre, the medieval mystery cycles were religious in origin and purpose. Every few years, community members, working through their guilds, re-created the story of Christianity in a series of playlets presented during the late spring festival of Corpus Christi. Plays were staged on pageant wagons that moved from place to place in the town. The conventions of the medieval theatre were derived from the shared, sacred language of signs and symbols used to evoke and represent Christianity. Stories were simple and told in episodic fashion, both in the plays and in medieval visual art forms such as stained glass windows; the works of playwrights and artists were anonymous and emphasized order and symmetry. In the medieval cycles, religious meaning merged with the humorous and exuberant performances to create an event that was highly entertaining as well as deeply moving. The plays reinforced the hierarchical structure of medieval society with stories that encouraged obedience and humility.

Topics for Discussion and Writing

1. The purpose of this exercise is to examine the way "personal performance" is used in everyday life. Choose "nonactors" for your observations. Where do you see people performing in daily life? That is, under what circumstances do people make some kind of switch in how they present themselves, taking on a different role, putting on a mask, or dramatically aggrandizing their behavior? What is the purpose of the "performance"? Observe people in five different situations. Write approximately one-half page for each observation.

2. Discuss the ways in which the Hopi kachina cycle benefits the Hopi community. Do you know of any dramatic ceremonial performances that are part of your community?

3. Greek tragedies involved a great deal of violence. However, all the violent incidents took place offstage and were then described in detail to the audience by messengers who had witnessed the violence. The dead bodies were also frequently brought onstage as a display of what had happened. What reasons might the Greeks have had to place the violence offstage? What do you think the effect would have been on the audience? What would happen to contemporary drama and films if the violence occurred offstage? What is the effect of onstage and onscreen violence on audiences today?

CHAPTER 2

Theatre as a Mirror of Society

The Professional Theatre

The Greek theatre of the fifth century B.C.E. and the medieval mystery cycles were both associated with religious festivals and appeared only seasonally. The plays in both cases were community endeavors involving large numbers of community members and resources. The production of plays was considered a civic and religious responsibility and brought together religious leaders, civic leaders, business interests, and community members. The participants in the performances themselves consisted of a few semiprofessional theatre practitioners, but the majority were nonprofessionals.

We turn now to two professional theatres with different aesthetics and different conditions of performance: the theatre of Shakespeare and the **Beijing Opera** (also called the Chinese opera). Unlike the Greek and medieval theatres, both of these theatres involved professional practitioners engaged full-time in the production of plays. Commercial considerations were vital to the financial well-being of each theatre. Attracting a regular and substantial paying audience and securing the patronage of the aristocracy were equally important. Although the theatres of Shakespeare and the Beijing Opera represent extremely different cultural traditions, they share staging conventions that focus on the abilities of actors working on a bare stage to engage the imagination of the audience.

The Elizabethan Theatre

Elizabeth I, the daughter of Henry VIII by Ann Boleyn, came to the English throne in 1558. She inherited the English crown when England was entering an era of adventure and expansion, when the spirit of the Renaissance was firing the English imagination. But her reign began in the shadow of English civil wars, the Wars of the Roses, that had bled the nation during the preceding century. And Elizabeth faced an ongoing religious struggle between Protestants and Catholics, initiated when her father, Henry VIII, broke with the pope in 1534 and established himself as head of the Church of England. Elizabeth reigned for almost fifty years, until 1603, and she did much to stabilize the nation, creating an atmosphere conducive to spectacular achievements in science, exploration, and the arts. But she held together a contentious society that would return to civil war some years following her death, and there was a price to be paid for the peace that she maintained.

The Theatre in Society

The Elizabethan theatre inherited much both from the Greek theatre and from the medieval theatre that immediately preceded it, but its place in the English society of the late sixteenth century and early seventeenth century was quite different from the place of those theatres in their societies. The production of Greek and medieval plays merged religious observation with performances that entertained as they reinforced community values. Regular citizens were involved at every level of the productions, so productions were community-based and amateur in nature. In both Greece and medieval Europe, theatre festivals were held at special times of the year when the normal life of the community stopped to allow the presentation of plays.

In contrast, Elizabethan theatre was a secular theatre operated by professional actors and playwrights who supported themselves with their theatre activities year-round. This secular theatre interpreted the ambitions and the tremendous changes in worldview of the age. Elizabethan theatre was fascinated by the power struggles of kings and the inner turmoil provoked by such struggles. But in spite of seizing on the political maneuverings of the human community as one of its principal subjects, the theatre was cautious in keeping its distance from the political debates that swirled around the throne of Elizabeth I.

IN CONTEXT

Tudor and Jacobean England

Date	Event
1455–1485	Wars of the Roses
1485	Battle of Bosworth in which Richard III is defeated by the first Tudor king, Henry VII
1509–1547	Reign of Henry VIII (father of Elizabeth I)
1534	Henry VIII breaks with the pope and founds the Church of England
1547–1553	Reign of Edward VI
1553–1558	Reign of Mary I
1558–1603	Reign of Elizabeth I
1588	Defeat of the Spanish Armada by the English navy
1564–1623	Life of Shakespeare
c. 1590–1610	Shakespeare's theatre career in London
1603–1625	Reign of James I (referred to as the Jacobean period)

The film *Elizabeth* (1999), with Cate Blanchett in the title role, chronicled the evolution of Elizabeth I into a monarch with an iron will, strong enough to withstand the threats to her throne and the power struggles surrounding her. In a remarkable performance, Blanchett begins as a lively and emotional girl and gradually builds up her defenses until she withdraws behind the mask of the invulnerable queen. Elizabeth I brought considerable stability to England, allowing the theatre, including the work of William Shakespeare, to flourish.

The unique circumstances of the late sixteenth century in England afforded the opportunity for a national theatre. The intellectual and artistic curiosity of the Renaissance prepared the way for sophisticated plays such as those of Shakespeare. The stability of the long reign of Elizabeth I allowed the economy to prosper, and with it the theatre. The patronage of the nobility protected playwrights and actors and allowed them to continue to work, even when some religious and civic leaders saw the theatre as either a moral danger or an actual physical danger through the spread of the plague. The growth of London—with a population of 200,000, the largest city in Europe—provided a lively audience eager for frequent theatre performances. And the English language, already rich in expressive words and rhythmic possibilities, was open to the playwright's inventive vocabulary and phrasing, unfettered by rigid rules or academic restrictions.

The Nature of Elizabethan Drama

Elizabethan drama focused on the complexity of human motivation. The human mind and human action were placed center stage. Human action was played out against a background of religious and political concerns, but it was the internal struggles of the characters that became the major subject of the drama. The most compelling characters from Elizabethan drama were those whose vision for themselves outreached their abilities to live the lives they imagined. It was the drama of an age of human possibility, full of startling opportunities for the expansion of human understanding, underscored by the expansion of the European nations on the high seas and on vast, distant continents. The unknowns were enormous, but the possibilities were exhilarating. A new view of human existence was emerging from Renaissance philosophy and science; at the same time, however, medieval thinking still persisted.

A play that offered an illuminating prologue for the Elizabethan dramas to follow, particularly the plays of William Shakespeare, was *Doctor Faustus*, by Christopher Marlowe. *Doctor Faustus* explores the mind of a man with a consuming ambition to understand the nature of the world and the universe. But his science proves to be no more than a magician's tricks. Faustus's hope for the mind of man shatters his faith in God. He dies in despair, unable to achieve the heights of human understanding that he envisions but also unable to repent for his desire to know. In his quest for knowledge, he is damned by his own conscience as well as the prevailing morality of his society. Faustus has lost the comfort of the medieval worldview, a view that he has yet to escape.

Doubts and questions also torment Shakespearean characters whose burning ambitions lead them to ill-conceived courses of action. Macbeth pursues a course of murder to gain the crown but cannot silence his conscience. King Lear divides up his kingdom in order to receive the adulation of his daughters and is driven mad by the consequences of his actions. In his greatest play, Shakespeare creates a character, Hamlet, who is forced to deal with the murderous ambition of his uncle Claudius. The play explores the questioning mind of a character who cannot make sense of the political and philosophical issues confronting him.

William Shakespeare

As we examine Elizabethan theatre, we focus on William Shakespeare, the playwright whose soaring achievements became synonymous with the age. A number of other playwrights, such as Christopher Marlowe and Ben Jonson, contributed to the vitality and brilliance of this remarkable period of theatre, but as the theatre became central to Elizabethan and Jacobean England, so Shakespeare became central to the theatre.

Although images of Shakespeare exist, he continues to be an elusive historical figure, known through the eloquence of his plays but not through substantial biographical materials. We can only imagine the life he led in London as a member of the Lord Chamberlain's Men who sometimes wrote as many as three plays a year to keep up with the demands of his company and his audience.

Shakespeare's Career Shakespeare's career in the theatre illuminates the characteristics of the professional London stage of the late sixteenth century and the early seventeenth. Between approximately 1590 and 1610 Shakespeare wrote thirty-seven plays that together are considered the greatest achievement of any playwright in the history of world theatre.

Shakespeare emerged from an obscure background in Stratford to become one of the important members of the Lord Chamberlain's Men, a small but prominent professional theatre company in London. As part of this company, Shakespeare was an actor, a shareholder, a part owner of the Globe Theatre, and, most significantly, a playwright. Shakespeare's membership and participation in the Lord Chamberlain's Men greatly facilitated his career as a playwright. He worked with a company that had a continuing need for new material, and he knew the strengths and weaknesses of the company, the specialized skills of individual members, and the range of the different actors. In fact, he knew who would play the roles as he wrote them—which actor excelled at comedy, which actor had a good singing voice, which boy actor was available to play a woman's role, and how many lines he could be expected to handle. There was a continuous interplay

Michael Cumpsty plays Richard III in this 2007 production at the Classic Stage Company, directed jointly by Cumpsty and Brian Kulick. Cumpsty plays Richard as a seductive villain who successfully overcomes his opposition with charm before he turns to murder. The play was performed on an open stage with the only scenic element large crystal chandeliers that were raised or lowered by the actors to create a throne room, a forest, or even an undersea environment. The use of the chandeliers was a modern variation of the flexible staging employed in Shakespeare's time.

between the playwright and the company as he crafted his work to take advantage of the gifts of his fellow company members.

The Sources of Shakespeare's Plays
Shakespeare was not an original story maker. Rather, he was a genius at taking materials from other sources—historical chronicles, romances, and even other plays—and dramatizing them for his company, his theatre, and his lively audience, which consisted of royalty, aristocrats, merchants, and laborers. Written histories of the dynastic struggles that led to the triumph of the House of Tudor provided the material for his

chronicling of the English kings. His comedies were modeled on the Latin comedies of Plautus and on Italian romances; his tragedies were derived from violent stories and plays of revenge. But no matter how indebted he may have been to his sources, Shakespeare's particular genius— his brilliant language, his facility with plot and action, and his deep understanding of human nature expressed through his unparalleled array of characters—allowed him to bring a series of dramas to the stage that made his company the most successful in London.

Although the struggle for political power was a prominent subject of his plays, Shakespeare generally managed to focus on character rather than on political analysis, which might have been seen as commentary on the national debate over succession. One of the most striking of his history plays, *The Tragedy of Richard III*, however, reveals the manipulation of history in the drama. Drawing on the distortions in Thomas More's biography of Richard III, also repeated in the Holinshed *Chronicles* (histories of England, Scotland, and Ireland), Shakespeare created a portrait of a monstrous, misshapen villain who murders the two boys who are the true heirs to the throne and slashes his way across England to revenge himself for his bitter life. As a study of evil, *Richard III* conveniently justifies the killing of Richard by Henry VII and Henry's subsequent usurpation of the throne. Henry VII was the grandfather of Shakespeare's sovereign, Elizabeth I. The portrait of Richard III immortalized by Shakespeare obviously justifies the presence of Elizabeth on the throne. That Richard was actually far different from Shakespeare's character has generally been lost to history, so vivid was Shakespeare's rendering of his villain.

Elizabethan Staging

The Globe and Other Theatres

A cluster of professional theatres was built across the River Thames from the city of London, just beyond the jurisdictional reach of a city government that was dubious about the wisdom of a growing theatrical presence. But theatre owners saw profit to be made from theatrical entertainments that drew 3,000 spectators at a time to their large, round, wooden theatres. The most famous of these public commercial theatres, the Globe, was the home of Shakespeare's company, the Lord Chamberlain's Men, from 1599 to 1609. The name of the Globe not only reflected the circular shape of the theatre but also described the way the physical structure of the theatre contained the universe as the Elizabethans saw it. And this point of view, encompassed by the theatre building, echoed the same combination of medieval and Renaissance thinking as did the structure of the plays.

Because the theatre was partly open to the sky, the stage was protected by a canopy that might have had stars painted on it to represent the heavens. The stage platform itself was the world, the level of human endeavor; and the area below the stage, accessible through trapdoors, suggested hell, with its ghosts and spirits. This hierarchical representation was similar to the understanding of the universe expressed by the medieval stage. The difference was the expansion of the human arena, where most of the action took place.

Of the three theatres discussed so far, the medieval theatre had the most elaborate scenic effects. The Elizabethan stage—like the stage of the Beijing Opera discussed later in this chapter—was an empty space with minimal stage properties: a table, a chair, banners. It was through the playwright's eloquent language that the Elizabethan actor defined the space.

Language as an Element of Staging

Like the Greek theatre, the Elizabethan stage relied on vivid, energetic, and evocative **language** to fill the stage space and shape the **action**. In scene after scene, the playwright framed the action with only a few poetic words to create setting or time of day. In *Hamlet*, the sunrise is created with the following memorable lines:

But, look, the morn, in russet mantle clad,
Walks o'er the dew of yon high eastern hill.[1]

In *King Lear*, a storm is created when Lear pours out a description of the weather that also describes the breaking of his heart:

LEAR: Blow, winds, and crack your cheeks! Rage! Blow!
You cataracts and hurricanoes, spout
Till you have drench'd our steeples, drown'd the cocks!
You sulph'rous and thought-executing fires,
Vaunt-couriers of oak-cleaving thunderbolts,

The Globe Theatre was built for the Lord Chamberlain's Men and was the site of the premiere performances of some of Shakespeare's most famous plays. This photo shows a reconstruction of the Globe, built on the south bank of the Thames River, that is now used for theatre performances in London. In Elizabethan times the Thames served as a boundary between the city of London and the theatres that by law were kept outside the city limits. This photo shows a production of *Coriolanus* with Jonathan Cake in the title role under the direction of Dominic Dromgoole, performed at the Globe Theatre in 2006.

Singe my white head! And thou, all-shaking
   thunder,
Strike flat the thick rotundity o' th' world!
Crack nature's moulds, all germens spill at once
That makes ingrateful man![2]

The entering or exiting of characters indicated a change of scene, and frequently characters referred to their next destination as they went. All the information needed by the audience to follow the action was contained in the language. The importance of the language points to an audience prepared to listen closely to the words and rapidly process verbal cues, although there were certainly visual cues as well.

The performance of Shakespeare depended on the imagination of the audience. *Henry V* opens with a prologue in which a character called Chorus asks the audience to fill in the images suggested by the actors so that the stage might become a battlefield where a few actors become armies led by kings:

Piece out our imperfections with your thoughts;
Into a thousand parts divide one man,
And make imaginary puissance;

Think, when we talk of horses, that you see them
Printing their proud hoofs i' th' receiving earth.
For 'tis your thoughts that now must deck our
      kings,
Carry them here and there, jumping o'er times,
Turning the accomplishment of many years
Into an hour-glass.[3]

As suggested in these lines, Elizabethan plays involved numerous characters acting out complicated events in rapidly shifting locations over extended periods of time. This expansiveness of space and time was a direct inheritance from the medieval stage, which told the entire history of the Christian world in a single production. The Greek drama, in contrast, generally offered a concentrated representation of human experience, portrayed by only a few characters in one location in a very compressed passage of time: human action reduced to its essence. Shakespeare and his contemporaries looked to show the variations of human action by writing complex plays with multiple plots or subplots. To accomplish this sweeping presentation of action, the Elizabethan stage depended on the alertness of its audience and the language of the playwright.

Acting in Elizabethan Dramas

The professional English actor was a master of speech. In discussions of Elizabethan acting, the most famous acting teacher was Shakespeare himself, who through the character of Hamlet instructs a group of traveling actors on their craft:

Speak the speech, I pray you, as I pronounced it
to you, trippingly on the tongue; but if you
mouth it, as many of your players do, I had
as lief the town-crier had spoke my lines.[4]

Hamlet goes on to emphasize a natural acting style, performed with moderation rather than exaggeration.

Nor do not saw the air too much with your hand,
thus, but use all gently; for the very torrent,
tempest, and, as I may say, the whirlwind

of passion, you must acquire and beget a
temperance that may give it smoothness. . . .
Suit the action to the word, the word to the
action; with this special observance, that
you o'erstep not the modesty of nature. For
anything so overdone is from the purpose of
playing, whose end, both at the first and now,
was and is, to hold, as 'twere, the mirror up to
nature; to show virtue her own feature, scorn
her own image, and the very age and body of
the time his form and pressure.[5]

In fact, the actor would frequently perform very close to the audience, again more like the medieval theatre than the Greek. The platform stage extended into the audience space, and audience members would have stood on three sides of the stage pressing close against it. The actor playing at the edge of the stage would have been able to address the audience easily and intimately in his soliloquies and asides. Even the audience seated in boxes placed around the walls of the audience space would have been close enough to the stage to observe the details of character action. The proximity of the audience to the actors suggests that broad gestures and exaggerated speech were unnecessary. Furthermore, the indication is that the speech was delivered with considerably more speed than it would be today, making a broad style of delivery impossible to maintain.

The Beijing Opera of China

China is a nation with ancient origins that date back to around 4000 B.C.E. The theatre has played a significant part in the rich Chinese cultural heritage for more than 3,000 years and has taken many forms over that remarkable span of time. The relatively recent form that we examine here, the Beijing Opera, draws on many earlier theatre movements or styles but is usually recognized as being established in 1790. It was at the eightieth birthday party of the reigning emperor in that year that new forms of performance were introduced to Beijing, the capital of China.

A Formal Society

The teachings of Confucius, who lived in the fifth century B.C.E., at the same time as the major Greek playwrights, provided the foundation for the organization of Chinese society. Confucian ideas of family, respect for and deference to elders, acceptance of one's place in the hierarchy, and the importance of formal codes of conduct evolved over a period of centuries into a society governed officially by a vast bureaucracy and internally by a complex and pervasive network of rules and obligations. Although Confucius adhered to ideals that included democracy, what resulted from the modifications of his principles led to a society committed to conformity as a way of maintaining social stability.

At the center of Chinese society was the extended family. The effective functioning of the family as the basic social and political unit depended on the observation of intricate rules that governed relationships and the demonstration of appropriate regard for the elders who headed the family and the ancestors who had preceded them. The dramas of the Beijing Opera took this organization of the family as one of its major subjects. The theatre developed its own precise rules of style and detailed codes for the presentation of character types in response to the formal organization of Chinese society.

Playwrights and Plays

Like the Greek dramatists and Shakespeare, the playwrights for the Beijing Opera drew on earlier sources, such as historical novels, myths, and legends. But the goal of the Chinese dramatist was not to create a work that would stand on its own philosophical or poetic merit but to provide a vehicle for the actor. The Chinese playwright was an anonymous arranger of a text, bringing together functional passages that would support the actor's creation. And the audience members who gathered in large restaurant-like theatres, drinking tea and eating during the performances,

did not hang on every word but paused in their noisy activity to pay close attention only to the most exciting or clever parts.

The plays were loosely divided into two areas of focus: civil plays that dealt with domestic and social situations and military plays that maximized the opportunity for the action of warriors, outlaws, and demons. Plays were constructed around a set of instantly recognizable stock characters: four categories—male, female, painted-face, and comic—were divided into representative types whose characteristics were predetermined through generations of performances. A male character could be the hero, the official, the warrior, or the patriarch. A female character could be the virtuous and demure woman, the lively but untrustworthy woman, the warrior woman, or the matriarch. As in the Greek, medieval, and Elizabethan theatres, men played the women's roles, and because these were professional actors, female impersonation became a highly refined art. The gender issues related to female impersonation were complicated further by the social and sexual position of the male actors who undertook these roles in Chinese society. We return to the issue of female impersonation later in the chapter.

The painted-face characters brought the fantastic, the grotesque, and the supernatural into the world constructed by the Chinese theatre. Animal gods, outlaws, and warriors were given a larger-than-life appearance with bold and colorful makeup applied in such strong patterns that it functioned much like a mask. Finally, the comic roles included characters who contradicted expectations: the elderly soldier who was foolish rather than wise, the peasant who was cunning rather than simple.

A Language of Gesture

Although the form of the Beijing Opera is absolutely distinct from the other major forms of theatre in Asia, such as the **kabuki** theatre of Japan,

IN CONTEXT

The Beijing Opera and Chinese History

Date	Event
1644	Manchus conquer China. China is ruled by Manchu dynasties until 1911.
1790	Beijing Opera introduced at the eightieth birthday celebration of Emperor Ch'ien Lung.
1911	Revolution breaks out against dynastic rule. After 1911, women slowly begin to appear on the stage in traditional plays as well as more Westernized drama.
1912	China becomes a republic. A period of great instability begins, involving continuous military and political struggles over the next thirty-seven years, including feuding warlords, Japanese invasion, and civil war between Chiang Kai-shek and the communists.
1921	Creation of the Communist Party.
1930/1935	The actor Mei Lan-Fang tours Japan, the United States, and Russia, where he is seen by Bertolt Brecht.
1937	War with Japan.
1942	Talks at Yan'an Forum on Art and Literature, during which Mao Zedong presents his theories of art and theatre serving the political cause.
1949	Communist takeover of China.
1966	Cultural Revolution. Harshest period of censorship of the arts under supervision of Mao's wife, Jiang Qing. Substitution of model plays for traditional Chinese theatre.
1976	Death of Mao. Overthrow of the "gang of four." Revival of traditional theatre forms.
1978	New openness.
1989	Massacre at Tiananmen Square. Crackdown against democracy movement.
1990s	Acceleration of social change.
2008	Summer Olympics in Beijing.

the **kathakali** theatre of India, and the dance drama of Bali, certain basic principles guide all the traditional theatres of Asia. Just as text is the dominating force in the Western theatre, so gesture is the language of the actor in the Eastern theatre. In the West, the scripts of famous playwrights have been handed down through the centuries, and theatre is largely a verbal, language-based art. In Asian theatre, the gestures, stylized and intricate, convey codes of meaning

that can be "read" by an audience just as plainly as we in the West can interpret the actor's speech.

The text of the Beijing Opera may lack the power of the finest writing for the Western stage; similarly, the use of character types may have precluded the development of highly individualized, psychologically developed characters such as Oedipus and Hamlet, whose struggles have made them central to Western culture. But the Beijing Opera developed a poetry of theatrical

The heroine prepares for battle in this scene from *The Peony Pavilion,* which demonstrates the way the intensity of the gestural acting style combined with brilliant costumes and elaborate makeup provides the visual expression of Chinese opera without the use of any scenic background. Women now perform in traditional Chinese theatre with the same impressive skills as men.

expression that we cannot yet approximate. And the speech of Asian theatre, which is totally unlike Western conversational stage speech, is as stylized and removed from the everyday world as the actor's movement patterns.

Acting and Staging

The movement and the speech or singing of the Asian theatre demand a technical proficiency achievable only after years of the most disciplined training, which begins when the actors are children. It is through such rigorous training that the physical interpretation of a role can be passed from generation to generation, even over centuries.

With the conventions of the Chinese theatre in mind, we can imagine a performance of the Beijing Opera in the mid-nineteenth century. The actor stood alone on a bare platform stage. Although elaborate scenery was in use throughout European and American theatres at this time, in the Beijing Opera there were no clever scenic elements to capture the audience's imagination, no special lighting effects to focus their attention. The actor had to use his own resources to create everything that the audience would see. And for this, the actor was singularly well prepared. With a few steps he crossed an invisible threshold and entered a new room or building. With a flick of his whip he rode a nonexistent horse; with a swaying motion he was carried down the river in an imaginary boat. Dressed in sumptuously embroidered robes and wearing an elaborate wig and headdress, the Chinese actor created a compelling presence.

Later in the performance the subtle pantomime that created both environment and action gave way to more spectacular choreography. A battle scene took place, and the combatants seemed to come flying across the stage. With enormous swords in hand, the actors performed acrobatic feats that had the audience shouting approval. Bodies hurtled about the stage at unbelievable speeds, performing multiple flips and somersaults in the air, akin to the flights of Olympic gymnasts. All the action, the entrances and exits, the pantomimed sequences, and the acrobatic choreography were accompanied by musicians seated in view of the audience playing drums, gongs, cymbals, flutes, and traditional Chinese string instruments. The actors' lines, which had their own stylistic patterns, were sung and chanted rather than spoken.

A few basic pieces of furniture were all that helped designate location. A table and two chairs in different configurations changed the scene from a palace to a law court to a bedroom or indicated a wall, a bridge, or a mountain. A stagehand whose invisibility was an accepted convention of the Chinese theatre appeared as needed to reposition the furniture or to add or remove the few additional props that gave further definition to the changing space. The flexible approach to staging meant that performances could easily accommodate multiple locations and shifting conditions, such as time of day and weather. This style of performance emphasized the bond between the actor's skill and the audience's imagination. It also depended heavily, as so many performance traditions do, on a body of theatrical conventions accepted and understood by all participants in the dramatic event.

The Beijing Opera and the Communist Revolution

The history of the Beijing Opera in the twentieth century was closely intertwined with the rise of the Communist Party to power and its subsequent cultural policies. In the first part of the twentieth century approximately 3,000 opera companies performed the traditional repertoire throughout China. A typical company was a private commercial endeavor organized around one or more star performers that played regular engagements in a theatre and also was hired to perform for various festivals, both public and private.

The most famous company was headed by the actor Mei Lan-Fang, who was revered throughout China for his brilliant performances and for the innovations he brought to the traditional theatre form. Mei Lan-Fang also achieved an international reputation by undertaking a series of tours with his company in the 1920s and the 1930s to Japan, the United States, and Russia. He made an enormous impression on Western theatre practitioners, particularly the German director and playwright Bertolt Brecht, who would become one of the defining forces in twentieth-century theatre.

The Chinese communists saw the arts as essential to their goals for transforming Chinese society. From the early days of communist activity in China, Mao Zedong and his followers encouraged the development of a political theatre that would serve the revolutionary cause. In 1942, seven years before the communists came to power in China, Mao officially articulated his theories about the relationship between politics and art and literature at the Yan'an Forum on Art and Literature. According to his view, the only acceptable function for art was to celebrate and serve the proletariat:

> If everyone agrees on the fundamental policy of art serving the workers, peasants, and soldiers and on how to serve them, such should be adhered to by all our workers, our schools,

publications, and organizations in the field of literature and art and in all our literary and artistic activities. It is wrong to depart from this policy. Anything at variance with it must be duly corrected.

The implications of this policy would be as wrenching for the Beijing Opera as the upheaval and strife generated by Mao and his wife, Jiang Qing, would be for the Chinese nation as they reformed what they perceived to be the corruptions of the past. Jiang Qing, who had been an actor before she became a communist leader, brought both personal and ideological concerns into her drive to dominate the arts in China. Because of its enormous popularity, the Beijing Opera was targeted as a major vehicle for communist propaganda. During the **Cultural Revolution** (1966 to 1976), the traditional Beijing Opera was almost completely suppressed and replaced with eight model plays that dealt with contemporary themes and emphasized heroic, sacrificial actions on behalf of the revolution and the workers. Enormous sums of money and human resources were lavished on the development of the model productions. Productions such as *The Red Lantern* and *The White-Haired Girl* demonstrated the class struggle at the heart of the Chinese revolution and clearly identified the corrupt, capitalist enemies of the people.

Although these plays are not without strong characters and rising tension, they are extremely didactic. And although the model productions held the attention of audiences during this intense period of upheaval in China, they undermined the ability of the opera form to sustain itself when the political winds changed. The old actors and stories were gone. Audiences became wary of overtly political theatre. The model productions had laid no groundwork for the development of new material, and the companies had no other plays available with which to attract audiences.

The manipulation of the Beijing Opera to present communist propaganda had the long-term effect of practically destroying the theatre form itself; this development was not unlike the elimination of the mystery cycles in Elizabethan England as part of the government's policy to create a nation removed from the pope's influence. In China, the Beijing Opera was appropriated to promote the social change envisioned by Mao Zedong and his wife, Jiang Qing.

These examples are far from unique. Many societies, past and present, have sought to manipulate the theatre for political ends. Some societies have persecuted and even murdered actors and playwrights, and some cultures have worshiped them, sometimes simultaneously. Actors and playwrights have been slaves and they have been military leaders and heads of state. They have been social outcasts and the confidantes of kings.

For example, in the United States in the mid-twentieth century, fear of communism prompted the United States Congress to call playwrights and screenwriters, actors and directors before the House Committee on Un-American Activities (HUAC) to answer questions about their political affiliations. Without due process or proof of laws being broken, theatre and film practitioners were sent to jail or were blacklisted. They were blocked from further participation in film or play making until this committee was discredited for its attempts to control the free expression of ideas, an overt contradiction of one of our nation's founding principles.

The Theatrical Mirror

The Chinese opera, like the Elizabethan theatre, the Greek theatre, and the medieval theatre, was at the center of its society. All four of these theatres functioned as the mirror that, in Hamlet's words, revealed the "form and pressure" of "the very age and body of the time." The performance traditions and the subjects of the plays reflected the concerns of the community and the way the community understood and expressed itself.

Thus far we have observed the way the theatre has reflected religious beliefs, political organization, and social relationships. As we try to understand what the theatre has to tell us about the past, we are struck particularly by one theatrical convention shared by all of these theatres from vastly different periods and with extremely different political and religious points of view: Although women characters appeared on the stage, all the female roles were written and played by men.

In the theatres that we have studied in the first two chapters, women did not participate in any way except as audience members. The exclusion of women from participation in the theatre reflected a significant aspect of a social organization that excluded women from the public discourse. Just as women did not vote, hold office, or participate in the educational system or the government—with the exception of Elizabeth I—so they were not allowed to be part of the theatre as playwrights or actors. Women characters were presented, but women did not represent themselves through writing or acting. The female behavior constructed onstage was considered appropriate or even ideal. But men created all the images that represented women, both physically and psychologically.

Today, some theatre historians and social critics see this representation of women by men as an absence. That is, any actual sense of women was completely missing. The female characters were part of a man's world but not part of a woman's world. The female characters may have become erotic objects for the male characters or they may have reflected male attitudes toward women, but they did not genuinely represent the actual nature and concerns of women themselves.

In the Greek theatre, masks and costumes designated the gender of the characters, and because three actors played all the individual roles, actors moved back and forth between male and female characters. In the unmasked Elizabethan theatre, boys or young men played the female roles. In the Beijing Opera, elaborate makeup, costuming, and wigs were used to complete the illusion. In the Asian theatre, Chinese or Japanese actors were designated at an early age to take female roles, and their whole training focused on techniques of impersonation. These actors, called *dan* in the Beijing Opera, then played female roles throughout their careers.

By being excluded from the early forms of theatre, women lost a valuable opportunity to participate in the life of the community. Their voices were not heard, and so there was a serious distortion of what both women and men in a given society saw as "believable" female behavior. Because the theatre functions as a major source of culturally accepted gender identity, ideas or models of behavior were generated that defined women's roles and women's nature, even though women had no part in their creation. Demeaning stereotypes are often substituted for truthful representation when people are not able to speak for themselves. Conversely, inclusion in the theatre, in the making of a community's stories, is one of the most powerful ways to change a society from within.

Theatre and Social Change

South Africa

We turn to another part of the world, South Africa, to examine a further dimension of the relationship between theatre and social change. Through much of the twentieth century, South Africa pursued some of the most repressive government policies in modern history. Blatant segregation based on race was used to divide black and white citizens, to determine where people could live and with whom they could associate. Employment conditions and labor options open to people of color were dictated by the white minority government to the black majority of South Africans. Extreme poverty, lack of

Timeline of South African History and Apartheid

Date	Event
Origins:	Research identifies South Africa as one of the earliest areas, possibly the earliest area, inhabited by human ancestors, millions of years ago. Modern humans have lived in South Africa for as long as one hundred thousand years or more.
1652	First European settlement.
1800	Acceleration of colonization by British and Dutch people resulting in land dispossession for African people.
1948	Apartheid institutionalized as the governing apparatus of South Africa by the Boer leadership, which legalized the systematic segregation of races that had been developing since 1910 when the Union of South Africa was established. Black citizens forced to live in townships and home-lands facing censorship and brutal repression involving imprisonment and murder.
1950s	Athol Fugard (born 1932) begins his work as a playwright and a director.
1960	Sharpville Massacre: killing of unarmed black Africans (69 killed, 180 injured) who protested against the pass laws which restricted where black Africans could live and what employment was open to them.
	International movement of sanctions against South Africa expands following Sharpville Massacre.
1961	Fugard's first major play, *The Blood Knot*.
1962	Nelson Mandela (born 1918), leader of the African National Congress, arrested and eventually sentenced to life in prison. Mandela served much of his twenty-seven years of imprisonment on Robben Island.
1963–64	Rivonia Trial in which 10 leaders (black and white) of the African National Congress were tried for acts of sabotage against the state for trying to overthrow apartheid.
1973	First performance of *The Island*.
1976	Soweto Uprising: massive student protests at being forced to use the Afrikaan language (Dutch derived) instead of native African languages. Of the eleven languages currently recognized as official South African languages today, Afrikaan is spoken as a mother tongue by 13.3% of the population; English is spoken as a mother tongue by 8.2% of the population. Most of the remaining people speak an African language as their first language.
1977	Law student and black power leader Steven Biko dies in police custody. Following the death of Steven Biko most nations embrace sanctions against South Africa with the exception of the governments of the United States and Great Britain, although many citizens of both nations joined in various forms of boycotts.
1986	The United States Congress votes in favor of sanctions against South Africa over the veto of President Ronald Reagan.
1990	Nelson Mandela released from prison.
1991	Nelson Mandela elected president of the African National Congress and apartheid begins to be dismantled.

Date	Event
1994	Nelson Mandela elected president of South Africa in the first democratic elections with black citizens granted voting rights.
1996	Truth and Reconciliation Commission hearings.
1998	*Ubu and the Truth Commission.*
2010	*The Girl in the Yellow Dress.*
2012	*Mies Julie.*

education and opportunity, separation of families, as well as brutal work and living conditions were the result of *apartheid*, a network of laws established to privilege and enrich residents of European descent through the exploited labor and enforced servitude of black citizens. Resistance to apartheid resulted in persecution, arrest, imprisonment, and sometimes death. The system of apartheid was so brutal that until 1990 South Africa was considered an outcast from the international community of nations. It is only in the last twenty-five years that South Africa has attempted to govern itself democratically and transform the living conditions of its people. We are witnessing a process of change that is ongoing; many of the traumatic consequences of South Africa's turbulent history still need to be overcome. But instead of erupting into civil war, South Africa has found the beginning of a path toward a peacefully constituted multicultural society with a redistribution of power and privilege. This is a story of social change for our own time in which we can see the power

of the theatre's contribution to the re-making of a nation: first through resistance and protest and then through the forging of a new identity.

The Island was first produced at a tiny, radical theatre called The Space in Cape Town in 1973. This photo shows a recent revival of the play in 2013 at The Market Theatre in Johannesburg, which is one of the leading theatres in South Africa. The original actors were John Kani and Winston Ntshona, who collaborated with the director Athol Fugard in writing the play. The current revival is being directed by John Kani, with his son, Atandwa Kani, now acting the role of John originated by his father. The other actor is Nat Ramabulana. Although much of the play presents the hostile world governed by irrational conditions at the Robben Island prison, this scene shows the intense comradery between the two characters. They have just finished an exhausting day of digging and transporting sand, "grotesquely futile labor." They have been humiliated and beaten by the guard they call Hodoshe, green carrion fly. "I was sentenced to Life brother, not bloody Death!" Now they attempt to revive their spirits by enacting an imaginary phone call to old friends in a bar they frequented in happier times. With resilient good humor, they joke with their imaginary friends, and then more poignantly, ask to be remembered to their wives and children.

In the 2013 revival of *The Island* at the Market Theatre, the two prisoners stage a scene from *Antigone* as an entertainment for the other prisoners. Winston, played by Nat Ramabulana, takes on the character of Antigone, which at first he refuses to do. "I didn't walk with those men and burn my bloody passbook in front of that police station, and have a magistrate send me here for life so that he can dress me up like a woman and make a bloody fool of me." But Winston comes to recognize that his act of resistance, burning his passbook, is like Antigone's act of resistance, burying the body of her dead brother, against the decree of her uncle, the king. The two actors express the ideas that Sophocles wrote two thousand five hundred years ago as a warning against tyranny in Greece. The words of Sophocles take on a haunted meaning when they are adjusted to the justice system that sentences men to life on Robben Island. The actor, Atwanda Kani, who plays John, also plays the role of Creon.

Theatre and Resistance to Apartheid

In 1970 a white playwright who was also a theatre director began to work with two black actors on a play about justice and the prison system in South Africa. The very nature of their collaboration, blacks and whites working together, was prohibited. The subject of their play was a dangerous one: the human rights violations and the brutality with which political prisoners were treated on Robben Island. Robben Island was an infamous and remote island prison, seven miles out to sea from Cape Town, where incarceration was used to suppress dissent. At the time that the play was presented, Nelson Mandela, the leader of the opposition to apartheid, had already been imprisoned on Robben Island for a number of years. The audiences for this play also gathered in contradiction to the laws of South Africa, which prohibited the mixing of the races in public assembly. The production of *The Island* was one of the boldest examples of theatre performances, occurring in a number of cities at this time, aimed at breaking down barriers between the people who participated and encouraging black and white resistance to the increasingly repressive measures of the South African government. The presentation of these plays was an act of courage and a form of empowerment.

The development of *The Island* was innovative for other reasons. It was not the work of a single playwright but was devised by the three participants through improvisation and then arranged as a written text. The participants were the playwright, Athol Fugard, and the actors, John Kani and Winston Ntshona. All three knew a number of people who were or had been imprisoned on Robben Island, so the details of the play were drawn from actual experience. And the three collaborators also drew on another source for their story about the resistance to tyranny, the play *Antigone* by the Greek playwright Sophocles. A member of their theatre company, the Serpent Players, had been arrested and sent to Robben Island while they were rehearsing *Antigone* some years earlier. He had performed speeches for the other prisoners from Sophocles' play, and this episode also became part of *The Island*. In *The Island* the two characters determine to put on a scene from *Antigone* as part of one night's prison

The Handspring Puppet Company of Cape Town produced *Ubu and the Truth Commission* in response to the actual hearings conducted by Bishop Tutu on the crimes committed during apartheid. The piece combined puppetry, performance by live actors, music, animation, and documentary footage. Puppets, such as the one in the photo, represented the witnesses who testified at the hearings. Live actors spoke verbatim testimony while the puppets performed restrained actions such as the stirring of soup. The puppets enlarged the presence of the witnesses to a metaphoric and universal stature. The simple demeanor of the witness puppets with their excruciating stories was juxtaposed with another performance dynamic. Two live actors played characters taken from an absurdist play by Alfred Jarry entitled *Ubu Roi,* first produced one hundred years before the South African adaptation. Pa and Ma Ubu are vulgar, obscene, loud, and greedy, a representation of corrupt leaders desperate to save themselves now that their power has been stripped away. Pa and Ma Ubu are grotesque and wildly funny, adding a surprising element of humor to a deeply painful subject. Jane Taylor wrote the text for the play.

entertainment. They stage the scene where the king, Creon, sentences his niece to death for defying his orders not to give her brother, who has been killed, an honorable burial. The play sets two different battles between the rights of the individual and the abuse of the power of the state against each other. In the foreground is the daily struggle of two humble prisoners not to be crushed by a prison system that would take away their identities as individual human beings of worth. Their struggle is amplified by the commitment of a young woman to love and honor her dead brother according to religious law even though the king believes her brother is a traitor to the state. And behind both stories, all audience members would have recognized the fight of Nelson Mandela, imprisoned on Robben Island, to bring about a new day in South Africa.

The Island inspired other politically engaged theatre pieces and theatre practices in South Africa and contributed to the growing resistance in South Africa to apartheid. And because it was

The Girl in the Yellow Dress is set in Paris where a French-Congolese student, Pierre, played by Nat Ramabulana, is studying English with a British teacher, Celia, played by Marianne Oldham. Inspired by Ovid's myth of Echo and Narcissus, the play is foremost about "a young man trying to survive a troubled relationship." The romantic struggle of the couple shifts between witty exchanges and damaging accusations and revelations. The male/female conflict can be seen in terms of a power struggle connected to gender, to politics, to class, and to race. Written by Craig Higginson and directed by Malcolm Purkey for the Market Theatre, the play premiered in 2010 at the Grahamstown International Arts Festival in South Africa before touring to Scotland and Sweden. Since then new productions have been staged in New York and Chicago.

also performed widely outside of South Africa, it helped further galvanize international public opinion that helped bring economic and cultural sanctions against the South African government.

Truth and Reconciliation

In 1989 the new leader of South Africa's government, William de Klerk, realized that the situation in South Africa was unsustainable with the disenfranchisement of so many of its citizens and world opinion unanimously opposed to its policies. In a stunning reversal, Nelson Mandela, whom many people feared would die in prison, was released. His political party, the African National Congress, which had been banned, was legitimized. Groups that had been violently opposed began to seek ways to work together.

Not only did new, inclusive democratic policies need to be implemented, but the terrible damage done by apartheid had to be recognized and redressed.

In 1994 Nelson Mandela was elected president of South Africa. Two years later in 1996, under the leadership of Bishop Desmond Tutu, the Truth and Reconciliation Commission (TRC) was established to hold hearings across the country where witnesses were at last given the opportunity to testify about the atrocities they had experienced and government officials, prison guards, police, and soldiers were offered amnesty in exchange for detailing and acknowledging their crimes. The Truth and Reconciliation Commission hearings were the beginning of a healing process that is still in its early stages. As the theatre was essential to the resistance during apartheid, now it has another role to play as South Africans reexamine their bitter history and work to establish new relationships between the racial, ethnic, and language groups that make up this richly multicultural nation. Jane Taylor, who wrote the text for the play *Ubu and the Truth Commission*, shown on previous page, says, "that through the arts some of the difficult and potentially volatile questions, such as why we betray or abuse each other, could be addressed without destabilizing the fragile legal and political process of the TRC itself."[6]

Mandla Mbothwe is a director working with the Magnet Theatre in Cape Town. In 2010, more than a decade after *Ubu and the Truth Commission* was first presented, he produced a play in collaboration with his actors entitled *The Wound of a Healer* (*Inxeba Iomphilisi*). Mbothwe emphasizes the significance of individuals telling their personal stories, an experience initiated by the Truth and Reconciliation Commission.

> All of us South Africans were given bandages to bandage our wounds. But our wounds were never healed; our wounds were never really attended to. At this point in South Africa, the bandage is leaking. The production rips off the bandage and deals with the wound, cleans it. It's going to be painful, but you can't pass that stage. You cannot put the stories in archives. It's very early. One can't do it alone. We need an audience to watch when we rip off the bandage.

South African plays have also begun to embrace other themes, moving beyond the focus on the terrors of apartheid and the catastrophes left in its wake. South Africa, often referred to as the rainbow nation, is a country that formally recognizes eleven different languages. Ethnic groups with substantial histories in South Africa include indigenous African peoples as well as descendants of English, Dutch, Lithuanian, Indian, and other immigrant groups. Plays have begun to explore the many identities and histories represented within the South African population, as well as the new perspectives on social relationships within this rapidly transforming nation and between South Africa and other parts of the world.

Malcolm Purkey has been the director of the Market Theatre in Johannesburg for the last nine years, which produced the revival of *The Island* shown in photographs in this chapter. The Market Theatre was a major artistic force in the opposition to apartheid and remains one of the leading theatres in South Africa today. Purkey emphasizes the seismic shift in the landscape of South African thought.

> We live in a society that's in a new kind of a crisis. Democracy has thrown up new ways of seeing the world, and our theatre must engage with those. People have a great hunger to see reflections of themselves, to have light thrown on where we are in the world, how we are making progress.

Craig Higginson, a playwright and dramaturg at the Market Theatre, explains that no one play can represent the experience of the nation.

> We sometimes say that it's not in any one play that you will see a picture of South Africa, but in the dialogue between the different plays.[7]

Because of the unique contribution that theatre in South Africa makes to its own country and the world theatre, we will return to other plays from South Africa in later chapters in the book.

Conclusion

When we look at nations like China and South Africa, we can see in contemporary situations ways that theatre is used for government propaganda or to bring about revolutionary social change. In the United States theatre has often been part of the debate about social issues. At the time of the American Civil War, dramatic versions of Harriet Beecher Stowe's novel *Uncle Tom's Cabin* were performed all over the country and had a significant impact on the struggle to abolish slavery. During the Vietnam War in the 1960s and early 1970s, theatre was an important part of the national dialogue about the legitimacy of that conflict and was a vital part of the efforts that brought that war to an end. Today as a nation we are involved in debates about subjects like immigration, gender identity, equal opportunity, substance abuse, and the environment, as well as issues of war and peace.

Many theatre practitioners believe that the stories we tell in the theatre should be part of our national discussion. The plays included in this book, *Joe Turner's Come and Gone*, *And the Soul Shall Dance*, *Angels in America*, and *Water by the Spoonful*, are first and foremost examples of strong theatrical storytelling concerned with the human condition. But each, in its own way, also focuses on different areas of the American experience and the challenges we face early in the twenty-first century.

Summary

Unlike the Greek and medieval theatres, which were basically religious and depended on community participation, Elizabethan theatre and the Beijing Opera were secular and professional. Elizabethan drama focused primarily on human motivation and the internal struggles of psychologically complex characters. Reflecting the curiosity and expansiveness of the Renaissance, Elizabethan drama took on the whole realm of human endeavor. The vitality of Elizabethan drama came from vivid and poetic language, most highly regarded in the works of William Shakespeare. Performing on a bare platform stage during Shakespeare's time, the actors were able to create a continually changing panorama of events and locations through the playwright's expressive words.

Before the Cultural Revolution (from 1966 to 1976), Chinese plays focused on domestic, social, and military situations, supporting the existing values of society. The Chinese playwright's goal, however, was not to create an immortal work but to provide a vehicle for the highly trained Chinese actor. The Beijing Opera was a theatre of stylized gesture and choreographed, acrobatic movement. The conventions of this theatre included a refined movement vocabulary that conveyed meaning just as spoken scripts do in Western theatre.

Theatre has always reflected religious belief, social organization, and issues of concern to the community. In the twentieth century, the theatre began to question the construction of identity in relation to race and gender. In South Africa the theatre played a vital role in exposing the catastrophic inequities of racial politics and has begun to explore the emerging identities of people whose position in society has been drastically altered. No matter what its specific concerns, however, theatre is a community endeavor with the power to reinforce, to celebrate, to challenge, and to sustain.

Topics for Discussion and Writing

1. On the basis of the examples discussed in the chapter, what differences do you find between religious and secular theatre?

2. What makes theatre a useful tool for propaganda?

3. The chapter discusses the exclusion of actual women from the theatres of the past. How were women represented on the stage? What conventions were used to create female characters? Are there any such conventions used today for the representation of women or men in the theatre, in film, or on television?

 For suggested readings and other resources related to this chapter, please visit www.mhhe.com/creativespirit6e

CHAPTER 4

The Art of the Actor

In Chapter 3 we studied the collaboration among playwright, director, actors, and designers in producing *Joe Turner's Come and Gone.* We began with the work of the playwright, August Wilson, but, in fact, at the center of the theatre is the work of the actor. If everything that was not absolutely necessary to the theatre were stripped away, we would be left with the actor, a simple playing space, and the audience. The impulse to perform, discussed at the beginning of this book, is the essential force of the theatre. The work of all of the other theatre practitioners builds on the impulse to perform: the creation of stories for the actor to play; costumes to enhance or define the actor's body; scenery and light to provide an environment for the action; music and sound to build atmosphere, mood, and energy.

In the 2005 Broadway production of Martin McDonagh's play *The Pillowman,* Billy Crudup plays Katurian, a character devoted to the gruesome fairy tales he invents. Here he attacks his disabled brother, Michal, played by Michael Stuhlbarg. Of his character Crudup says, "I've never played someone who was as grotesquely distorted by his own history."[1] Crudup's character, part enthusiastic storyteller and part monster, draws the audience through the twists and turns of the play with black humor that shocks in its savage details. Crudup must invest this character with the passion and intensity to account for Katurian's startling actions.

The Presence of the Actor

In Chapter 1 we examined the transformation of the Hopi when they are inhabited by the kachina spirits, and we considered the transformation of the Greek actor through the mask. Whether or not an idea of the supernatural or a mask is part of the process, the actor always undergoes a transformation when appearing onstage in front of an audience. The actor becomes more than an ordinary person going about daily life. The actor in performance becomes a presence charged with energy and vitality who transmits a heightened sense of life to the audience. As the actor opens up to greater emotional and sensory awareness, the audience members also experience heightened awareness. The actor is able to project a sense of character life across the stage space and the auditorium space to reach the audience. The actor invents a world onstage that audience members may also inhabit through their imaginations.

David Warrilow, an actor known for his adventurous work in the plays of Samuel Beckett and in exploratory theatre forms, sees the actor-audience relationship as a matter of trust:

> If I as an actor invest myself to the best of my ability in the work I have chosen to present—if I give it my best energy—then there's a chance that the audience can trust what is going on on stage. If I hold back, if I sit in judgment on myself or the material or the audience, then there is less chance that the audience is going to be justified in trusting and therefore joining the experience. If the actor is willing to go through some kind of transmutation, then the audience can, too.[2]

Frequently the actor's presence is described as a kind of double or triple existence. On the stage the actor is always present in his or her own person. In addition to this elemental self, the actor creates a character who has his or her own boundaries separate from those of the actor's own person. The performer projects a double representation of self and character. A third layer of the actor's presence might be considered a critical facility that the actor uses to step back from the performance and view it from the audience's perspective, making adjustments and modifications as necessary. BW Gonzalez, who played Mattie Campbell in *Joe Turner's Come and Gone*, describes the actor's state of mind as one of "hyperawareness."[3] Stephen Spinella, who played Prior in *Angels in America* at the Eureka Theatre, at the Mark Taper Forum, and on Broadway, discussed in Chapter 10, says that he is always aware of his own presence on the stage and the presence of the audience:

> I am absolutely, completely conscious of the audience. I feel what they are doing. I'm completely conscious of what's going on in my body. It's the height of reality. I actually feel as though I'm suspended above myself or in back of myself and my body. Everything is moving and doing exactly what it should be doing. And I'm saying to myself, "Now do this," making little tiny artistic choices.[4]

In a solo show entitled *9 Parts of Desire,* Heather Raffo plays nine different Iraqi women characters. She must shift between ages and character circumstances, between speech patterns and physicality. Each character is so vivid that they all seem to be present onstage by the end of the performance, listening to the stories of the other characters. Raffo developed the text for the play by drawing on her interviews with ordinary Iraqi citizens over a period of ten years. The play creates a social document about life in Iraq before and after the American military intervention through the characters' different perspectives on the upheavals that define their lives. The play, which has toured widely, was first performed at the Manhattan Ensemble Theater in 2004 under the direction of Joanna Settle.

The actor commands the attention of the audience by bringing concentrated and explosive energy onto the stage. The actor brings the stage space to life and sweeps the audience up in the

Summary of the Actor's Responsibilities

- To study the text
- To memorize lines and blocking quickly
- To bring new ideas to the rehearsal process on a daily basis
- To work openly with the director and other actors
- To be creative in rehearsal
- To constantly refine and adjust character development
- To work with consistent high energy
- To maintain health and flexibility of voice and body
- To sustain freshness in performance and execute repeated performances at a consistent level of quality

vitality of the performance. This energy is part of the actor's charisma. In this respect, the actor is like an athlete or a rock star. For the actor, the energy may be less overtly displayed than for a football receiver leaping to make a catch or a popular singer dancing in front of the microphone. But high-voltage energy is present nonetheless, and the audience senses the electricity generated by the actor's presence.

Because of the unique nature of live performance—with the very real connection between performer and audience—the actor receives energy from the audience just as the audience is energized by the actor's presence. For BW Gonzalez, the energy generated by the audience contributes directly to her readiness to begin the play.

> Before I say my first line, once I feel the energy of the audience, I feel perfectly at home on the stage.[5]

Sean McNall, who recently played Hamlet, believes Shakespeare intended a personal relationship between Hamlet and the audience to be an essential part of the play, particularly in the soliloquies such as the one presented in the photograph on page 116:

> In *Hamlet* you reach out to the audience and you cast the audience in a certain way so you know to whom you are speaking and the reason why you need to address them at this moment. With this particular part, the audience became a kind of conscience, a touchstone. Having the audience on my side was of great importance. But I had to assume that they weren't simply on my side. So when I had the opportunity to reach out to them, I was always making a case. Suddenly, I had all this different energy coming at me.[6]

Stephen Spinella sees the audience energy as a major catalyst for his performance:

> The theatrical event requires the overwhelming focus of the audience. The actors, who have acquired that attention through control of the space and the moment, have power, and if the muse is with them, that power makes them soar.[7]

The actor Heather Robison, whose photograph appears on page 123, sees the audience as the final defining factor in the theatre event:

> The play doesn't work without the audience. That's when the play first lives. The audience is the last character of the play and you live and breathe with them.[8]

James Earl Jones also uses the analogy of flight to describe the propulsion that the audience brings to the performance:

> All acting, at its best, is about entering the stage and, spiritually, going to the edge of that cliff that is the proscenium, acknowledging there is an energy there, and like a sky-diver, pushing yourself off. You trust the thermal waves of energy that the audience is and you soar.[9]

The Actor's Craft

The vitality and talent of the actor are contained and shaped through the development of technique. We expect musicians to study and practice for many years to perfect skills on the piano, the cello, or the saxophone and to acquire subtleties of musicianship. Dancers, too, commit themselves to a training schedule of many hours a day to develop their physical abilities and artistry. In the same way, technique is essential to the actor working on the stage.

We can easily summarize the skills that most actors work to achieve and maintain. The vocal technique of the actor involves the ability to control and project the voice, to speak with richness of tone and nuance of expression, to enunciate with clarity at all times, to use dialects and accents with authenticity, to maintain a healthy voice that doesn't succumb to overuse, to give the language of Shakespeare or August Wilson its own style and rhythm, to speak for the characters and the playwright with authority and imagination. Physical technique allows the actor to move with grace; to command the stage space; to change posture, gestures, and body rhythms to create a range of characters; to present a sense of period style; to perform at a high level of intensity every day; to achieve the appropriate degree of relaxation and freedom from tension; to dance or juggle or walk on stilts.

However, performance skills alone do not make an actor. The words *alchemy* and *magic* are frequently used to describe the way the actor animates the skills of performance and gives life to a dramatic text or situation. Analogy is often used to describe acting because it is difficult to define the actor's process with precision. First, many forces intervene: the text, the director, the other actors, the rehearsal structure and duration, the playing space. Second, acting is such a personal and individual endeavor that it can be impossible to identify with certainty what has taken place internally to produce the result that the audience sees. Some choices are conscious; some are the result of intuitive responses to the text or the rehearsal situation. To investigate the components of the actor's work, we begin with the phases the actor goes through before arriving at a performance in front of an audience: the audition, individual preparation for the role, and the rehearsal.

The Work of the Actor

Competing for Roles: The Audition

One of the harshest and must grueling aspects of the actor's profession is the **audition.** Acting is a highly competitive business. There are many more actors and aspiring actors than there are acting opportunities at every level of theatre

The actors warm up in rehearsal for a production of *Apollo* directed by Nancy Keystone at Portland Center Stage in 2009. The actors perform a complex sequence of exercises that build stamina and flexibility and also provide a way for them to connect to the images in the play and physically and emotionally to one another. One of the cast members, Richard Gallegos, explains: "The warm-up brings us into the rehearsal room, into a collective energy, and it establishes a common vocabulary. It encompasses the body, the breath, and the psyche. It completely makes us a unit."[10]

The professional actor is a kind of magician who can do what we, the audience, cannot. Bill Irwin has an extensive background in mime and dance that also includes studying at the Clown College of Ringling Brothers Barnum and Bailey Circus. In fact, he began his acting career as a clown with the Pickle Family Circus. He then began to develop his own magical "new vaudeville" pieces, such as *Largely New York* (1989) shown here, that have no spoken text and depend on the broad, comic physicality of the actor to communicate.

and film production, in part because of the passion that actors feel about their work and in part because of the large rewards for the few "stars." To enter the competition for roles or places in training programs, actors must participate in auditions.

The audition allows directors and casting directors to see how different actors may fill a certain role or to see which actors complement each other as a group to make an **ensemble.** Because auditions are usually set up to screen a large number of people, the actors are allotted very little time to convince those making the casting decisions of their "rightness" for the part and the depth of their talent. For example,

the Yale School of Drama auditions 900 aspiring actors for its graduate training program. Of those 900, only 16 students are offered places. Likewise, hundreds of dancers and singers may audition for the roles in the chorus of a Broadway musical, and smaller theatres attract scores of actors to their auditions.

Furthermore, auditions may call for unique combinations of talents. Susan Stroman auditioned actors for both the recent revival of *Oklahoma!* (1999) and the new production of *The Producers* (2001). For *Oklahoma!* the actors had to sing and dance and then do a monologue. For *The Producers* they also had to be able to tell jokes. Richard Gallegos, who appears as the Ghost of

Sean McNall is a young actor who won an Obie (Off Broadway) award in 2008 for sustained excellence in performance. He is shown here playing Hamlet in the Pearl Theatre's 2007 production directed by Shep Sobel. McNall has been a member of the Pearl Theatre's resident acting company since 2003, which reflects his goal of being an actor in an ongoing repertory company rather than participating in a continuous sequence of auditions. "What I don't like about the way the business of theatre works is that every production and every performance, particularly in New York, is an audition for the next performance. Some people are able to be creative with the thrill of that. But I think that is a detriment to the creative spirit because that's where people find out what they're good at and then they craft and hone exactly what they're good at, in much the same way that we try to make the best "product." We turn ourselves into a product and we sell that product. This is the model that many of us work with and I'm just not attracted to that. So being in a company gives me this opportunity to be bad, to fail, to do something radically different for a change. Time and time again, that is rewarding."[11]

the Prisoner of Camp Dora in the photograph of *Apollo* on page 130, recalls a memorable audition experience:

> For six years I did the *Wild Wild Wild West Stunt Show* at Universal Studios. When I auditioned, I didn't know what I was getting myself into. I thought they wanted me to tumble and do a couple of cartwheels. They took us into this big warehouse at Universal Studios. There were about 300 of us. They unveiled this huge platform that was about twenty feet high and there was a big fall pad. They wanted us to climb up there and do a forward fall. I was scared out of my mind. The majority of them were actual stunt men. Somehow I weaseled myself into this audition and made the cut. I was there and I just had to breathe in. I remember climbing the ladder and saying to myself, "waiting tables, stunt show, waiting tables . . ." and the next thing I knew, my body was in the air and I did it and I got the job. It was crazy.[12]

Directors pride themselves on being able to recognize almost instantly the qualities that they seek for a certain role. Gordon Davidson, former artistic director of the Mark Taper Forum, says, "I have a feeling within a minute of the audition that you know whether you're in the presence of talent or not."[13] The composer and lyricist Stephen Sondheim can judge singing ability in sixteen measures, or even in eight or four bars of a song.[14] This tendency toward immediate judgment puts enormous pressure on the actor in the audition to deliver a knockout performance. Actors, in fact, study auditioning techniques as part of their career preparation and constantly work to hone their auditioning skills.

Some auditions may involve the presentation of set pieces that the actors have had a chance to study and prepare in detail in advance of the audition. Actors perform monologues or songs of their own choosing for graduate training programs, repertory theatre, or summer stock opportunities—all situations that require actors to take multiple roles. Actors try to choose

Sage Howard and Brandon Zerr-Smith audition for a production of *Anna in the Tropics* at Lewis and Clark College with scripts in hand. They receive feedback from the director before reading the scene again. Actors are strongly encouraged to study the full text before auditioning for a play.

one of the most important factors that directors try to ascertain in the audition:

> Directors want to come away from an audition knowing that they're going to be able to work with the actor, and that the actor is imaginative enough and well-trained enough to handle different directions. They also need to get a feel for what the actor will be like to work with for an extended period of time.[15]

material from well-respected plays and musicals, but also material that directors may not have already seen hundreds of times. The pieces also need to be well suited to the actor and show the range of the actor's abilities.

A dramatic audition consisting of two contrasting monologues is frequently limited to four minutes. A singing audition may be limited to thirty-two measures of music. In that scant time, actors must show their understanding of the text, their speech or singing skills, their energy, and their ability to reach an audience. The actor must jump into the heart of the character and the play and deliver the lines or the song with all the passion and intensity of a performance, usually without the help of a supporting cast, set, or costumes. The audition also reveals how much training the actors have, their stage presence, and their openness. Jack Bowdan, who casts for Broadway and television, emphasizes that the ability to take direction is

Some auditions focus on cold readings of scenes from the play that is going into production. In this situation, with minimal preparation, actors must read from the script, often with a stage manager or some other member of the production staff who is not an actor as their scene partner. The producer Stuart Ostrow believes that although the cold reading is "the best of a worst lot," its benefits outweigh the drawbacks:

> What it does first and foremost is tell you about the intelligence quotient of the actor. And I would always opt for an intelligent actor, even though he may be wrong for the part. In the creation of a play, that cold reading leads to an understanding about the actor's capacity for imagination and creativity.[16]

If the actor gets through the initial phase of the audition and is called back for further readings, then the process opens up in interesting

James Earl Jones transformed his physical appearance to play the boxer Jack Jefferson in *The Great White Hope* (1967) at the Arena Stage in Washington, D.C. The physical training involved in preparing for the role of a boxer also provided psychological insight into the character. James Earl Jones and Jane Alexander, shown here, also re-created their stage roles for the film version of Howard Sackler's play.

ways, depending on the type of production and the producing company. Interviews, group improvisations, and extended readings with other potential cast members may all be part of the "callback." But first, actors must show that they have enough talent, skill, flexibility, and commitment to stand out from the crowd. No matter how stressful or disappointing the audition process may be, all actors must struggle through the ordeal of auditioning if they are to work. Tamu Gray, who played Bertha in *Joe Turner's Come and Gone*, summarizes the feelings of many actors when she says, "You must raise an amazing amount of courage to go out and audition, but that makes you even stronger because you do it."[17]

Preparing for the Role

When a part has been secured, actors may go to extraordinary lengths to prepare for their roles. They might read histories and biographies or study real-life situations, or they might immerse themselves in the actual circumstances of characters' lives before they try to re-create or interpret those circumstances on the stage or in front of the camera. Sometimes actors transform themselves physically, losing or gaining weight or participating in intense physical training to reshape their bodies or learn difficult physical skills.

James Earl Jones is an actor known for his distinguished performances in the plays of Shakespeare, the South African Athol Fugard,

The Necessary Skills and Talents of the Actor

- Interest in human nature
- Keen observation
- A good memory
- Concentration
- Imagination
- The drive to appear on the stage in front of an audience
- The ability to create characters and interpret dramatic situations
- A strong, expressive voice
- An expressive face and body
- High energy and physical stamina
- The ability to work openly as part of a group process
- Discipline

and August Wilson, as well as for his film work, including the famous voice of Darth Vader in *Star Wars*. To play the role of Jack Jefferson, a boxer, in *The Great White Hope*, by Howard Sackler, Jones undertook the training of a fighter:

> I didn't have the bulk of a fighter but I had the sinewiness, the flexibility. In Washington D.C., when we were at the Arena Stage, I had a trainer named Bill Terry who was a former fighter. He took me through the life of a boxer-in-training. Every morning you get up, you run a certain number of miles, you go to the gymnasium, you consume certain kinds of liquids and foods that are good for strength and endurance.

Jones then shaved his beard and his head as part of his mental and physical preparation:

> At this point the physical training I had been doing came into focus and I was a different person. By then I had learned, with the director Ed Sherin's encouragement, to walk and behave physically, unconsciously like an athlete, which I'm not. By the time I finished the run of the play and the film, I hated the training. I was not good at diets and I wanted to be free to eat what I thought my body was crying out for in terms of sustenance.[18]

The Rehearsal Process

In Chapter 3, we reviewed the work of the actors as they rehearsed *Joe Turner's Come and Gone*. We saw them studying the text, memorizing lines, seeking the characters' motivation, developing the characters' relationships, rehearsing blocking patterns, and finding the speech rhythms that would give authenticity to their characters and bring passion and eloquence to the playwright's words.

What happens in rehearsal is a very intricate process of give-and-take between the actors and the director. For a production to have vitality and originality, the rehearsal must be a time of exploration. Discoveries must be made about the characters and their relationships. Staging ideas are tested and discarded. Rhythms and pacing are built and adjusted.

The Actor's Commitment   Acting is extraordinarily hard work. It is a physical and mental process that requires great physical stamina and high energy. Actors must be able to remember their lines, work creatively, and be open and receptive to one another and the director. They must come to rehearsal well rested and fully alert, able to concentrate intensely on the work at hand, whether it is repeating a sword fight many times or discovering the intimate rhythms of a love scene. At each rehearsal, actors must be prepared to try out new approaches to line readings and blocking or to refine choices that have already been made. Rehearsals demand at least as much from the actors as performances; and, for some, rehearsals are the most satisfying part of the production process.

In *Hamlet*, the actor playing Ophelia must find a way to express the character's desperation resulting from the death of her father and her rejection by Hamlet. But the reactions of the other characters are essential to building the belief that she is, as Claudius says, "divided from herself," and in her brother Laertes's words, "a document in madness." In this photo, Laertes reacts with dismay as he tries to comprehend his sister Ophelia's incoherent speeches. Laertes is played by David L. Townsend and Ophelia by Jolly Abraham in the 2007 Pearl Theatre production of *Hamlet* directed by Shep Sobel.

Kathleen Chalfant, who played multiple roles in *Angels in America*, including the part of Ethel Rosenberg, describes rehearsals as a way of pulling a role or a text apart in order to put it back together again:

> In order to learn to act you must take apart something that happens faster than thought, break it into its component parts, and then put it back together. That's also what rehearsal is, breaking down a speech or a reaction, and then getting it close to the speed at which a human being actually does it. Quite often, plays are just a little slower than life because you've added a step, the breaking down. The trick is to act as quickly as you think, which is not necessarily a function of speed. When you're doing it properly, it often feels as though you have all the time in the world. Then you can allow yourself to be entirely taken, with no conscious control. That's what being in the moment means. In order to be prepared to give yourself over to the moment, you have to have done all the work beforehand: knowing the words backwards and forwards, knowing where you're supposed to stand, and more importantly, knowing what the character is doing at every turn and why she does it.[19]

Action and Reaction   In rehearsal, actors discover their actions and their reactions. Much of their work depends on playing actions that communicate a passionate expression of life's defining moments. The action may be contained in a speech such as Hamlet's "To be, or not to be, that is the question," or Bynum's story of the "shiny man." The action may be physicalized through gesture—for example, when the actor playing Herald Loomis cuts himself with the knife or when the actor playing Juliet drinks the sleeping potion.

But as important as the actors' actions are the actors' reactions. Much of what actors create comes through reaction, through response, through seeing and believing. Actors bring a sense of the environment onto the stage; they feel the weather—the cold wind blowing through the cracks of a dilapidated house or the stifling heat of an urban summer. They experience the weariness of the passing of time, see the opulence of a ballroom or the emptiness of a Beckett landscape. Most of all, through reaction, actors give reality to the characters of the other actors onstage. They make these characters believable for the audience by the way that they watch and register the truth of what they have seen. They recognize loss, and they recognize triumph. They feel a threat and respond to an invitation. The art of acting has to do with creative expression and with the construction of belief.

Improvisation

Improvisation is a useful rehearsal method for enhancing belief and creating imaginative actions. It is used with increasing frequency in many different kinds of production situations. Improvisation can be defined as spontaneous invention that goes beyond the scripted material to explore aspects of character or situation. Actors may do group improvisations at the beginning of rehearsals as a warm-up. They may also use improvisation to solve acting problems or to generate staging ideas. Improvisation is also an important method for establishing creative rapport between actors. Most acting students now have considerable exposure to improvisation as a fundamental part of their training.

One of the most common improvisations involves playing a scene in the actors' own words instead of the playwright's scripted words. This technique allows actors to work through scene content and to explore areas of the characters' relationships. For example, there may be an argument between two characters that lasts two minutes or less in the actual play. The two actors involved might then improvise a much longer argument to explore the sources of the tension between their characters. Their improvisation might even involve extreme physical interactions to help shape the verbal exchange. The scripted

In this photo from *The Piano Lesson,* Boy Willie has persuaded his friend Lymon to help him move the piano so that it can be sold. However, the characters find that they are unable to budge the piano from its spot. The two actors must be convincing in their efforts to push or lift the piano and they must react to one another's attempts as if they are using all of their strength and still failing to move the piano at all. Jason Dirden, to the left of the piano, plays Lymon, and Brandon J. Dirden plays Boy Willie in the 2012 production directed by Ruben Santiago-Hudson for the Signature Theatre.

argument might be set at a dining room table or in a court of law, where restrained behavior is expected, but to get to the strong feelings underlying the situation, the two actors might improvise some physical interaction while saying their lines. They might begin a tug-of-war or shoving match to heighten their responses to each other. The actors then use the intensity generated by the physicalization of the conflict in their verbal exchanges when they play the argument as scripted in the more confined situation.

Improvisation can also take the form of a game. Actors often invent situations in which, for example, the weather, the age of the characters, or the nature of the relationships keeps changing. Actors also improvise stories in which one person begins with a single word or a sentence and then the other actors add pieces to the developing narration. Improvisation can also involve invented languages in which the actors communicate for long periods of time through made-up words. Susan Stroman, whose work as a director and choreographer is discussed in Chapter 11, on musical theatre, has dancers who have no lines to speak create "back stories" to give each of them more character detail and a sense of individual development when they dance their roles.

Improvisation is also used with increasing frequency today to create the actual play text or dramatic structure. Instead of a playwright who provides a complete script before the rehearsal process has begun, the actors, in collaboration with the director, invent both the plot elements and the text together. *The Island,* discussed in Chapter 2 was developed through improvisation as were many parts of *Apollo,* a large-scale performance piece considered in this chapter.

Improvisation is a liberating technique for actors that encourages spontaneity and quickness and can deepen relationships with the other actors in a production. Most of all, by immersing themselves completely in the given circumstances, actors use improvisation to increase their commitment to the truth of the situation.

The Rehearsal Schedule   In **equity theatres** (theatres with more than 100 seats in which all actors are paid according to a union contract), rehearsals last eight hours a day. At the Oregon Shakespeare Festival, which must rehearse several plays at once because actors perform in repertory, rehearsals are held in four-hour units. Actors may rehearse two different plays in one day or rehearse for one play during the day and perform a different play during the evening. In **equity waiver theatres** (theatres with fewer than 100 seats that are not governed by union regulations), rehearsals may last several hours each evening after actors finish their other jobs.

The standard rehearsal process for a play begins with the reading aloud of the script by the company. Sometimes the actors read their parts; sometimes the director reads to the actors. The objective of the reading is for all the actors to hear the words as a starting point for their work. The actors are neither expected nor encouraged to have defined their characters at the first reading. Decisions made too early in the process may impede the work to be done. First readings are not meant to be performances and can sometimes seem very flat.

The work done after the first reading is usually referred to as "table work." It involves the kind of discussion, questioning, and rereading of the play that we observed in the early rehearsals of *Joe Turner's Come and Gone.* During the table work, the director might present the actors with background materials as well as establish the directorial concept or interpretation of the play that will be pursued.

Collaboration with the Designers   Sometimes the designers participate during this phase by showing the actors a model of the set and costume sketches, or "renderings." The participation of the designers helps the actors to imagine the world of the play being constructed and contributes to their own work on their characters. The costume designer's interpretation of a character in terms of silhouette,

For *The Belle's Strategem* produced in 2005 at the Oregon Shakespeare Festival under the direction of Davis McCallum, Heather Robison played a character that she says "asked her to be three different people." The play originally written by Hannah Cowley in 1780 is about views of love and marriage and involves the central character disguising herself to test the heart of the man she hopes to marry. Robison says the role "pulled on every bit of training I've ever had, from movement and speech and text analysis to dance and all of my circus training." Robison collaborated closely with the costume designer Deborah Dryden and found the costume designs were essential to the shift in her character from a proper member of society to a "gauche, country bumpkin," appearing in a petticoat, "with all of her formality and the preconceived ideas of what a lady should be in that time period stripped away. I found it very freeing to wear something so risqué and dangerous. Then she has permission to do anything."[20]

color, weight and texture of fabric, and accessories has enormous implications for the actors' own work in defining character. The presentation of the designers' work gives the actors a sense of the visual style of the production and makes clear the physical realities and practical requirements of the set and costumes: how many steps they will have to navigate, how long a skirt will be, what colors their character will wear. Joe Mantello, who played the role of Louis in *Angels in America*, found costume choices to be an important part of the foundation for his character work:

> Louis is always looking to be judged. Tony Kushner, the playwright, and I always saw Louis wearing oversized boy clothes that he could disappear into when things got hard, when he was being judged. . . . Louis is swimming in his clothes. They make him look like he just wouldn't grow up. . . . In rehearsal

I always wore an overcoat or a scarf that I made sure was too big for me.[21]

Early on in the rehearsal process, the actors will start wearing **rehearsal costumes.** Doing so allows them to practice with the limitations created by their particular costume pieces and also to experience the feelings generated by wearing particular items of clothing and undergarments. The difference between wearing a baseball cap and wearing a bowler hat or between a cotton bandana and a velvet hat with feathers is enormous. Likewise, a change in shoes from cowboy boots to wing tips or from tennis shoes to high heels makes a huge difference not only to posture and style of walking but most significantly to how the actor feels. The designers' input feeds the actors' creative process. BW Gonzalez recently played Lady Macbeth in *Macbeth*, written by William Shakespeare. She began the rehearsal process wearing boots but found that the boots made her "too masculine." They "stopped her energy and blocked the sensuality" she and the director had determined were central to the character. Ultimately she wore sandals for most of the play and was barefoot in the famous sleepwalking scene.[22]

Approaches to Acting

Actors take many different approaches to their work on a role. Frequently, for the same production, actors work in different ways and use a combination of techniques they find useful. Ultimately, the style of acting throughout the production must be consistent. That is, the audience must perceive that all the actors are in the same play.

The Internal Approach

In a simplified overview of approaches to acting, we can distinguish between a psychological, internal approach and a technical, external approach. The **internal acting approach** involves identifying as closely as possible with the character

The actors in *Dying City* must deal with a very complicated subtext. Kelly is the young widow of a soldier killed in Iraq. Peter, the twin brother of Kelly's husband, has arrived unannounced at her apartment. The play unravels a secret past as it explores the sexual relationships of the characters. Diane Davis, seated, plays Kelly and Ryan King, standing, plays Peter, in *Dying City* by Christopher Shinn at Hartford Stage under the direction of Maxwell Williams in 2008. Ryan King also plays Peter's twin brother Craig in flashbacks to the past.

to be played. This internal approach is associated with the acting innovations developed by Konstantin Stanislavsky (see Chapter 7). Actors using a psychological method look for areas of the character's life that somehow correspond to their own experiences. They draw on their own personal histories and reactions to contribute to the life they create for the character. Actors working internally view the character as having a life beyond what is contained in the play text; they may develop an autobiography that provides them with a sense of the character's past. They investigate motivation in great depth to discover what the character wants from the other characters at any given moment in the play. They fill in the "subtext"—that is, what thoughts occur behind or between the character's lines but go unspoken. The subtext is translated into a stream of consciousness called the "inner monologue" that becomes the actor's silent text. The subtext is not expressed verbally but is communicated through vocal tone, gesture, or facial expression. The actors work to feel the emotions of the character's situation as if they were in the character's place. They are constantly asking why, constantly seeking the source or cause of behavior. Physical choices follow from psychological exploration, and it is this physicalization that reflects the character's state of mind.

The External Approach

In contrast to the internal approach, some actors work technically to give characterization a clear, external shape. Much of our discussion of acting thus far has centered on the actor's identification with the character. When actors seek ways of linking their inner lives with the inner life of the character, they are in the realm of psychological acting. Because so much of American theatre and American actor training depends on an internal, psychological approach, it is harder for us to understand the nature and validity of external, technical approaches to acting.

The **external acting approach** has more to do with conscious choices about how language is to be spoken, which physical details to emphasize, and how emotional content is to be expressed. The actor creates a structure for character through imagination and analysis but not through psychological identification. Under such circumstances, a character's emotion may be created through the manipulation of the actor's expressive abilities rather than through the actor's actual emotional response. For actors who begin with an external approach, the speaking of the text is frequently the foundation for their work. Character emerges from the investigation of the language, the content and sounds of the words, the rhythm and phrasing. Brandon Dirden, seen in the photo of the two actors moving the piano on page 121, says that actors must follow the rhythm that August Wilson writes into his language. "I think Wilsonian actors can embrace all of the beauty of the language and know it's in the language and not outside . . . This is not me doing something to the language, this is the language doing something to me."[23] Bill Irwin begins by creating an oversize physical reality for the character. But actors who work externally can also be conscious of the needs and goals of their character, what we have called objectives or motivation; although Irwin takes a physical approach to characterization, he acknowledges that he is always aware of what his character wants. An external choice often unlocks a strong emotional response.

Acting Cordelia in *King Lear*

To further explore the concepts of internal and external acting approaches we consider here possible approaches to the role of Cordelia in Shakespeare's *King Lear*. In the opening scene of the play, Lear's youngest daughter, Cordelia, faces the most difficult decision of her life. Her father, King Lear, has decided to give up his throne and divide his kingdom among his three daughters. He has assembled his daughters and the entire court to make a public ceremony out of his abdication of the throne. But he is looking for a show of adulation from his children in exchange for his apparent generosity in giving them a share of the lands and property. The king insists that his three daughters respond to his demand, "Which of you shall we say doth love us most." In responding to this manipulative ploy, Cordelia must either compromise her own beliefs to satisfy her father's vanity, or she must

This photo shows the moment early in Act 1 of Shakespeare's *King Lear* when King Lear asks his daughter Cordelia to declare how much she loves him. King Lear is played by Len Cariou and Cordelia is played by Blair Brown in the 1974 production directed by Michael Langham at the Guthrie Theater in Minneapolis. The stage picture makes clear who holds the power in this scene and underscores the vulnerability of Cordelia's position as she tries to find a truthful answer to her father's perplexing question.

disappoint him publicly to maintain her own integrity. Her two sisters, Goneril and Regan, make elaborate declarations of love, and Lear rewards them each with a third of his kingdom. But although Cordelia loves her father far more than do her sisters, she cannot offer the kind of false praise he seeks.

In the following two speeches, Cordelia tries to explain her position. She loves her father as a devoted and faithful daughter, but she knows that human beings have multiple loyalties and multiple claims on their affections. Because she is about to be married herself, she is acutely aware that her love must be divided.

CORDELIA: Unhappy that I am, I cannot heave
My heart into my mouth. I love your Majesty
According to my bond, no more nor less.
. . . .
                    Good my lord,
You have begot me, bred me, loved me. I
Return those duties back as are right fit,
Obey you, love you, and most honor you.
Why have my sisters husbands if they say
They love you all? Haply when I shall wed,
That lord whose hand must take my plight shall carry
Half my love with him, half my care and duty.
Sure I shall never marry like my sisters,
To love my father all.[24]

An actor playing Cordelia who works internally might carefully consider and construct a family history, particularly focusing on Cordelia's relationship with her father. She might invent situations in which Cordelia has acquiesced to her father in the past, encouraging him in his belief that she will follow his desires in this scene. The actor might even imagine situations in which Lear and Cordelia have clashed before in order to explore the dynamics of the power struggle between them. The nature of the relationship might be worked out together by the actors playing Lear and Cordelia. Then when Cordelia speaks to Lear, the actor can use this history as a reference point; she can work to project a sense of what has already passed between them.

As part of an internal process, the actor might also look for her own emotional connections to the situation in two different ways. She might imagine what it would be like to be faced with such a dilemma. By making the pressures of Lear's demands seem real, feelings of her own might surface. The actor might also go back through her own personal history to a time when she faced a difficult choice or defied an authority figure with whom she had a close relationship, such as her own father or mother. This process is called "substitution"—the actor uses feelings she recalls from her own experiences as the foundation for the character's responses in the play.

The actor might also work on the character's thought process to create a flow of ideas and responses that we have identified as the inner monologue. She might create a stream-of-consciousness dialogue with herself and the other characters. An example of a brief inner monologue might come before the line "Unhappy that I am." The actor might think but not speak, "His moment of glory . . . that look on his face . . . he will never forgive me for this." She might even improvise parts of the inner monologue aloud during some rehearsals.

The actor who approaches the role of Cordelia externally might begin with the language, the rhythm and sounds of the words. For example, the line "I cannot heave my heart into my mouth" expresses the essence of Cordelia's anguished situation. The words *heave*, *heart*, and *mouth* have long vowel sounds and soft consonants, giving the words weight and emotional depth as the starting point for the presentation of the character. The phrasing of the line "you have begot me, bred me, loved me" is answered by the rhythm in "I . . . obey you, love you and most honor you." The repeated "me" of the first line is linked to the repeated "you" of the second line, tying Cordelia's life to her father's. The insertion of "and most" before the third verb in the sequence adds emphasis to Cordelia's expression of respect for her father. Cordelia's straightforward declaration of her position in short, patterned syllables is followed by a question, "Why have my sisters husbands . . . ?" which offers a distinct contrast to the tone of the preceding three lines, challenging her sisters' sincerity. Careful analysis of the linguistic structure and the meaning of the words—as well as intuitive responses to the sounds and patterning of the words—yields a character foundation that emerges from Shakespeare's language rather than from an analysis of situation and character psychology.

In either case, before an actor can play Cordelia, there are many questions to be answered. How much control is the character consciously exerting over her own emotions? Are the two speeches played directly to Lear, or is part of the longer speech played to the two sisters? Is Cordelia challenging her father's authority, or is she warning her father of the consequences of taking her sisters' speeches for the truth? Is Cordelia trying to plead her case or prove her point? Is the longer speech a passionate accusation directed at the hypocrisy of Regan and Goneril or a restrained defense of principle? Does she want to expose her sisters as liars or force Lear to see his own vanity? In order to play these few short lines, the actor has many choices to make, whether she uses internal or external techniques for creating character.

Gestural Acting

Today is an explosive time for the actor. Method acting, associated with Stanislavsky and American realism, is being reconsidered from many sides. Experimental theatre companies, performers, and directors are exploring intriguing alternatives to or variations on traditional internal approaches to acting. Acting programs now offer remarkably eclectic courses of study that include dance, Asian theatre, improvisation, games, circus techniques, singing, and speech as well as character analysis and development. The actor has various sources to draw on, some of which strongly reject psychological motivation as part of character development.

In the production of *And the Soul Shall Dance* at East West Players, discussed in Chapter 8, hooded figures dressed in black who are identified by the Japanese term **kuroko** act in a style that does not have a psychological base. Although a primary function of the kurokos is to change the scenery, these actors are far more than stagehands. Their performance is choreographed; their expressive language is based on movement, not words. They embody forces such as the wind rather than detailed human characters. The technique they use in production is based on dance training and the disciplines of Asian theatre.

Asian theatre forms and acting techniques have had a growing influence on many Western theatres and theatre artists, not just on theatres with an Asian cultural base such as East West Players. Some actor training programs teach forms of Asian martial arts in combination with a movement vocabulary influenced by the kabuki or nō theatres of Japan, the Beijing Opera, or Indian kathakali. Eastern approaches to performance may be combined with Western dramatic literature—for example, in kabuki productions of Shakespeare.

Acting in *Apollo*

Drawing on new directions in actor training and theatre production, the director Nancy Keystone and a group of actors have formed a theatre company, Critical Mass, to develop theatre pieces in which movement is as important to the performance as the text. Nancy Keystone explains her goals for the staging of *Apollo*, their most recent production:

> Theatre is a very physical medium. But most of the time what we see is people acting from the neck up. The body is forgotten. Actors as living beings in front of a living audience have great potential for physical expression. One of the goals of *Apollo* was to create a piece in which movement told as much of the story as anything else, to present information—narrative, aesthetic, thematic information—nonverbally. A life lived onstage is a full and extreme life. An actor will do extraordinary things as a character living the events of the play. When we are creating and developing the piece, what I do to prepare, since there is no script, is to write a foundation for the play through exercises. The exercises explore physical states and psychic states which we believe are at the core of the story we're trying to tell.[25]

For this 2009 production, the actors used their bodies to convey actions such as astronauts floating weightless in space, living characters haunted by the dead, or confrontations over civil rights. Gestures combined with simple props constructed themes through their repetition from character to character, such as the use of handkerchiefs to wipe hands and consciences clean or the wrapping and unwrapping of bundles of ashes

Space flight is celebrated in Part 1 of *Apollo* as the characters imagine a rocket trip to the moon. The weightlessness of the astronauts is created only through the actors balancing upside down on plain metal chairs with their floating arms and legs magnified by the light in this 2009 production at Portland Center Stage, directed by Nancy Keystone. The actors are Richard Gallegos, Andy Hirsch, Jeffrey Johnson, Nick Santoro, and Christopher Shaw.

Apollo: Thematic Development

Apollo, an epic theatre piece composed in three parts, develops themes rather than building a tightly knit plot. The themes are connected to key aspirations in American history: the desire to conquer space and the struggle for civil rights. Geographically, the production moves between Germany in the 1930s and 1940s and the United States in the 1950s and 1960s. But ultimately the focus is on Huntsville, Alabama, where German scientists and engineers were brought following World War II to help develop the American space program and where African Americans were engaged in attempts to integrate public institutions and secure voting rights. The desire to glorify human ingenuity through sending rockets to the moon is seen against the desire to honor human dignity through fighting for equal rights. A consuming quest for power is seen against a consuming quest for freedom. The text for *Apollo* is drawn from historical documents, as well as the improvisation of the actors and the scripting of the director. The production depends on elaborate uses of sound and music, projected slides and film, and choreographed stage movement, in addition to spoken text and character action.

Part 1: *Lebensraum*

Part 1 celebrates a fantasy view of rocket history with glimpses of the development of German technology before and during World War II and America's love affair with space flight. Werner von Braun, a key character, appears with both Hitler and Walt Disney as he sells first Germany and then the United States on his vision to reach the moon.

Part 2: *Gravity*

The mood of the play shifts, as Part 2 uncovers the history of the slave labor used by the Germans to build their V-2 rockets and the war crimes of Germans brought to the United States to satisfy America's desire to win the space race and put a man on the moon. U.S. prosecutor Eli Rosenbaum confronts German engineer Arthur Rudolph about his past, as they examine the contents of some of the 3,000 file boxes that form the set for Part 2 of the play. The revelations bring to light the way the U.S. government put its determination to succeed in space ahead of the nation's laws.

Part 3: *Liberation*

The Nazi "rocketeers" begin their work in Huntsville, Alabama, at the same time that the momentum of the civil rights struggle is increasing, with attempts to integrate lunch counters and then the University of Alabama. Although many historical figures appear in the play, such as Werner Von Braun, Governor George Wallace, Robert Kennedy, and the Reverend Ralph Abernathy, the play focuses, in the end, on a fictional character, David McCadden. He becomes one of the first black students to integrate the University of Alabama and eventually joins NASA to work on the Apollo space program.

to recall lives lost to violence. Sometimes the actors played characters exchanging dialogue; sometimes they were part of an abstracted choreographic sequence. Some scenes were emotionally charged; some were parody. Each of the twelve actors played multiple roles and they needed to shift instantly between characters and between different uses of their acting skills. In

order to develop their approach for *Apollo,* Keystone and the actors spent eight years studying research materials and exploring ideas through exercises and improvisations that were distilled and refined to become the scenes of the play.

One of the characters played by Richard Gallegos in *Apollo,* the Ghost of the Prisoner from Camp Dora, is seen kneeling on the table

An American prosecutor, Eli Rosenbaum, one of the characters played by Andy Hirsch, interrogates Arthur Rudolph, one of the characters played by Christopher Shaw, about his past as director of an underground factory in Germany which built V-2 rockets in *Apollo* (2009). The Ghost of the Prisoner of Camp Dora, Richard Gallegos, represents the atrocities of the past, which have been evaded while Rudolph was a leader in the American space program.

in the photograph on this page. This character represents the many people who worked at forced labor building rockets for the Nazis during World War II. In *Apollo* the "Prisoner" has returned from the dead to personify the past of a German rocket scientist, Arthur Rudolph, who faces deportation from the United States for war crimes. Richard Gallegos describes the external process involved in developing the presentation of his character:

> In the beginning Nancy Keystone told me, "you're not reliving these moments; you are now of the other world. You are drifting by. You are here for a purpose and then you leave. You are simply telling, so you can't have too much emotional connection."
>
> I found the physicality of the character first, the master gesture, the voice. The center of him is the core of my body, just above the pelvis. I wanted to find a gliding quality for him physically. So when he's walking, it's almost like he's moving through space without even touching the ground. He's just an energy that is hovering and not really quite in time movement-wise with everybody else.[26]

A synopsis of *Apollo* is included in this chapter for reference, since we discuss this production here and in Chapter 5.

Whatever the style of the play, the actor's process is both highly individual and subject to fluctuation. Actors usually combine various techniques in their work, and there may be many subtle shifts in the degree of actual emotional engagement in the role at various stages of the rehearsal and performance process. Actors constantly integrate various sources of information and inspiration into their creation of a role. All the work focuses on the creation of stage life that is original and truthful and that the actor can play with maximum conviction. No matter what the approach, good actors achieve complete concentration on the moment being played. As Valerie Spencer, a member of the *Apollo* cast, says:

> For me, I have to be completely in the now. Completely in the present, just in my body, on the stage, or backstage doing what I'm doing. I can't start thinking, "what if, what if, what if," or it will be a train wreck. If I'm changing my clothes, I'm listening to what's going on onstage. I can't be thinking ahead or daydreaming. I can't let my mind wander. I have to be completely focused on the task. It requires absolute concentration and focus and determination. A complete giving myself over to the ride.[27]

Mary-Louise Parker, seen here in *Dead Man's Cell Phone* by Sarah Ruhl (2007). Parker emphasizes that process is the way actors sustain the freshness of their work when doing a long run. "The idea that I've got a role completely doesn't fit in with my philosophy. It's never something to be fully arrived at. It's just something to experience, to keep flexing and testing and to grow with, rather than to fully find."[28]

The Performance

The purpose of all the actor's training and all the work in rehearsal is to provide the foundation for performance. A well-rehearsed play provides the actor with the control and confidence to give a fully energized and completely detailed performance, to be open to audience responses and to make adjustments for the unexpected that always occurs with live performance. Sometimes the run of a play lasts a few weeks or a few months. Sometimes an actor may appear in the same play for years. The final, crucial element of the actor's work is finding ways to sustain the performance over the entire run no matter how long that may be.

Theatre and Film

Far more than other theatre practitioners, actors working in the United States today frequently alternate between the theatre and film work. Most actors appreciate the depth and variety of the characters written for the stage and the way acting in the theatre stretches their skills. Prominent actors who appear in both theatre and film include Cate Blanchett, Billy Crudup, Clare Danes, Charles Dutton, Bill Irwin, Laura Linney, Liam Neeson, Mary-Louise Parker, Kevin Spacey, and Meryl Streep.

The difference between acting in the theatre and acting on film is usually described in terms of scale. In film acting, the camera comes to the actor. Actors then work to open their responses but not to enlarge them. In the theatre, the actor crosses a distance to reach the audience. The size of the performance must respond to the size of the stage and the auditorium. Stage actors need to contain their instincts to be expansive when they are working on a film, and film actors must increase their energy and the breadth of their response when they appear on the stage. Ray Ford, who appeared in *Apollo*, trained as a stage actor and then found he needed to acquire new techniques to act in film and television:

> For the theatre, my intensity needs to land at the back of the house. In a TV show, my intensity just needs to make it a few inches away from my face. So it's the same work, the same preparation, but the delivery is different. It took me two years in L.A. to learn how to do that.[29]

The film actor is aware at all times of the camera lens, both the width of the shot and the focus. Acting must be concentrated in the body parts seen by the camera—the face or a hand, for example, in a close-up. Film actors compose their actions and reactions in synchronization with the size and movement of the lens. Like so many other aspects of the actor's craft, working with the camera is a technical skill to be learned and practiced.

VALERIE SPENCER: In film you're playing to a lens and are always conscious of being watched and photographed; of how your image is being picked up; how you look and the angle of your head. You have to be considerate of that stuff because it's splayed on a huge wall.[30]

Some actors find the financial rewards and the exposure of film acting to be more attractive than the work itself. For actors, film work usually involves more waiting than acting. Setups for stunts or special effects require an extraordinary amount of preparation. Sometimes the waiting depends on the weather or the light. Sometimes huge numbers of extras must be organized. Although the work of the actor is usually the most visible expression of the medium, the actor's work is scheduled around the needs of an elaborate technical process.

Films are frequently shot out of sequence. Actors may have to play a climactic moment at the end of the story before they have filmed the incidents that lead up to that point. The film actor learns only the lines that are necessary to the scene currently being filmed. There is no need to learn all the lines at once or to retain lines from scenes that have been completed. The film editor is responsible for organizing and making sense of the pieces of film that have been shot. The editor constructs what the viewer sees of the plot and the actor's progression. Of this fragmented way of working, Cate Blanchett says, "The challenge is to be able to shape a performance when the process is so piecemeal."[31] Sometimes actors who appear in the same movie never meet during the filming process.

Although the amount of rehearsal time for films varies widely, there is never as much rehearsal time as there is for most plays, and sometimes there is no rehearsal time at all. Sarah Jessica Parker says, "In the theatre, everything you do is about acting. In the movies, it's about a fifth, or an eighth."[32] Valerie Spencer brings us full circle to the connection with the audience in explaining what the film experience lacks for the actor:

> First and foremost it's the connection to the audience. You are telling a story and communicating essential truths about the human condition. If you are brave enough and have the opportunity, you can look out and see the faces of the people, read their reactions, and feel the pulse of their energy coming back to you. Perhaps theatre is the most human art form because it communicates from person to person in the same room.[33]

 # Summary

The art of the actor is the primary force of the theatre. For theatre to exist, in its essential form, only an actor, a playing space, and an audience are required. When actors appear on the stage, they undergo a transformation. Because actors convey concentrated energy and heightened awareness, they seem larger than life. Through their charismatic presence, they inspire the audience's belief in the stage action.

Years of demanding training in voice, movement, textual analysis, character development, and improvisation lay the foundation for performance in front of an audience. Beyond the challenges of actor training, the opportunity to work in the theatre depends on successfully competing for roles in the audition process. Once an actor has been cast, prerehearsal preparation may involve physical training or body reshaping in addition to research and study of the text. Actors immerse themselves in their roles during the rehearsal period.

The rehearsal is a collaborative process of discovery guided by the director. Approaches to character development during rehearsals may include improvisation as well as psychological acting techniques and external acting techniques. Improvisation involves the spontaneous creation of character, action, and dialogue. Improvisation may be used as a way to explore the playwright's text, to develop rapport between actors, or to generate staging ideas. The goal of internal acting is identification with the character that grows out of the actor's own personal experience as well as the actor's imaginative placement of himself or herself in the character's situation. External technique refers to the shaping of character through the manipulation of language and the construction of physical details of posture, movement, and appearance. Gestural acting, a more stylized form of acting that uses abstracted movements to capture the essence of character,

reflects the growing influence of Asian performance styles on American theatre.

Many actors today work in both theatre and film. Acting in the theatre demands a more expansive presentation that is scaled to the size of the theatre. In contrast, acting on film emphasizes subtleties and nuances, which the camera can capture close up. Acting in the theatre involves an integrated, sequential process of rehearsal and performance. Film acting, on the other hand, is a more fragmented process in which action is often shot out of sequence. Actors working on the same film may never meet. On the stage, the actor organizes the details of the performance; in film, the editor has considerable control over how the actor's performance will ultimately be seen.

 # Topics for Discussion and Writing

1. What is meant by the actor's presence? How would you describe your own response to performances you have witnessed that you would call charismatic?

2. Attend a theatre performance at your university or college. Where do you notice the actors' success in creating belief through their reactions? What do they help you to see or be aware of? Look for reactions to physical circumstances and to the actions of the other characters.

3. Choose one of these short scenes from *Joe Turner's Come and Gone:* Seth and Bertha (page 60) or Molly and Jeremy (page 84). Explore the subtext in the scene you have chosen. What thoughts may be behind the lines that the characters do not verbalize? Choose a section of lines and write an inner monologue that an actor might think as he or she plays the lines. How might the inner monologue affect the way the lines themselves are spoken?

● For interviews with some of the actors in this chapter and *"Apollo* in Performance," as well as suggested readings and other resources, please visit **www.mhhe.com/creativespirit6e**

CHAPTER 5

The Director

The actor brings the playwright's characters to life and secures the vital connection to the audience. The designers create an environment for the actor's presence. Uniting all the elements of the performance—script, acting, set, costumes, lights, music, and sound—into a meaningful whole is the business and the art of the director. The director Libby Appel says, "It is the director's job to illuminate the play for the audience."[1] The director creates a theatrical language, a language of space and movement and sound that coherently communicates the ideas of the production to the audience. The director and critic Harold Clurman, one of the founders of the Group Theatre (the American theatre of the 1930s dedicated to new realistic plays) and a major force in the American theatre for fifty years, calls the director the "author" of the stage action:

> That action speaks louder than words is the first principle of the stage; the director, I repeat, is the "author" of the stage action. Gestures and movements, which are the visible manifestations of action, have a different specific gravity from the writer's disembodied ideas. Theatrical action is virtually a new medium, a different language from that which the playwright uses, although the playwright hopes that his words will suggest the kind of action that ought to be employed. The director must be a master of theatrical action, as the dramatist is the master of the written concept of his play.[2]

The History of the Director

The actor and the playwright are as old as the theatre itself. The designer, in the form of a stage machinist, mask maker, or costumer, is also connected to ancient traditions in the theatre. But the position of the director is a relatively recent addition to the process of theatre production. In earlier times the playwright or a leading actor was responsible for coordinating the production and placing the actors on the stage. In the Greek, medieval, Elizabethan, and Chinese theatres, traditions and conventions were firmly established, and therefore questions of stylistic interpretation were not an issue. Productions did not strive for historical authenticity in representing earlier periods; nor was there an array of acting approaches to choose from.

The Director and the Development of Realism

The position of the director came into being in the Western theatre during the nineteenth century in response to certain shifts in the nature of the theatre. The director filled needs created by (1) an interest in a more detailed representation of place and character history—the movement called realism, which attempted to put a sense of daily life on the stage—and (2) the profusion of theatre styles that arose in response to realism.

As playwrights such as Ibsen and Chekhov began to write realistic plays in which environment deeply affected character feeling and action, the authenticity of the environment became very important. Exact details of costume were also necessary to place the characters accurately in their situations. Actors couldn't simply go to their own wardrobes and choose costumes they thought would be suitable or glamorous. And the psychological motivation and subtext implied by the plays needed careful development by an ensemble of actors, not a presentation by individuals all eager to draw attention to their own particular expertise. Someone was needed to coordinate the production elements of the realistic stage, and this is where the director first appeared.

The Duke of Saxe-Meiningen   George II, duke of Saxe-Meiningen (1826–1914), the leader of a small duchy in what would become Germany, contributed considerable resources and energy to

Stanislavsky's production of *The Seagull* for the Moscow Art Theatre demonstrates the profusion of details in early realism. Rooms were fully structured with walls, doors, and windows. Furnishings and accessories defined character background and also provided many opportunities for naturalistic character action. Stanislavsky maintained that the settings were as important for the actors as for the audience in providing a sense of the environment.

Anton Chekhov (center) reads *The Seagull* to the actors of the Moscow Art Theatre. The director Konstantin Stanislavsky sits immediately to Chekhov's right. Poor health curtailed Chekhov's participation in the development of these famous first productions of his plays. Much of his interaction with the company was reduced to correspondence.

the development of the Meiningen court theatre. Taking on the role of director himself, he was determined to reclaim the theatre from haphazard production practices and the excesses of popular leading actors indulged by a star system in which all elements of a production were dedicated to showing off their talents. In collaboration with his third wife, Ellen Franz, an actor, and with Ludwig Chronegk, who functioned as codirector, the duke built his company on principles that became influential throughout Europe. The actors were hired to be part of an ensemble; an actor who played a leading role in one production might be part of the crowd in the next. Costumes and settings were carefully researched and constructed with great attention to period detail. All the elements of the production were

coordinated in a unified presentation. Between 1874 and 1890, the company toured from England to Russia, eventually presenting forty-one plays. European theatre practitioners who subsequently pursued the nuances and subtleties of realism in acting and staging had the integrated productions of the Meininger Players as a foundation for their efforts.

Konstantin Stanislavsky The most famous and influential director of this early realistic period was Konstantin Stanislavsky. As we observed in our discussion of the internal approach to acting in Chapter 4, Stanislavsky's psychological approach to character development asked actors to behave onstage as if they were living the circumstances of the characters' lives. Stanislavsky defined himself as a director in 1898, when he and his partner Vladimir Nemirovich-Danchenko undertook the direction of Anton Chekhov's first major play, *The Seagull*, at their theatre, the Moscow Art Theatre.

The Seagull had failed in its first production at another theatre because no one had recognized that changes in production methods were necessary to make a success of Chekhov's play. In its initial production, Chekhov's delicate play, which involves the struggles of a small group of characters to be recognized as artists while they also seek to resolve failed love relationships, was performed at the footlights with speeches played melodramatically out to the audience. Stanislavsky recognized the need to turn the characters toward each other. Stanislavsky saw that building an ensemble of the actors would help to create the links between the characters' lives so crucial to Chekhov's dramatic intent. An ensemble could create the essential rhythms of action and speech that together would build a rhythmic structure for the play and draw the audience into its rising and falling breath. Stanislavsky believed that ensemble acting would give the lives of all the characters equal weight and interest rather than having the dramatic material be dominated by the performance of a star.

Stanislavsky also worked to physicalize in small, realistic details the inner, spiritual lives of the characters and to create an atmosphere of setting and sounds that would give the appearance of reality and provide a believable environment for the action. Here he was very concerned about the objects handled by the actors, such as cigarettes and walking sticks, as well as with sound effects such as birdcalls and cricket chirps.

Stanislavsky built a recognizable world for the play through a profusion of details taken from daily life. But to make sense of the physical details and the characters' realistic actions, Stanislavsky recognized the need to discover or identify what he called the **spine** of the play—that is, the central action or central idea that draws together all the smaller plot incidents and all the separate character actions.

As a young director, Stanislavsky followed a method of preparation that some directors still use. He made copious notes of actions and business, diagrams of the actors' placement onstage, sketches of settings, and lists of sound effects and properties. He determined the details and the shape of the production in advance of the rehearsal period with the idea that the actors would be told or taught what to do. The process of discovery was his alone. Later in his directing career, however, Stanislavsky came to see the need for the actors to assume more responsibility for the creative work of building characters. Stanislavsky's revised view of the discovery process is one that many directors adhere to today. Although most contemporary directors immerse themselves in a process of preparation for months or even years before they begin rehearsals, they view the rehearsal process as a journey of discovery that is embarked upon in a spirit of partnership between the actors and the director. The British director Peter Brook, known for his bold interpretation of classical works and highly original new pieces, stresses the importance of spontaneity in the rehearsal process:

> I make hundreds of sketches of the scenery and the movements. But I do this merely as an exercise, knowing that none of it is to be taken seriously the next day. . . . If I were to ask actors to apply the sketches that I did three days or three months earlier, I would kill everything that can come to life at the moment in rehearsal.[3]

The Director and the Determination of Style

Although the position of director emerged in response to developments of realism, the role of the director as a theatre artist who gives a production a clear stylistic point of view that integrates all the elements of the performance became fundamental to the multiplicity of styles that

For this production of Chekhov's play, *Uncle Vanya,* the designer David Borovsky dispensed with the walls and the interior details of realism that we see in the photograph of Stanislavsky's production of *The Seagull* shown on page 136. The house in which the characters live is suggested by a few pieces of furniture. The rural atmosphere of the play is indicated by the haystacks that hover around the characters. The production, directed by Lev Dodin for the Maly Drama Theatre of St. Petersburg, was first produced in 2003 and is shown here in a photograph from a performance at the Brooklyn Academy of Music in 2010. The actors include Sergey Kuryshev and Elena Kalinina. Dodin says of the spatial arrangement in an interview in *The Village Voice,* "We both wanted the space to breathe, to convey the ringing purity of the change of seasons." There is a sense that the characters are suspended in the environment, rather than confined by it.

followed realism. It is the director who decides how a play is to be interpreted, whether it is a classic play from an earlier era or a new play. For example, a director can choose to set *Hamlet* in twelfth-century Denmark, in seventeenth-century England, in a contemporary time frame, or in the future. A production can follow Elizabethan staging practice that frankly acknowledges the presence of the audience, or it can use the convention of the "fourth wall" (an imaginary barrier between the actors and the audience across the front of the stage) to seal the characters in their own world. A director can choose to emphasize the central character's philosophical questioning or the struggles of power politics. In the words of Brook:

> Many years ago it used to be claimed that one must "perform the play as Shakespeare wrote it." Today the absurdity of this is more or less recognized: nobody knows what scenic form he had in mind. All that one knows is that he wrote a chain of words that have in them the

Peter Brook has done his own adaptation of *Hamlet,* in collaboration with Marie-Helene Estienne, in which he cut and rearranged the text. The entire play was performed by only eight actors, without intermission. In the Brook production, the play became even more tightly focused on Hamlet himself, played by Adrian Lester. The stage was defined only by an orange carpet with a few large stools and cushions moved around by the actors to provide a sense of the change of scenes.

possibility of giving birth to forms that are constantly renewed. There is no limit to the virtual forms that are present in a great text.[4]

And the plays of Anton Chekhov, for whom Stanislavsky created intricately realistic productions full of detailed properties and sound effects, could be interpreted with abstract settings that emphasize the symbolic content of the plays. Although some, including the playwright himself, have disagreed with Stanislavsky's interpretations of Chekhov's plays, Stanislavsky defined the position of the director as one who interprets the playwright's creation. Other directors have moved beyond the idea of collaboration with a playwright to view themselves as the primary creators of the theatrical event.

The Visionary Director: Jerzy Grotowski and the Poor Theatre

In 1959, sixty years after Stanislavsky began his work on *The Seagull,* Jerzy Grotowski, a Polish director, began an experimental theatre in Opole, Poland. Six years later, in 1965, Grotowski's Laboratory Theatre moved to the larger city of Wroclaw, Poland. Throughout its existence, the experimental Laboratory Theatre would be subsidized through state and city resources. Although the subsidy was hardly lavish, it did provide a level of basic support that such an experimental company could not expect

in the United States. The following discussion of Grotowski's theatre practice is based on his career in Poland, before he shifted the site of his work to the United States and then to Italy.

Like Stanislavsky, Grotowski was devoted to reforming actor training. But instead of employing Stanislavsky's internal acting system, aimed at producing the most naturalistic performance, Grotowski sought an approach to acting that would maximize the expressive power of the actor's total instrument. Grotowski wanted to train actors to use their voices and bodies in astonishing ways to communicate a heightened expression of human experience:

> At a moment of psychic shock, a moment of terror, of mortal danger or tremendous joy, a man does not behave "naturally." A man in an elevated spiritual state uses rhythmically articulated signs, begins to dance, to sing.[5]

Grotowski's rigorous and athletic program of actor training was based on his own studies of Western acting styles and methods, including Stanislavsky's; and Eastern theatres, including the Chinese opera, the Indian kathakali, and the Japanese nō theatre. Although the training depended on stretching vocal and physical capacity to extraordinary limits, the goal was not simply technical brilliance. Grotowski

In this photo from the 1964 Grotowski production of *Akropolis* (version III, Opole), we see the stripped down nature of the "poor theatre." The actors wear costumes made from burlap bags with holes torn in them and lined to suggest the naked bodies of the actors underneath. They are all dressed identically in heavy work boots and cloth hats to indicate the uniform of the concentration camp where all individuality has been lost. The stage is merely wooden boards, the set made of old wires and pipes. The acting style relies on extreme gestures and grimace-like facial expressions, abstracted expressions of grief and suffering. The characters are going though the motions of living. The violin, the one actual musical instrument in the play, is used as counterpoint to scenes of brutality, a hint of a former civilization. The actors are Zygmunt Molik and Rena Mirecka.

In his 1904 play, *Akropolis,* Stanislaw Wyspianski examined the relationship of Poland to the forces of Western culture. In the play statues representing religious, literary, and historical icons come to life, culminating in the resurrection of Christ. Grotowski placed scenes from Wyspianski's play in a Nazi concentration camp, to show the collapse of human civilization rather than its resurrection. In this photo, a grotesque wedding procession takes place, with the pipe carried by the actor in front used to represent the bride. During the course of the play, the actors use pipes like the one they are carrying to build a crematorium, which they climb into at the end of the play. Grotowski demanded a total commitment from the participants to his methods of actor training and this production was rehearsed for two years before being given public presentations. The actors are Zygmunt Molik, Ryszard Cieslak, Mieczyslaw Janowski, Andrzej Bielski, Gaston Kulig, and Rena Mirecka in *Akropolis* version III at Opole in 1964.

encouraged a process that would allow actors to reveal themselves, to strip away the "life-masks" that they use to protect themselves, so that the spectators would be encouraged to look deeply into themselves as well.

The actor training was essential to Grotowski's own work as a director, which involved staging plays with an entirely different emphasis from that used in the realistic theatre. Grotowski was interested in creating theatre performances that explored myths and archetypal characters as they confronted or illuminated the experiences of the members of his theatre company and the experiences of his audiences, the people of Poland:

> I am very fond of texts which belong to a great tradition. For me, these are like the voices of my ancestors and those voices which come to us from the sources of our European culture.[6]

He was particularly concerned, for example, about the legacy of World War II for Poland and about the presence of Nazi concentration camps such as Auschwitz on Polish land and their effect on the collective Polish psyche. For one of his plays, *Akropolis*, Grotowski arranged a text—based on the play by Stanislaw Wyspianski—that brought together mythical figures from throughout Western history who, in the production, became inmates in a concentration camp. During the course of the production, the characters constructed a crematorium that they all entered at the end of the performance. Ludwik Flaszen, who was the literary adviser of the Laboratory Theatre, writes that the production of *Akropolis* asked the question, "What happens to human nature when it faces total violence?"[7]

As a director, Grotowski believed that the text should be part of the production but not necessarily the dominating force. He maintained that a director should be able to reshape a text or bring several texts together and create a collage of pieces of plays. With this approach, the director goes beyond being the partner of the playwright in developing the production of a play. The director essentially becomes the author. It is the director's imagination that creates the foundation for what happens on the stage.

Grotowski believed that the director should also shape the stage space, the actor–audience relationship, as he or she shapes the text and the actors' work. In his own attempt to bring the actors and audience as close together as possible, Grotowski created a new spatial arrangement for each of the productions of the Polish Laboratory Theatre. For a production of *Doctor Faustus*, the audience sat at long tables while the actors moved around the tables and even performed on top of them. The tables were to suggest the Last Supper. For *The Constant Prince*, the audience members looked down from their seats, raised slightly behind a fence, as if they were at a bullfight or in a surgical operating theatre. The fence was used to suggest that the audience was looking at something "forbidden."[8]

Through the Laboratory Theatre, Grotowski was able to control all the elements of the performance to realize his vision of the theatre. Like the spatial arrangement of the actor-audience placement that we have just discussed, all the physical elements of set, costumes, and

properties had an abstract and symbolic quality. Grotowski was adamant that the theatre should leave lavish and high-tech production values to the film industry and focus instead on the most stripped-down, basic materials that could support the actors' work. Found objects, reworked fabrics or clothes, and bare lights served as the design elements of his **poor theatre.** Only those objects or costume pieces that served the actor were incorporated. Nothing was used merely for the purposes of decoration, mood, or background.

The Playwright as Director: Athol Fugard

Stanislavsky's approach to directing was based on finding a truthful way to present the work of the playwright. Grotowski saw the writing of the playwright as material to be manipulated to suit the vision of the director. Another major figure of twentieth and twenty-first century theatre brings the work of the playwright and the director together in a third way. Athol Fugard, introduced in Chapter 2, was initially an actor and then a director before he became one of the leading playwrights of the modern era. When he began to write plays, he also continued his career as a director, directing most of the premieres of his own plays and a number of their subsequent productions. Between 1956 and 2010, Fugard wrote thirty-three plays and directed numerous productions of them. He continues as an active playwright and director today. Adapted to his own purposes, Fugard followed some of the realistic foundations of Stanislavsky and at the same time he was inspired, like Grotowski, to reduce the elements of theatre production to their simplest forms.

The early plays of Athol Fugard were produced under very difficult circumstances. There was no money to purchase materials, hire designers, or pay for theatre space. Sometimes the actors' names were announced from the stage because there was no money for programs. The actors were often under police scrutiny and some of their participation resulted in arrest and imprisonment. Keeping the sets and costumes to a bare minimum

Athol Fugard is shown here with the actors Zeljko Ivanek (Harold), Danny Glover (Willie), and Zakes Mokae (Sam) at the first rehearsal for the world premiere production of *Master Harold and the Boys* at Yale University in 1982. This was the first of the plays written and directed by Fugard that had its premiere production outside of South Africa. The character Harold is based on Fugard's memories of himself as a young man, a character who is caught between two visions of the world. In one vision, he reciprocates the kindness and familiarity shown to him by Willie and, most of all by Sam, who has become his surrogate father. In the other, he embraces a racist perspective, lashing out at these two generous characters and humiliating them to try to offset his own emptiness. The play is set simply in the tea room owned by Hally's parents where Sam and Willie are waiters, arranging the furniture and dishes for the next day's customers, and Harold is doing his homework. Central to the physical action of the play, the two older men practice dance steps for a ballroom competition they plan to enter. In his review of the production in the *New York Times*, Frank Rich writes, "Mr. Fugard's point is simple enough: Before we can practice compassion—before we can, as Sam says, 'dance life like champions'—we must learn to respect ourselves."

was a necessity. What was important was the presentation of stories that revealed the struggles of characters trying to survive in a world rapidly losing its humanity. Fugard was concerned with the brutality of life in apartheid South Africa, but his focus was not specifically on a social critique so much as on the nature of human connections and ultimately human isolation. He wanted to make a place for actors to create and for audiences to see

stories that touched their own lives. "My aesthetic probably comes out of having a theatre in South Africa with nothing, but even if I had resources, my inclination may not be to use them."

Stanislavsky was interested in the details of everyday human behavior and he used a profusion of reference points in elaborate sets, costumes, and properties that gave the appearance of actual places. Fugard selected a few basic objects, the most utilitarian furnishings for set, and basic clothing pieces for costumes. Grotowski was interested in rough found materials to create his environments and properties, and in contrast to Stanislavsky's realistic presentation of human behavior, Grotowski used theatricalized metaphors. Old pipes and pieces of metal became a crematorium. Fugard also used a rough aesthetic, but the few pieces he chose had a much closer correspondence to actual life. The idea for a play or an acting exercise might come from an object like a coat, taken off at the last moment by a man about to be sent to prison, to be left for his family, or a camera used to preserve the identities of common people, or a passbook that must be carried at all times with official stamps in it declaring where a person might live or work. The rehearsal work for *The Island* represented by production photos in Chapter 2 began with Fugard repeatedly folding a blanket in half for the two actors to stand on until there was barely room for both of them to fit on it. The small square of fabric became the space of the play, a prison cell that was both physical and mental.

Fugard explains through his notebooks and in interviews that he has written plays in order to work with actors and, furthermore, that the gestural possibilities of the actor are as important in expressing the ideas of his plays as the words. Essential to composing his plays are the theatre space itself and the silence that surrounds the words. "I would take away the words from him if a simple gesture,

Angels of Swedenborg, originally produced by Ping Chong in 1985 and again in 2011, is a mixed media theatre piece focusing on the conflict between the search for spiritual enlightenment and the temptations of the material world.

a simple pause—the way he put on a sock, the way he took off his scarf and rolled it and put it into his raincoat pocket—said it all."[9] "I have always regarded the completed text as being only a half-way stage to my ultimate objective—the living performance and its particular definition of space and silence."[10]

Directing the Theatre of Mixed Media: Ping Chong

Thus far we have identified three models of approaches to directing: the director who is committed to a partnership with the playwright (Stanislavsky), the director who draws on a variety of sources but is the primary creator of the theatrical event (Grotowski), and the director who is also the playwright (Fugard). Ping Chong is a director who has yet another approach to the creation of work for the stage. He believes in guiding a collective of artists to devise the performance and being free to draw on all the resources of the theatre to lift the audience into an otherworldly view of human existence when appropriate. Ping Chong (1946–   ) is an American theatre director with an international perspective and an extensive

Undesirable Elements is a series of works produced by Ping Chong since 1992. It is an example of the docudrama form, which uses the testimony of actual people. Each new installment represents a form of collective storytelling by a group of individuals in a different city—in the United States or elsewhere—drawn together by Ping Chong to explore their concerns with identity and isolation. The staging is the essence of simplicity: the actors seated in a semicircle of chairs, in order to put full emphasis on the stories they tell of their own lives. In *Cry for Peace: Voices from the Congo,* Congolese refugees offer first-person testimony about their own experiences of "brutality, loss, and regeneration" in Congo to promote "healing, reconciliation, and justice," in material arranged by Ping Chong and Kyle Buss in 2010. The performers are Cyprien Mihigo, Emmanuel Ndeze, Beatrice Neema, Kambale Syaghuswa, Mona de Vestel, and Dina Ndeze Mahirwe.

background in dance, film, and the visual arts. In fact, he identifies himself "as an artist *in* the theatre, not a theatre artist."[11] Chong was born in Canada and raised in New York City's Chinatown. He studied filmmaking and graphic design before joining Meredith Monk to collaborate with her on experimental dance theatre pieces. In 1975, he founded Ping Chong and Company, dedicated to creating theatre works that address cross-cultural issues and explore new means of theatrical communication. He rejects what he sees as an outdated reliance on realism in the American theatre.

A lot of what goes on in the theatre isn't theatre, in my opinion. It doesn't transform the stage. It doesn't turn it into magic or poetry. The American theatre is largely nineteenth-century naturalism and that's antiquated. We live in a cyber world, a fragmentary world, a world of electronic sound.

Chong and his collaborators—writers, actors, designers, dancers, puppeteers, animators, and video artists—set out to address contemporary issues with contemporary forms, unafraid to integrate ancient storytelling devices with the most recent technology or to combine adventurous uses of the three-dimensional stage space with imaginative projected imagery from video or animation.

As a director, Ping Chong is interested in changing the terms of theatrical communication. He therefore willingly seeks out new collaborative partners and stages performances in new locations. Thematically Chong has been concerned with exploring what it means to be an outsider, how we are affected by perceptions of difference, and what the consequences of those perceptions may be for individuals and communities. He has moved from reflecting on the condition of being apart in his early pieces to work that articulates the need for connection. Recently, Chong's work has embraced two different kinds of storytelling: one that offers a highly theatrical and symbolic form of the presentation through puppets, intricate scenic arrangements, and projected animation; and one rooted in the actual words of people who appear onstage to speak of their own personal experiences.

Elizabeth LeCompte

The director Elizabeth LeCompte leads a collective process with the Wooster Group, an experimental theatre company that also devises

The Wooster *Hamlet* is a recent production directed by Elizabeth LeCompte. The actors perform the play of *Hamlet* in front of a famous, earlier filmed version of this play starring Richard Burton. The Wooster actors mimic the staging and gestures of the film, creating a dialogue between the live action and the film. LeCompte and the Wooster Group work with complex technology that is a major factor in the company's aesthetic. Scott Shepherd plays Hamlet, with Richard Burton seen behind him on the screen.

new theatre works. The performances of the Wooster Group interweave materials from many sources, including play texts, autobiographies, poetry, letters, personal biographical contributions from the actors, and group improvisation. All of the members of the group help generate material for their pieces, but LeCompte makes the final decisions about what will be included.

> I like to run a tight ship. I like to have the final say, not so much because I want the power of it, but because otherwise I lose my way. These workers bring this material to me, and I sift and siphon through it. It isn't that some material is better than other material. I use it when it links up to something very particular with me, when it extends my vision.[12]

A collaborative approach to devising material has become increasingly prominent in the development of new work for the theatre, and directors engaged with this process have a variety of ways of providing leadership.

The Director at Work

We will now continue to explore the work of the director identified in the first model, in which the director is committed to truthfully interpreting the work of the playwright. However even the role of this director is still in flux, and there is much disagreement about how much a director should impose on a production and how much should emerge from collaboration. Declan Donnellan directed the London production of *Angels in America: Millennium Approaches* by Tony Kushner, which preceded the play's Los Angeles and New York productions. (*Angels in America* is presented in Chapter 10.) The playwright, Tony Kushner, participated in the rehearsal process in London, and his presence led to considerable tension between Kushner and the director. Donnellan reports that he and Kushner "almost killed each other," in part over a disagreement about the role of the director:

> I was much freer with the actors than Tony expected. There was one great row when Tony asked why a certain actor was standing to say a line when it was very clear from the written line that she should be sitting down. I said that I hadn't even noticed that she was standing up because the scene varied from day to day, and Tony couldn't believe that I wouldn't control whether an actor should stand or sit. He thought this showed a terrible lack of respect for detail. But I told him that on the whole it was for the actor to make the detail, it's up to me to make sure that the actors know what they are doing, which is very different from telling them to stand or sit.[13]

The director Bertolt Brecht was outspoken about his theories of epic theatre as they applied to acting methods and scenic presentation. But in rehearsal he was famous for sitting quietly while the actors worked and making only brief suggestions when they had finished.

Describing the process the director uses is even more difficult than pinning down the process and methods that actors use to create roles and give performances. Directing is studied and discussed less than acting is. Far fewer people are involved as directors than as actors, and the path of the director is a highly individual one. We can identify only the kinds of tasks that a director must accomplish, and we can form an overview of the directing process by describing the approaches used by some prominent directors. Frequently, the views and the methods used by one director contradict those of another director.

Choosing the Play

Directors usually have some choice about what they are going to direct, and they tend to choose plays they care deeply about. They choose plays that connect to their understanding of the world, plays that make sense to them. A play that is a good choice for one director may not work for another. A director may admire and enjoy a particular play and yet lack an inner understanding of the work that would lead to a successful

Summary of the Director's Responsibilities

- To choose the play
- To study the play and the historical context, possibly in collaboration with a dramaturg
- To develop a "concept" for the production in collaboration with the designers
- To audition and cast the actors
- To guide the work of the actors:

    To establish an acting style

    To block the play

    To clarify character development and the characters' relationships

    To build the play's rhythm in order to maximize audience involvement

- To maintain an atmosphere that is conducive to the creative work of all involved
- To guide the work of all participants to a timely and coherent readiness for performance

production. Although some directors are hired for a theatre season for which the plays have already been selected, most theatre practitioners and producers recognize the importance of the connection between the director and the script. If the director is to interpret the world of the play for an audience, then the playwright's vision must appeal to the director's imagination and understanding of human nature.

Davis McCallum, who directed *Water by the Spoonful*, the play that is the focus of Chapter 13, explains why he was drawn to an earlier work of the playwright, Quiara Alegría Hudes.

> I remember reading the play on the subway and getting just ten pages into it, the very first scene, which involves three different time periods and these three different men

remembering their war experiences and I thought this is a playwright who is musical and poetic and yet you believe the characters are real and you could walk up on stage and introduce yourself to them. I would be thrilled to work on this play.

Marc Masterson, the artistic director of South Coast Repertory Theatre, chose to direct *Eurydice* by Sarah Ruhl, a production to be explored through its design in the next chapter because of the challenges presented by its lyrical construction and the open-ended nature of the decisions to be made. The play offered a process of discovery.

> I love the material with its many challenges. The play kept opening up where the possibilities of how to do the story kept us all engaged through a four-week rehearsal period, which is a great sign of an interesting and worthy play.

Lloyd Richards, who directed the original productions of many of August Wilson's plays, found that the beliefs articulated by Wilson's characters coincided with his own understanding of human nature. Richards says of reading the plays for the first time:

> There were characters in the play that were well delineated. And the things that they were talking about, I believed. So the playwright, in a sense, was speaking for me as well as to me.[14]

Richards was drawn to Wilson's artistry in expressing a moral position: "He has a very deep sense of social responsibility. He is a repository of unlimited stories which reveal human experience."[15] And the rhythmic structure of the plays inspired Richards's directorial approach: "August Wilson is music. I directed all of his pieces as if they were music."[16]

When directors have a feel for certain material, they sometimes direct a play more than once. Libby Appel, who first directed *Macbeth* in 1987, felt compelled to return to it at the Oregon Shakespeare Festival in 2002 because she had come to a new understanding of this work.

In Part 2 of *Apollo* at Portland Center Stage in 2009, the actors search in the file boxes for evidence about the past of Arthur Rudolph. Three thousand boxes filled the stage and were moved by the actors to create the stage environment. All of the props used by the actors were discovered in the boxes. Andy Hirsch, standing center, plays the prosecutor, Eli Rosenbaum. Chris Shaw, seated with the magnifying glass, plays Arthur Rudolph. Valerie Spencer, holding the bundle of handkerchiefs, plays the daughter of Arthur Rudolph, and Jeffrey Johnson, standing with his back to the audience, plays the ghost of Werner von Braun. The director Nancy Keystone was also the scene designer for *Apollo;* the metaphoric use of the boxes informed both her work with the actors and her shaping of the space.

I've always wanted to do it differently, in a way that would focus on the psychology of the event. I wanted to take it out of the spectacular epic and put it in a smaller space to concentrate on the thought processes of the characters.[17]

Since directing *Joe Turner's Come and Gone* at the Oregon Shakespeare Festival, Clinton Turner Davis has directed Wilson's play for the Milwaukee Repertory Theatre and the New Federal Theatre in New York City. Tisa Chang, the artistic director of the Pan Asian Repertory Theatre in New York, directed *And the Soul Shall*

Dance, discussed in Chapter 8, twice and produced a third production over a period of fifteen years. She says that she is drawn to Yamauchi's work because of the truth she recognizes in the characters:

And the Soul Shall Dance is so special because it has very strong women's roles. Emiko is a woman who is utterly unfulfilled, unsatisfied, but has great yearnings, intellectual yearnings, artistic yearnings, and very deep feelings, emotional and sensual. There's nothing false, the sexuality, the brutality. Yamauchi really is the central figure and she was writing about issues that were very daring. *And the Soul Shall Dance* is also remarkable because it seems to speak to so many different people at once. We've had audiences, Italian, Jewish, all say, "This is my story."

The play is an actor's paradise. These roles are so meaty. And until then most of the roles for Asian actors on the American stage were abysmally stereotypical images.[18]

The Director's Initial Response to the Play

Just as actors go through a process of discovering the essence or inner life of the characters they will play, so directors go through their own process of discovering the essence or inner life of the play. They build their own understanding of the world of the play before they attempt to communicate their responses to other members of the production team. Directors use many approaches for exploring a play's images, textures, rhythms, characters, and possible meanings. Directors analyze characters' motivation, but they also listen to music and look at paintings. They study thematic developments, and they also read history. They travel to cities and even foreign countries in search of landscapes or ways of life or performance traditions that may serve the needs of the production. The directorial process is analytical, but it is also intuitive and imaginative.

Creating Metaphors

As a director approaches a play, he or she begins a process of discovering a metaphor, or image, that will translate the ideas of the play into a stage language. The metaphor is a way of expressing the most compelling ideas of the play in a concentrated form that will become a guide for the work of all the theatre artists involved in the production. A metaphor is an analogy, or comparison, a symbolic way of expressing the action of the play. The founding director of the American Conservatory Theatre in San Francisco, William

Ball, emphasizes the need for a single, strong metaphor to guide the work on the production:

> I have learned from my own experiences and from my observations of the work of other directors that the more clear and striking the metaphor, the more unified and powerful the production.[19]

Building metaphors was central to the director Nancy Keystone's work on the production of *Apollo* that was introduced in Chapter 4. One of the subjects of this play was the history of the German scientists who were brought to the United States to work on the American space program after World War II.

> When I'm thinking about a play, metaphor is one of the key ways of developing the work. An example would be Part 2 of *Apollo*. When we first developed Part 2, we were dealing a lot with history, with the Holocaust, and with concentration camp victims, and crimes of the Third Reich. Approximately 20,000 people died in the V-2 rocket factory where some of the German engineers worked. This was the key ethical issue of the story. My first thought was could we have 20,000 of something onstage? What would that be? And then, also, what's the main action of this piece? The main action is the search for the truth. When we started, there were two characters who were researchers, who were searchers. It felt to me like they were digging through archives, digging through the past. So I thought, what if we have a bunch of file boxes onstage, and the file boxes create the environment and everything comes out of the file boxes. That thought is what led to this design. The first time that we performed this part of the play was a workshop in a very small theatre. We had 200 file boxes, and they really filled up the space. Justin Townsend, who is the lighting designer, is also a very close collaborator. He had the idea of creating a wall with these boxes at the front of the stage. The piece would start with this wall and the actors would then remove the boxes. We found that just thrilling to contemplate.

Robert Wilson creates a vivid and horrifying image of violence using the actor's body position and the light to convey the intensity of the moment in his 2002 production of *Wozyeck,* produced in collaboration with the Betty Nansen Teatret of Denmark, with music by Kathleen Brennan and Tom Waits. Wilson is known for his use of visual metaphor as a central expressive device in his productions.

The actors then become manipulators of the environment. That's how it started. I think now we have almost 3,000 file boxes. That's an example of how the conception of the set and the ideas of the piece intersect.[20]

The formulation of a metaphor is a process initiated by the director but very much dependent on the collaboration between the director and the designers. Exactly who will define the nature of the stage imagery, and at what point in the process a central metaphor can be determined, varies from production to production and depends on the working dynamics of the production team.

For a new production, the process of formulating a metaphor, involving the director and the designers, is usually begun well in advance of the work involving the actors. However, in certain situations when the production process takes months or even years, the designers may work in rehearsal with the actors and make design decisions and changes as the production evolves. Theatrical metaphors must be strong enough to provide a physical shape to a production and open-ended enough that they will engage the imaginations of the theatre artists and the audience members.

Directorial images have a visual component that is crucial to the designers, and the images usually include a sense of the stage action as well that will guide the director in the blocking of the actors. At the Oregon Shakespeare Festival in 2002, the director and designers for the production of *Macbeth* looked for a simple, concentrated image around which to build their work. Shakespeare's *Macbeth* is about the ambition of the title character to become king and then to keep the crown at any cost. This ambition transforms Macbeth from a heroic soldier into a bloody murderer who strikes king and servant, friend and foe, woman and child in a desperate course of spiraling violence. The first key decision made by the director, Libby Appel, was to do the play in the round with the audience surrounding the stage (see page 167).

> I knew that I wanted an empty space and that it was just about the actors telling the story. I wanted the audience to be as "cabined, cribbed, confined" as Macbeth is—so that they would feel the claustrophobia of the small space with Macbeth. There's no escape.

Aware that only minimal visual effects would be possible, the director and the designers turned to the language of the play, the many references to blood, summed up in the following lines spoken by Macbeth, as the source for the production's guiding metaphor:

**Will all great Neptune's ocean wash this blood
Clean from my hand? No. This my hand
    will rather
The multitudinous seas incarnadine,
Making the green one red.**[21]

First they decided that a bucket or pool of blood would be placed center stage, and all the action would revolve around it.

> It grew into this pool of blood that became the cauldron, "fire burn and cauldron bubble." And the whole of the round, the theatre, is the cauldron. And we're all in this cauldron together.

Once the idea of placing a pool of blood onstage was established, the costume designer, Deborah Dryden, concluded that the costumes should be white in order to show the blood. This decision then evolved into the idea that the "blood should be accumulated all the way through the play with every bloody deed multiplied." The costumes became a canvas that would be painted with the murderous actions of the characters. Finally, the movement director, John Sipes, responsible for staging the fight sequences, saw that the pool

of blood onstage should govern the fight choreography. Rather than using swords, the fighting was stylized, with the characters dipping into the pool and marking each other with blood where a blow would have opened a wound.

Working with the Actors

Casting

The first crucial contact the director has with the actors comes during the auditions. Choosing actors wisely is essential to the success of the entire enterprise. Sometimes actors will be chosen at the kind of open auditions discussed in Chapter 4. Sometimes actors are invited to read for a play, and

BW Gonzalez is seen here as Lady Macbeth in the sleepwalking scene wearing the white costume designed by Deborah Dryden to show the bloody misdeeds committed by the Macbeths during the course of the play. The production was directed by Libby Appel at the Oregon Shakespeare Festival in 2002.

sometimes actors whom the director has worked with before are simply asked to take a part. Actors in a repertory situation such as the Oregon Shakespeare Festival are cast in several parts for different plays, all at the beginning of the season.

The director must choose actors who are suited to the roles in the play, who have good work habits, and who will work well in the particular configuration of the cast. The right balance and chemistry among the cast members are as important as the talents of individual actors. **Typecasting,** the selection of certain actors because they have a certain physical appearance and personality, is still entrenched in some areas of the American theatre, particularly in musicals and summer stock. Although a presence that makes the character believable is essential, more and more directors seek actors who will bring insight and creativity to a role rather than a preconceived physical appearance.

Nontraditional Casting

A recent development in the American theatre involves a rethinking of approaches to casting in terms of race. This shift has resulted in part from the increased participation in the theatre of actors and directors from diverse ethnic groups as well as increased social awareness on the part of theatre producers and directors.

Contemporary productions frequently combine actors from different racial backgrounds— even when they are playing members of the same family. Such casting is currently referred to as "nontraditional" or "color-blind casting." The director assumes in this kind of casting that the best actor should be cast for the role and that the audience will respond to the group of characters, not to the racial difference of the actors. In some productions, characters are cast specifically with race in mind to bring out certain ideas in the text. As we reevaluate where we are as a nation in terms of race, casting in the theatre will serve as a way of expressing and addressing the diversity of the U.S. population.

The Work Environment

At the heart of the director's responsibilities in the production of a play is his or her work with the actors. This process begins with the audition and continues through the rehearsal period and the first performances. From the beginning of the auditions, the director is responsible for creating an atmosphere that is conducive to the creative work of all involved, that ensures respectful consideration of the actors' efforts, and that recognizes the vulnerability inherent in the acting process. Because the actors' progress during the rehearsal period depends on their making open and honest responses, the director must be protective of the working environment. Rehearsals are usually closed to outside observers, who might make inappropriate commentary or inhibit the actors' work by making them feel that they are "performing" before they have completed their foundation work. The actors must trust the director; otherwise the process is imperiled. The director who shouts or humiliates an actor immediately shuts down the lines of communication.

The rehearsal should be a time when risks are taken and discoveries are made about the characters' deepest feelings and most compelling motivations. Hidden desires, buried secrets, burdens of the past, and ambitions for the future must be teased out during the rehearsal process. The actors must be open not only to the director and themselves but also, perhaps most of all, to each other. The connections between the actors drive a play forward and create a sense of an imagined world come to life. And it is the responsibility of the director to encourage the bonding of the actors and to guide them in making sense of the characters' relationships.

We have already looked at a number of directorial approaches in our discussion of the production process at different theatres and in the chapter on acting. Although the director usually has a planned structure for the rehearsal process, involving table work, blocking, and character development, the creativity and spontaneity

The lunch counter scene in *Apollo* directed by Nancy Keystone was developed through improvisation. In this violent encounter, played out in slow motion, the man standing repeatedly mimes hitting the seated characters, who, each time they are hit, fall forward. The stage picture makes clear the relationship between the characters and the shift in who is occupying the space and the price to be paid to take a seat at the table. The actors include Ray Ford, J. Karen Thomas, Richard Gallegos, Nick Santoro, Angie Browne, Valerie Spencer, Lorne Green, Brandon Ford Green, and Russell Edge.

of the director in rehearsals are as important as the creativity of the actors. The director must respond in the moment to the contributions and questions of the actors and the progress of the work. The director may stop a scene that is problematic to set up an improvisation in an attempt to get at deeper, more committed responses from the actors. Or the director may make suggestions for stage business that will physicalize a character's motivation.

The director always functions as the actor's audience to confirm what is being clearly communicated and to help clarify moments when the actor's intention is unclear. The director must maintain the company's focus and do whatever is necessary to inspire a continuous high level of energy and creativity. Although the director may be watching the action quietly, in fact she or he must match and encompass the energy of everyone on the stage.

Improvisation

Nancy Keystone, the director of *Apollo*, used improvisation to generate both the text and staging for many of the scenes in this production. The photograph on this page shows a moment from a scene in Part 3 of *Apollo*, representing the attempt

The Necessary Skills and Talents of the Director

- A visual sense
- A rhythmic sense
- The ability to analyze dramatic structure
- The ability to interpret through image and metaphor
- The ability to work with actors
- The ability to compose stage action
- Strong managerial skills
- Physical stamina
- Discipline

to integrate lunch counters in Alabama during the civil rights movement. The finished scene was performed with no words and structured through the precise repetition of the gestures of a group of archetypal white characters used to eating in a segregated restaurant. The characters repeat the motions of entering the diner, eating, and exiting, all in speeded up time, until the rhythm and pace of their movements is broken by the entrance of an African American character. The pace then shifts to extreme slow motion as more African American characters take seats at the lunch counter in spite of the hostile responses with which they are met. The actor Ray Ford, who appears seated at the table on the left in the front, describes the development of the scene:

> The lunch counter sequence was born as an improv. Nancy came in and said, "Ok, here's two tables, it's a lunch counter. You be the chef, you be the cook, you be the waitress, and everyone else be the customers." So we did that improv for a couple of hours. It starts off just as an acting exercise, but there comes a moment where your reality sort of

drops away and you're really there. When you're doing an improv for two hours, your defenses are down, and it completely shifts the energy, not just in the actor, but in the entire room. I remember leaving that night and we were all just completely wiped out and exhausted. But you just go there. You completely go there. It's just about that action of walking into this diner where you're not welcome, and what that feels like on both sides. That was all we had to work with for a long time. There still are no words in that scene, you know, it wasn't like we were playing it out. And we would flip roles, blacks played whites, whites played blacks, to see what that felt like. It's all about the feeling underneath all of that.[22]

Staging the Play

The director's own particular eloquence is expressed through the staging of the play. The director must arrange the actors in the theatrical space and develop sequences of actions that account for the necessary actions required by the script. But this staging of action through spatial relationships goes far beyond serving the practical needs of the script. Like designers, directors should be spatial artists. They compose in space and time with the actors and the scenic elements to interpret the ideas of the play.

The director arranges what is called the **stage picture,** the arrangements of actors onstage to communicate character relationships. But unlike a photograph, the stage picture cannot remain static and still hold the audience's attention. Characters cannot appear like posed statues. The stage picture must be dynamic, ever-changing. And the composition of the stage picture must direct the audience's attention to the important character or characters while also making clear the relationships among the group of characters. Blocking a play is far more complicated and subtle than merely getting the actors on and off the stage and getting them to do interesting things.

Focus

One of the most important components of directorial composition is focus. By the arrangement of the actors' bodies in the theatrical space the director must guide the audience's attention to a specific actor or to the point on the stage where key actions, reactions, or line deliveries will take place. A film director uses the camera to focus the spectator's attention. With a close-up shot, the camera singles out the significant actor and makes sure that the slightest response is registered clearly for the audience's appreciation. A long shot is used to give a view of the whole scene and then, through editing, the film cuts from actor to actor as the director wishes the spectator's attention to shift from character to character.

Stage directors, however, cannot employ such editing techniques. The audience views the

In this photograph, one character reads to a group of workers, sitting at imaginary tables cutting tobacco and rolling cigars, to help them pass their work day. Focus is directed to the character of the reader because he is standing while the other characters are seated and he is also elevated above them. The reader is dressed more formally than the workers and he is placed center and looks directly out while the chairs of the workers are angled in different directions. By placing the reader behind the other characters, the audience can also see their responses as they listen to the story. By raising or lowering lights on individual characters, including the reader, focus can be heightened or shifted. The reader Juan Julian is played by Francisco Gattorno. The other actors are Denise Quiñones, Tatiana Vecino, Grettel Trujillo, Raúl Durán, and Gil Ron. The production is the Spanish language translation of *Anna in the Tropics* by Nilo Cruz, *Ana en el Tropico*, produced in 2004 at Repertorio Español under the direction of René Buch.

full stage space continuously and remains at a constant distance from the stage. The director achieves focus through the placement of characters in relation to one another on the stage. Contrast in the visual presentation of the characters is one of the director's most important compositional tools. A character dressed differently from all the other characters and placed prominently attracts focus. A character separated from a group of characters becomes the focal point. Contrast can also be achieved by elevating or lowering the position of the actors onstage. A character who stands while everyone else sits receives focus; and as long as the character is plainly visible, a character who sits or even falls to the floor while everyone else stands receives the focus. A character raised up higher yet on stairs or an elevated platform will receive the focus if the other characters onstage are on a lower level. The focus of the actors will also direct the focus of the audience. If all the actors are looking at one character, the audience's attention will follow. Actors may also lean their bodies toward a particular character, or they may hold objects that direct the audience to look in a particular direction. The photograph of Herald Loomis on the floor at the end of act 1 of *Joe Turner's Come and Gone* demonstrates several of the principles of stage focus (see page 101).

Spatial Composition and Character Development

In addition to focus, another major function of directorial composition is the communication of character relationships and character development. William Ball compares his spatial work with actors to choreography:

> Picturization is similar to choreography in that the body positions reveal the relationships, independent of the words. My productions usually bear a slight resemblance to ballets, because I tend to picturize as intensely as possible. For example in my production, when the script calls for two people

Black Watch is drawn from the lives of members of a 300-year-old Scottish Army regiment that saw repeated duty in the Iraq War as allies of the United States. The play begins in a pub setting where the characters have gathered on their return home. The audience is shocked when suddenly a hand punches through the top of the pub's pool table and men in combat uniforms begin climbing up out of the table. This is almost like a reverse image of the figures at the end of *Akropolis* climbing down into the crematorium. Drawing on both military formation marches and fight sequences, the co-directors Steven Hoggett and John Tiffany place the characters in individual and collective battles with enemies that continue long after the troops are back on Scottish soil. Originally a production of the National Theater of Scotland in 2007, *Black Watch* has toured widely in the United States.

seated on opposite sides of a table, the one who is winning is usually climbing over the table, and the one who is losing is sliding under the other side.[23]

For the 2013 production of *The Glass Menagerie* at the American Repertory Theatre in Cambridge, Massachusetts, John Tiffany and Steven Hoggett used the images of glass and reflection to build a fragile world of memory. Far from the explosive movement used in *Black Watch*, they focused instead on the repetitions of small actions that play continuously in the memory of the narrator, Tom, who abandoned his mother and sister years ago. A moat surrounds part of the stage, separating the characters from both the larger world and the present, and the moat allows the characters to be reflected like glass figurines set on a mirrored surface. Zachary Quinto plays Tom; Cherry Jones plays Amanda Wingfield. The set and costumes are by Bob Crowley; the lighting designer is Natasha Katz.

By expressing the essence of character relationships and individual character development spatially, the director provides a visual telling of a play's story or a visual score just as the playwright's script provides a verbal score. The audience reads the nature of relationships or changes in relationships by the placement of the characters in space and their physical interactions. How close together or far apart are the characters? Do they face each other, or do they face away? Do they touch each other or avoid physical contact? Do the play's events bring the characters together, or do they push the characters apart? Does one character dominate the space while the other shrinks into a less important or a restricted part of the space? Does one character move freely through the space while the other is hesitant? Does one character lead while the other follows? *The progression*, the evolution of the spatial placements, is crucial in defining the progression of the character relationships or character development. Does an independent character who has kept herself apart come to depend on the character she has avoided? Does a character who has moved aggressively through the whole stage space come to occupy a smaller and smaller part of the stage as his power is stripped away?

Plays frequently have strong spatial implications built into their structure that give directors the starting point for their work. A battle for the stage space occurs in a number of plays. The confrontation between the Angel and Prior in act 2, scene 2 of *Perestroika* is a fight for Prior's soul that is realized in physical terms. In *Joe Turner's Come and Gone*, Seth wants to force Loomis out of his house while Loomis is determined to keep his place. In contrast, the sharing of the stage space is central to the supportive character relationships of a play such as *And the Soul Shall Dance*.

Recently a British choreographer and director, Steven Hoggett, has become known for taking a new approach to spatial composition and character development through a movement vocabulary that pushes recognizable physical interactions to extreme or even dangerous dimensions. Starting with the emotional crises of the characters or the difficult predicaments in which they find themselves, he works with the actors to generate gestures or movement sequences that approach the psychological and physical edge. Hoggett uses neither a traditional dance style nor a fixed idea of actor training. Rather he seeks to find the deepest and most truthful physical response to the characters' circumstances. Steven Hoggett is the co-director with Scott Graham of a British company called Frantic Assembly. His work has also been widely seen in the United States. He has served as the choreographer in collaboration with director John Tiffany of a group of diverse theatre pieces that have each broken new ground in the expressive use of movement and spatial composition in theatrical storytelling. These pieces include *Black Watch* in which explosive combat encounters give reality to the lives of Scottish soldiers in Iraq; *Peter and the Starcatcher*, a super-charged comedy where the actors change size, change gender, change from humans to animals, from children to pirates, by only transforming their physicality to account for their new characters; *Once*, the 2011 Broadway musical in which all of the actors are also musicians and all of the movement must be done with musical instruments in hand; and most recently, a 2013 production of Tennessee Williams's *The Glass Menagerie*, that finds original rhythms and gestures to open up the fragility of each character and to locate the play as an inescapable and haunting memory.

Rhythm and Pacing

A play progresses through character development and conflict, through visual imagery, and through rhythm. The rhythmic development and pacing of a play are also the director's responsibilities. A play has a number of rhythmic components. Each actor's speeches have a certain rhythm, as do each actor's movements. Rhythm is in fact an important part of character development. Character rhythms feed into the overall rhythm and pace of the play. Pace is simply the speed at which the production moves. The pace of the play must be slow enough for the audience members to comprehend the information they are receiving but fast enough to maintain a sense of forward drive and excitement. Plays frequently accelerate in pace to build the intensity of conflict or certain moments of revelation. Or the pace may be slowed considerably to allow the characters and the audience to reflect on some catastrophic event. Pacing that is relentlessly fast is exhausting for an audience, just as pacing that is too slow drains away the audience's energy. The pacing of a play is a crucial way of drawing the audience into the drama unfolding before it.

Preparing the Play for Performance

The goal of all the work on a production is always performance. The rehearsal process has its own accelerated pacing as the production moves toward opening night. According to schedule, rehearsals shift from exploration to a tentative shape, from changing and adding details to a completed form. "Run-throughs" of acts and then the whole play take the place of minute work on character and scenes. Rehearsals during which the actors may call for their lines are replaced by rehearsals without interruptions or lapses of concentration. The director brings the play to a point where the actors have confident control of their material and pacing just in advance of the "technical rehearsals."

During the **technical rehearsals** the actors' work receives less focus as the director's attention shifts to the lighting **cues,** the final appearance of the costumes, and the look and movement of the set. It is during the technical rehearsals that all the details of the production, so long in the planning and development phases, are brought together to create the effect that the director has envisioned. Lighting cues may need to be adjusted and set changes rehearsed until they take an acceptably brief amount of time. The director's capacity to attend to myriad details while moving toward performance is most severely tested at this stage of the process.

After the technical rehearsals and dress rehearsals, **preview** performances are given to allow the actors to finish their work on the play in the presence of an audience. (The preview audience consists of people who have been invited or those who have bought tickets at reduced prices.) The director continues to work closely with the actors during the preview performances to refine pacing and timing and to make sure that clarity has been achieved. This is the final stage of the director's involvement. When the play officially opens—the moment that all the director's energies have been focused on—the production belongs to the actors, who will continue to draw on the foundation built during the rehearsal process. The director's work is finished.

The Director's Training

Becoming a director is not unlike training to become an orchestra conductor. Conductors usually study several musical instruments for years before they take on the responsibility for a whole group of musicians. Similarly, directors must have expertise in several areas of theatre before they assume responsibility for coordinating an entire production. Sometimes directors begin their work in the theatre as actors, and their preparation then includes their own work in performance as well as their observation of the methods of the different directors they have worked with. Sometimes directors

begin as stage managers, obtaining a foundation in the organization of production details as well as production oversight. Some directors start as scene designers, gaining experience that gives them a strong visual sense. And there are also examples of successful directors who begin as dancers and choreographers. Choreographic skills are extremely important in the placement of actors on the stage and in the development of spatial relationships. Many directors also have a strong musical background, either as practicing musicians or as scholars of periods and styles of music. Whatever the director's starting point, the successful director must develop skills in all the areas mentioned.

In addition to those directors who work their way up through theatre companies, there are directors who receive their training from undergraduate and graduate theatre programs. Graduate study in directing usually focuses on the M.F.A. degree, although there are Ph.D. programs that also have a directing component. Frequently, graduate schools expect students to have worked in the theatre as directors before entering their programs. In graduate school, directing students study the analysis of plays and directing methods and often scene design, costume design, and lighting design. Studying the design areas not only builds visual skills but also provides a vocabulary and a point of view that facilitate the crucial dialogue between directors and designers. Graduate programs in directing usually involve a minimum of three years of study.

Summary

The director is the "author" of the stage action, the theatre practitioner who unifies all the elements of performance. Sometimes the director functions as the primary interpreter of the playwright's work, and sometimes the director

composes both the drama and the theatrical presentation of the drama.

The modern history of the director began in the late nineteenth century with George II, duke of Saxe-Meiningen. Directing numerous productions that were influential throughout Europe, the duke emphasized the integration of the elements of spectacle and the authenticity of period costumes and settings. At the turn of the century, Konstantin Stanislavsky developed his directorial approach in his work with the plays of Anton Chekhov, which Stanislavsky believed required an ensemble of actors and a more "natural" acting style than had been used previously. Stanislavsky began as a dictatorial director but gradually involved the actors in a more creative partnership.

During the 1960s, Jerzy Grotowski developed the Laboratory Theatre in Wroclaw, Poland. Grotowski had as much influence on the theatre of the latter part of the twentieth century as Stanislavsky had on theatre earlier in the century. Grotowski used the texts of playwrights as a springboard for his own ideas and frequently combined more than one source. He was committed to what he called the "poor theatre," using only the simplest, roughest materials for sets and costumes. The actors trained by Grotowski practiced a physical form of acting heavily influenced by Asian performance techniques. Athol Fugard exemplifies the playwright who directs his own plays. Ping Chong draws together live actors, puppets, and various forms of electronic media to create multidisciplinary works tied to the experiences of different communities who participate in the performances.

Today, directors take widely differing approaches to staging plays and working with actors. Directors such as Clinton Turner Davis work to interpret the playwright's text. Robert Wilson structures a visual presentation of an idea to which he adds text. Elizabeth LeCompte directs the productions of the Wooster Group in which all participants contribute to the shape of the text and the interpretation of that text. Many directors rely on the creative contributions of the actors, although some expect the actors to follow the director's expressive choices.

Directors prefer to have the freedom to choose plays that they find inspiring. Through a collaborative process, the director and the designers evolve a metaphor, or image, that guides the work on the production. The director selects actors who are suited to the roles of the play and the style of the production. The director is responsible for creating a rehearsal atmosphere that encourages the actors to be open with one another and to take creative risks.

In rehearsal, the director faces two major tasks: to guide the interpretive work of the actors and to stage the play's action. Through the arrangement of the actors on the stage, the director clarifies the character relationships and the plot elements. The director pays close attention to the expression of the play's rhythms through the actors' speeches, movements, entrances and exits, and the pacing of their interactions. During the technical rehearsals and preview performances, the director works with the designers, the technical staff, and the crews to finalize all details of the production.

 # Topics for Discussion and Writing

1. Review the principles of directorial composition related to focus. Find photographs and paintings of groups of people in which the composition is arranged to focus on one or only a few people. Use magazines, newspapers, collections of photographs, or books on painters, but do not use photographs of theatre productions. Bring five pictures to class that clearly establish focus, each through a different element of composition and contrast. Examine the pictures together to see the range of possibilities for spatial

composition assembled by the class. What kinds of statements about relationships do the photographs convey? If space and time permit, select some of the most striking compositions and re-create the relationships between the people in the photographs using members of the class.

2. Observe people in different situations and environments to see how they respond to each other in terms of space. Choose one situation that involves a significant negotiation over space, and write a short paper in which you describe the nature of the interaction. For example, you might observe someone trying to maneuver someone else to get the largest share of the space or the most comfortable chair. Someone conducting a job interview might dominate the space while the interviewee takes up as little space as possible. People involved in an argument might try to assert themselves by expanding their physical position. Find a spatial interaction that you think communicates strong motivations, and write a detailed description of approximately one page.

For interviews with some of the directors in this chapter and "*Apollo* in Performance," as well as suggested readings and other resources, please visit www.mhhe.com/creativespirit6e

CHAPTER 6

The Designers

Stage Design—the work of the scene designer, the costume designer, the lighting designer, the sound designer, and the video or projection designer—is an essential part of what makes the audience experience in the theatre a magical one. Stage design, together with the presence of the actor, creates a world apart from the day-to-day existence outside the theatre's boundaries. The designers create a poetry of space, visual and aural, that brings the stage to life with startling images and creates an eloquent foundation for the actor's work.

The stage speaks with color and shape, with light and shadow, with music and sound. The flight of an angel, a boardinghouse seen against a city skyline, a rolling piece of tumbleweed, the haunting sound of a Japanese *shakuhachi* flute, the lyrics of a blues song— these images from productions discussed in this book appeal to the senses. The designers engage the audience with sensory information to locate the actor physically and psychologically and to support the ideas of the text.

The photo on this page represents a central image in the play *Eurydice* by Sarah Ruhl. On the day of her wedding to Orpheus, Eurydice falls from the upper story of a highrise apartment building. The stage directions indicate that Eurydice is transported to the underworld in an elevator and inside the elevator it is raining. In collaboration with the director, the designers must imagine what this moment of transition from the world above to the world below looks like and sounds like. Is there an actual elevator? How strange or terrifying is this journey for the character who is a very young woman? How does the style of the elevator fit in with the rest of the design elements for the play? Where is design necessary for the most vivid telling of this story, where would it get in the actors' way? In 2012, Marc Masterson, the artistic director of South Coast Repertory, and a group of designers set out to solve the special challenges of Sarah Ruhl's play in a process we will highlight as we analyze the art and craft of design for the stage.

In the photo on the opposite page, Eurydice's arrival in the underworld is meant to surprise the audience. Only moments before, she was seen on a bare stage in her wedding dress. All of a sudden, the light turns to deep shades of purple and green and a whirring sound is heard from high above. The elevator, which has been invisible to this point, appears and begins to descend from 45 feet above the stage floor. The door opens and Eurydice re-enters, now dressed for a journey, her umbrella open, the rain falling down. Eurydice is played by Carmela Corbett. The scenic design is by Gerard Howland; the costume design is by Soojin Lee; Anne Militello is the lighting designer. The sound design is by Bruno Louchouarn.

Stagecraft and the Theatre

The actor and the director are artists who are made for the theatre. Their skills and talents are wholly claimed by the theatre itself. Designers, on the other hand, have skills and talents that they share with other visual artists, sound artists, and craftspeople. Scene designers have drafting and construction skills. Costume designers work with fabrics and have cutting, sewing, and dyeing skills. Many scene and costume designers also have extensive training in drawing, painting, sculpture, or architecture. Lighting designers create with a broad range of electrical instruments and control systems. Sound designers work with music, sound effects, recording equipment, and amplifiers. Video and projection designers have expertise with cameras, digital editing, and image manipulation. If designers do not sew or do carpentry or work with electricity themselves, they must clearly understand the

The characters in this photograph are called the Stones. In Sarah Ruhl's play *Eurydice,* they inhabit the underworld. According to the director Marc Masterson, they are "the embodiment of the dead, complacent, and craving quiet. Over time, they have become part of the rock the earth is set on."[1] The designers were faced with the challenge of creating an environment for characters who are fixed in place, have a limited ability to move, and need to seem as they have been in this place for a very long time. The actors are Michael Manuel, Bahni Turpin, and Patrick Kerr.

properties of the materials they incorporate in their designs. But no matter how many overlapping abilities designers share with visual artists, musicians, digital technology experts, or craftspeople, like actors and directors they are interpretive artists whose creativity must be used to shape the world of the play or the theatre piece. A designer's work of art does not stand alone onstage as an individual creation but interprets the ideas of the play with materials just as the actors shape ideas with their voices and bodies.

Much of our discussion of the theatre has to do with the serious interpretation of serious subjects. But whether the subject is comedy or tragedy, spontaneity and playfulness are crucial to theatre work and part of the theatre's great appeal to its participants. The possibility for creative problem solving, for tackling curious challenges that most people never have the opportunity to take on, is part of the basic work of the stage designers and technicians. The following examples demonstrate some of the intriguing problems designers and technicians are called on to address.

- For *Eurydice* one of the design problems was to provide a visual interpretation of characters who are meant to represent stones.

- For the New York production of *Angels in America*, discussed in Chapter 10, the staff faced the problem of flying the angel in such a way that she could perform her aerial gymnastics without catching her wires in her very elaborate costume.

- For *Apollo* (Chapters 4 and 5), for each performance the crew needed to stack 3,000 boxes across the stage, many of which would then be moved by the actors. The boxes needed to be arranged in a precise order because some contained props that had to be accessed by the actors.

- For the Wooster *Hamlet* (Chapter 5), the technical director Boskurt Karusu had to dress in a costume at each performance in case he needed to go onstage and fix malfunctioning media equipment.

- For the production of *Macbeth* discussed in Chapter 5, the costume designer Deborah Dryden needed to find white fabric for the costumes that could be stained with "blood" at each performance and then washed and dried for the next performance, sometimes on the same day when there was a matinee as well as an evening show.

- For *Water by the Spoonful* (Chapter 13), the scene, lighting, and projection design needed to guide the audience in tracking scenes that alternated between actual time and space, where the characters faced each other, and virtual space, where the characters were communicating online.

Bodies need to disappear and ghosts walk the earth; costumes and sets must be changed in a matter of seconds; ships must sail across the sea; or a mountain must give the appearance of snow and ice. Theatrical design requires continuous imaginative thinking, first to visualize the image in response to the needs of the play and then to come up with the technological solution that will make it possible.

The Theatrical Space

The first condition that governs the work of all the designers is the nature of the theatrical space, the relationship between the audience and the stage. The size and atmosphere of theatres in the United States vary widely, from the traditional elegance of Broadway to the modern comfort of large regional theatres such as the Oregon Shakespeare Festival and the Mark Taper Forum to the small and sometimes cramped spaces of equity waiver theatres such as East West Players (Chapter 8) and the Eureka Theatre (Chapter 10).

The common denominator for all theatre spaces is their three-dimensionality. In contrast, movie audiences sit in front of a large flat screen on which filmed images give the impression of dimensional space, but that sense of depth is in fact an illusion created by the camera. In the theatre, the dimensionality of the stage space is actual. For this reason, the audience space and the stage space can be arranged in different configurations. The audience relationship to the screen at the movies, however, always remains the same.

The Proscenium Theatre or End Stage

In many large theatres, such as the Oregon Shakespeare Festival's Bowmer Theatre and Broadway theatres, the audience sits opposite the stage, facing what is called the **proscenium** or **end stage.** A proscenium theatre is a theatre constructed in a rectangular form with the stage at one end of the rectangle. The stage opening follows the rectangular form of the space as if the audience were looking through one end of a box. The audience's view is shaped by a framing device that defines the rectangular opening called the **proscenium arch.** The proscenium arch is like a picture frame. The stage frame of the proscenium masks the mechanics of the backstage operations and creates a clearly defined theatrical space that is particularly suited to realism. The opening of the proscenium arch can be covered by a curtain,

The Argyros Stage is a contemporary version of a proscenium theatre that is part of the group of theatre spaces that make up South Coast Repertory in Costa Mesa, California. This is the theatre in which the production of *Eurydice* we are studying was staged. Because it holds only 336 seats, the Argyros is ideally suited for intimate theatre productions. The proscenium stage began its evolution in the Italian court theatre of the sixteenth century at a time when painted scenery and lavish special effects became an increasingly important part of stage spectacle. The audience members in a proscenium theatre all share the same view of the performance.

The theatre shown in this photograph is part of the Hartford Stage Company in Hartford, Connecticut. This theatre can be transformed into either a thrust configuration or a proscenium configuration. The play being performed in the thrust configuration is *Water by the Spoonful,* which we will study in Chapter 13. Notice the depth of the stage platform, where characters can be seen one behind the other at some distance, and the minimal use of scenic elements except in the upstage area. The thrust stage is historically connected to the Greek and Shakespearean theatres, where the audience was placed around three sides of the stage. A thrust stage allows for a close relationship between actors and audience members.

which also functions as a masking device to allow scene changes out of the view of the audience. Today, however, many styles of theatre other than realism are presented on proscenium stages, such as the surreal and lyrically written play *Eurydice*. Rectangular stages that lack a curtain or even a defined frame are referred to as end stages.

Thrust, Arena, and Black Box Stages

In contrast to the seating arrangement in a proscenium theatre, some theatres are designed to allow the audience to sit on three sides of the stage, which may be rectangular or rounded in its shape. The three-sided arrangement is called a **thrust stage.** The thrust stage extends into the audience, and different sections of seating look across to other seating areas. The audience members in a thrust situation are much more aware of the presence of other audience members than they would be in an end stage arrangement and are therefore more likely to be conscious of their own presence in a theatre watching a play. When the audience sits surrounding the entire stage space, the configuration is referred to as **arena staging** or **theatre in the round,** whether the

The Oregon Shakespeare Festival has three different stage spaces including a flexible space shown here in an arena configuration for the production of *Macbeth* in 2002. The pool of blood in the center was the only constant scenic element in this production except for the structure of the stage itself. Two chairs were brought on for the banquet scene to suggest the thrones of the Macbeths. Arena stages are surrounded on all sides by audience seating. The arena stage emerged from performance traditions in which ceremonial plays were performed in community plazas. The morality plays of medieval times, at which audience members sat on the hillsides of a natural amphitheatre, are one of the best-known historical uses of arena staging. Today the arena stage provides an intimate relationship between actors and audience members. Scenic elements must be carefully scaled and arranged to protect the audience's view.

stage space is an actual circle or a square with the audience on four distinct sides.

Theatre architecture is frequently permanent; that is, a theatre building is constructed so that the actor–audience relationship always remains the same. Sometimes a theatre plant will have more than one stage as South Coast Repertory and the Oregon Shakespeare Festival do; this arrangement allows the staging of plays in different kinds of spaces. Sometimes a theatre space will be constructed specifically so that the stage space

itself can be flexible. Small theatres and colleges frequently have what are called **black box** spaces that can be arranged differently depending on the needs of the specific production.

An exciting opportunity for theatre practitioners occurs with the use of **found spaces** as performance venues. Rather than fitting the production into a traditional configuration of stage and audience, found spaces inspire creative approaches to the actor–audience relationship and unique design possibilities. Found spaces may be inside or outside, public or private. Churches, department stores, factories, garages, train stations, packing plants, and armories have all been turned into theatres. Sometimes the space not only provides architectural opportunities but also carries with it historical and sociological significance that relates to the themes of the play.

The Implications of Theatre Architecture for Designers

Thrust and arena stages have neither the masking of the proscenium arch nor curtains that can block the stage from the audience's view. Therefore, all set changes must be done in view of the audience. In the production of *And the Soul Shall Dance* at East West Players (Chapter 8), the set changes were performed by costumed actors, kurokos, whose choreographed movements were an integral part of the play and were important for the audience to see. In *Angels in America* (Chapter 10), the actors themselves changed the set, but during scene changes they projected a neutral persona rather than portraying one of their characters from the play. In other productions, the lights are dimmed for the set changes,

This production of *Waiting for Godot* was staged in a ruined house in the Gentilly neighborhood of New Orleans shortly after Hurricane Katrina. The actors used both the house and the street to perform Samuel Beckett's play about characters waiting for a figure of salvation, who never comes. Setting the play in an abandoned house and the street is an example of using a found space to produce theatre. The producers wanted to call attention to the sense of abandonment felt by many who remained in New Orleans after the hurricane and provide a way for residents to gather together to support each other. Wendell Pierce plays Vladimir and J. Kyle Manzay plays Estragon in the production directed by Christopher McElroen in 2007.

which are performed by stagehands in dark clothes who move quickly and quietly across the stage space, changing or rearranging the set as efficiently as possible. In theatres with sophisticated physical plants and large budgets, scenic units may be moved mechanically across the stage or on a revolving platform, or they may be flown in from above. The movement of scenery in musicals is frequently choreographed to the music and becomes part of the visual spectacle.

Each spatial configuration makes different kinds of demands on the designers. In an end stage arrangement, the audience cannot see the back of set pieces, which therefore do not have to be finished; in theatre in the round, however, every object on the stage has to be completely finished because it can be seen from all angles. Towering set pieces or backgrounds can be used on proscenium stages or at the back of a thrust stage, whereas set pieces on an arena stage must be designed not to block the view of anyone in the audience. All kinds of ingenious solutions have been developed for arena stages to allow the audience to look over or through stage objects. Costumes and properties become the design focus in arena or thrust staging. The size of the stage and the size of the audience area are also important factors in determining the scale of the scenery and the detail of the sets and costumes.

Three-Dimensional Space

Although the shape of each stage configuration presents unique problems and opportunities, the basic notion of three-dimensional space remains the same. The director and the designers are composing in space. The costume designer and the lighting designer are particularly concerned with shaping the body of the actor. The costume designer creates a silhouette; the lighting designer molds that silhouette. The scene designer creates the physical environment that contains and defines the figures shaped by the costume designer and the lighting designer. The director creates meaningful relationships between the figures of the actors within the space defined by the set designer. Ultimately, the lighting designer unifies all the stage elements, including the figure of the actor.

The History of Scene Design

The history of scene design moves back and forth between periods featuring open theatre spaces with little scenic definition and periods when the scenic environment was of utmost importance to the presentation of the drama. The Greek theatre in the fifth century B.C.E., the Elizabethan theatre, and the Chinese theatre are all examples of theatres that used neutral playing spaces defined through character action, language, or minimal use of properties. The Roman and the medieval theatres began to show considerable interest in scenic effect. But it was in the court theatres of the Renaissance and Baroque periods throughout Europe that stage design generated great enthusiasm and remarkable ingenuity. Some of the leading inventors and artists of the time—including Leonardo da Vinci—contributed their skills to the theatre.

To imagine the energy and resources that went into the effects of the Renaissance theatre, the contemporary film industry provides a useful comparison. Film studios spend tens of millions of dollars on intergalactic special effects, stunts, models of cities or spaceships, hundreds or thousands of elaborate costumes, and the most advanced technology in cameras and sound. This was the kind of fascination that swept the court theatres and later the public theatres. During the Renaissance not only was perspective scenery painted lavishly with palatial interiors or mythical lands, but stunning special effects were also executed, with dazzling results. Fifty angels at a time could rise to the heavens on cloud units called **glories.** The stage floor could be made to resemble the ocean, with dolphins and whales diving through the waves. Mythical figures flew across the stage on the backs of animals or birds.

Buildings collapsed, and actors appeared in the midst of flames. Stupendous costumes matched the scenic invention.

In the nineteenth century, the introduction of scenic realism was a continuation of the Renaissance ideal of an integrated scenic background or environment for the drama. But the realistic stage focused on the limitations of human existence rather than on the fantasies dramatized in earlier centuries. And in the hands of American directors and designers of the late nineteenth century and the early twentieth century, such as Steele MacKaye and David Belasco, realism turned into a spectacle of its own, with rivers running across the stage and fifteen-minute sunsets.

Design for the contemporary theatre includes the aesthetics of both the open, neutral playing space and some form of elaborate scenic background. Broadway musicals usually use very elaborate scenic effects, as do the productions of Robert Wilson, although with different goals and a different impact on the audience. Contemporary productions of Shakespeare are frequently, although not exclusively, produced on some kind of open stage, relying on the talents of the actors and the language they speak to express the essence of the world of the play. And elements of the two approaches can be combined in different ways. In both types of staging, the work of the costume and lighting designers has a great deal to do with completing the visual statement of the production. On an open stage, however, the costumes and lights take on particular expressive significance.

At the beginning of the twentieth century, when a fusion of realism and spectacular effects dominated the European and American theatres, a quiet Swiss scene designer, Adolphe Appia (1862–1928), proposed a radical change in scene design. Appia was an idealist searching for a way to merge music, acting, scenery, and light into an integrated expression of the drama. Appia's research in the theatre was aimed at finding the most eloquent way to stage the operas

of Richard Wagner. His conclusions about the possibilities of the stage space in combination with new uses of lighting had a lasting effect on the development of scenic and lighting practices throughout the twentieth century.

Appia advocated a return to the idea of the open playing space and the elimination of painted scenery and all realistic objects. However, rather than the flat platform of the Elizabethan or Chinese stages, Appia thought that the stage floor should be broken up into various levels that would help shape the movement of the actor. Through a combination of ramps, steps, and playing areas of different heights, Appia designed a **terrain** for the action of the drama that would have rhythmic as well as visual implications.

A multilevel stage provides many expressive possibilities for arranging groups of actors. The stage picture formulated by the director is greatly facilitated when the possible positions for the actors are increased vertically as well as horizontally. Steps and ramps also provide for movement patterns and in fact dictate a rhythm of movement through the number of steps and the distances that may be measured in the actors' movements. Appia was interested in supporting the moving figure of the actor as the focus of the performance. He believed in stripping away unnecessary details of spectacle because they detracted from a focus on the actor.

He encouraged the use of light instead to bring color to the stage and create mood and atmosphere through the creative use of shadows. Foremost in his writings on the theatre were his observations on the way that light can define and reveal the moving figure of the actor. Experimentation with the expressive possibilities of light was in its infancy. Appia understood the potential of light as a transformative element in theatre design that would take on a new partnership with both the drama and the actor. The photo of *The Glass Menagerie* at the end of Chapter 5 reflects the influence of Appia on modern stage design.

Scene Design Today

Eurydice at South Coast Repertory

Scene design today may emphasize an elaborate scenic background or an architectural shaping of space. The scenic elements may be realistic or abstract; they may be constructed of simple or highly finished materials. The design may acknowledge the architectural definitions of the theatre or attempt to disguise or transfigure the space. The design may incorporate digitally produced, projected images or use only dimensional, tactile materials. To explore some of the concepts of theatre architecture and scene design that have been introduced thus far, we return to the scene design for *Eurydice* at South Coast Repertory.

First we must begin with the script that is the foundation for the production. To craft her play *Eurydice*, the playwright, Sarah Ruhl, turned to the myth of Orpheus and Eurydice. The story has been told in many versions since its origin in ancient Greece and later in the re-telling by the Roman poet, Ovid, in his collection *Metamorphoses*. In the traditional story, Orpheus, who is known as the world's greatest musician, falls deeply in love with Eurydice. On their wedding day, a catastrophe occurs. Eurydice is bitten by a snake and she dies. Determined to bring Eurydice back to life, Orpheus travels to the underworld to find her, where he plays such beautiful music that Hades, lord of the underworld, relents. Eurydice may leave the underworld as long as she follows behind Orpheus during their return journey to the world of the living, and he does not look back at her. But Orpheus is unable to keep from looking at Eurydice, and when he does, Eurydice dies a second death and is lost to Orpheus forever.

The director, Marc Masterson, points out that Sarah Ruhl's version of *Eurydice* "is a traditional story unconventionally told." Ruhl changes the plot in two major ways. Historically, the story is told from Orpheus's point of view. But as the title of the play tells us, this is Eurydice's story. And Ruhl introduces a new character into the mix, Eurydice's father, who is waiting for her when she arrives in the underworld. In fact, as the playwright acknowledges, she wrote this play in part to work through her grief at the loss of her own beloved father who died when she was twenty. Ruhl explains, "I wanted to write something where I would be allowed to have a few more conversations with him." For the director, "that is where the heart of the story lies. When Eurydice reaches the underworld and is able to reconnect with her father and her memory and her childhood, she has the connection with her father that she never really had in life. Orpheus is more or less a supporting character." Ultimately, this is a story of a daughter's love for her father, which she must address before she can move on in other ways. When Eurydice comes to know her father better during their shared time in the underworld, she also comes to know herself.

As important as the plot is to the work the director and designers will do on this play, the tone and style of the playwright will guide them in the choices they make. The playwright approaches with a light touch a sequence of events that could be relentlessly disturbing for the audience. The characters are odd and quirky, comic moments occur frequently in the dialogue and the action, and the language is lyrical, full of poetic images.

> MARC MASTERSON: The poetry is not just linguistic. She does some wonderful things to ignite your visual imagination. When Orpheus reaches the gates of hell, she has a stage direction that says, "raspberries, peaches, and plums drop from the ceiling." And another stage direction says, when Orpheus turns around and looks at Eurydice on his way back up, "the world falls away." These kind of stage directions lead you toward a kind of visual poetry. We ended up not having any raspberries, peaches, and plums. But the writer is creating surreal images that gave us permission to render the world in a particular way.

Summary of the Designers' Responsibilities

- *Costume and scene designers*—prepare sketches and then color renderings of sets and costumes to provide visual definition of designs; develop complete designs that meet the needs of the production, the theatre, and the budget

- *Lighting designer*—prepare a light plot that indicates the position and angle of all lighting instruments; arrange for any additional instruments or materials for special effects

- *Sound designer*—identify cues and collect or compose sounds or musical pieces

All designers:

- Read the play carefully and research possible sources

- Collaborate with the director and the other designers to arrive at a production concept

- Prepare appropriate breakdown of design elements (blueprints, elevations, hookups) to allow support technicians to construct sets and costumes and to hang lights and prepare cues

- Attend rehearsals to monitor necessary changes in designs

- Maintain a dialogue with other designers and the director

- Supervise the construction of sets and costumes, and where appropriate, execute the most difficult processes such as painting and dyeing

- Work through the period of technical and dress rehearsals to make all necessary adjustments

Masterson began his work with the designers four or five months before *Eurydice* was to open at South Coast Repertory in September of 2012. Previous to his joining SCR, Masterson was the artistic director for eleven years of the renowned Actors Theater of Louisville. Since he had moved recently to a new part of the country, he was eager to collaborate with west coast theatre practitioners, and so the designers he invited to work on *Eurydice* were all new to him and new to each other, although some had worked previously at SCR. They didn't yet have a shorthand for communicating with each other that some creative teams develop when they have spent years working together. But what was most important to Masterson was finding "people who were eager to think outside the box, who could do a complex collaboration involving different mediums." In the early developmental process, the designers met individually with Masterson, who communicated the evolving design ideas to the rest of the group. The work with the scenic designer, Gerard Howland, came first.

Design that Supports the Action of the Play

The first task of the scene designer is to support the action of the play. A playing space must be shaped that will provide for the specific actions called for in the play. Do the actors need to run in and out of many doors? Is there a mountain that must be climbed? In the case of *Eurydice*, two underlying actions must be accounted for: in some way the characters must be able to move from up to down, and there must be a way to express simultaneous action in the upper and the lower worlds. A third crucial need has to do with water. In mythology and in Sarah Ruhl's play, there is a River of Forgetfulness. Characters must dip themselves in the river to wash away their memories of the world above and take their leave of life.

For the 2012 production *Eurydice*, Gerard Howland, the scene designer, needed to create a terrain that would allow the director to stage all of the essential moments of this play. The creation of this terrain was both conceptual and practical. After a number of meetings, Howland and Masterson spent one afternoon walking

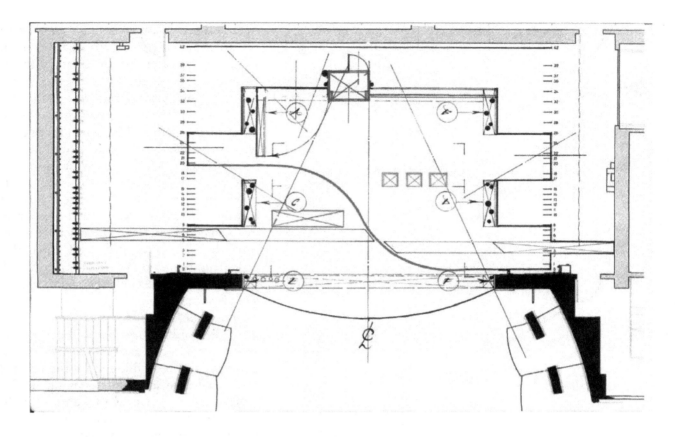

around the stage together, discussing ways that the actors could travel between two worlds that would represent states of mind as much as they represented physical places. From this session, the basic design ideas emerged that are represented in the **ground plan** shown above.

The floor of the stage itself was built to account for the shift in locations. Note the blue line that curves across the stage from **stage right** to **stage left.** This line represents the River of Forgetfulness and divides the stage into two sections, one of which is elevated 6 inches above the other. There are now two major playing areas of different heights, which could be used to indicate different locations. And when the contoured edge of the upper platform was lit, the river appeared. To the downstage right of the curving line is a rectangular platform outlined in red. When Orpheus lay down on this platform, it tipped up on a steep angle and he slid beneath

the stage floor as if he was shooting down into Hades, where he could search for Eurydice. The three boxes outlined in green represent openings cut into the floor through which the Stones emerged in their mirrored boxes. All of these logistical arrangements could be achieved because there is considerable depth underneath the playing level of the stage and the scene shop had the resources to build a complete stage floor just for this production with its special traps and moving pieces. In the upstage center area of the ground plan is a larger square outlined in purple. This represents the elevator shaft that extended up 45 feet to provide for Eurydice's dramatic descent into the underworld. Together these elements provided the director with the fundamental stage positions to tell the story of the play, with both eloquence and with the simplicity that he thought was in keeping with the evocative nature of the script.

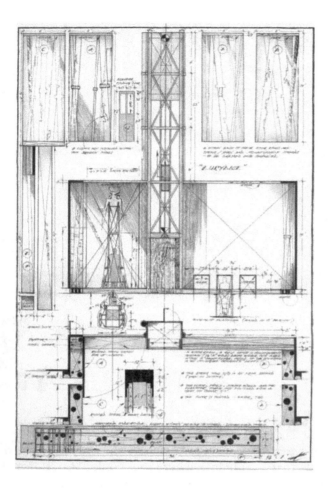

As the design process moved forward, Marc Masterson made the decision to include video as part of the language of the production. From the beginning he knew that sound and music would be needed to create an "aural landscape" for the story. When he determined that video would also be used "in the form of underscoring" like the music, another challenge was created for the scene designer, to build screens into the stage space that could be seen by all audience members and complement the positioning of the actors. Two screens were installed, one on either side of the elevator shaft. The use of video created its own set of logistical complications as well as interesting opportunities for expressive images, to be discussed later in the chapter. One of the challenges for the scene designer occurred in creating an effect of falling rain. Water images are an essential part of the texture of this play, sounds of dripping water, a faucet from which Eurydice drinks, the river in the underworld, and many instances of rain, not just in the elevator. To provide rain as a backdrop to significant parts of the action, Howland designed a water wall constructed of lines of monofilament along which water would run to create a sense of rain. The water wall needed to be positioned so the video projects could be seen clearly enough through these lines. And sometimes a rain effect was projected onto the video screen at the same time that actual water flowed down the water wall, heightening the effect. Look at the close-up photo of the Stones on page 163 to see the water lines behind them.

Sometimes the scene designer provides a great deal of imagery that will define the world of the play. In the case of *Eurydice* much of the imagery was to be filled in by the other designers. What Howland did focus on in the scene design was the imagery of water. In addition to the water wall, he designed a framing device for the stage that responded to an idea for the set stated simply in the script as "some rusty exposed pipes." Howland created a sculptural effect of drainpipes that surrounded the entire stage space. These pipes suggested the continuous presence of water, but not water that is a renewal of life, water that wears away at life. The rain pipes conjured water that seeps into the ground and travels to underground places, such as the River of Forgetfulness. The endless drip of loneliness or longing, the falling of water that obscures the view and dampens the spirits.

Costume Design

The costume designer creates through fabric, color, and texture. The materials used range from sumptuous brocades and hand-painted fabrics to clothing found in thrift shops, from delicate laces to metal. Hats, wigs, feathers, and jewelry are just some of the many accessories that add detail and style to a character's presentation. Distortion of the actor's body may be achieved through padded costume pieces, masks, or makeup. Costumes may present a dazzling vision of a fairy-tale world or show poverty and deprivation. The costumes may place the characters in terms of time, place, and social status, or the costumes may be symbolic rather than realistic.

The costume designer Angela Wendt begins her work by asking herself questions:

> Who are these people and what do the clothes mean to them? How do they decide to put on a particular piece of clothing? What does it say about their attitude toward other people and the world? Even though I do research beforehand, I always leave myself the freedom to wait until I've seen the actors themselves, gotten to know them a little bit, so I can pick costumes that support their artistic choices.[2]

Stylistic Unity

Whatever period and style are established for the costumes in a play, the costume designer must approach the characters as a group. Costumes usually have a coherent sense of style as a unit and clearly express visual relationships between the characters in terms of color, line, shape, and texture. Within the group, individual identities are established through contrast and variations in the silhouettes, colors, and materials. Together a group of costumes can be "read" to reveal hierarchical relationships based on wealth or power, differences in age and background, and relationships between smaller units of characters, such as families.

The Psychology of Character

The costume designer has a most interesting responsibility in helping the actor to define what could be called the psychology of character. The clothes we wear have a great deal to say about how we see ourselves and about how we wish to be seen or perceived by others. Joe Mantello, who played Louis in *Angels in America*, imagined his character choosing clothes that were too big for him, clothes that the character "could disappear into when things got bad." On the other hand, Molly Cunningham in *Joe Turner's Come and Gone* is a character who wants to be noticed. The other characters comment on the appeal of her appearance, but she is also careful not to go too far with the impression that it creates. She says of herself, "Molly don't work. And Molly ain't up for sale." The image she presents of herself through the choices the costume designer makes is quite different from the costume image for Mattie Campbell, who is filled with self-doubt, even though the two characters are both young women and come from very similar socioeconomic backgrounds.

There are people who gain security by carefully following social conventions. Dressing "correctly" in the most acceptable manner, therefore, could be an important character statement. For a rebellious character, choosing the way the character breaks the rules in terms of clothing becomes an interesting challenge for the costume designer. For example, Hamlet continues to wear mourning attire out of respect for his father after the rest of the court, particularly his mother and his uncle-stepfather, have returned to their everyday clothes. His solemn clothes become a point of contention between him and his uncle, Claudius; and their disagreement is a very important issue for the costume designer. In consultation with the director, the costume designer must connect the individuation of the characters to internal as well as external considerations.

The Costume Designer and the Actor

The character definition expressed through costume must support rather than impede the actor's work. A character grows and changes during the course of a play. The audience should be surprised by revelations as the play progresses. The costume designer must allow room for character development rather than make such an obvious statement that the actor's choices are limited or entirely predictable. The definition of character becomes a collaboration between the designer and the actor, with the designer's work enhancing and focusing the creativity of the actor. In the musical *Contact*, the lead dancer wears a yellow dress that was redesigned and constructed nine times during the last two weeks of rehearsal to make sure the fabric and the cut of the dress would accommodate the actor's movement, shown on page 368.

This photo shows the first meeting of the Nasty Interesting Man and Eurydice on her wedding day. His appearance strongly suggests that she should beware. But Eurydice is drawn away from her relationship with Orpheus by the pull of a message from her father. The Nasty Interesting Man is played by Tim Cummings; Eurydice is played by Carmela Corbett. Soojin Lee is the costume designer.

Costume Design for *Eurydice*

For *Eurydice*, the costume designer Soojin Lee was faced with a set of challenges that would have a major influence on both the work of the actors and the choices to be made by the other designers. Some of the characters in the play come from what we would consider the real world and some come from a netherworld that is in large part defined by the characters who reside there: the Stones and the Lord of the Underworld. The playwright, Sarah Ruhl, offers the director and the designers a significant and tantalizing clue to her view of the underworld. In the stage directions she writes, "The underworld should resemble the world of Alice in Wonderland more than it resembles Hades." In fact, in this production the costume designer's responsibility for determining the nature of the underworld was increased because the set design was more

After Eurydice arrives in the underworld and is reunited with her father, she receives a visit from the Lord of the Underworld who comes to visit her riding a red tricycle and dressed as an overgrown child. He both threatens her and tries to seduce her and finally forces her to whisper in his ear, all the creepier for his bizarre appearance. At this point, we see a hint of the playwright's reference to Alice in Wonderland in Eurydice's suit, which could be seen as an adult version of what Alice might have worn when she went down the rabbit hole in Lewis Carroll's story, and the child's costume which could suggest Tweedledum and Tweedledee.

This photo shows the full power of the Lord of the Underworld when he has attained overwhelming size and authority. He dwarfs the stage and all of the other characters. Eurydice's father has washed away his memories and lies dead in the River of Forgetfulness in the contoured part of the stage. Eurydice appears extremely vulnerable with her jacket removed and her arms bare, as the Lord of the Underworld insists that he has grown into a man and that she will become his bride. Ultimately, this is a choice that Eurydice rejects. When the Lord of the Underworld exits to prepare for this bitter wedding, Eurydice makes her final farewell to Orpheus and joins her father in the river. In addition to the other actors already named, Eurydice's father is played by Timothy Landfield.

structural than imagistic. Together, the director and the costume designer had to imagine a visual expression for the Stones that would weigh down the mortal characters who encountered them, and a set of incarnations for the Lord of the Underworld that was genuinely threatening.

Furthermore, in designing the characters from the underworld, Lee was faced with additional problems. In this production the director determined that the Stones would be fixed in place. Therefore all the information that could be communicated about them visually needed to be built into their first entrance. And because the actors' movement would be limited and they are only seen from the waist up, she needed to give their costumes a great deal of detail to help the actors sustain their performances. In developing her design ideas for the Stones, Lee began by researching images of "stones and rocks that appeared to have human qualities such as rock formations in Arizona and coastal rocks shaped by wind and surf." She then integrated ideas about rocks with a mixture of costume elements from different time periods to create a sense of characters who have lived through hundreds of years of history and like stones have

In sequence, the moment in this photo comes before the previous scene with the enormous figure of the Lord of the Underworld. Eurydice is following Orpheus out of hell when she turns to him and calls his name, which causes him to turn and look at her. Here we see the impact of the simple approach to the costumes for Eurydice and Orpheus, particularly in comparison to the previous scene. The characters are young and very human, both grappling with what it means to be in love and to commit yourself to a lifetime with another person. In this moment, Eurydice fully realizes that this is not a decision she is ready to make. She cannot yet take leave of her father. The costumes sequenced here demonstrate the way the surreal and symbolic telling of Sarah Ruhl's story fits with the human struggles of the central characters. Orpheus is played by Alex Knox.

accumulated various bits and pieces from the forces they have encountered. This presentation of an archaeological layering extended to the wigs and makeup of the Stones as well, with all of the pieces stiffened to complete the rock-like state of the characters' existence. The costumes were also actually constructed in gray and brown earth tones related to rocks in nature. Their green appearance in the photos and throughout the play was the result of a lighting design choice to use saturated green as one of the fundamental colors of the underworld.

The most disturbing character in the play, the Nasty Interesting Man who is also the Lord of the Underworld, goes through an extensive metamorphosis during the course of the play, in distinct contrast to the unchanging appearance of the Stones. He wears four different costumes that represent different stages of Eurydice's interactions with him. She first encounters him in the real world on her wedding day when he persuades her to leave her wedding for a party at his high-rise apartment by promising to give her a letter sent by her father. It is during this episode that Eurydice takes her fateful fall into the underworld. He then appears to her as a petulant and manipulative child riding a tricycle. From the child, he grows into a rock and roll guitarist, ready to challenge Orpheus in the realm of music making. This third version of the character was an addition of this production that is not described in the script. And finally he expands into a towering figure of the devil himself.

Soojin Lee interpreted the characters of Eurydice, Eurydice's father, and Orpheus as everyday mortals and used the hints of the time period that Ruhl provides in the script from the 1930s to 1950s as the guideline for the style of their clothes. By keeping these costumes quite simple, she provided starting points for character development, but gave the actors a great deal of room to build their roles through their acting choices in order to draw the audience members into a deepening awareness of what is at stake for them. Orpheus and Eurydice's father change very little in terms of their appearance. Eurydice's costume goes through subtle but important changes that support but don't define the growth of the character, leaving the actor in control of her psychological journey.

Lighting Design

Light is one of the most powerful influences on human existence. The rhythm of our lives is guided by the cycles of day and night and the lengthening and shortening of days as the seasons change. Summer light is different in intensity from winter light. Light that is filtered by trees and leaves is different from uninterrupted light that glares off water or sand or snow. The light of dawn is often seen as a promise, a beginning; the light of dusk may be seen as a closing or a fading. The beauty of sunrise and sunset offers unending variation and inspiration. Moonlight suggests romance, but a shadow across the moon may seem ominous. We gather around candles and fires because they break the darkness. Light is one of the most expressive tools available to the theatre, and audience members carry with them thousands of impressions and associations with light.

Light has always been a central metaphor in the drama because the effects of light are deeply embedded in the human psyche. Blanche DuBois in Tennessee Williams's *A Streetcar Named Desire* is frightened by the light. She needs to cover the lightbulb to soften the marks of age on her face but also to hide the signs of fear. Ibsen's characters are strongly affected by the Norwegian light; the short winter days of a northern country made gloomier yet by constant rain coming off the fjords play a significant part in the characters' outlook and the mood of the plays. *The Oresteia*, by Aeschylus, begins with the flare of a beacon that signals the end of the Trojan War. The metaphor that guides the entire trilogy is that of light coming out of the darkness. Romeo is drawn to the light in Juliet's window. For him, she becomes the sun and the "envious moon" grows "pale with grief."

The History of Light in the Theatre

It is easy to divide the history of light in the theatre into three periods. Early theatres were located outdoors and relied on natural light. Beginning in the Renaissance there were indoor theatres, which were lit by candles and eventually by gaslight. The modern era of theatre can be dated from the introduction of electric lighting on the stage. With the auditorium darkened and intense light focused on the stage, the realm of the audience became separated from the realm of the actors. And the nature of theatre spectacle was completely transformed by the ability of light to isolate, to create contrasts of light and shadow, to mold the body of the actor, to project a dimensional sense of color rather than the flat color of painted scenery.

However, expressive uses of light surely predated the modern theatre. There is some speculation that in ancient Greece *The Oresteia*

The Necessary Skills and Talents of Designers

- Interest in a collaborative process
- Fascination with dramatic literature and the work of actors
- Strong imagination
- Curiosity
- Flexibility
- Stamina and discipline
- Openness to varied materials and approaches
- Advanced artistic abilities
- Advanced technical abilities

would have been staged early in the morning to allow the natural dawn to express the daybreak that begins the play. The earliest versions of the Christian mystery plays were sung as part of church services and therefore would have been dimly lit by candles and the filtered light coming through windows, thus creating a mood of mystery and reverence far different from the mood set by the late spring light that would have shone brightly on the more exuberant outdoor productions. Lanterns and torches have been used throughout the history of the theatre. But the lighting technology that began in the nineteenth century and has advanced exponentially since then has given light in the theatre an entirely new expressive capacity.

The Lighting Designer's Materials

The lighting designer works with electrical instruments of different shapes and sizes that are placed at various angles to create a design through light. Side light shapes the actors' bodies. Front light illuminates their faces. Follow-spots

are used, particularly in musicals, to highlight and isolate an individual character.

Colored gels are placed across the lighting instruments to change the mood of the light and to interact appropriately with the color choices of the scene designer and the costume designer. Blue is usually considered a cool color, and yellow and straw are warmer, more cheerful colors. A choice from hundreds of gel colors allows the lighting designer to achieve very subtle gradations of color effect. Patterned stencils, or gobos, can also be placed inside lighting instruments to fragment the light and create special effects on the floor or other flat surfaces. Backlighting of actors behind scrims can create a dance of shadows. And projections can be used on various surfaces to provide moving imagery.

The Light Plot and Light Cues

The lighting designer is responsible for creating a light plot, which charts the placement of lighting instruments to meet the needs of the production. Following the completion of the light plot, the lighting designer works closely with the director in developing a sequence of light cues for the production. Each change in light during the course of a production is recorded as a separate cue. In a realistic production, lights may change to indicate changes in the time of day or the weather or to reflect changes in onstage light sources such as candles or chandeliers. Lights also change to reflect mood, to shift focus to different parts of the stage, to emphasize an important entrance, or to create a special effect.

Visibility

Although the lighting design is the last piece of the production puzzle to be fitted into place, it is by no means less important than the work of the scene and costume designers. The light unifies the stage space and the figures of the actors. The visibility of the actors, particularly their faces, depends on the proper use of light. Sometimes lighting designers and directors are drawn to moody, dimly lit effects. But audiences cannot appreciate what they cannot see, and eyestrain rapidly increases general fatigue, making otherwise attentive and involved audience members restless.

Focus

The lighting designer and the director work closely together to guide the audience members' focus. The lighting designer reinforces the director's arrangement of the actors to highlight crucial characters or stage locations. A musical comedy star about to start her song is lit by a spotlight. A doorway receives a special light in anticipation of an important character's entrance. The central figure in a group is picked out with light. As important as the presence of light in establishing focus is the absence of light. Lowering lights on one area of the stage and bringing them up on a new area will redirect the audience's focus.

The Rhythm of Light

The lighting designer Joan Arhelger says that the lighting designer makes a large contribution to building the rhythm of a play, musical, or opera.

> The light breathes. Without movement of the light, the stage and the piece, itself, become static. Our eyes expect change. Every piece has a rhythm to it like music. Is it a love song? Do things flow like a gentle rain or like lightning or thunder? Where are the stepping-stones in the telling of the story? Which ones need a memorable visual moment? The lighting designer must be concerned with how fast things change, the length of the builds, and the timing of the climactic moments.[3]

The lighting for *A Chorus Line* was shaped in response to the dancing and the music. All of the 128 cues were called (initiated) by the stage manager in time to the music. Rather than following a verbal script or cueing the lights off

lines spoken by the actors, the stage manager followed the music score and called the cues so that the change in lights would coincide with changes in the music or moments in the dance. The timing of the light cues is a critical aspect of performance and is as carefully set and rehearsed as anything that happens on the stage.

Light usually has a rhythmic function in the theatre even for plays that are not musicals. The rhythm of the lights is created not only through the timing of the changes in the lights but also through the length of time taken for each cue. Light cues are done on timed counts, and the pace of the counting must respond to the pacing of the

In this close-up photo of Eurydice's arrival in the underworld, the angle of the light turns the actor's face into a mask. Notice also the way the light hits the rain falling in the elevator, which together with the face lighting makes the figure appear ghostly.

performance. Sometimes a light cue will be executed rapidly to give visual punch to the moment being played. In contrast, fading up the light on a ten count or longer gives an entirely different effect. Robert Wilson is known for the very slow, meditative movement in his productions. Extremely long, meticulously counted light cues are an enormously important part of his aesthetic.

Here we see the Lord of the Underworld in the third stage of his character progression when he has become a heavy metal guitarist. He is lit as a garish Las Vegas-style entertainer. The sound designer Bruno Louchouarn used rock and roll themes throughout the play in association with this character. At this moment in the play, Orpheus has arrived at the gates of hell and the Lord of the Underworld tries to overwhelm him with the pulse of his musical attack. Note also the hand extensions with elongated fingers that have been added to the costume, further distorting the character.

Although we can summarize the equipment used in theatrical lighting and the basic functions of light in the theatre, Anne Militello, the lighting designer for *Eurydice*, explains that working with light is neither predictable nor easy. The light is alive in ways that scenic and costume materials are not and consequently it brings an extremely important dynamic to the stage.

> When you're a lighting designer, you've got nuts and bolts to deal with, you've got electricity, you've got loads of equipment, you've got budget. And when you put it together, sometimes you've got unknowns. A light doesn't always behave like you think it's going to. You have to be able to roll with it and shape it and mold it and conform it to what you want to do. You've got to fight with the beast and tame it. It's wild! It's an electromagnetic form of energy. It's not a hard piece of scenery, or a piece of fabric, that you know what it's going to do. So there's a magic that goes on when you are making a lighting design.

Conceptualizing with Light

The light in *Eurydice* was essential to establishing the kind of world in which the play takes place. The movement of the actors through the space, down the elevator or through the floor, told us this is a surprising place where the usual rules of human existence do not apply. Space is fluid and can change instantly from the world above to the world below. The costumes of the Stones and the Lord of the Underworld also contributed to the strangeness of Eurydice's journey, funny at times, but also grotesque. Through color changes, variations in degree of saturation, shadows, shifting the angles of the instruments, changes in the rhythm of the light cues, and special effects, the light had a major function in establishing how much separation there was between the world above and the world below, how threatening the forces were that beset Eurydice, and when she had control over her own circumstances.

Here Eurydice and her father dance together in the string house that he has made for her. The space is further defined by the bright rectangle of light on the floor. Their faces glow and the Stones fade somewhat into the background.

Mood, Atmosphere, and Psychology of Character

For a play like *Eurydice* with rapidly changing moods as well as locations, the light became a principal part of the storytelling, guiding us through the journey of the characters, placing them both geographically and emotionally. Strongly contrasting colors were used in association with different characters and different kinds of situations. Militello describes her work on this play as a way of painting with light. For example, Militello says she saw the underworld as a "lonely place, where time is forgotten." With the lights she wanted to "capture some kind of isolation, a feeling of being trapped." When Eurydice enters the underworld

she was lost, foreign. I lit her face from below with soft light, making her look not like herself. I wanted her eyes to be dark; the world that she was coming into was empty. So I hollowed out her eyes. I took away her sparkle and gave her a very cold light; it was raining and dank. But at the same time, around the elevator shaft was a kind of magic, green crystal color. As if she had brought in the light with her. I wanted it to look like a surreal painting.

In consultation with the director, Militello decided to use a deeply saturated green for the Stones.

Because they're stones, they are stuck, they're confined, they can't move very well. So they are only in one atmosphere, which we decided should be a kind of sickly green.

They are gathering moss, they are not being wiped, and they are in the ground, like mold growing. I wanted to light them from below so the light source they had was buried with them in the ground.

Militello added a deep red to the lighting palette with the entrances of the Lord of the Underworld.

When the Lord of the Underworld comes in and is offering all these wonderful vices, I just made it as garishly colorful as possible. Almost like Las Vegas, it is sin city and garish and horrible. But it's in the guise of being this sparkly, colorful, enticing atmosphere. In the upper world, he's camouflaged himself. But we don't want to give it away until we see where he lives.

In contrast to the saturated light of many of the moments in the underworld, Militello interpreted the scenes of Eurydice and her father with a brighter, cleaner light. Although their time together also takes place in the underworld, these characters find a way to create a protected space for themselves. Eurydice's father makes a small house for her from string to shelter her from the turmoil outside. Obviously the string is a fragile form of protection.

I felt that there was a sweetness to the confinement. They are in a house where they are happy together. But they're sheltered and they're separated. So I shuttered the light in and I actually made a hard rectangle on the floor, so it was bright white within the space, with blue around them that didn't seep into their little string room. They were illuminated by their own excitement with each other. But for me it wasn't a warm happiness. It was weird, distorted. There was something foreboding about it. Confinement and coldness.

Finally, Militello created a lighting approach for Orpheus that set him off from the other characters, as if he is ultimately separated from the drama of Eurydice and her father.

In this photo Orpheus studies the globe looking for Eurydice. His face is lit by the light source in the globe as well as the front light described by lighting designer Anne Militello. These lighting effects combine to create the sensation that Orpheus is suspended in space.

With Orpheus, I was trying to keep him separated and keep him romantic. And as a lighting designer, you also take your cue from the facial structure of an actor. He has a beautiful face, with deep-set eyes. I really wanted to see his eyes so I had to lower the angle of the light a little. His eyes were difficult to work with because I had such high angles with the front light, which I was trying to keep off the projection screen. So I had to be strategic about how I lit him, because I wanted him to appear as the angelic hope of the whole thing.

In addition to her conversations with the director about his vision of the play, Militello was strongly influenced in her design choices and the rhythm of her cueing by the sound design of Bruno Louchouarn. During the late rehearsal process, she made a number of adjustments to the lights in order to interpret what she was hearing musically. In part because she also designs rock and roll tours, she says, "I'm used to hearing music and reacting instantly. Sometimes instinct and impulse is what fuels some of the most effective work. So as I heard it, I lit it. In rehearsals."

Video Design

Exploring the Character's Unconscious

Before the lights dim on the audience for the opening of the play, a pair of narrow eyes with a yellow tinge, haunting and mysterious, appear on the stage right projection screen. They hint of a cat's eyes or perhaps a snake or possibly the devil. A much larger eye appears on the other projection screen. It is a woman's eye filling half of the screen. The face that holds the eye is blended into abstraction, only the eye is clearly from a human face. At first the image seems to be still, but then extremely slowly

the eye blinks. The eyes dissolve into clouds, then waves. Bird-calls blend with sounds of the ocean. We are at the beach. The actors playing Orpheus and Eurydice enter and the play begins with Orpheus proposing to Eurydice by tying a string around her finger. In the next scene, Eurydice's father enters imagining that he is in attendance at Eurydice's wedding. Behind him on the projection screen, Eurydice's face appears as if it is suspended in a drop of water. Eurydice's face returns to the projection screen in different versions throughout the play haunting both Orpheus and her father.

Video, exemplified by the images described above, was the fourth crucial design component in building the visual environment for Sarah Ruhl's play. The director chose to incorporate video into this production because of the way it could be used to explore the unconscious of the characters, their memories, and fragments of thought too elusive to be represented by words. The video designer, John Crawford, was concerned about the "non-narrative elements" of the play that created a "multi-layered exploration of relationships between human beings that went well beyond the story of Orpheus and

This photo represents the way the play and the production bring together the living and the dead, and actuality and memory. Orpheus and Eurydice dance at their wedding. Eurydice's father who is dead dances upstage of her, suggesting that she may be missing his presence at her wedding and remembering him. He, too, has his own longing for her, as she appears behind him on the video screen in a diffused film version of the dance being done in real time on the stage.

Eurydice or Eurydice and her father." Projected images of interior moments could "provide a livening of the set and the lighting in a way that only video could do." John Crawford spent ten years as a theatre director and then ten years studying computer science before embarking on a career that brought both fields together in the area of intermedia design for the arts.

The photo on page 185 shows a video image of Eurydice dancing at her wedding that relates to her father's attempts to reconnect with her across the vast chasm created by his death. He is imagining what her wedding would be like at the same time that the wedding is actually taking place. Father and daughter continue to seek each other in spite of the apparent finality of his death. Crawford used video to add visual detail to the characters' perceptions of each other and themselves in the father–daughter relationship and in the relationship between Orpheus and Eurydice. He wanted to explore what he saw as both physical and emotional distance. He says of Eurydice and Orpheus, "Maybe they didn't know each other that well and the play might have some connection to Orpheus's projections of who he thinks Eurydice is and Eurydice's projections of who she thinks Orpheus is."

When Eurydice dies and is transported to the underworld, Orpheus writes her a sequence of letters which he reads aloud. As their separation continues, he begins to question his certainty about everything. Orpheus says, "I thought: Eurydice is dead. Then I thought—who is Eurydice? . . . and I thought: who am I?" John Crawford explains, "I felt it was important to show how Eurydice was inhabiting, not so much his memory, but his vision of her, who she might be."

To amplify the sense of Orpheus's struggle to keep hold of some part of Eurydice following her death, Crawford created a different view of Eurydice's face to be projected during each one of the letters Orpheus reads. The faces become the woman Orpheus is trying to envision and whom he continues to lose as the play progresses.

In composing these strange faces, Crawford drew on the imagery of string used in the construction of the string house, which provides a temporary dwelling for Eurydice in the underworld (see page 183) and in the stringed instruments that Orpheus plays—string that is fragile, string that can break or unravel. Crawford discusses the process through which he created Orpheus's visions of Eurydice's face, just one of the sets of imagery he created for the production.

I began by shooting some close-up video of Eurydice's face. She is looking *for* Orpheus or imagining that she is looking *at* Orpheus. And then I chose several sections that I was particularly interested in. We only shot two or three minutes of video and I used the computer technology to create super slow motion, where instead of having a two second chunk of video, we would have a 30 second chunk of video. So the first step was creating the super slow motion. And then I used the technology called the particle system to create these strings, which I composited with the face in such a way that it started to look like the face was made of string. Or maybe, more accurately, I think it looked like the face was sketched on a string background. I wanted to come up with the feeling of something hand drawn, something not representational, but a little bit sketchy, the way our memory can sometimes be, where parts of it come in and out of our consciousness. I also had this idea of sand-memory, the way sand can kick up and obscure things. I created what I am calling the sand of memory by compositing dots with the string face in a way that gave you the feeling that the face was disintegrating. And these rendered faces were alive because they were not just a static frame, they were this super slow motion. We would get to see something like very slow blinking that put us into a different time world. I think sometimes that's when video can be most effective; when it's not competing with the real world and trying to show us real time and real space, but where it gives us the ability to perceive time slowing down or time speeding up.

The Integration of Video into the Production Process

The use of filmed imagery, including live figures in action, still images, and animation, is seen in a range of theatre productions today. From Broadway musicals to experimental site-specific pieces to a theatre work such as *War Horse*, discussed in Chapter 9, that combines large puppets with actors to an intimate play such as *Eurydice*, theatre practitioners are exploring the opportunities that filmed imagery offers to heighten theatrical expression. The use of video introduces another complex element with its own special properties that must be brought into balance with the rest of the production.

JOHN CRAWFORD: It's very important to find ways that the video supports the vision of the production rather than competes with it. And in this we really have to use two languages: the language of film and the language of the theatre. It's hard to create video that doesn't steal attention away from the production. You have to think of the time scale; you have to think of the size of the video, the fact that a video screen is almost always bigger than the actors. For example, if you put someone's face on a video screen, the nose of that face on the video screen might be as big as the whole actor is in real space. If all we're doing is watching a film, the scale is not a problem because we get used to the fact that a face can be large on the screen in the cinema or on the screen of our TV at home. But when you're trying to combine real three-dimensional people with these two-dimensional synthesized images, it becomes necessary to pay close attention to scale and to time. If you have video that is in the same tempo as the stage time, there can be a feeling of competition. Sometimes video can be most effective when it goes into a different time, when it stretches or compresses time.

Like the choices of the lighting designer, the video designer will see how the video pieces work with the production for the first time during technical rehearsals. Therefore a great deal of fast paced, creative video composition needs to be done shortly before the production opens.

JOHN CRAWFORD: I was making a lot of adjustments all the way through the tech process. Because almost all of the images are synthesized to one degree or another, they are rendered on the computer, sometimes laboriously one frame at a time. I was rendering through the entire tech process. We would finish tech at ten or eleven each night. Then I would go back to my studio and work on editing the video elements for a couple of hours and then I would set them up to render on the computer overnight. I would bring the new versions into rehearsal, see how things were working, and then after the rehearsal go back and do some more rendering. I also had multiple computers in the theatre, so I was able to do some changes to the video design as the rehearsal progressed. It was a race against time to get—not so much the big strokes—but the subtleties that are crucial to making the piece work.

Unifying the Production Through Sound

Music and sound effects have always been fundamental to theatre performance. Musical accompaniment or onstage orchestras are associated with almost all theatre traditions. Simple but ingenious solutions to sound effects can be traced to the earliest performances. A storm effect was created by snapping or shaking a metal thunder sheet; rolling wooden balls simulated the hooves of approaching horses; a slapstick accompanied the mock violence of comedy. These are all faithful elements of backstage equipment from centuries past. However, the technological advances in electronic recording equipment—first records and tape recorders and then compact discs and computerized sound applications—have completely revolutionized the way sound is produced and used in the theatre.

The sound designer now creates a sound score for a performance just as a lighting designer creates a light plot and a sequence of lighting cues. In fact, sound design shares many key functions with lighting design in the shaping of a production: deepening the mood of a scene, building the rhythm of the action, guiding transitions, providing special effects to define or punctuate important moments. For the production of *Eurydice*, the sound was as important as the light in drawing all of the elements of the production together.

The Materials of Sound Design

Sound design encompasses all of the **aural** components of a theatre production not created by the speaking voices of the actors. The sound designer may compose music for traditional instruments or on an electronic keyboard or synthesizer. The sound designer may record actual sounds such as a car door slamming or a dog barking or produce sounds through the creative manipulation of sound-producing objects. To create the score for *Eurydice*, the sound designer Bruno Louchouarn did all of these things.

Bruno Louchouarn is an accomplished musician with a broad interest in musical styles from many different cultures and from classical music to rock and roll. He plays a variety of instruments: guitar, viola, clarinet, saxophone, flute, and numerous percussion instruments. There is even a bagpipe in his studio. He is also a composer and a computer scientist and he delights in experimenting with either ordinary or unusual items that have the capacity to make interesting and convincing sounds.

In addition to the composition of music and sound, the sound designer is responsible for the amplification of sound through microphones and speakers. For some theatre productions, such as musicals, all of the actors are miked throughout the performance and wear visible microphones as part of the production aesthetic. For *Eurydice*, the actors wore hidden microphones that were used in only a few moments to create special effects such as vocal reverberation. But the placement of speakers was very important to the *Eurydice* sound design even though the play was performed in a relatively small theatre. Just as the actors entered from different places and the light shifted from area to area and came from different angles, to achieve the effect of sound that was integrated into the movement of the storytelling, the sound needed to originate in different parts of the stage space. Therefore a number of speakers were located strategically around the space. A speaker was placed at the top of the 45-foot-high elevator shaft that was used to play the first cue in the sequence of cues accompanying the descent of the raining elevator. Other speakers were placed at different heights, on the sides of the stage and at the back, as well as on the floor.

BRUNO LOUCHOUARN: All the stream sound comes from speakers that are placed at ground level, so the sound basically is slithering, is hugging the ground. And reinforced by the visual, your mind hooks on it and you really feel they are in the water.

Composing and Producing the Score

For a production like *Eurydice*, Bruno Louchouarn saw himself as a storyteller who was developing musical themes to support the character arcs and action of the play.

BRUNO LOUCHOUARN: There are a few big themes that are in the sound. They are traceable and they will help people relate. I think very structurally. I do sound design as part of the whole thing. But you can't have more than a few themes or people get very confused.

Louchouarn developed four major themes or motifs for the *Eurydice* score. The first theme was generated by the idea that Orpheus is a musician who is composing a gift of music for Eurydice. This theme began with gentle harp music and built into a construction of twelve melodies. The instrumentation used had a "floating" quality "because the whole world where they are is so ethereal and immaterial." The brash and vulgar Lord of the Underworld had a theme that contrasted sharply with the ethereal music associated with Orpheus. Louchouarn composed a progression of rock and roll to parallel the development of the character from a grotesque child to the immensely threatening figure at the end of the play. For the Stones, he used percussion instruments and the sounds of stones rather than a more traditional composition to create a sound that was "dry and different and rustling." And finally Louchouarn was particularly struck by the action of the play with the downward movement of all of the characters from the world above to the world below. "So there was this idea of coming down forever and ever and that being eerie and unsettling. So I worked out the descent musically." For all of the themes the music was produced through a blend of real instruments, most of which Louchouarn played himself, and instrumental music that was re-synthesized.

In addition to the four major themes related to the characters, one of the other major contributions of the sound score was to help establish the water imagery that is foundational to the play. Louchouarn had a number of strategies for creating sonic impressions of water. He recorded live sounds of rain falling, of water running through downspouts, even of water in his bathtub. He says water is "gentle and terrifying." He created cascades of water and drops of water. He used pebbles to "*imitate* drops of water because they have a very definite sound that is more energetic than (actual) drops of water." He used bells, and the harp, and glasses to make pinging sounds of water that are different than the "spooky sound of dripping reverberating in a cave." He also explains how important it was to shape the sound of water with interruptions.

> Water sounds are noise. So it can be a disaster. It can cover the voice of the actors. It can really fatigue the listener. So you want to have details that come in and out. So it has spaces: you read it and then it disappears.

Integration of the Sound Design into the Production

The musical score for *Eurydice* was so important to the production that it was introduced into the rehearsal process in advance of the technical rehearsals so that the actors would be familiar with the timing of the cues and also be able to use the sound to help build their performances.

> **BRUNO LOUCHOUARN:** You really want the actors to like the sound and the music so they will play with it and lean on it. They're going to spend a while with it and they can actually modulate their performances, which is hard.

For the composer, being present during rehearsals provided the opportunity to hear the music in conjunction with the actors' voices and experience the rhythms of the spoken language and the tempos of the actors' movements. Louchouarn attended rehearsals weekly from the beginning and then brought the score into the final week of rehearsals before tech.

> **BRUNO LOUCHOUARN:** I will have my ear buds and I will play music in my ear buds with their voices, because the voices of the actors will decide everything, the quality, the energy, where they are in the scene. The music is modulated by what the actors are saying. And sometimes I think, this is going to work, and it doesn't work and sometimes I think this is going to be great and it works. You don't want to cover the actors.

The early introduction of the music provided a testing process that supported the ongoing discussion between the director and the composer about the development of the score. And working with such a complex sound score during rehearsals allowed the stage manager to become familiar with this set of cues before also having to work with both the light cues and the video cues. Once the technical rehearsals began, Louchouarn still had many adjustments to make.

BRUNO LOUCHOUARN: This is sort of my specialty, these really complicated shows with a lot of music. Right from the get go, I write many variations of what I'm going to have in various tempos, all on separate tracks. In rehearsal, I am able very quickly to take away some instruments, move things, move entry points. It's very flexible. So I'm able to change things very quickly.

The work that Bruno Louchouarn does with musical instruments, synthesizers, computers, and sound amplification equipment is highly technical and relies on years of training and experience. But he speaks for all of the designers whose work is discussed in this chapter when he emphasizes that the starting point for their creative efforts in working in the theatre begins with the ideas in the play.

> Technique is always important in music, in sound, in everything. But technique will always follow the concept and the imagination. It starts with ideas. What you're going to do on every project is you're going to learn. Listen to your collaborators. Collaboration is the hardest thing and the most wonderful thing.

 # Summary

Stage designers communicate the essence of a play through visual and aural forms. Although designers share skills with visual artists, craftspeople, and musicians, the goal of the stage designer is to provide a foundation for the actor, not to create art that exists for its own sake. Designers are highly imaginative in their selection of materials and their uses of technology. They may use advanced electronic and computer technologies and sophisticated methods for forming plastic or metal. They may engage in time-consuming sequences of painting, dyeing, distressing, or otherwise transforming fabric or wood. They may scavenge old material or objects from secondhand sources. Designers must combine a capacity for creating eloquent images with a capacity for practical, technological applications. They are inventors as well as artists.

The designer's work is heavily influenced by the nature of the theatrical space. The proscenium theatre is constructed in a rectangular form with the stage at one end of the rectangle. The proscenium arrangement provides the greatest degree of separation between audience and actor. In a thrust theatre the audience sits on three sides of the stage, and an arena stage has audience members on four sides of a square or completely surrounding a circular stage space. A black box theatre is a flexible space that can be arranged in any of the preceding configurations. Large pieces of scenery and complicated scenic effects are appropriate on a proscenium stage. For thrust and arena stages, scenery must be designed so that it will not block the view of audience members. The back of scenery for a proscenium stage need not be finished. In contrast, a scenic piece on an arena stage must be finished because it will be seen from all angles.

The costume designer is concerned with establishing the period and background of the characters through silhouette and the textures of the fabrics. The costume designer establishes the individuality of characters as well as the relationships between groups of characters. He or she enhances the actor's presence without restricting the possibilities for character development.

The lighting designer unifies all the visual elements of the performance, bringing together the costumed figure of the actor and the scenic environment. The lighting designer is concerned with visibility, atmosphere, focus, and rhythm. Lighting contributes to the movement of the performance in time and also shapes stage space.

The video designer adds to the visual communication developed by the scene, costume, and lighting designers through the projection of images that can include film of live action, still photographs, or animation. Video can be projected onto screens integrated into the set design or on other surfaces including elements of either the set or the costumes. Video can provide specific information about location or historical context, but it can also add a special dimension to theatre production through the exploration of psychology or the unconscious of the characters through the inventive manipulation of imagery.

Because of rapidly advancing technology, sound design is becoming an increasingly important part of theatre production. Sound design includes the expressive area of environmental sound, such as music and sound effects; and the area of reinforcement, which involves the amplification of the actors' voices. Sound design parallels lighting design in unifying the expressive elements of the production.

Stage designers work closely together to develop a coherent production in which the design elements complement each other in terms of style, color, scale, degree of detail, and mood. The designers interpret the world of the play through visual and aural images that communicate to the audience members' senses and intellects. The stage design may be dazzling and opulent or simple and suggestive. Theatre production depends on the imagination of the designers to transform the stage space into a magical world that reveals the play in physical terms and that enhances the actors' potential.

 # Topics for Discussion and Writing

1. *Costume:* The following writing assignment explores the concept of the psychology of character used by costume designers. Begin by observing the clothing choices made by people in different locations and situations. Consider the impressions created by the clothing choices that you observe, and consider what you perceive to be the intended impressions. For example, one person may choose clothes to create an impression of power but instead project a sense of uncertainty; yet another person may be very effective in creating an aura of power. Select three people who have made distinct clothing and style choices that project a strong sense of character. Describe the choices in detail. Include your own interpretation of what is communicated to you about each person by the construction of his or her appearance. Write a one-half-to-one-page description of each observation.

2. *Light:* Bring notes to class for discussion on the following: (a) Choose an interesting outdoor location. Observe the light at three different times during the day and, if possible, under different weather conditions. (b) Choose three interior locations—such as a store, restaurant, or house—with distinctly different lighting. What kind of lighting is used in each location? Are the light sources natural or artificial? How bright is the light? Is the light soft or harsh? How does the lighting affect the appearance and mood of each space?

3. *Sound:* (a) Over the course of several days, keep a log of sounds that you hear. How many sounds did you hear that you are not normally aware of? How did the various

sounds affect your mood? What kinds of qualities do you associate with the different sounds? What sounds are soothing? What sounds are irritating? What emotional characteristics does a specific sound convey? For example, what emotion does a loud automobile horn in a traffic jam convey? Make a list of sounds that seem to have an emotional component. Include some that involve the human voice and some that do not. (b) Creating a soundscape: Work in groups of four or five. Bring interesting soundmakers to class. Using the soundmakers, as well as vocal sounds and hand sounds, compose a "soundscape" that suggests a specific location, such as a harbor, an amusement park, or a bar. Your soundscape may have individual words in it but no descriptive phrases. Think of your composition as a collage in which sounds will be layered. Some will repeat; some will fade in and out. Each soundscape should last thirty seconds. While performing the soundscapes for class members, have them close their eyes.

(c) Creating a sound story: After warming up with the soundscape, create a short dramatic story with a beginning, middle, and end, using only sound. The sound stories can be performed live or taped. Use dialogue sparingly or not at all. For example, the subject of a sound story could be a burglary that begins with the sound of cautious footsteps, followed by the rattling of a doorknob, the prying of a lock, and the breaking of glass. Other sounds might include drawers being opened and closed, papers being shuffled, and coins clinking. Breathing and muttered voices might also be used. The story could conclude with a police siren, running footsteps, and shouting. Experiment with different soundmakers to create the most interesting and vivid sounds, keeping in mind that the actual object being represented may not make the most convincing sound effect. The sound story should last from thirty to ninety seconds. Length, however, is not as important as creating an intriguing sequence of sounds.

For interviews with some of the designers in this chapter and music segments from *Eurydice*, as well as suggested readings and other resources, please visit **www.mhhe.com/creativespirit6e**

CHAPTER 9

Understanding Style: Theatricalism

The two plays we have examined in depth—*Joe Turner's Come and Gone* and *And the Soul Shall Dance*—are largely realistic, both in their dramatic construction and in their staging. Although realism has had a prominent position in theatre and film since the early twentieth century, another style of theatre, nonrealistic theatre, has provided a different way of expressing many of the tensions and uncertainties of modern life. Nonrealistic theatre takes a variety of startling forms that continue to be invented. Audacity and challenge are fundamental to the highly theatrical expression of **nonrealism,** which theatre practitioners and audiences alike find energizing and compelling, as well as sometimes puzzling and disturbing.

As we discussed in Chapter 7, the period of realism in the theatre began with the work of European playwrights and theatre practitioners in the second half of the nineteenth century. Realism continues to be a popular style today, particularly in Western theatre and film and also in many non-Western nations. Realists have sought to focus on the social problems engulfing ordinary people by examining psychologically coherent characters placed in detailed environments.

Shortly after the advent of realism, however, some theatre practitioners rejected the idea that constructing an illusion of reality was the most revealing way to examine the human condition. Other styles arose in the arts and in the theatre that were inspired both by the limitations of the realistic theatre and by the tremendous changes in social organization and in scientific and philosophical thought. The Industrial Revolution, for example, drastically changed the nature of human labor and threatened individual identity. The increasingly destructive weaponry of World War I and World War II brought the human community closer to annihilation. Religious skepticism increased in the face of the meaningless slaughter of millions. Changing views of the nature of the universe, such as that provided by Einstein's general theory of relativity, contributed to growing uncertainty about the existence of absolute truths. All these developments prompted the emergence of new styles in the theatre.

These new theatre styles have been referred to collectively as "nonrealistic theatre" or "antirealism" because of their specific reaction against realism. However, they have more in common than just their opposition to realism. If the realistic theatre depends on carefully chosen surface details, then the nonrealistic theatre seeks ways of going beneath the surface to identify something essential about human existence and then to express that essence through theatrical imagery. The theatrical image is an abstraction of or a poetic metaphor for some aspect of life. In the next play we read, *Angels in America* (Chapter 10), an angel appears on the stage. The angel is presented not as part of an actual event in the lives of the characters but as a fantastic creature in both appearance and behavior who symbolizes the characters' struggle to change. The angel is an imagistic way of expressing a complex structure of ideas about religion, psychology, and politics. Although the styles that make up the nonrealistic theatre take many forms, most of these forms rely on bold **theatricalism** that interprets the human condition in concentrated images. Theatricalism expands the concept of nonrealism by indicating a theatre composed of images. *Eurydice* by Sarah Ruhl is such a play, in which the complexity of human relationships is expressed through a highly symbolic journey. For our purposes, we use the terms *nonrealism* and *theatricalism* interchangeably.

Plays that use the style of theatricalism are often concerned with expressing the interior journeys of their characters. Frequently the point of view is expressed subjectively; that is, we see the world as the character sees it. Distortion, grotesque images, and nightmare visions are projected onto the stage from the character's mind, such as Eurydice's encounters in the underworld. In contrast to the realistic concrete world of work, home, and everyday activities in which the characters are viewed objectively by the playwright, the subjective landscape is often bizarre and highly personal. In *Angels in America*, one of the characters is seen largely through her hallucinations; she places herself in a frozen landscape of ice to avoid confronting fears that threaten to destroy her.

Theatricalism also often involves poetic or extravagant language, which frequently blends with the visual imagery to heighten the play's expressiveness. Many twentieth-century nonrealistic plays that focus on the failure of human beings to communicate with each other use fragmented or even nonsensical speech to explore the absence of meaning in human interactions.

The production of *Apollo* that has been discussed in two previous chapters is another example of theatricalism. The story that is told about the efforts to put a man on the moon is presented as a collage pieced together with fragments of history, fantasy, and parody. Images composed of movement, language, music, props, light, and projections are layered to build themes rather than a tightly knit plot. Large questions about American principles and ideals tie together the wide-ranging episodes. The visionary quest for the moon is expressed through many differing views of rockets, which are sometimes seen as playthings, sometimes as powerful missiles. The rocket images are crafted through props, costumes, and projections as well as through movement sequences like the astronauts floating in space (see page 128 and the online slide show). The loss of life associated with the Nazi rockets is expressed through metaphoric objects: the appearance of a pair of small white shoes; a bundle of ashes untied and poured from hand to hand. When the performance shifts to consider the quest for civil rights, the small white shoes and ashes reappear. Like a musical composition, motifs recur and transform. The dramaturg Tom Bryant observes that the director Nancy Keystone is working with certain instances of history but not relying on "realism" as the means of presenting the past. "She's translating these historical transactions or these historical events in theatricalized ways."

Exposing the Mechanics of the Theatre

In addition to concentrated imagery, the subjective point of view, and exaggerated speech, theatricalism changes the actor–audience relationship that is the goal of realism. Although we as audience members always know at the deepest level that we are in the theatre, the realistic theatre tries to make us forget where we are, whereas the nonrealistic theatre tends to remind us that what we are watching is a theatrical creation. In the realistic theatre, the tricks of the theatre are hidden. We do not watch the set changes or the costume changes. Certainly, the East West Players' production added nonrealistic elements of kabuki theatre to the scene changes of an otherwise realistic production of *And the Soul Shall Dance*. But in the Oregon Shakespeare Festival's production of *Joe Turner's Come and Gone*, the backstage areas were blocked off or masked so the audience would not be distracted by what was going on in the wings. The audience's awareness of such activity would have broken the illusion that was being carefully constructed onstage.

Additionally, in realistic staging the actors consciously remain in character the entire time they are onstage. Sometimes offstage sound effects are used in realistic theatre to suggest that the characters' fictional lives continue even when they have exited the stage. We can then imagine them in conversations or actions that continue their stage life when they are no longer in view. The intrusion of the mechanics of the theatre into the realistic illusion onstage would be like watching a film in which a microphone hanging above the actors is accidentally shown on camera. We are instantly taken out of the fictional world of the film and reminded of the devices used to construct the illusion.

In the nonrealistic theatre, the mechanics of the theatre are frequently exposed or the stage effects are so obviously executed that they call attention to themselves as theatrical gestures rather than as subtle elements of a realistic whole. The descent of the raining elevator in *Eurydice* is such a gesture as is the metamorphosis of the Lord of the Underworld from a bizarre stranger to a child to an enormous figure of the devil. In the nonrealistic theatre we may see the ropes that support the scenery or the movements of the stagehands. In *Angels in America*, the actors themselves change the scenery in view

of the audience. A scenic effect such as moonlight, which might be handled in the realistic theatre by a soft light coming through a window, might be presented in the nonrealistic theatre as a cardboard cutout of a moon attached to a stick.

The words *representational* and *presentational* are used to identify the distinction between realistic and nonrealistic theatre. **Representational staging** refers to the creation of a completely realistic illusion, and **presentational staging** refers to staging that recognizes the audience's awareness of theatrical manipulation. Presentational staging demands more of the audience's imagination than does representational staging, in which all of the details have already been filled in. The presentational, nonrealistic theatre frequently uses bold images, and abstract ideas or concepts are given symbolic expression through character, character action, and design as well as through language.

Expressionism

In the early part of the twentieth century, a loosely knit group of theatre artists and visual artists experimented with a form that would become known as **German expressionism.** Although the movement of German expressionism itself lasted from 1905 to 1922, the influences of the German expressionists extend until the present. For example, a contemporary experimental Japanese form, *butoh*, was inspired by the work of the German expressionists.

The word **expressionism** is also frequently used in a more general way to indicate the various developments in Western painting, sculpture, architecture, dance, film, and theatre that were concerned with the abstraction of form. The painters Pablo Picasso and Marc Chagall, the composer Igor Stravinsky, and the choreographer Martha Graham are all included in a long list of expressionist artists. The playwright August Strindberg, whose work is discussed in Chapter 7, turned to a more subjective, abstracted form of theatre in his plays *The Ghost Sonata* and *The Dream Play*, which broke ground for the later expressionists. Early in his career,

The film *Metropolis* (1927), by Fritz Lang, drew on many of the techniques developed in the German expressionist theatre to create the bitter mechanical world inhabited by oppressed workers. The style and scale of the images have been influential ever since the film was made.

Bertolt Brecht was part of the German expressionist movement. The innovations and concerns of the expressionists can still be seen in a play such as *Angels in America*.

German Expressionism

German expressionist theatre was infused with a sense of anguish. It has even been called the theatre of the shriek or the cry; its aim was to put into theatrical terms the feeling that was expressed in Edvard Munch's then highly influential painting *The Scream*. The German expressionists were horrified by the arms buildup in Germany and the militarization of their country. Their theatre

performances were a cry for humanitarianism to replace the brutality they saw around them. The expressionists, of course, proved to be prophetic. Many of them fled Germany during Hitler's rise in the 1930s, but those who didn't died in the concentration camps.

The silent film *Metropolis*, by the great German filmmaker Fritz Lang, uses many of the techniques developed in the German expressionist theatre. At this point we briefly examine the techniques used in *Metropolis* because this classic film is readily accessible on video and provides an excellent opportunity to experience the fundamental principles and themes of the German expressionist movement.

The plot of *Metropolis* focuses on the attempt of an industrialist's son to stop the manufacture of poison gas in his father's chemical plant. The film is dominated by striking visual images of the gleaming modern city above ground, inhabited by the unthinking rich; and the brutal factory below, where the workers live out their hopeless days. The workers have become dehumanized cogs in the operation of the vast factory. Almost lifeless, dressed in identical clothes like prisoners, they go through choreographed sequences that integrate their stylized, repetitive, robotlike movements with the workings of the wheels and pulleys of the machinery and the giant hands of a huge, regulatory clock. The enormous scenic images of the factory below and the skyscrapers above dwarf the tiny human characters, who have become insignificant in the world of relentless machines.

The scenes are presented as a sequence of episodes enacted by characters without names who are meant to be types rather than individuals and who speak (in subtitles) in abbreviated bursts of dialogue. The actors' stylized movements and the visual images are as important as the spoken language—or even more important. Although some of the acting is humorous by today's standards because of the exaggerated facial expressions and body language, the power of the workers' segments is undiminished by time.

American Expressionism: Eugene O'Neill

Early in the twentieth century, a number of American playwrights were drawn to expressionism as a style suited to exploring the contradictions and anxieties of American life. Elmer Rice wrote about the dehumanization of the machine world in *The Adding Machine*; Sophie Treadwell explored gender conflicts in *Machinal* (1927); and Eugene O'Neill used expressionistic elements in a number of his plays. Of these playwrights O'Neill has had the most lasting influence.

Eugene O'Neill (1888–1953) grew up in an Irish American family dominated by his father, James O'Neill, a well-known actor. James O'Neill played the lead in *The Count of Monte Cristo* for years, unable to give up the role for fear of financial failure. Thus Eugene O'Neill's youth was steeped in nineteenth-century melodrama. O'Neill remains a seminal figure in the American theatre because of his attempt to lift the level of the medium above nineteenth-century melodrama and spectacle and find an authentic American voice in playwriting that would approach the eloquence of the Europeans Ibsen and Strindberg.

No established form of serious American drama existed when O'Neill began writing one-act plays for the Provincetown Players in 1915. O'Neill's career as a playwright was marked by his experimentation with form, as he searched for the language and dramatic structures that would express his understanding of the American experience. He was concerned with the way human beings deceive themselves with illusions of success or love and then become paralyzed when those illusions are shattered.

Early in his career, in his plays *The Emperor Jones* (1920) and *The Hairy Ape* (1922), O'Neill used expressionism to present the distorted, nightmarish worlds of his characters. Borrowing a convention of the ancient Greek theatre, O'Neill used masks in *The Great God Brown* (1925). And in *Strange Interlude* (1928), which took many hours to perform, he had the characters speak their **inner monologues** and **subtext** aloud. He turned in yet another direction when he wrote *Mourning Becomes Electra* (1931), a trilogy modeled on Greek tragedy. Set during and after the Civil War, the three plays explore the destructive passions of the Mannon family.

O'Neill finally came to a bitter kind of realism in his last and most successful plays, *The Iceman Cometh* (produced posthumously in 1956), *Hughie* (produced posthumously in 1958), *A Moon for the Misbegotten* (1947), and *Long Day's Journey into Night* (produced posthumously in 1957).

Willem Dafoe and Kate Valk appeared in a new production (1997) of Eugene O'Neill's *The Hairy Ape,* produced by the Wooster Group and directed by Elizabeth LeCompte.

The Irish American personages of his youth figure prominently in O'Neill's work, and in the last two plays, he turns to the searing history of his own family, destroyed by alcoholism and drug addiction. These four late plays continue to draw the participation of America's finest actors on Broadway and in regional theatre.

Epic Theatre: Bertolt Brecht

Bertolt Brecht (1898–1956) was a prolific playwright and director who began his work in the theatre as part of the German expressionist movement. Brecht envisioned a new theatre experience to replace what he perceived as the failings

of the realistic theatre. Brecht's **epic theatre** has achieved an influence on the development of the modern theatre equal to the influence of Stanislavsky's system on the development of contemporary psychological acting. Following World War II, Brecht moved to East Berlin. There he founded the famous Berliner Ensemble theatre, where he directed highly regarded performances of his plays. We investigate Brecht's theories of theatre here at some length because of their continuing importance to the modern theatre and because of their influence on the major playwright we study in Chapter 10, Tony Kushner.

Brecht believed that there was a danger in the audience becoming too deeply engrossed or

Bertolt Brecht, who began his theatre work in Germany, became an exile in the United States during World War II. The repressive political climate in the United States following the war encouraged Brecht to return to East Germany, where he founded the Berliner Ensemble, which became one of the most distinguished theatres of the century.

lost in the story of a play. For Brecht, the goal of realism—to make the audience members forget that they were in the theatre—made the theatre into a kind of anesthetic. He wanted to find ways to make the audience step back from the drama in order to encourage analysis rather than empathy or identification. He wanted to provoke questioning so that audiences would maintain an active, internal dialogue with the performance. From Brecht comes the idea, then, of interruption, of breaking the narrative to snap the audience out of what Brecht saw as a hypnotic state.

Brecht also did not want the experience of the play to be completed within the time and space of the performance. Rather, he saw theatre as a call to action. He hoped the performance would be a beginning point or part of a process in which audience members and actors would become engaged in social action. Therefore, Brecht did not look to provide the audience with the kind of experience that involves empathy and then the emotional release often referred to as **catharsis.** Brecht wrote:

> The spectator was no longer in any way allowed to submit to an experience uncritically (and without practical consequences) by means of simple empathy with the characters in a play. . . .
> The dramatic [realist] theatre's spectator says: Yes, I have felt like that too—Just like me—It's only natural—It'll never change—The sufferings of this man appall me, because they are inescapable—That's great art; it all seems the most obvious thing in the world—I weep when they weep, I laugh when they laugh.
> The epic theatre's spectator says: I'd never have thought it—That's not the way—That's extraordinary, hardly believable—It's got to stop—The sufferings of this man appall me, because they are unnecessary—That's great art: nothing obvious in it—I laugh when they weep, I weep when they laugh.[1]

Brecht's Concept of Alienation

To bring the audience to this receptive or alert mental state, Brecht employed techniques to achieve an **alienation effect,** or, in German, the *Verfremdungseffekt (V-effekt)*. In Brecht's vocabulary, *alienation* did not mean "withdrawal"; rather, it meant "to make strange." He saw this strangeness as a way of interrupting the audience's involvement in the fiction created onstage.

As a director and a playwright, Brecht used a number of theatrical devices to create the alienation effect. The mechanics of the theatre were exposed to destroy any sense of magic or illusion.

In this 2007 production of Brecht's *Mother Courage* at the Berkeley Repertory Theatre, the action of the play is broken with cabaret-style singing. Here Yvette, played by Katie Barrett, sings one of the songs composed by Gina Leishman, with Mark Danisovszky at the piano, in the production directed by Lisa Peterson.

do in British and American musicals, songs in Brecht's plays change the mood and demand the audience's attention. Brecht's goal was to separate the music from the other elements of the drama, whereas in musical or lyrical theatre the goal is to integrate the music into the drama. According to Tony Kushner, the music in Brecht's plays provokes thought rather than provides a mental break:

> When it's good, [Brecht's music is] harder to listen to than the dialogue. It's more upsetting and more difficult. Which sort of reverses the traditional notion of musical theatre, at least American musical theatre, where the music is sort of your rest from thinking. And I think that really great composers for Brecht respond to the lyrics by writing something ugly and hard and difficult.[2]

Set pieces and props were simple and suggestive. Titles posted at the beginning of each new scene told the audience in advance what would happen to interrupt the development of suspense. Slide projections and films were introduced to provide information that clarified or contradicted the situations of the characters. In Brecht's conception, epic theatre encourages spectators to question why the characters make the choices that they do.

Brecht also used music to interrupt the action and to comment on the situation. Rather than heighten the emotional mood of scenes as songs

Brecht's Approach to Acting

Brecht's approach to acting was one of his most intriguing and challenging ideas about changing the nature of the theatre. Brecht was opposed to Stanislavsky's idea of complete identification with the character. Brecht suggested a new approach to performance in which the actor would comment on the character, that is, stand both inside and outside the character—as if the actor were describing his or her conduct and in some way engaging in a dialogue with the

Lynn Nottage has written a new play, inspired in part by *Mother Courage,* entitled *Ruined,* which won the Pulitzer Prize for drama in 2009. Nottage moves the location of the play to the Congo, where an ongoing war currently brutalizes that country. In fact, the playwright interviewed Congolese women in preparing to write the play. In Brecht's version of the play, the character Mother Courage is a peddler who sells food and other goods to the warring armies. Lynn Nottage sets the action in a brothel, where Mama, the Mother Courage figure, played here by Saidah Arrika Ekulona, prepares Sophie, Condola Rashad, to sing for their customers. The play's premiere shown here is a co-production by the Goodman Theatre of Chicago and the Manhattan Theater Club, directed by Kate Whoriskey in 2009.

audience about the character. This technique is sometimes referred to as **acting in quotes.** In Brecht's words:

> The actor does not allow himself to become completely transformed on the stage into the character he is portraying. He is not Lear, Harpagon, Schweik; he shows them.[3]

Brecht is very clear in his writings that he did not mean that the actor should not be emotionally invested in the characterization or that the emotions of the audience should remain disengaged.

Instead, he wanted both the actor and the audience to bring a critical attitude to their participation in the theatre event so that they could consider what was possible under the circumstances:

> Human behavior is shown as alterable; man himself as dependent on certain political and economic factors and at the same time as capable of altering them. . . . The idea is that the spectator should be put in a position where he can make comparisons about everything that influences the way in which human beings behave.[4]

Brecht focused his plays on characters forced to make difficult choices. The plays are written in long sequences of short scenes that reveal the various forces affecting the characters' decision-making process. Brecht also presented a comprehensive history of the situation rather than entering the story line at a late point, as did Ibsen, whose plays begin just before the characters' major crises. For example, *Mother Courage*, which Brecht wrote in collaboration with Margarete Steffin, takes place during the Thirty Years' War of the seventeenth century. Concerned with the devastation of war, Brecht and Steffin created some historical distance so that the audience could consider the effect of all wars. The central character is a peddler who crosses back and forth over the battlefields, selling her wares to both sides in the conflict. She is a pragmatist who is committed to her own survival. But during the many years of the war, she ends up losing her own children because of decisions she makes about the family's economic welfare. Brecht's play *Galileo* demonstrates the influences on the central character Galileo as he first proposes his notion that the earth revolves around the sun and then recants his position after being threatened by the Catholic Church.

Theatre of the Absurd

In the 1950s another dramatic style evolved in response to the devastation of modern warfare, this time World War II. Based more on philosophical or metaphysical explorations than was the overtly political German expressionist theatre, the **theatre of the absurd** was created by a group of international playwrights who all lived and wrote in Paris: the Irish Samuel Beckett; the Romanian Eugène Ionesco; the Russian Arthur Adamov; and the French Jean Genet, who began writing in a prison cell.

In the face of the horrendous slaughter of World War II and the complicity of various segments of European society in the extermination of huge groups of innocent people, the playwrights of the absurd found traditional value systems bankrupt. They wrote about the meaninglessness of human existence and the inability of language to communicate in an effective way. The ultimate isolation of human beings shaped the images of futility that emerged from the absurdist movement. In his definitional study on absurdism, Martin Esslin writes:

> The Theatre of the Absurd . . . tends toward a radical devaluation of language, toward a poetry that is to emerge from the concrete and objectified images of the stage itself. The element of language still plays an important part in this conception, but what happens on the stage transcends and often contradicts the words spoken by the characters.[5]

The most famous play of the theatre of the absurd is Samuel Beckett's *Waiting for Godot*. Two tramps wait by the side of the road, essentially a physical "void" interrupted only by the presence of a shriveled tree. In the play the two characters wait for another character, named Godot, who never comes. While they wait, they struggle to fill the empty time with patter and activity reminiscent of clowning routines from vaudeville. But each attempt at interaction is more futile than the last. Long silences surround and break their speeches. The tree is the only visual detail that breaks the bleakness of the physical space, just as their meaningless chatter may be seen as only a brief interruption of the vast silence of the universe.

Although the two characters speak of parting from each other, they don't. They speak of leaving, yet they are unable to exit from the stage. They simply go on waiting. The nature of Godot is never defined; he is a puzzle that has led to intense speculation about what he may represent. Interpreted simply, Godot represents a reason for the characters to go on waiting, and that must suffice. In his play, Beckett constructs a powerful and disturbing image of life itself: Life is reduced to the act

Endgame is another major play by Samuel Beckett that, like *Waiting for Godot,* explores the futility of human existence and the trivial activities which people concoct to pass the time. And like *Godot,* the vivid language of the characters presents the bleakness of their situation at the same time that it offers biting humor and opportunities for theatrical brilliance. Here Alvin Epstein plays Nag and Elaine Stritch plays Nell, two characters confined to garbage cans for the entire play, in a 2008 production directed by Andrei Belgrader at the Brooklyn Academy of Music.

of waiting for something that never comes. Beckett's plays are extremely dark in spite of their humor.

Eugène Ionesco also wrote about the uselessness of human activity, but sometimes in a more playful way than Beckett. Ionesco delighted in creating situations in plays, such as *The Bald Soprano*, in which characters speak to each other at length in various forms of nonsense. Ionesco was particularly concerned with the failure of language to provide us with a means of reaching one another, as is Tony Kushner, whose *Angels in America* includes a scene in which an assembly of angels blather empty phrases simultaneously.

A Revolution in Movement: Martha Graham

The expressionists and the absurdists made major changes in the use of language, in plot structure, in characterization, and in the nature of stage action. It would require an artist of a different sensibility to contribute a way of approaching stage movement to match the other innovations of expressionism and absurdism. Martha Graham (1893–1991) stands out as one of the most innovative and influential artists of the twentieth century, comparable to Picasso in visual art and James Joyce in literature. Her work has changed the way we understand the expressive possibilities of the human figure in space and the interactions of the figure with objects and costumes. Although Graham's contributions are most evident in modern dance and theatre, her influence, like that of other seminal artists and thinkers, spreads across many disciplines.

Martha Graham was a dancer, choreographer, actress, and playwright. Dance was her language, but her compositions took the form of drama. Graham was an actor who communicated through her body her own versions of Greek and American myths. She began her independent

work as a choreographer in the early 1930s and continued to compose dramatic dance works until her death in 1991. The enormous output of this visionary artist spanned the twentieth century.

A New Dance Vocabulary

All the innovators of modern theatre in the West, from the realists to the expressionists to Brecht to the absurdists, sought new styles of acting that would fully engage the body of the actor as well as the voice, to make performance more

Early in her career, Martha Graham choreographed and performed *Lamentation,* a dance of grief that recalls images of the German expressionists.

than posed figures declaiming speeches. Many of these theatre practitioners were inspired by the brilliance of the moving actor in the Asian theatre but frustrated by the lack of a comparable movement tradition in the West. Graham revolutionized what was possible in movement on the stage. Strongly influenced by Asian forms, Graham developed a movement system that contributed to both the technique and the climate that would enable Western experimentation with Eastern forms.

Until the early part of the twentieth century, the available dance vocabulary came from the ballet. In Graham's work, the bare, flexed foot replaced the pointed foot in ballet toe shoes. Angular, asymmetrical movement contrasted sharply with the symmetrical elegance of ballet. The pelvis and abdomen became a primary center for movement so the body could contract and then release rather than always maintain a vertical line. And fundamental to the movement of both women and men was the expression of the body's weight. The floor became a partner in this exploration of the substance of the human body rather than a springboard. The fall, the pull of gravity, was central to Graham's movement system; dancers pressed up from the floor, using their visible power to oppose gravity. Graham herself was a virtuoso performer with an astounding technique and a riveting dramatic presence. She opened the way for much of what would follow in the twentieth-century experimental theatre.

Costume and Set as Partners in Dance

Graham also approached scenic and costume elements as partners to the dancers rather than as decorations or representations of period, although they also served both of these functions. Sewing her own costumes and working with designers such as Isamu Noguchi, who created sculptures for her settings, Graham used design elements to give further definition to the

dancing figure and to provide for the development of character through movement. In an early piece entitled *Lamentation*, the dancer is cloaked and hooded by a piece of draped fabric. In this dance of grief, the dancer pushes with angular, stretching gestures against the fabric that surrounds her. The tension of the dance and its emotional content are generated by the way the fabric resists the efforts of the dancer to displace or break through its binding force.

An example of a sculptural set piece by Noguchi is a free-form metal frame bed that he created for a dance about Jocasta, the mother and wife of Oedipus, in Graham's work *Night Journey*. The bed has a strong symbolic presence. It serves first as the place where Jocasta gave birth to Oedipus, second as the site of their incestuous relationship, and third as the funeral bier that carries Jocasta's body to her grave. The bed has physical importance as well. It is central to the movement of Jocasta and Oedipus as they dance out their relationship on its slanted surface. The hard metal frame supports the dancers' bodies and sets in relief the strength and the vulnerability of their characters: Oedipus, who will lose his eyes; and Jocasta, who will lose her life.

Total Theatre: Robert Wilson

Another American theatre artist, Robert Wilson (1941–   ), has become one of the dominant figures shaping today's theatre of images. Wilson's theatrical style is connected to a movement called **total theatre,** a form that stretches back to the mid-nineteenth century and the operas of Richard Wagner. Since Wagner's time, many theatre artists have been drawn to a vision of theatre that fuses music, dance, language, scenic image, and light; this is exactly what Wilson aims at. He creates works on a very large scale in terms of (1) the numbers of performers and collaborators involved, sometimes more than 150; (2) the duration of the performances, which can last up to twelve hours; and (3) the size and complexity of the images he constructs. Wilson begins his theatre pieces with scenic images and with music and dance. Language is frequently used, but text is neither the starting point nor the foundation of what is communicated.

Wilson's expectation of the audience experience is very different from that of most of the other theatre artists we have discussed so far. Wilson is not attempting to build a visible and coherent structure of ideas or to interpret character psychology; nor is he offering a social critique. He seeks to trigger associations in the minds of audience members. Rather than consciously constructing work that interprets themes, Wilson and his collaborators present loosely related images that the audience members must then organize and interpret according to their individual responses. Wilson creates stage images that seem to come from the world of dreams and hallucinations.

Wilson's Experience

Robert Wilson brings to his work a unique combination of training and personal experience. A brief consideration of his background is helpful in understanding his point of view and his approaches to his theatre pieces. Wilson studied painting in Paris before he returned to the United States to earn an undergraduate degree in architecture. He experimented with various visual art forms, including large outdoor installations. His first involvement in the New York theatre was as a scene designer. Wilson is a visual thinker; he develops scenes through long sequences of drawings rather than dialogue.

Another profound influence on Wilson's life is dance. As a child Wilson had a pronounced stutter, which inhibited his ability to communicate verbally. At seventeen he began to study dance with a remarkable seventy-year-old teacher, Bird Hoffman. Through controlled movement and relaxation, Wilson was able to overcome his stutter. His studies with Hoffman inspired Wilson's work with children and adults with disabilities, in

which he encouraged creative responses, in part through the use of slow, controlled repetitions of patterned movement. Eventually he incorporated this approach to movement into his theatre performances. He also invited the participation of some of the children he worked with, and he used their contributions onstage. Wilson frequently communicates nonverbally with the performers in his pieces as he works with them on stylized gestures and abstract movements. There is none of the discussion of character or motivation that is so important to the realistic theatre.

The Interior Landscape

Wilson's work includes *The Life and Times of Joseph Stalin*, *A Letter to Queen Victoria*, *Einstein on the Beach*, and *The Life and Times of Sigmund Freud*. As the titles suggest, Wilson uses large subjects that can be interpreted in many ways. He frequently focuses on a major historical figure whose influence has been felt across generations and continents; he builds collages of images in response to the impact of the central figure. The images relate to each other thematically, often in a very loose sense. The critic John Rockwell summarizes Wilson's approach to these subjects:

> What Wilson really is concerned with is deeper questions of authority, terror, fear and hope and the smaller (deeper?) human quirks of such seemingly overpowering figures.[6]

In Wilson's work one image slowly dissolves to the next: immense architectural backgrounds; enormous figures; characters in elaborate costumes from different periods; dancers; animals such as bears, elephants, and fish; suspended objects and people; burning houses. Various pieces of text are read or spoken, sometimes in several different languages. Exploratory work that was done for a production of *King Lear* involved a complete reordering of Shakespeare's text, spoken sometimes in English and sometimes in German, with an early Russian film version of *King Lear* playing in the background. Music also

Time Rocker, designed and directed by Robert Wilson with music by Lou Reed and based on H. G. Wells's *Time Machine,* is the last piece of a trilogy of rock operas. Wilson produces his work more frequently in Europe than in the United States, and *Time Rocker* was created in Hamburg, Germany, before being produced at the Théâtre de L'Odeon in Paris.

takes a prominent role in Wilson's work. Some of his work has featured the compositions of the **avant-garde** musicians Philip Glass and Laurie Anderson and the voice of the opera singer Jessye Norman. Through the intersection of abstract scenic imagery, hauntingly strange music, hypnotic dance, and pedestrian and poetic fragments of text, Wilson pushes back the boundaries of theatrical expression to reveal, in Martha Graham's words, "the interior landscape."

A New Meeting of East and West: Shen Wei

Both Martha Graham and Bertolt Brecht were deeply influenced by Asian performance styles. Graham's movement vocabulary and Brecht's approach to playwriting and acting reflect their contact with dancers and actors from India, Japan, and China. As Western theatre practitioners adopted ideas from Asian sources, Western performance traditions also have had a major impact on Asian culture. The Japanese perform Shakespeare in the kabuki style, and the Chinese have been exploring realistic spoken drama through performance of plays, like Arthur Miller's *Death of a Salesman,* translated into Chinese or new plays written by Chinese playwrights that use Western-style spoken dialogue instead of dialogue sung in the style of Chinese opera. Most recently, the fusion of Eastern and Western traditions has achieved a striking new direction in the work of Shen Wei.

From Opera to Modern Dance

Shen Wei (1968–) is a Chinese-born dance theatre artist now working in the United States. His father, an actor and a director, and his mother, a producer, both worked in the Chinese opera company in Xianying and were displaced by the Cultural Revolution. Some of Shen's early childhood was spent in harsh circumstances while his parents were forced to do agricultural work in the countryside. He says, "After the Cultural Revolution, the government tried to get back all that had been lost" and some of the Chinese opera schools and companies were reopened.[7] At the age of nine, Shen Wei left his family to study at the Hunan Arts School and prepare for his own career as an opera performer. Classes began at 5:30 in the morning and continued until 8:00 at night. They included movement, acrobatics, martial arts, acting, speech, singing, and learning the roles of different characters. "It was difficult as a young child to get up at 5:30 in the

Shen Wei created *Folding* on a visit to China in 2000 and then re-created it for his company Shen Wei Dance Arts in the United States. Taking his inspiration from the action of folding paper or fabric or any other item, he choreographed a work in which the dancers engage in slow folding and unfolding of their bodies. Dressed in long, draped costumes of red and black and wearing shaped headdresses to extend their height, the dancers have a sculptural quality as they move across a white floor and in front of a huge painting of fish swimming through a mysterious sea. Shen Wei is responsible for the choreography and the set, costume, and makeup design. The lighting is by David Ferri.

morning, to do your own laundry by hand with no hot water. I saw my parents twice a year. You had to be independent very early. It was really, really hard."

In 1984, at the age of sixteen, Shen started his professional career in the theatre. For the next five years he performed with the Hunan State Opera Company, where he specialized in the roles of the acrobatic warrior hero. By this time, not only was Shen an accomplished actor and singer, he was also skilled in music, calligraphy, poetry, and painting. He explains that he was raised in a tradition where an educated person was expected to develop multiple artistic abilities

in order "to achieve spiritual development." And in addition to his mastery of traditional Chinese art forms, he began to teach himself to paint in the Western style that was becoming visible as Chinese society became more open. Just when his interest in painting had become the focus of his creative energies, on a trip to Beijing in 1987, Shen was exposed to yet another art form, Western modern dance. The restless young artist had found the basis of his future work.

The first Chinese modern dance company, Guangdong Modern Dance Company, was established in 1989. Shen Wei was the only member of the new company who did not have

In contrast to the slow meditative movement of *Folding, Rite of Spring* demands the dancers to move with lightning speed while they execute complicated sequences of turns and falls. Choreographed to music by Stravinsky, the movement draws on vocabulary from both the Chinese opera and contemporary dance. The costumes and set including the floor are realized in colors of black, white, and gray as the dancers perform abstract sequences of movement connected to Stravinsky's phrases and rhythms.

a firm background in ballet or classical Chinese dance forms. "I was the only one from Chinese opera. But the director saw my paintings and recognized that I had an open mind, so even though I lacked classical dance training, I was accepted." Studying with visiting teachers from the Martha Graham, José Limón, and Paul Taylor companies, Shen quickly became as interested in choreography as he was in dancing.

The evolution of Shen Wei's artistic journey reflects the rapidity of change in China in the last twenty-five years and the way that change is transforming its culture. However, in 1995 Shen Wei decided to leave China for the United States in search of more opportunities and greater artistic freedom. Drawing on his training in both modern dance and Chinese opera; his skills as a painter; and his knowledge of music, makeup, and costuming, Shen formed his own company in 2000 and began to create new theatre works that merge East and West, performing arts and visual arts.

Choreographer and Designer

In creating his theatre works, Shen is like Martha Graham in the way he choreographs and dances in the pieces and then also designs the makeup and costumes, which are very important to shaping the movement. And like Robert Wilson, he designs his own sets. However, as a choreographer, Shen Wei is unique in an important way. Rather than defining himself through a signature movement style that forms an identifiable foundation for his pieces as a group, he attempts to develop a new dance vocabulary for each new work he undertakes. So the rehearsal process always begins with training the dancers in the new movement he has invented or is exploring. He is known for some works that use very slow, repetitive, meditative movement passages in which stillness is an essential part of the composition. In these works, the dancers seem to inhabit a dreamlike world in which their bodies change shape and have the ability to move in entirely new ways. In other pieces, the movement is lightning-fast and percussive, with the dancers leaping or rolling on the floor with breathtaking speed. Uniting the different pieces is a sense that the dancers' bodies and movement patterns are clearly connected to the world of painting and sculpture. In *Connect Transfer*, a canvas covers the entire stage floor and the dancers have paint on their bodies, with which they color the floor in the patterns of their movements. In *Folding* and *Deep Resonance*, the dancers' bodies themselves seem to be the evolving sculptural forms. A more recent work, *Second Visit to the Empress* (2005), offers a restaging of a prominent opera from the Chinese repertoire in which Shen Wei returns to his roots. But now the traditionally costumed singing characters share the stage with contemporary dancers, an interplay between forms of East and West and the past and the present. In 2008 Shen Wei brought his talents and international perspective to the world stage as the principal choreographer for the spectacular opening ceremonies of the Beijing Olympics.

Handspring Puppet Company

To be surprised by a performance is one of the greatest gifts the theatre can give us. The play *War Horse* works this particular magic when we see horses on stage that are clearly puppets, but at the same time seem completely real. *War Horse* tells a story of the part played by horses in the battles of World War I with the focus on one heroic horse, Joey, and the boy who loves him. Stories of animal and human interactions are frequent subjects of film and television, from highly realistic adventures filmed in nature to absurdly rendered creatures dreamed up through animation. But the horses of *War Horse* are neither live animals nor cartoon figures. They exist in another dimension entirely, the world of the puppet. And the puppet brings with it a unique theatricality different from any of the heightened forms we have considered thus far.

War Horse was developed in a collaborative production by the National Theatre of Britain and the Handspring Puppet Company of South Africa. *War Horse* was first presented in England in 2007 and then across the United States and around the world. As the production enters its seventh year of continuous performance, it has proven to be a remarkably popular theatre event for adults and children and a vivid demonstration of the ingenuity of the Handspring Puppet Company in crafting new approaches to an ancient form.

A total of nine horses make up the puppet cast of *War Horse* with one of them, Joey, a stiff-legged colt who flies apart in pieces when he is transformed into a galloping adult. The horses are scaled to appear full-size in comparison to the numerous human characters, first English villagers and then soldiers, who share the stage with the horses. In addition to the actors playing characters, there are three puppeteers onstage for each horse. The puppeteers do not double as actors playing other roles in the play. They have a dedicated responsibility. Each horse has two puppeteers manipulating it from the inside and one puppeteer on the outside adding further refinements to the horse's movements. The puppeteers also vocalize all of the horses' sound effects from neighs and whinnies to snorts and other sounds of breath. All three puppeteers are

In this photo, the puppet horse, Joey, is startled by a tank on the battlefield, while another horse lies dead on the stage. The future of warfare is clear. The old strategies of soldiers on foot and on horseback will be replaced by more terrible and destructive weapons of war. The open cane work of the horse construction is repeated in the tank. The 2007 production of *War Horse* was directed by Tom Morris and Marianne Elliott. The set design was by Rae Smith. The play was adapted by Nick Stafford from a novel by Michael Morpurgo.

always visible. No effort is made to hide them. The horses and puppeteers move freely around the entire space. They are never presented behind some kind of limiting puppet stage. They can gallop, rear up, carry soldiers into battle on their backs, pull wagons loaded with weapons, and die from injury, starvation, and exhaustion in the midst of all of the human characters.

The puppeteers are dressed in keeping with the environment in which the horses are placed. When the horses are on a rural farm in England, the puppeteers are dressed as stable hands. When the horses are on the battlefield, the puppeteers are costumed as soldiers. The horses are fabricated from molded cane and nylon mesh, which depending on the lighting can be opaque or transparent. The articulation of their leg joints, the movement potential of their ears and tails, and the sense of their breathing created through the rising and falling of necks and backs, give the horses a compelling sense of life. When the puppeteers are on the stage, they look only at the horse they are animating. They never look at another actor or at the audience. This specific style of

Adrian Kohler and Basil Jones stand in front of the prototype of the horse puppet designed by Kohler for *War Horse*. The brilliant horse puppets were the culmination of thirty years of experience and experimentation with puppet design and manipulation. Kohler and Jones have not only co-directed the Handspring Puppet Company since its founding, they have been two of the principle puppeteers in many of the productions.

puppet performance has been evolving since Adrian Kohler and Basil Jones, together with Jill Joubert and Jon Weinberg, founded the Handspring Puppet Company in Cape Town in 1981.

We first considered the work of the Handspring Puppet Company in Chapter 2 when we discussed theatre and social change in South Africa. The same company that is currently dazzling the world with a heartwarming, universal story about horses and war also produced one of the most compelling pieces of theatre about apartheid, *Ubu and the Truth Commission* (see page 41). Over its thirty-year history, Handspring has

explored the way puppets, often in combination with live actors, can express complex ideas about the human condition in theatre pieces that are created for an adult audience.

The work of the Handspring Puppet Company has been distinguished by a number of factors. Key participants have been leading visual artists as well as theatre practitioners. Adrian Kohler, the company's artistic director and principle puppet designer and sculptor, and Basil Jones, the executive producer, both trained as visual artists before committing their careers to "the artistry of the performing object."[8] In addition to experimenting continuously with new expressive possibilities, Kohler and Jones have also turned to the rich heritage of mask and puppet traditions in Africa through collaborations with the Sogolon Puppet Troupe from Mali and Koffi Koho from Benin. And they have invited leading South African avant-garde theatre directors such as Malcolm Purkey and William Kentridge to join in their process of developing new work that would do justice to the conflicts in their society. Like other South African theatre practitioners working during apartheid, they were determined to create pieces that addressed the precarious nature of life in their country. The vexing problems of identity in South Africa compounded by the views and restrictions of apartheid offered rich material for a theatre using both puppets and humans as actors.

One area of prolonged exploration involved the development of a new style of puppets to be used in combination with animation. William Kentridge, who had trained in theatre as well as in visual art, worked with Adrian Kohler and Basil Jones on four groundbreaking productions: *Ubu and the Truth Commission*, *Woyzeck on the Highveld*, *Faustus in Africa*, and *Il Ritorno d'Ulisse*, an opera. Kentridge is known for his hand-drawn charcoal animations that are now shown in museums around the world that he calls "drawings for projections."[9] Some of the early investigations that he did into this form of animation were undertaken to provide visual imagery for the plays he was producing with Handspring. The creative

The crocodile puppet appears with Ma Ubu, Busi Zokufa, in *Ubu and the Truth Commission* performed at the Market Theatre, Johannesburg, in 1997. The crocodile's head was carved from wood. His body was made from an old briefcase, appropriate to his consumption of vast quantities of documents. Busi Zokufa, who was both a puppeteer and an actor in this production, is a central member of the Handspring Puppet Company. The director and animation designer was William Kentridge.

partners found that the animations "could assist the audience in reaching into the thoughts of the puppets."[10] Kohler began designing wooden puppets in human form that expressed concentrated emotions augmented by the animations and strange versions of animals that presented human qualities through association: a crocodile, a hyena, a rhinoceros. The rough and provocative Kentridge animations intersected with the carving aesthetic used by Adrian Kohler on the wooden puppets in these pieces, which clearly showed the marks of his chisel, and the junk-like found objects that were used as props or even became part of the puppets.

Each of the four plays that Kentridge worked on with Handspring examined the struggles in South Africa from a different perspective, perspectives that were specific to South Africa but universal at the same time. These plays also connect directly to theatre movements discussed earlier in this chapter. *Ubu and the Truth Commission*, arranged by Jane Taylor, uses characters and text from *Ubu Roi* by Alfred Jarry, a play that is often considered as the beginning of the absurdist movement. The grotesque characters from *Ubu Roi* are used in the South African version to parody corrupt leaders such as the character Pa Ubu, played by a human actor, who is

In *Woyzeck on the Highveld,* performed at the Market Theatre, Johannesburg, 2008, Woyzeck reaches for his baby while his lover Maria stands in the background. The puppeteers are Louis Seboko and Adrian Kohler. The animation of the night sky on the projection screen reflects Woyzeck's anguish as he considers Maria's infidelity. The animation was by William Kentridge, who was also the director.

accompanied by a puppet of a three-headed dog. Another *Ubu* character is a crocodile whose body is a briefcase. The crocodile serves as a kind of paper shredder, voraciously eating incriminating documents. *Ubu and the Truth Commission* also draws on a number of Brechtian devices to set off the testimonies of witnesses at the hearings of the Truth and Reconciliation Commission. *Woyzeck on the Highveld* is an adaptation of a German play by Georg Buchner that is a foundational text in the development of expressionism. The Buchner play examines the mental disintegration of a poor soldier who eventually

kills his lover with whom he has a child. *Woyzeck* is one of the most frequently produced plays in the international repertory. The oppressive conditions for workers of color in South Africa provide a poignant environment for the desperation of Buchner's central character.

By using puppets to reinterpret these well-known plays, Handspring opens up a wider conversation by challenging how we understand the nature of the actor in the theatre. The puppet characters/actors of the Handspring plays provoke a different kind of relationship with the audience than we have seen in other styles of performance.

First of all, puppet performance depends on audience members projecting deep feelings onto inanimate objects. And then the essential starting point for character creation is neither the playwright nor the actor, but the hand and the imagination of the puppet sculptor. The sculptor determines how the puppet will look, the materials to be used, the style of carving or fabrication, and the kinds of movements that are built into the puppet's basic construction. The details selected for the puppet's appearance and the style and capacity of the puppet's body for articulate movement is a form of script writing. Basil Jones points out that the work of the puppet sculptor is a kind of "authorship."[11] The story of the character is embedded in the puppet's figure. That scripted figure is then given life by the puppeteer, the energy of the entrances and exits, the quality of the gestures large and small, the rhythm and timing, and a sense that the puppet has its own breath. These inanimate objects which we endow with life in a magical transformation can then conjure new worlds that are both human and beyond human.

WORKING IN THE THEATRE

Festivals—Grahamstown

Many of the productions from South Africa discussed in this book, including the plays of the Handspring Puppet Company, have something in common besides their national home. Their premiere performances were presented at the National Arts Festival of Grahamstown in the Eastern Cape in the southern part of the country. Grahamstown is a university town that sponsors an annual arts festival which draws together experienced and emerging theatre practitioners, musicians, dancers, and visual artists to share their work with each other and audiences from around Africa and the world. Thousands of performances fill every possible presentation space in the small community, which explodes each July with artistic energy. For decades the Grahamstown festival has served as a crossroads for artistic exchange where artists could receive support and encouragement. During apartheid and afterward, the festival provided an arena for the presentation of new ideas that challenged the status quo aesthetically and politically.

Arts festivals take place in a variety of locations around the world and take numerous forms. The best-known and largest festival takes place at the end of each summer in Edinburgh, Scotland. In fact, the Grahamstown festival is second in size only to Edinburgh. Other major festival sites include Avignon in France and the Spoleto Festival in Charleston, South Carolina. Arts festivals provide the opportunity for new artists to be seen and for major new works to be developed.

*To learn more about the National Arts Festival in Grahamstown and its significance for young artists, see the film on our Web site.

 Summary

In response to what many saw as realism's failure to completely reveal the human condition, new theatre styles arose in the early twentieth century. These theatrical forms communicated through overtly theatrical images, through stylized movement and poetic language, through the abstract rather than the concrete, through a concentration of expression rather than through the accumulation of detail. Although these theatre styles are often grouped under the category of nonrealism, or theatricalism, no single term adequately defines the many forms of theatre that seek to express the inner life of human beings.

Since the beginning of the twentieth century, many playwrights, choreographers, and directors have taken various approaches to theatrical expression. In the theatre of the German expressionists, plays often took the form of protest against war, industrialization, and inhumanity. Characters and language were reduced to their essence and supported by stylized movement and distorted scenic images to produce an effect of anguish. The American playwright Eugene O'Neill used expressionism in much of his early work. Bertolt Brecht sought an alienation effect to interrupt the audience's emotional involvement in the drama in order to encourage analysis of the dramatic event. Absurdist playwrights such as Samuel Beckett and Eugène Ionesco used theatrical imagery to explore philosophical rather than social issues.

Other theatre artists have created unique styles through the use of movement, music, and scenic image rather than language. Martha Graham invented a movement vocabulary to explore the passions of archetypal characters engaged in mythic dramas. Robert Wilson creates a dreamlike total theatre in which enormous scenic images, evocative music, and dancing figures suggest mysterious relationships. Shen Wei draws together theatre, dance, and visual art traditions of China and the West. The Handspring Puppet Company explores the potential of puppets in combination with actors and animation to challenge perceptions about human identity and create deeply felt, concentrated expressions of human experiences.

 # Topics for Discussion and Writing

1. Research the works of such artists as Edvard Munch, Pablo Picasso, Salvador Dalí, and Käthe Kollwitz that distort and fracture the represented figures, landscapes, or environments. What kinds of commentary about the human condition do these paintings make? How do they diverge from more realistic image making?

2. What changes in the nature of the actor–audience relationship were proposed by Bertolt Brecht? How do Brecht's ideas about acting contrast with those of Stanislavsky outlined in Chapter 7? We frequently see evidence of Stanislavsky's approach to acting in theatre and film today. Cite some examples of Brecht's approach to acting, in which actors call attention to themselves as actors.

3. Compare the plot of *Waiting for Godot* with that of *Joe Turner's Come and Gone* or *And the Soul Shall Dance*. What is the difference in the kinds of actions performed by the characters, and what is the significance of those actions? What is the difference in the endings and what we imagine will happen to the characters after the plays have ended?

● For suggested readings and video resources related to this chapter, please visit www.mhhe.com/creativespirit6e

CHAPTER 11

The Musical Theatre

Music and dance are forms of human expression that respond to some of life's most intensely felt moments, when it is neither enough to speak nor to remain silent. Through rhythmic movement or by lifting our voices in song, we express joy or heartache. The blues, Celtic ballads, country music, work songs, rap, and reggae are all connected to essential life experiences.

Music and dance mark our observations of life's defining occasions. At weddings we celebrate through music. Music and dance accompany courtship, from the prom to the nightclub, from rock and roll concerts to moonlight serenades. Fight songs inspire battles and sporting events. The Maori of New Zealand still dance the ferocious *haka* that once motivated their warriors. Most religious worship includes musical expression, from the solemnity of a restrained hymn to the exuberance of gospel. Ecstatic dancing that liberates the spirit is also associated with religious observation throughout the world. We mourn the dead through music as well, in the form of a solemn requiem or the livelier music of a wake or the spontaneous keening and wailing of individual mourners.

Much of our musical expression is formalized in its association with particular events, from worship services to sporting events. We also organize musical participation through orchestras, bands, and choirs. However, spontaneous musical expression is one of life's great pleasures, whether it is the hip-hop danced on street corners or the singing of a lullaby to a child. If music and dance were eliminated from our lives, we would find human existence greatly diminished.

Music and dance have been fundamental to many of the world's great theatre traditions: the Greek choruses danced and sang; bands played before and during the medieval mystery cycles; and Elizabethan theatres had a special place built for musicians. Most forms of Asian theatre involve onstage musicians who play throughout the performances, and many of the actors' lines are sung. The theatre has always recognized the emotional and dramatic expressiveness of music.

Song and dance together give the actor two of the most powerful means of communicating a heightened sense of human experience. The emotional possibilities of the singing voice fusing words with melody and the visual language of the body propelled through space provide a lyrical way of enacting a story that carries the audience beyond everyday reality. Rhythmic structures build the drama and drive the action forward, pulling the audience into their energy and their pulse. The musical is another major example of theatricalism and has its own unique history in the United States.

Origins of Musical Theatre in America

The immigrant groups that made up the U.S. population of the nineteenth century and early twentieth century brought many music and dance traditions with them. Musical entertainment of all kinds grew out of the free-swirling mixture of cultures. For example, tap dancing developed in part because of the incorporation of Irish clog dancing into the developing black tradition of dance.[1] The young nation enjoyed entertainments in which song and dance routines were laced with comedy, and novelty acts brought together the latest in musical styles and dance steps. Minstrel shows and then musical revues and vaudeville eventually led to the development of a **musical theatre** form that presented the popular dancing and singing in a dramatic plot with characters who played out a complete story. A collection of loosely connected routines or variety acts gave way to an integration of spoken text, singing, and dance that developed a dramatic idea. The evolving musical theatre drew on diverse talents and diverse backgrounds. Entertainers from the world of jazz and vaudeville eventually intersected with ballet choreographers and classically trained composers and musicians to create the American musical theatre.

The term *musical comedy* was used for years to describe this theatre form because most of the early works followed the pattern of a troubled love relationship that was accompanied by comic variations and that ended with reconciliation and celebration. In fact, musical comedy in this version fits nicely into the definition of comedy discussed in Chapter 14. However, the musical theatre form has grown and expanded beyond the formulaic romance to include a variety of subjects and situations that do not always lead to reconciliation. We use the term *musical theatre* to include the most open definition of this form.

The Broadway Theatre

Our discussion of musical theatre focuses on Broadway, which continues to be the heart of musical theatre production. For much of the twentieth century, most musicals originated on Broadway. Over time, however, the musical theatre too has been affected by the decentralization of the American theatre. New musicals today are often developed in regional theatres and then move to Broadway, or they may develop in not-for-profit theatres or workshops before achieving a Broadway production. Nonetheless, the goal in most musical theatre is still a Broadway engagement.

Broadway consists of a group of large, elegant theatres located on or close to Broadway and Times Square in New York City. Most of the theatres are found between 41st Street and 50th Street. Broadway theatres usually seat more than 1,000 audience members in an orchestra and two balconies and are equipped with state-of-the-art technology. The price of a ticket for a Broadway musical at $75 and higher makes attendance at this "popular" form of theatre a very expensive proposition. Half-price tickets can be purchased on the day of performance at the TKTS booth in Times Square, and some musicals reserve a number of lower-priced seats for students.

As we examine some of the most celebrated musicals of the American theatre, we focus primarily on the original productions. There we can see the work of the composer, lyricist, and librettist joined to the work of the director and choreographer. In contemporary American theatre, the choreographer has become a major theatre practitioner, contributing significant new ideas to the staging of the drama.

Oklahoma!

Opening on Broadway in 1943, *Oklahoma!* was a musical about farmers and cowboys that reinforced traditional American values at a time when the nation was in the middle of its participation

The dream ballet from *Oklahoma!* features the "Post Card Girls," who suggest another side of life on the American frontier in the choreography by Agnes de Mille.

in World War II. The musical tells a simple love story set against the progression of Oklahoma toward statehood. *Oklahoma!* represented nostalgia for the past at a time when war made for an anxious and uncertain present. Songs such as "Oh What a Beautiful Morning," "The Surrey with the Fringe on Top," and the title song "Oklahoma!" created an onstage sense of optimism and faith in rural American life. *Oklahoma!* was a retreat from the sophisticated subject matter of earlier musical theatre but an advance in the integration of theatrical materials. Each song in *Oklahoma!* contributed to the development of the plot or the emotional state of a character.

Known for its enduring musical score, *Oklahoma!* also established new possibilities for the use of dance in the musical theatre form. Instead of serving as a break in the action to provide variety and show off the skills of talented performers,

dance was used to develop character and express ideas nonverbally. Cowboy posture and movement that derived from actions such as horseback riding and roping were combined with square dancing to give the choreography and the play a distinctive flavor. Significantly, the dance went beyond filling the stage with charming western idioms to accompany the songs. In the most innovative use of dance, a prolonged choreographic sequence was used for psychological development. The central character, Laurey, has foolishly encouraged the attention of Jud Fry, to provoke the hero, Curly. Jud is a hostile, threatening figure, and Laurey's fear of him is played out in an elaborate dream ballet. Curly and Jud fight, and Curly is killed. Laurey is carried off by Jud to live in his sleazy world of violence and used-up dance-hall girls.

Oklahoma! was the first creation of the partnership of Richard Rodgers, who composed the music; and Oscar Hammerstein II, who wrote the **book** (script) and lyrics. Together, Rodgers and Hammerstein later created such popular musicals as *Carousel, South Pacific, The King and I,* and *The Sound of Music.* All of the Rodgers and Hammerstein collaborations are known for their use of music to define character and to contribute to the structure of the plot. Each of their musicals tells the story of characters, usually in love, who overcome conflicts and obstacles to reach a triumphant ending. Sentimental but inspired melodies and good-humored characters carry the Rodgers and Hammerstein musicals.

For *Oklahoma!* Agnes de Mille joined the Rodgers and Hammerstein team as choreographer. She brought her considerable ballet background into the musical theatre but also drew on tap and folk dance forms. De Mille continued to choreograph Rodgers and Hammerstein productions and became one of the first choreographer-directors. Her approach to the integration of choreography into the musical opened the way for the brilliant innovations in the musical theatre to come. It is interesting to note that the choreographer Susan Stroman, whose work is discussed later in the chapter, restaged Agnes de Mille's original dances for *Oklahoma!* in a new Broadway production that opened in 2001.

West Side Story

Oklahoma! reflected the sensibility of a nation engaged in war abroad that looked to the stage for a comforting, rural view of the home front. In

Jerome Robbins's explosive choreography distinguished *West Side Story* and brought the musical theatre to a new level in the integration of drama and movement. For the Broadway revival of *West Side Story* in 2009, Joey McKneeley reproduced the original Robbins choreography. Here Anita, Karen Olivo, and Bernardo, George Akram, perform in the "Dance at the Gym" during which the Jets and the Sharks continue their rivalry on the dance floor.

The gang tension in *West Side Story* erupts in a deadly knife fight between Bernardo, George Akram, and Riff, Cody Green, in this recreation of Jerome Robbins's choreography by Joey McKneeley.

1957 a new musical, *West Side Story*, would take on our own urban warfare. Based on the feuding families that doomed the love of Romeo and Juliet, *West Side Story* dramatizes the gang conflict between Puerto Rican and Anglo youths in an impoverished New York City neighborhood. The choreographer-director Jerome Robbins originated the idea for the production and invited the collaboration of the composer and conductor Leonard Bernstein. Robbins and Bernstein had already worked together successfully on a ballet, "Fancy Free," that became a Broadway musical and then a film, *On the Town*. Each had extensive experience in the musical theatre in addition to Robbins's work in the ballet and Bernstein's contributions to the world of classical music. They were both at the top of their professions and were able to merge their formidable talents to create one of the great American works of the modern theatre. The playwright Arthur Laurents adapted Shakespeare's *Romeo and Juliet*; and a young songwriter, Stephen Sondheim, wrote the lyrics. Sondheim would go on to become one of the foremost composers and lyricists of the musical theatre, creating such works as *Company*, *Sweeney Todd*, and *Sunday in the Park with George*.

The young lovers in the 1950s version of Shakespeare's play are Maria and Tony, on opposite sides of the gang conflict. Tony is a former member of the Jets, the gang made up of the sons of European immigrants; Maria is the sister of Bernardo, leader of the Sharks, the Puerto Rican gang. As in its Shakespearean source, hostilities and misunderstandings lead to the deaths of several young men. Yet in the musical version Maria lives. As with much contemporary gang violence, the woman is left to face the consequences of the fighting alone. The entire play focuses on the young people involved: the limitations of their circumstances, their reliance on one another, their alienation from the larger society, their aspirations, and their love.

West Side Story has very little dialogue. Almost the entire story is told through songs and dances, with dance playing a much more important part than it had previously in the American musical theatre. The Bernstein score has an edgy, urban dissonance influenced by jazz and Latin rhythms. Some of the most memorable love songs of the musical theatre come from *West Side Story*, such as "Maria," "Tonight," and "Somewhere." The score is also notable for its use of counterpoint. For example, a love theme is introduced and then returns to be played against the theme of the impending gang fight. The score is percussive, with a drive and urgency that would be adopted by many later musicals.

Matching the intensity of the music, the choreography had the actors flying across the stage and at each other for much of the production. The characters were in constant motion, cruising the streets, looking for fights, dancing at the gym. Intricately choreographed sequences defined character and dramatized the action of the play. Robbins combined a ballet base with a heavy use of jazz and gymnastics to create a tough, jagged street-smart choreography for the gang sequences and a sexy, competitive choreography for the men and women. Latin dance styles were integrated into the movement of the Puerto Rican characters in the "Dance at the Gym" and "America" to physicalize the difference between the backgrounds of the two groups of characters. The raw dancing of the gang members and their girlfriends formed a contrasting background for the softer, lyrical duets of Tony and Maria. Robbins's position as director and choreographer ensured the complete integration of all the staging elements, with dance becoming the central force around which the rest of the production was built.

My Fair Lady

In the mid-1950s, two musicals based on classics of drama from different eras—*Romeo and Juliet*, by Shakespeare; and *Pygmalion* (1912), by George Bernard Shaw (1856–1950)—brought the musical theatre to a new level of artistry. *West Side Story* fulfilled the dance possibilities suggested by *Oklahoma!* and *My Fair Lady* introduced brilliant language to the musical stage. Both used the unique advantages of the musical theatre to create dramas of substance and style.

My Fair Lady (1956) represents the collaborative efforts of another well-known Broadway team, Alan Lerner and Frederick Loewe. Their third collaborator, the English playwright George Bernard Shaw, is sometimes overlooked as one of the creators of this most witty of all Broadway musicals. In *West Side Story*, although the situation resembles *Romeo and Juliet* and some of the plot incidents coincide, the language and terms of expression are entirely reworked. In contrast, much of the strength of *My Fair Lady* derives from the characters and the language written by Shaw.

My Fair Lady tells the story of the transformation of Eliza Doolittle, who sells flowers in Covent Garden, from a "guttersnipe" and "a squashed cabbage leaf" into a young woman of such distinction that she can be passed off as a princess at a royal ball. Her two mentors in this unlikely venture are both noted linguists: the abrasive Professor Henry Higgins and the milder Colonel Pickering. Their project to reinvent Eliza grows out of a bet over how much work it will take to eliminate Eliza's cockney speech patterns and instill in her instead the speech of a lady.

As the lessons proceed, Eliza and Henry engage in a battle of wills and wits that creates one of the more original female–male relationships in the musical theatre. Their verbal sparring is expanded to include the contributions of Eliza's father, the opportunistic Alfred Doolittle, a dustman; and Henry's eminently sensible mother, Mrs. Higgins. The score, which includes the popular

Henry Higgins (Rex Harrison), Eliza Doolittle (Julie Andrews), and Colonel Pickering (Robert Coote) celebrate Eliza's newly achieved mastery of proper pronunciation in "The Rain in Spain" from *My Fair Lady*, with choreography by Hanya Holm and stage direction by Moss Hart.

favorites "I Could Have Danced All Night" and "The Street Where You Live," also has a series of brilliant character songs that are as engaging musically as they are dramatically. Higgins and Eliza carry their skirmishes into musical attacks that are filled with humor and bite.

The casting of Rex Harrison and Julie Andrews in the lead roles became one of the celebrated partnerships of the musical theatre. The director, Moss Hart, who was an exceptional comic playwright himself, staged the play with a sophistication that matched the brilliance of the material. Another major dance figure of the mid-twentieth century, Hanya Holm, did the choreography. The choreography complemented the clever staging by Moss Hart. But it was the

music and language that carried *My Fair Lady* to the heights of the musical form.

Cabaret

The 1960s saw major changes in the U.S. political scene and in the theatre. The divisiveness of the Vietnam War and student protests marked the decade, as did new theatre companies concerned with both political issues and new forms of expression. *Cabaret*, a musical first produced in 1966, expressed some of the anxieties of the times and the upheaval in traditional forms while turning back to an earlier era for its subject.

Cabaret draws on *The Berlin Stories* (1945) of Christopher Isherwood and the play *I Am a*

Alan Cumming, as the Master of Ceremonies, is surrounded by the jaded dance girls of the Kit Kat Club in the 1998 revival of *Cabaret* directed by Sam Mendes at the Henry Miller Theatre in New York City, which was turned into a nightclub for the production.

Camera (1951), by John Van Druten, based on the Isherwood material. *Cabaret* presents a sleazy picture of Berlin in the late 1920s, just preceding the Nazis' and Hitler's rise to power in Germany. The musical is set in a trashy nightclub, the Kit Kat Club, inhabited by tacky dance girls dressed in skimpy torn stockings and underwear. These women go through the motions of nightclub routines under the control of the bizarre Master of Ceremonies, a bitterly flamboyant character who directs the false gaiety of all the proceedings. At the Kit Kat Club we come to meet a young American writer, Clifford Bradshaw, who is at first attracted to the decadence that pervades Berlin, symbolized by the Kit Kat Club, and then repelled by it as he realizes that the Nazis are gathering power while

careless people indulge their jaded appetites. The world of the musical is seen through Bradshaw's eyes as he becomes involved with a young English expatriate, Sally Bowles, a singer at the Kit Kat Club. When Bowles becomes pregnant, Bradshaw offers to marry her and move with her to the United States, but Bowles chooses an abortion and the chance to go on being part of the Kit Kat Club. The fate of the Jews is particularly focused in the subplot of a Jewish grocer who insists, in the face of increasingly violent anti-Semitism, that normality will return to Germany.

The book for *Cabaret* was written by Joe Masterhoff, the music by John Kander, and the lyrics by Fred Ebb. But rather than telling a straightforward story in the style of *Oklahoma!*

or *My Fair Lady*—which are designated as **book musicals** because of their reliance on traditional dramatic plotting—*Cabaret* created a new style for expressing its content. In collaboration with the director, Harold Prince, the writers created what is called a **concept musical**—a musical that emphasizes a theme in which scenic and performance elements are of greater significance than the plot. This innovation is not unlike the emphasis on imagery in German expressionism and the theatre of the absurd discussed in Chapter 9. In the case of this play, the idea of the world defined as a cabaret shaped the basic concept. And the jangling cabaret music, recalling the jarring music composed by Kurt Weill for Brecht's early plays, became the framing structure for the drama itself rather than a device to complement or fill out the play's dialogue. In his review of the original production for *The New York Times*, Walter Kerr wrote:

> Instead of telling a little story about the decadence of Berlin just before Hitler came to power into which casual musical numbers can be sandwiched whenever politeness permits, *Cabaret* lunges forward to insist on music as mediator between audience and characters, as lord and master of the revels, as mocking conferencier without whose ministrations we should have no show at all. We are inside the music looking out, tapping our feet to establish a cocky rhythm and a satanically grinning style to which the transient people of the narrative must accommodate themselves, through which—in irony and after the fact—they can be known.[2]

The play's tone established by the music was continued in Ronald Field's choreographed sequences set in the Kit Kat Club, which were vulgar and suggestive and backed by a large mirror in which audience members could watch themselves watching the show. Under Harold Prince's direction, the staging shifted the audience's sense of being detached from the action to becoming part of the audience in the Kit Kat Club itself. In the Broadway revival of *Cabaret* in

1998, the audience involvement was heightened by turning the entire seating area of the audience into an extension of the nightclub with tables and chairs, red lamps on the tables, and food and drink served and consumed by audience members during the performance. The atmosphere in that revival emphasized the cheap, harsh sexual exchange that underscores all the action and the bleak, abusive world of the Kit Kat Club. With *Cabaret*, the musical left the romance of the form far behind.

Among the actors in the original production, Joel Grey created a sensation as the Master of Ceremonies and went on to re-create the role in the highly regarded film, which starred Grey and Liza Minelli. Lotte Lenya, who began her career acting with Bertolt Brecht, played the role of Fräulein Schneider, who runs the boardinghouse in which Bowles and Bradshaw live and who ultimately rejects her Jewish suitor when the Nazi presence becomes too ominous. In the revival of 1998, Alan Cumming was scintillating as the Master of Ceremonies, with a more vicious quality yet than that of Joel Grey, a reflection perhaps of our own times. And Natasha Richardson gave the most complete interpretation of Sally Bowles since the musical was first produced. This revival was directed by Sam Mendes, following a production of the same play, which he directed in London in 1993.

Stephen Sondheim

The contributions of Stephen Sondheim to the musical theatre cannot be represented by a single defining work. From his earliest effort as a composer of both music and lyrics in *A Funny Thing Happened on the Way to the Forum*, the works of Stephen Sondheim have followed no formula or pattern. Rather, he is known for his experimentation with subject and form, for being adventurous in a field that has tended to favor predictability. During his time as theatre critic for *The New York Times*, Frank Rich observed that Sondheim was "persistent" in trying "to transform the Broadway musical" and considered him "as adventurous and as accomplished an author, playwrights included, as Broadway has produced over the last two decades."[3] Sondheim has spent his career in the musical theatre, from 1957 to the present, exploring new ways of creating musical dramas.

Stephen Sondheim was a committed student of music composition at Williams College, which he followed with three years of study with the avant-garde composer Milton Babbitt. He wrote his first musicals in high school and was always focused on the goal of composing for the musical stage. As a family friend of Oscar Hammerstein II, he had the unique opportunity of being mentored by the author of some of the most compelling and successful song lyrics in the musical theatre. Sondheim learned much from Hammerstein, but Hammerstein wrote optimistic lyrics about overcoming adversity, the "golden sky and the sweet silver song of a lark" that followed the storm (*Carousel*), and the sustaining power of love, "younger than springtime am I with you" (*South Pacific*). Sondheim would move in a very different direction.

Steeped in musical theatre tradition, Stephen Sondheim began his professional career as lyricist first for *West Side Story* and then for *Gypsy*, collaborating with other major figures in the musical theatre such as Jerome Robbins, Jule Styne, and Harold Prince. When he began to write his own complete scores as well as the lyrics, Sondheim placed increasing responsibility on the music and lyrics as the driving force in the creation of the drama. The book that in earlier musicals told a story through dialogue augmented by songs was replaced by the score itself. Building his works around a theme or an idea rather than a highly structured plot, Sondheim was a major influence in the development of the concept musical.

The subjects of the Sondheim musicals are challenging for audiences: examining the stresses and disappointments of urban life, the difficulties in building satisfactory relationships, the painful and sometimes bitter path to maturity, and the contradictory nature of American values. Whereas many musicals are written and produced to provide audiences with a form of escape from their concerns, Sondheim musicals ask audiences to participate in a thoughtful process. For example, *Pacific Overtures* explores the forced opening of Japan in the nineteenth century to Western commerce and the consequences for Japanese society as it underwent enormous social change. *Sunday in the Park with George* considers the nature of artistic creation, and *Assassins* takes on the disturbing subject of violence in American public life. Music and lyrics in combination are used as social commentary, as narrative, and as reflection or debate as well as the expression of a character's state of mind. In *Pacific Overtures* traditional Japanese instruments create a texture of life in sound whose rhythms are interrupted and distorted by the demands of outside forces. In *Assassins* the style of folk ballads usually associated with a positive sense of American character is used as a point of departure for the confusion expressed by those trying to rewrite U.S. history through murder.

The work of Stephen Sondheim demonstrates particularly the way song lyrics can be seen as poetry set to music. The lyrics are a condensed and eloquent expression of a significant moment in a character's life. The lyrics contain the particularity of the character's voice as well as an intricate verbalization of the changing or developing circumstances of the drama. The sung lyrics must be listened to as carefully as or more carefully than any of the spoken dialogue, and the audience members cannot simply lose themselves in the melody or the staging of a song.

> You try to make the language dance, not only to your own tune, which is a metaphor, but to the actual tune that's there. You try to make the words sit on music, to rhyme them, to make jokes land, to use literary techniques. It's technical, like poetry or any creative art is technical. But, because lyric writing makes you deal with so few words and the language is not so elastic when sung . . . it becomes very crossword puzzle-like.[4]

In 2005 *Sweeney Todd* by Stephen Sondheim was produced on Broadway under the direction of John Doyle, with Michael Cerveris and Patti Lupone playing the central characters. Doyle employed a unique approach to staging a musical by having the actors double as the musicians who accompany each other's singing. Doyle developed this concept of the actor-musician in England before re-staging his interpretation of *Sweeney Todd* in the United States.

Here is the final section of the song "Four Black Dragons" from the musical *Pacific Overtures* (1976) in which the local people and the narrator, the Reciter, sing of their terror at the arrival of U.S. warships off the coast of Japan.

(Townspeople)
Four black dragons
Spitting fire!
    (Reciter)
Then the hooves clattered
And the warriors were there,
Diving quickly through the panic
Like the gulls.
Hai! Hai!
And the swords were things of beauty
As they glided through the air—
Hai!
Like the gulls.

Hai!
    (Townspeople)
Hai! Hai!
Four black dragons,
Spitting fire!
    (Thief and Company)
And the sun darkened
And the sea bubbled,
And the earth trembled,
And the sky cracked,
And I thought it was the end
Of the world!
    (Reciter)
And it was.[5]

Through the lyrics Sondheim furthers the drama in a number of ways. He creates the action of the arrival of the ships, the "four black dragons." He captures the fear of the community as the people record this invasion of their private world. He creates explosive visual imagery of the upheaval that it represents, and he foreshadows the transformation to come.

Sondheim's songs have not had nearly the success of the work of other composers as popular songs performed outside their plays, because of the deep connection of the words to the ongoing drama. And Sondheim's works can be hard to appreciate without their proper instrumentation because of the close integration between the lyrics and the score. In spite of the fact that the music and lyrics dominate Sondheim musicals, Sondheim has chosen not to write the spoken dialogue of his plays, relying instead on a series of collaborators. Some of his work has suffered as a result of dramatic construction that lacks the sophistication and skill of the score.

But there is no doubt that Sondheim has created a body of work that is a major force in shaping the musical theatre at the beginning of the twenty-first century. Recent productions of Sondheim musical theatre pieces reflect his continuing importance for the American theatre. In 2002 Sondheim was represented on Broadway by a well-received revival of *Into the Woods*, and *Pacific Overtures* was presented at the Lincoln Center summer festival in a new production by the New National Theatre of Tokyo. At the same time, a major retrospective of six Sondheim musicals was produced at the Kennedy Center in Washington, DC. In June 2003, the Goodman Theatre in Chicago premiered Sondheim's newest work, *Gold*, which returns to U.S. history to look at the lives of the Mizner brothers, trying to grasp the opportunities available to the adventurous as they travel from Alaska to Florida at the beginning of the twentieth century. And a highly regarded production of *Sweeney Todd: The Demon Barber of Fleet Street* began a successful Broadway run in 2005.

A Chorus Line

Before *West Side Story*, musicals relied on a chorus of singers and dancers to dress the stage and carry the choreographic responsibility of the big production numbers. There was a clear delineation between principals and chorus members, and the groups even rehearsed separately. In *West Side Story*, Jerome Robbins essentially eliminated the chorus by making all the roles singing and dancing characters, thereby assigning importance to all the performers. For the first time, the musical cast became an ensemble.

In his musical *A Chorus Line* (1975), with music by Marvin Hamlisch and lyrics by Edward Kleban, Michael Bennett made the chorus the subject of the play. The premise of this musical is based on the endless auditioning required of performers seeking employment as chorus members. Bennett created a musical that told the stories of young singers and dancers desperately hoping for their big break. In a time-honored tradition, the theatrical performance was about the theatre.

Bennett began dancing as a child and served his apprenticeship dancing in the choruses of musicals before becoming a choreographer. Always focused on a theatrical career, he dropped out of high school to become one of the Jets in the international touring company of *West Side Story* and to learn from the master, Jerome Robbins. Bennett's theatre education and training took place in the musical theatre. In 1970, he joined Stephen Sondheim and Harold Prince as the choreographer of *Company* and then became the choreographer and codirector of *Follies*. When he turned to the lives of dancers as the subject for a new musical, he was able to draw on his own experiences from many productions as well as those of a group of dancers he invited to brainstorm with him in a workshop at the Public Theater, then under the direction of Joseph Papp.

In creating *A Chorus Line*, Bennett reduced the musical form to its essence, in the words of one of its famous songs, "the music and the mirror, and the chance to dance." Gone were the sets that had become increasingly lavish for musical theatre production; gone were the

At the end of *A Chorus Line,* the vulnerability and anxiety of the individual actors hoping to be cast is replaced by the confidence and unity of the chorus line. In the musical's finale, the actors have the chance to pull out all the stops as they sing and dance their triumph, wearing the production's signature gold tuxedoes and top hats. *A Chorus Line* is a tribute to the musical form itself.

elaborate costumes and the cast of "thousands." A group of young characters stood in a line at the front of the stage wearing a combination of leotards, tights, jeans, and T-shirts. One at a time, they told the stories that had brought them into the theatre, beginning with spoken words that segued into song and then into dance. Because the play took the form of a fictional audition, the stories were addressed to the character of the director, who was placed at the back of the auditorium behind the audience seats, allowing the actors to speak out directly to the audience.

A Chorus Line has a very thin plot, involving a relationship between the dancer, Cassie, and the director, Zach. Like *Cabaret, A Chorus Line* is a concept musical. But the heart of the piece is in the characters' stories and their quest for approval and for a chance to show their worth and to follow their dreams. *A Chorus Line* became a metaphor for a new era of life in the United States.

New Directions for the Musical Theatre

Four musicals have once again turned the musical theatre in new directions at a time when some critics were suggesting that the form had exhausted its possibilities. *Bring in da Noise, Bring in da Funk* (1995) explores historical and contemporary perspectives in black American life through tap dancing. *Rent* (1995) chronicles the lives of artists and their impoverished friends living in the East Village in New York City. *The Lion King* (1997) introduces a style of integrating puppets and moving sculpture into a musical production that makes the director-designer the principal author of the story told onstage. And *Contact* (1999) features the work of the director-choreographer who composes the entire piece through dance and music with spoken dialogue but without songs. Both *Bring in da Noise, Bring in da Funk* and *Rent* deal with serious, sensitive, and controversial issues: oppression and self-determination in *Bring in da Noise, Bring in da Funk* and drug addiction and AIDS in *Rent*. *The Lion King* and *Contact* are recognized more for innovations in style than subject matter. But all four musicals are noted for their high spirits and originality. They were created by young authors and feature very young cast members, some without traditional theatre backgrounds. Although the sound and style of these productions are completely contemporary, these new musicals are tied to musical theatre traditions that are clearly still evolving.

Savion Glover and *Bring in da Noise, Bring in da Funk*

Savion Glover grew up in Newark, New Jersey, but in the shadow of Broadway. By the time he was twelve years old, he was already recognized as a dance prodigy. He tap-danced his way through *The Tap Dance Kid*, *Black and Blue*, and *Jelly's Last Jam* before he was eighteen years old. Dancing with Gregory Hines, Honi Cole, and Jimmy Slyde provided Glover with an education in American tap styles that he merged with his own

sense of rap and reggae to create a new approach, called "the beat."

Savion Glover performs with a style of dance distinctly different from the light and graceful approach frequently associated with African American tap dancers. Glover's dancing is forceful and appears self-involved. He drives his feet into the floor and uses the whole foot in new ways. He dances on his toes and on the sides of his feet. The focus of the dance is in his legs and feet; his head is often down, and he doesn't use his torso or his arms to extend the range of movement. The dancing is very athletic and includes gymnastic and break-dancing elements. This is dance that can express anger and sorrow as well as joy and freedom. Savion Glover represents the tap dancing of a new generation.

George C. Wolfe, the former director of the Public Theater, was the creator and director of *Jelly's Last Jam*, whose premiere production featured Glover as the young Jelly. After this production Wolfe began to consider the significance of African American tap dance as a folk form and its possibilities for expressing the African American experience. He proposed a collaboration with Glover in the development of a performance without a script. Glover brought to the developmental process at the Public Theater four young men with whom he had danced (the oldest among them was twenty-six) and two drummers. They were joined by Ann Duquesnay, an actor and singer who would collaborate on and eventually perform the songs for the show; and Reg Gaines, a poet who was working on the text. Together they evolved a series of scenes, focused in dance, that each addressed a different aspect of black life in the United States.

In *Bring in da Noise, Bring in da Funk*, tap dance is used to depict a lynching, the post-slavery migration to the North, and even the attempts of black men to flag a cab in New York City. *Bring in da Noise, Bring in da Funk* has an episodic organization of scenes related to a theme rather than a traditional plot made up of connected incidents. Like *A Chorus Line*, the show is about the dancers themselves. But in

Savion Glover and his fellow dancers bring the choreography of *Bring in da Noise, Bring in da Funk* into the present. The dancers and drummers celebrate one of the musical's fundamental themes, "In the beginning there was . . . da beat!"

A Chorus Line the dancers are always in character, even though much of the content of their characters' lives may be close to their own. In *Bring in da Noise, Bring in da Funk* the dancers speak for themselves. Their taped voices describing the place of dance in their lives accompany one sequence of their dancing. The actual lives of the actor-dancers are seen as the final movement of history that the play presents.

The black musical was a significant part of the early history of musical theatre in the United States. Musicals such as *Ain't Misbehavin'* and *Jelly's Last Jam* have reinterpreted a tradition that has deep roots in the American theatre. *Bring in da Noise, Bring in da Funk* makes a place for young dancers in the musical

theatre and brings an entirely new sensibility to a choreographed, dramatic form. At age twenty-three, Savion Glover joined Jerome Robbins and Michael Bennett as creators of modern, choreographically created musical theatre pieces at the same time that he reached back to the traditions of African American dance and musical theatre.

Jonathan Larson and *Rent*

Like *Bring in da Noise, Bring in da Funk, Rent* grew out of a workshop production, in this case at New York Theatre Workshop; it then moved to the Nederlander Theatre on what is considered the outer perimeter of Broadway. *Bring in da Noise, Bring in da Funk* was the work of young creators

The cast of *Rent* sings and dances "La Vie Bohème" on the tables of the Life Café with choreography by Marlies Yearby. In "La Vie Bohème" the characters sing of their social rebellion. Unlike the more structured choreography of *West Side Story* and *A Chorus Line,* the dancing in *Rent* has an informal, improvisational quality.

and performers but had the very experienced and well-connected hand of George C. Wolfe guiding the process. *Rent* was sustained by the energy and commitment of its creator, Jonathan Larson.

Larson studied acting and musical composition in college; and with encouragement from Stephen Sondheim, he committed himself to a career of writing for the musical theatre. It took fifteen years of living the life represented by the characters in *Rent* to bring his vision of a new musical to the stage. Larson sought to merge the tradition of the musical theatre with music of the 1990s and the sensibility of young people raised

with MTV, film technology, and rapidly changing social values. He wanted to place the heart of rock-and-roll culture on the musical stage in order to tell the story of young people struggling to make sense of life in the midst of poverty and the AIDS epidemic.

Larson found the starting point for what would become *Rent* in a nineteenth-century opera, *La Bohème* (1895), by Puccini; and in the novel *Scenes de la Vie Bohème*, by Henri Murger, on which *La Bohème* was based. From *La Bohème* he took the situation of a group of artists struggling with poverty and illness but sustaining themselves through their friendships and their faith in life. Many of the plot incidents and the characters are suggested by the opera; an example is Mimi, who in the opera dies of tuberculosis and in *Rent* is dying of drug addiction and AIDS.

But *Rent* is definitely a late-twentieth-century creation: a rock band is placed on the stage; the characters all wear head mikes; one of the characters records everything on a video camera; and drug addiction underscores the troubled lives of the characters. The music reflects the mix of pop music culture, all with a rock-and-roll beat. Instead of the slickness and polished finish of most musical theatre productions, Larson sought a roughness and rawness in the performance, in terms of both the singing and the visual presentation. The set appears to be made from found pieces of junk; the costumes are a grungy compilation of worn and frayed cast-off garments or the cheapest of the new. The staging has an improvisational feel. Where there is choreography, there is a sense of looseness and invention in the moment rather than the highly crafted dance structures of Jerome Robbins, Michael Bennett, or Savion Glover.

The story behind the creation of *Rent* is as dramatic as what occurs on the stage. The night before the production's final dress rehearsal, thirty-five-year-old Jonathan Larson died suddenly of an aortic aneurysm. The grief-stricken cast "went on with the show," which met with great success. But the success was mixed with sadness for the young playwright and composer who didn't live to see his music and lyrics lighting up Broadway.

Julie Taymor and *The Lion King*

In 1997 a new musical opened on Broadway that once again took the form in a major new direction. *The Lion King* was adapted from the extraordinarily popular Walt Disney film of the same name and followed the Disney recreation of *Beauty and the Beast* as a stage musical. The stage version of *Beauty and the Beast* was guided by the cartoon imagery of the film, but the stage production of *The Lion King* broke new ground in the musical theatre. The avant-garde director and designer Julie Taymor was invited by Walt Disney Theatrical Productions to interpret the story of *The Lion King* in her own way. Impressed by Taymor's previous intercultural work using astounding sculpted puppets and cinematic design effects, the Disney organization provided the opportunity for highly imaginative exploration in a commercial context. *The Lion King* continues the tradition of Broadway musicals that rely on lavish sets and costumes but integrates these elements into the telling of a story in a significantly new way. The designer-director becomes the driving force behind the expressive elements of the production.

Taymor became a serious student of theatre as a child and expanded her awareness of non-Western theatre traditions when she traveled to India and Sri Lanka during high school. During college she was part of the same experimental theatre company as Bill Irwin at Oberlin College. She also studied mime in Paris, improvisational acting in New York, and puppetry with the Bread and Puppet Theatre. Taymor was always concerned with the anthropological origins of theatre and with mythical subjects. She also showed talent early on as a painter and sculptor as well as a performer, talents that she continued to nurture as she apprenticed with different theatre companies and traditions.

After graduating from college, Taymor spent four years in Indonesia studying its brilliant movement theatre and observing the cultural conditions out of which it emerged. In Indonesia she became part of the Bengkel Theatre, which encouraged her to create a production with the company actors. Her first major work, *Way of Snow*, began her lifelong experimentation with theatre expressed through masks, puppets, live actors, and startling visual effects drawing on myth and ritual to probe the human condition. And she continued to build her design and construction skills in the areas of scene, costume, and puppet design at the same time that she refined her vision as a director. Taymor worked for twenty

Tsidii Le Loka is seen here as the shaman Rafiki in *The Lion King*. Her costume and makeup were designed to suggest the physical characteristics of a baboon.

years directing and designing original works, Shakespeare, and opera before being invited to bring her imaginative approach to *The Lion King*.

Taymor first worked with the original screenwriters of the film to expand and strengthen the narrative of the young lion, Simba, who must undertake a complicated journey to earn his place as king. She became a collaborator on the script itself at the same time that she began to envision the form that the characters should be given and a staging concept that would allow for the extremely adventurous nature of the action. The music from the film also required considerable augmentation, with particular attention

paid to its African sources. Elton John and Tim Rice, the original composers who had worked with the South African performer Lebo M, wrote two additional pop-style character songs; Lebo M, Hans Zimmer, and Mark Mancina filled out the score, drawing on Zulu chanting and African rhythms and musical instruments. Just as Taymor's production style would draw on international sources and performance traditions, so the score would be an eclectic blend of American, European, and African styles. But as important as the music and the script were to the production, the greatest excitement would come from the visual presentation.

Taymor determined that various forms of puppets inhabited by actors would bring the animal characters to life and give her the flexibility to create magical action sequences, such as stampeding wildebeests or characters who could fly. The actors were not to be hidden by the puppet forms but rather to exist in puppet form and human form at the same time. The faces of the actors would always be seen. The actors playing lions would wear large masks placed above their own faces and be dressed in gowns of African-inspired fabrics rather than animal bodies. The hippopotamus was designed in full animal form for two actors whose bodies would be inside the large animal but whose heads would appear above the huge puppet. The character of Zazu, the comic bird, was designed as a fully realized rod puppet to be worn on the head of the actor who would sing and dance the role but who would be dressed in a suit that suggested the attitude of the bird character rather than in any kind of costume representing a bird. Human figures were designed into costumes representing plants, vines, and grass. Contraptions were invented such as the Gazelle Wheel, which would allow an actor to push across stage a wheeled vehicle that provided the momentum for the seven leaping figures of gazelle that were attached to it. Other "corporate" puppet forms were designed to enable one actor to present other groups of animals such as a flock of birds. Some of the puppets in *The Lion King* recall the inventions of the Handspring Puppet Company discussed in Chapter 9. Taymor explains her reasons for keeping the actor-puppeteers visible:

> When we see a person actually manipulating an inanimate object like a puppet and making it come alive, the duality moves us. Hidden special effects lack humanity, but when the human spirit visibly animates an object, we experience a special, almost life giving connection. We become engaged by both the method of story telling as well as by the story itself.[6]

Taymor also conceptualized a method of changing scale that would help develop the sense of movement across vast spaces. Characters would be represented by small puppets when they were meant to be seen at a distance, what she calls a "long shot," and then would be played by human actors when they had traveled far enough to be seen in a "close-up." For the wildebeest stampede, the first image seen by the audience is created by painted figures on cloth being turned on rollers at the back of the stage. As the stampede approaches the audience, larger and larger masks are used to create the sense that the animals are coming closer and closer.

Developing this visually stupendous musical involved the creative collaboration of many theatre artists. Michael Curry codesigned the puppets and was responsible for engineering and constructing them; and Taymor was responsible for sculpture and aesthetics. Richard Hudson created the actual scene design after Taymor developed the basic staging concept. Seven of the actors who ultimately appeared in the production were involved in experimentation with puppets and masks throughout the development process to see what would work and what would communicate effectively. In fact, Taymor incorporated puppets in the audition process:

> I also brought puppets to auditions to see how performers would look in relation to specific puppets and how they would respond when asked to animate an inanimate object. And though performers would not be totally immersed within the puppets nor hidden behind the masks, they would have to be willing to accept that the audience is not going to be looking at them alone. Attitude is a very important part of my casting decision. I want an actor who is going to enjoy the challenge and not view it as a burden. Rather than expressly hiring puppeteers, I look for inventive actors who move well. A strong actor gives an idiosyncratic performance, because he infuses the puppet characters with his own personality instead of relying on generic puppetry technique. The thrill of working with a good actor who is new to this medium, is that he will take the form further than I ever imagined.[7]

Designers have frequently created spectacular environments for musicals in the past with astonishing special effects. However, in *The Lion King*, Julie Taymor has investigated ways in which the work of the actor may be extended through her puppet and mask creations. She has returned to ancient theatre traditions and brought them into contemporary performance to challenge the imaginations of both actors and audiences.

Susan Stroman and *Contact*

Susan Stroman called her theatre piece *Contact* (1999) a "dance play" because the essential medium for storytelling in this work was choreographic. Despite the facts that there was no actual singing in *Contact* and that the music for the dancing was recorded rather than played live, the Broadway community chose to extend the term *musical* to include this performance of three loosely related stories, each in its own way based on the central human need for emotional and physical connection to other people. In *Contact* the work of the choreographer, which had become a major force in earlier American musicals such as *West Side Story*, *A Chorus Line*, and *Bring in da Noise, Bring in da Funk*, replaced the work of both the playwright-librettist and the lyricist. Although John Weidman collaborated with Stroman to provide the actor-dancers with small segments of spoken dialogue, it was dance that shaped the characters, the characters' relationships, and the actions of their stories.

In 1997 Andre Bishop, who was the artistic director of Lincoln Center Theater, invited Susan Stroman to create an original piece for his theatre because he admired the excitement and energy her choreography had brought to more traditional musicals such as *Crazy for You* (1992) and the revival of *Show Boat* (1994). Bishop provided rehearsal space and resources to enable Stroman to develop material of her own choosing. *Contact* was inspired by Stroman's own experience in a late-night swing club in which she

Deborah Yates, the girl in the yellow dress, confident and flirtatious, dances with two of her many admirers while Boyd Gaines looks on from the background, unable to join the dance. *Contact* was choreographed and directed by Susan Stroman with costume design by William Ivey Long.

observed the magnetism of a stunning dancer in a yellow dress. From this seductive image evolved a story of a man who has lost the will to live until he dances with the woman in the yellow dress. The writer John Weidman explains that dance became salvation for a man betrayed by the failure of words: "The character came from a world that was all about language and language was something that failed him. He was going to have to escape from language to get saved."[8]

The story is danced out in the man's lonely apartment, which, in a dreamlike way, keeps changing into the swing club where he first watches from a distance and then finally, overcoming his inhibitions, dances with the woman in the yellow dress. Much of the piece consists of high-voltage swing dancing by characters who have discovered a world of dance that the alienated man is unable to enter. Because the story is set in a dance club, Stroman chose to use recorded jazz and swing music to reinforce the atmosphere of being in a club. When the work was expanded to include two additional stories, Stroman decided to use recorded music for all three vignettes.

The choreography of Susan Stroman is distinguished by invention and by the way dance movement creates character. For example, the first vignette of *Contact*, entitled "Swinging," consists of a playful and exuberant romantic encounter between lovers on a swing. The young man first pushes the woman on the swing and then joins her, sometimes sharing the seat and sometimes doing gymnastics on the ropes holding the swing. As the swing sails back and forth suspended high above the stage, the lovers find numerous ways of using the swing as part of their romance.

Stroman's ability to develop character through dance is exemplified by the second of the three *Contact* pieces, "Did You Move?" The essence of composing dance drama depends on conceptualizing the needs of the characters and the conflicts between them as physical problems. In this piece the central conflict is between a man trying to control his wife by imprisoning her in stillness while she tries to take back

her freedom through movement. The woman begins the short story seated opposite her surly, gangsterlike husband in an Italian restaurant. Hunched over his food, he discourages her attempts at conversation, and when he leaves the table to get more food from the buffet, he barks at her, "don't move." The woman overcomes the paralyzing effect of his threats, and during each of her husband's absences she dances out her fantasies with increasing abandon. Gradually she engages all the other people in the restaurant, diners and waiters, in a wild celebration of human connection. Full of humor, the dance evolves into a broad conspiracy involving actor-dancers and food and serving trays to confuse and outwit the joyless, thuggish husband.

Since the success of *Contact*, Susan Stroman has gone on to work as the director-choreographer first of a revival of *The Music Man* and then most notably of *The Producers* (2001). Starring Nathan Lane and Matthew Broderick, *The Producers* was adapted by the comedian Mel Brooks from his film of the same name and is a comedy about the theatre itself. *The Producers* tells a simple story of a down-on-his-luck theatre producer who hits on an outrageous scheme to make money. He persuades a large number of older women, foolishly susceptible to his charms, to invest in his next show, selling each of them a half interest or more, percentages that are clearly too large to be paid back. Then he guarantees that the show will be a catastrophic failure by choosing the most offensive and tasteless material possible, a cheerful musical about Nazi Germany. He is certain the show will close after one night, and he will be able to keep his elderly investors' money. However, audiences believe the show must be a satire and find it so amusing that it becomes a huge success. This success, of course, means that the producer, Max Bialystock, is exposed as a fraud, dashing his fortunes but not his survival instincts. *The Producers* enjoyed a notable success in the months after September 11, 2001, providing audiences with the much needed release of laughter during disturbing times.

The Musical Theatre Today

Large-scale musical productions continue to be mainstays of Broadway and national tours. In addition, regional theatres and smaller New York theatres have become increasingly interested in developing both traditional and new approaches to theatre works that use sung music as a foundational element. Popular music forms from rock and roll to hip hop to reggae to folk music to jazz invigorate the older styles of musical theatre composition. Many musicians who have established careers with bands or as recording artists are finding the musical theatre provides opportunities to add a dimension of storytelling or narrative performance to their music. The pop composer and singer Duncan Sheik wrote a score for an updated version of a German expressionist play, *Spring Awakening* (see page 380). The soul guitarist and singer Stew developed an autobiographical musical performance piece, *Passing Strange* (see page 466). Lin-Manuel Miranda, a rapper and lyricist who wrote *In the Heights* (see page 389), is currently working on developing his song cycle, concept album, *The Hamilton Mixtape*, into a musical biography of Alexander Hamilton. The renowned jazz trumpeter Wynton Marsalis is embarking on a collaboration

The musical *Once* (2012) is based on the 2006 independent film about the love affair of two young folk-rock musicians. The actors in the film, Glen Hansard and Marketa Irglova, are in fact the composers of the music and the love story is their story. Adapted for the stage through a series of workshops at New York Theatre Workshop, *Once* now stars Steve Kazee and Cristin Milioti, with a book written by the playwright Enda Walsh.

The two principal actors in *Once* are musicians as are the members of the ensemble. All of the music is played on the stage with violins, accordion, mandolin, guitars, cello, and piano. The set is a pub designed by Bob Crowley. The director is John Tiffany and the movement is devised by Steven Hogget, whose unique approach to stylized, choreographed movement was discussed in Chapter 5.

with Stephen Sondheim. Bands are developing musical theatre pieces from within their own groups such as Lisps' *Futurity*.

Theatre companies interested in presenting new work regularly invite musicians into developmental processes following the models exemplified by the Public Theater, the New York Theatre Workshop, and Lincoln Center Theater. Theatre practitioners and musicians realize that there is unexplored potential within the musical theatre form to incorporate new uses of music and new subjects. Through voices raised in song, the collected energy and range of musical instruments, the pulse and rhythm of dance, and the heightened use of text, the musical theatre form offers unique storytelling possibilities that can respond to the significant changes in contemporary culture.

 # Summary

Works of musical theatre integrate singing, spoken text, and dance to communicate the drama. The musical theatre is a unique development of the American theatre that has had widespread influence throughout the world. The musical theatre grew out of the minstrel shows, revues, and vaudeville of the nineteenth century, which drew heavily on the various immigrant groups that made up the U.S. population.

Oklahoma! made major advances in drawing together the expressive elements of musical theatre. All the songs in *Oklahoma!* were necessary to the development of plot or character, and dance was also used in a new way to further the ideas of the work. In *West Side Story*, based on William Shakespeare's *Romeo and Juliet*, Jerome Robbins made the choreography equal in importance to the singing. *My Fair Lady* drew on its source, *Pygmalion*, by George Bernard Shaw, to bring brilliant language to the musical stage. *Cabaret* turned the musical theatre away from the carefully plotted book musicals represented by *Oklahoma!*, *West Side Story*, and *My Fair Lady* to a new form, the concept musical, in which theme expressed through scenic and performance elements is of greater importance than the plot. Stephen Sondheim contributed major innovations in subject matter and

dramatic construction and set new standards for the writing of lyrics. *A Chorus Line* continued the evolution of the concept musical with its prominent use of dance to tell the stories of actors auditioning for a musical. New directions in theme and style have been provided by recent musicals such as *Bring in da Noise, Bring in da Funk; Rent; The Lion King;* and *Contact*.

The use of popular music to convey dramatic ideas and to build character and the centrality of dance in telling a story distinguish the musical theatre form. The popular music of each era has been embraced by the musical theatre, including, most recently, hip-hop and rock and roll. The choreographer-director has emerged as a new theatre creator, as exemplified by Jerome Robbins, Michael Bennett, and Susan Stroman. In *The Lion King*, it was the designer-director, Julie Taymor, who contributed a startling new vision for musical theatre by extending the actors' expressive possibilities through puppets and masks.

 # Topics for Discussion and Writing

1. Discuss the ways that music is an integral part of student life today. What kinds of music do you listen to or participate in creating? In addition to concerts, where music is the focus of the event, what events that are significant to you have some kind of musical association? What experiences in your life involve some kind of musical expression?

2. How does experiencing musical theatre differ from experiencing the spoken text of

   a nonmusical play? Draw on the musicals seen by members of the class, whether on the stage or on film, to discuss the way music changes the nature of theatrical expression and the audience's response. What kinds of material is music especially suited to?

3. What subject material and style of music in a musical production would appeal to an audience of your peers?

● For suggested readings and other resources related to this chapter, please visit **www.mhhe.com/creativespirit6e**

CHAPTER 13

Innovations in Dramatic Structure

Looking at *Water by the Spoonful*
by Quiara Alegría Hudes

Quiara Alegría Hudes is a young American playwright who began writing plays at an early age but focused her formal studies in music. She became an accomplished pianist and as an undergraduate at Yale University turned her attention to composition. She composed for a number of different

types of performance including musical theatre, dance, and small and large instrumental groups, and she also played with a band. Her musical interests were broad, ranging from classical European music to American jazz to the traditional music of her family's heritage in Puerto Rico. An early mentor was her aunt Linda Hudes who composed regularly for the Big Apple Circus, and so popular circus music was also part of the extensive world of music in which she grew up.

Following her college graduation, Hudes decided that as much as she loved music, storytelling through characters on the stage was the form of expression that made the best use of her talents and brought her the most satisfaction. Then as she embarked on her playwriting career, first as a graduate student in playwriting at Brown University, and later through the development of her craft as a professional playwright, she found that her study of musical forms and traditions and her experience as a composer exploring musical structures strongly influenced the way she approached dramatic structure.

In one of her first major successes as a playwright, Hudes collaborated with Lin-Manuel Miranda on the book for the musical *In the Heights,* drawing on her abilities to bring language and music together in dramatic form. *In the Heights* won the Tony in 2008 for the best Broadway musical. Working on *In the Heights* provided Hudes further impetus to continue exploring new territory in developing theatre pieces that would reflect her own personal history integrated with a range of musical traditions.

In the Heights tells a story about the Washington Heights neighborhood of New York City and the Latino families living there whose heritage includes Dominican and Puerto Rican roots. This musical was originally developed by Lin-Manuel Miranda when he was a college student. Later, Miranda invited Quiara Alegría Hudes to rewrite the book for *In the Heights* before its Off-Broadway (2007) and then Broadway (2008) runs. As a musical, the play is distinguished by its Latin and hip hop styles.

Elliot, A Soldier's Fugue: A Quartet for Actors

Before writing *In The Heights*, Hudes had completed an adventurous play inspired by the transformation of her cousin Elliot Ruiz during his tour of duty as a marine fighting in Iraq. She renamed her cousin Elliot *Ortiz* when she created him as a character in a play about what it means for a generation of young American men to go to war. Hudes was inspired to write the play when she met Elliot for the first time after his return from Iraq.

> **QUIARA HUDES:** I just remember the instant I saw him, there was just something changed in his eye. You know, he was still absolutely the same young clown of a cousin I had always known and had grown up with, loving, but there was something different. And I felt that I might never understand it. And that's the simple spark that it came from.[1]

THE AUTHOR SPEAKS

Quiara Alegría Hudes

One of the best classes I ever took in my education was orchestration. As a pianist, I learned how all the woodwinds sound, how all the strings sound, how the percussion sounds, in all of their registers. High register flute sounds extremely different than low register flute. High register clarinet sounds wildly different than low register clarinet. You learn the rules of how high and low they can go, what key signatures are trickier and more natural among them and then to experiment with various combinations. What's a piece for four violins versus what's a piece for violin, clarinet, tuba, and percussion? You're going to get two very different results. So I really hear the voices in the play, the characters in the play, like it's orchestration. Each one is its own instrument with its own sound and range and limitation.[2]

The cast of *Elliot, A Soldier's Fugue* appears together in the 2006 premiere production directed by Davis McCallum for Page 73 Productions. From left to right the cast is Elliott, Armando Riesco; Pop, Triney Sandoval; Ginny, Zabryna Guevara; Grandpop, Mateo Gomez. Page 73 Productions focuses on the development and production of new work by "early-career" playwrights.

This play, *Elliot, a Soldier's Fugue* (2006), presents the unfolding consciousness of an eighteen-year-old marine as he is confronted by the realities of war. At first the play focuses on his deployment, and through his dialogue and the narration of two other characters only his experience is presented. He appears to be alone, with the play's action shifting between actuality and his recurring nightmares. But soon Elliot is joined, onstage, by two other soldiers from two different wars: his father, Pop, in Vietnam, and his grandfather, Grandpop, in Korea. The meaning of the word "fugue" from the play's title quickly becomes clear. As a musical term, **fugue** indicates a piece of music in which a theme is introduced and then repeated with some variation by three or four other voices. There is a sense that these instrumental or sung "voices" are answering each other. In the play, the stories of the three

IN CONTEXT

American Military Engagement and *Elliot, A Soldier's Fugue*

Korean War

*Dates of American Involvement: 1950–1953

Warring Nations: American led United Nations Forces versus North Korea and China

**Casualties: U.S. Troops Killed: 54,229
             U.S. Troops Missing in Action: 8,142

Character from Play: **Grandpop,** Elliot's Grandfather (65th Infantry Regiment of Puerto Rico)

Vietnam War

*Dates of American Involvement: 1960–1973

Warring Nations: United States and South Vietnam versus North Vietnam

**Casualties: U.S. Troops Killed: 58,220

Characters from Play: **Pop,** Elliot's Father (3rd Cavalry Division)
                      Ginny, Elliot's Mother (Army Nurse Corps)

Iraq War

*Dates of American Involvement: 2003–2011

Warring Nations: United States and Coalition Forces versus Iraq

**Casualties: American Troops Killed in Iraq: 4,488
             American Troops Killed in Afghanistan: 2,061
             American Troops Wounded: 50,569
             Suicides Amongst Returned Veterans in 2012: 349

Character from Play: **Elliot** (1st Marine Division)

*These dates are open to interpretation. Some analysts would expand the time periods depending on the arrival date and departure date of all American forces.

**The casualty figures are for U.S. troops only. In each conflict many thousands of additional troops, both allies and enemies, were also killed. These figures also do not reflect the enormous loss of civilian life. In Iraq, for example, estimates vary from 600,000 to 1,500,000 civilian lives lost.

soldiers are woven together, each echoing the other: the loneliness and fear of young men far from home, the damage done to bodies by the weapons of war, the damage done to minds by the taking of lives. These are personal stories, not political statements: three generations of men from one Puerto Rican family, repeating variations of the same stories of war. The three men are joined by a fourth character, Ginny, an army nurse who will tend to the wounds of her future husband, and later tend the wounds of her son, Elliot.

Time and space in this play are entirely fluid. The play can be happening in all three war zones at the same time or shift back and forth between them. Sometimes the characters speak for themselves, sometimes they narrate each other's actions. The play is constructed like a piece of music with themes that echo and repeat, voices that are presented in counterpoint. Music is also built into the characters' actions. The grandfather has taken his flute to Korea and plays the music of Bach in a major key when one of his comrades receives a letter from home and in

Elliot relives the moment when he fired at a man he believed to be an armed Iraqi. The staging is suggestive. The actor, Armando Riesco, leans across a bench as if he is handling a rifle.

a minor key when a soldier is lost. The father calls out his own versions of military cadences while Elliot sings along to the rap music on his Walkman. The play can be seen in part as an innovative and poetic continuation of the expressionist movement discussed in Chapter 9.

In the following scene, Elliot is on patrol in Iraq talking casually with his partner when he sees "some hostiles." A similar situation is occurring at the same time with his father in Vietnam. In this scene, Elliot and his father, Pop, are the main characters performing the action of the play. Ginny (Elliot's mother) provides narration for Elliot; Grandpop provides narration for Pop. At the end of the scene, both Elliot and Pop will be faced with removing the identification from the bodies of the men they have killed.

Elliot, A Soldier's Fugue

QUIARA ALEGRÍA HUDES

6. FUGUE

The empty space. Two wallets are on the ground.

GINNY: In my dreams, he said.

> Everything is in green.
>
> Green from the night-vision goggles.
>
> Green Iraq.
>
> Verdant Falluja.
>
> Emerald Tikrit.

(Elliot enters. He puts on night-vision goggles.)

ELLIOT (*To unseen night patrol partner*): Waikiki man, whatchu gonna eat first thing when you get home? I don't know. Probably start me off with some French toast from Denny's. Don't even get me near the cereal aisle. I'll go crazy. I yearn for some cereal. If you had to choose between Cocoa Puffs and Count Chocula, what would you choose? Wheaties or Life? Fruity Pebbles or Crunch Berry? You know my mom don't even buy Cap'n Crunch. She buys King Vitaman. Cereal so cheap, it don't even come in a box. It comes in a bag like them cheap Jewish noodles.

GINNY: Nightmares every night, he said.

> A dream about the first guy he actually saw that he killed.
>
> A dream that doesn't let you forget a face.

ELLIOT: The ultimate Denny's challenge. Would you go for the Grand Slam or the French Toast Combo? Wait. Or Western Eggs with Hash Browns? Yo, hash browns with ketchup. Condiments. Mustard, tartar sauce. I need me some condiments.

GINNY: Green moon.

> Green star.
>
> Green blink of the eye.

Green teeth.

> The same thing plays over and over.

(Elliot's attention is suddenly distracted.)

ELLIOT: Yo, you see that?

GINNY: The green profile of a machine gun in the distance.

ELLIOT: Waikiki, look straight ahead. Straight, straight at that busted wall. Shit. You see that guy? What's in his hand? He's got an AK. What do you mean, "I don't know." Do you see him?

(Elliot looks out.)

We got some hostiles. Permission to shoot.

(Pause.)

Permission to open fire.

(Pause.)

Is this your first? Shit, this is my first, too. All right. You ready?

GINNY: In the dream, aiming in.

> In the dream, knowing his aim is exact.
>
> In the dream, closing his eyes.

(Elliot closes his eyes.)

ELLIOT: Bang.

(Elliot opens his eyes.)

GINNY: Opening his eyes.

> The man is on the ground.

ELLIOTT: Hostile down. Uh, target down.

(Elliot gets up, disoriented from adrenaline.)

GINNY: In the dream, a sudden movement.

ELLIOT: Bang bang. Oh shit. That fucker moved. Did you see that? He moved, right? Mother f. Target down. Yes, I'm sure. Target down.

GINNY: Nightmares every night, he said.
> A dream about the first guy he actually saw that he killed.

(Pop enters, sits on the ground. He's trying to stay awake. He looks through binoculars.)

GRANDPOP: In my dreams, he said.

GINNY: Walking toward the guy.

(Elliot walks to the wallet.)

394

GRANDPOP: Everything is a whisper.

GINNY: Standing over the guy.

(Elliot looks down at the wallet.)

GRANDPOP: Breathing is delicate.

GINNY: A green face.

GRANDPOP: Whisper of water in the river.

GINNY: A green forehead.

GRANDPOP: Buzz of mosquito.

GINNY: A green upper lip.

GRANDPOP: Quiet Dong Ha.

GINNY: A green river of blood.

(Elliot kneels down, reaches for the wallet on the ground. He puts his hand on the wallet and remains in that position, frozen.)

GRANDPOP: Echo Vietnam.

POP: Joe Bobb. Wake up, man. Tell me about your gang from Kentucky. What, back in the Bronx? Yeah, we got ourselves a gang, but not a bad one. We help people on our street. Like some kids flipped over an ice-cream stand. It was just a nice old guy, the kids flipped it, knocked the old guy flat. We chased after them. Dragged one. Punched him till he said sorry. We called ourselves the Social Sevens. After the Magnificent Sevens.

GRANDPOP: Nightmares every night, he said.

A dream that doesn't let you forget a voice.

The same sounds echoing back and forth.

POP: Guns? Naw, we weren't into none of that. We threw a lot of rocks and bottles. And handballs. Bronx Handball Champs, 1964. Doubles and singles. Hm? What's a handball?

GRANDPOP: The snap of a branch.

POP: Shh.

GRANDPOP: Footsteps in the mud.

POP: You hear something?

GRANDPOP: Three drops of water.

A little splash.

(Pop grabs his binoculars and looks out.)

POP: VC on us. Ten o'clock. Kneeling in front of the river, alone. He's drinking. Fuck, he's thirsty. Joe Bobb, man, this is my first time. Oh shit. Shit. Bang. *(Pause.)* Bang.

GRANDPOP: Whisper of two bullets in the air.

Echo of his gun.

A torso falling in the mud.

POP: Got him. I got him, Joe Bobb. Man down. VC down.

(Pop rises, looks out.)

GRANDPOP: Hearing everything.

Walking to the guy.

Boots squishing in the mud.

(Pop walks to the second wallet.)

Standing over the guy.

The guy says the Vietnamese word for "mother."

He has a soft voice.

He swallows air.

A brief convulsion.

Gasp.

Silence.

Water whispers in the river.

POP AND ELLIOTT: Military code.

Remove ID and intel from dead hostiles.

(Pop kneels in front of the dead man's wallet. He reaches out his hand and touches the wallet. Elliot and Pop are in the same position, each of them touching a wallet. They move in unison.)

POP: The wallet.

The body.

The face.

The eyes.

(Elliot and Pop open the wallets.)

ELLIOT: The photo.

The pictures.

Bullet.

(Elliot and Pop each pull a little photo out of the wallets.)

POP: Dog tags.

The wife.

ELLIOTT: The children.

(They turn over the photo and look at the back of it.)

Black ink.

POP: A date.

POP AND ELLIOT: Handwriting.

A family portrait.

(They each drop their photo. They each find a second photo. Lights fade.)[3]

A New Trilogy

Although Hudes received considerable acclaim for her work on *In the Heights*, a successful Broadway musical, it was the world of Elliot Ortiz that called to her. She believed there was more to Elliot's story that should be told and she was eager to experiment further with the integration of musical structures into her playwriting.

> QUIARA HUDES: I wanted to live in that writing world a little more. What I found out was that I couldn't go back, couldn't retrace my footsteps. I wanted to do something new. So I thought about working with music in the same way but using a different type of music so that I would be experiencing the same type of process writing-wise but would be moving forward with a new play. And so I thought about jazz. At the same time my cousin Elliot had some pretty incredible stuff happening in his life. I wanted to continue with this story and use jazz as a musical background.[4]

Hudes determined to write two more plays about her cousin Elliot's return from Iraq and use a different musical foundation for each. And the scope of the work would be expanded with new characters, some based on her family, and some characters of her invention, who shared the experiences that would be central to each play. Including *Elliot, A Soldier's Fugue*, the three interconnected plays would make a new trilogy for the American theatre, that we will call the Elliot trilogy.

> QUIARA HUDES: I love long form. I'm one of those rare audience members who wants things to be longer as opposed to shorter. A trilogy affords a long form without making someone sit through six hours of theatre straight. I think that it's the same attraction to serialized drama over cable. There will be a story arc that will last an entire season or that mini series model where you can really stretch a story for a longer amount of time. And then with the separation of the three different pieces within that long form, there's more room to play. Because each piece is its

own event too, I can play with different ideas in each one. Each play has a different style and a different structure, a very different tone; so it doesn't feel too repetitive.

The History of the Trilogy

The **trilogy** is one of the earliest forms in the history of Western drama. At the time of the Greek theatre in the fifth century B.C.E., which we studied in Chapter 1, the Athenian playwrights frequently composed plays in the trilogy form using the three-play structure to develop complex themes. Separately, the individual Greek plays often used remarkable economy in the plot (a single unified action), the setting (one place), and the time frame (twenty-four hours), but the trilogy allowed playwrights to show the evolution of an idea across a broader range of characters and situations. In spite of evidence that many trilogies were written at this time, *The Oresteia* by Aeschylus is the only surviving trilogy from the classical Greek theatre.

The Oresteia tells the story of the return of a general, Agamemnon, from the Trojan War, his subsequent murder by his wife Clytaemnestra, and then the revenge killing of Clytaemnestra by the son of Agamemnon and Clytaemnestra, Orestes. Orestes is pursued by the Furies for his crime until he is brought to a trial by jury. The overarching theme of *The Oresteia* is the search for a system of justice that will stop the cycle of vengeance begun when Agamemnon sacrificed his daughter, Iphigenia, in order to secure favorable winds that would allow the Greek fleet of ships to set sail for Troy to begin the Trojan War. *The Oresteia* has received a number of recent productions around the world because of the way it addresses the cycles of revenge and brutality that we continue to witness in many geographic regions, including our own participation in military conflicts in the Middle East. It is one of the oldest plays and yet it has proven to speak forcefully to our contemporary circumstances. The best-known American trilogy is Eugene O'Neill's *Mourning Becomes Electra*, written in 1931. In fact O'Neill's work is an adaptation of *The Oresteia* that he placed in the American Civil War. Both the Greek and American versions of *The Oresteia* were written to be performed in one continuous presentation.

The trilogy is not a form of dramatic structure that is frequently employed. However, we have seen two major recent experiments in the American theatre with plays that are structurally connected: the two plays that make up *Angels in America* and the ten plays that together create August Wilson's cycle for the twentieth century. Certainly we see a number of experiments with connected episodes in contemporary television and Internet drama.

The Elliot Trilogy

The three plays in the Elliot trilogy are *Elliot, a Soldier's Fugue; Water by the Spoonful;* and *The Happiest Song Plays Last.* Together they trace the story of Elliot's participation in the war and his injury in Iraq and the stages he goes through as a returned veteran who is traumatized and unsure how to find his way forward. Each play looks at a particular time in Elliot's life and then expands and deepens the meaning of his experience by placing it in the context of his relationship to other members of his family. The form of each play is shaped by the significance of these family connections and a form of musical composition that is both a metaphor for the experience

Ginny narrates Elliot's thoughts during the scene in which he is injured outside Tikrit.

represented and a structural component that expresses the nature of the characters' interactions and the human condition being explored.

Elliot, A Soldier's Fugue demonstrates the repetition of young soldiers at war from generation to generation, and the form is shaped as a fugue. *Water by the Spoonful* examines an issue affecting both Elliot and a larger group of other characters, all in recovery from substance abuse. This play is written as three duets for characters discovering ways to support each other. Where the first play in the trilogy is very carefully and economically constructed, *Water by the Spoonful* is a more expansive development of a theme through variation and longer, individual stories. The structures of jazz composition, particularly the music of John Coltrane, are used to reinforce the turmoil experienced by individual characters and the dissonance and conflict within the character relationships.

John Coltrane is recognized as one of the leading jazz musicians of the twentieth century. He rose to prominence during the 1960s and was known as a brilliant performer on both the alto and tenor saxophones. He experimented with the production of sound on his instruments, with extended improvisation, and with both melodic and dissonant compositions. Although he was born in North Carolina, Philadelphia became his musical home. Coltrane died at the age of forty in 1967. His reputation continued to grow following his death and his legacy was an inspiration to Quiara Hudes when she was a young music student in Philadelphia during the 1980s and 1990s. Two of Coltrane's most influential works, *A Love Supreme* and *Ascension*, became touchstones for Hudes when she was writing *Water by the Spoonful*.

QUIARA HUDES: With jazz and Coltrane, one of the things I was interested in was improvisation. He's exploring something about abandon. Just letting oneself go. And I wanted to give myself freedom to make big, bold statements at the risk of being messy. I listened to *Love Supreme* by Coltrane over and over again and I started thinking about what the play was going to sound like, the rush of energy, the movements.

In the last play, *The Happiest Song Plays Last*, Elliot moves toward a form of personal forgiveness. He performs an act of atonement for the taking of human life. He buries the passport that he took in the scene included above from *Elliot, A Soldier's Fugue* and that haunts him throughout *Water by the Spoonful*. He has tried to bury the passport in Jordan and then tried to return it to the widow of the man he killed. Finally, with the help of his cousin Yazmin and his new wife, Shar, who is of Arab heritage, he is able to bury the passport in his mother's garden.

The geographical setting of the third play shifts between Jordan, where Elliot is making a movie about the Iraq War, and Philadelphia, the home of Elliot's family. The play is written to be accompanied by two or three live musicians and includes a number of lively, traditional Puerto Rican songs. The Spanish-language lyrics of these songs augment and punctuate the content of the characters' dialogue and actions. The instruments called for are the guitar and the *cuatro*, central to Puerto Rican music. The playwright also recommends using an *oud*, an instrument from Iraq, which would further underscore the theme of mutual understanding that builds through the play.

Together the parts of the trilogy move from crisis to recovery to agency and reconciliation. Davis McCallum has directed the premieres of both *Elliot, a Soldier's Fugue* and *Water by the Spoonful*. He sees the character of Elliot taking on a larger significance than an isolated individual.

DAVIS MCCALLUM: He's just a guy who grew up in the barrio and went to Iraq, like a lot of other people, and came home, like a lot of other people. What's so inspiring about what Quiara has done is to see a cousin, whom she loves, as a kind of everyman. It becomes more than just one guy's story. The trilogy becomes the quintessential American coming-of-age story. Over three plays, we see this guy struggling with what it means to be a man, and to be an American man.

As McCallum points out, Elliot is an ordinary young man caught in circumstances not of his making. He is elevated by his journey of suffering and introspection. And in his struggle to become whole by taking responsibility for his actions, he becomes a representative for the nation.

The Playwright's Sources: Family

Particularly for the Elliot trilogy, Hudes has found the sources for her characters, their stories, and their cultural context in her own family.

> QUIARA HUDES: I have to feel that personal connection, at least thus far. It has to come from somewhere in me. When I was at Brown, I took a course with Holly Hughes who is a performance artist. She gave us ten minutes to write a list of our identities. At the end of ten minutes, I had thirty things written on my paper, and as I shared it, I realized only about the first three or four were really *my* identities. The rest were identities of people I was really close with and especially family members. I think I've always taken on the identities of those around me too. So I feel like when I write about family, in some ways it's as personal as autobiography.

In one sense the three plays are something of a family history.

Hudes is inspired by the struggles, the strength, and the wisdom of the people that she has known best and draws on their experiences as the foundation for these plays. In addition to Elliot, another cousin inspired the character of Odessa in *Water by the Spoonful*. Odessa is a recovering addict whose struggles with addiction had "serious repercussions" for other family members. Some characters can be identified specifically; some are composites of two different family members. In the second two plays, some characters are pure inventions. A central character for the entire trilogy is Ginny, who appears only in *Elliot, A Soldier's Fugue*. She is the figure of healing in

that play and her presence guides the development of the other two plays even though it is her death at the beginning of *Water by the Spoonful* that precipitates much of the action. Quiara Hudes, in fact, has an Aunt Ginny for whom this character is named. But the character's spirituality also reflects Hudes' mother and her connections to Taino and Afro-Caribbean rituals as well as her community activism.

In *Elliott, A Soldier's Fugue*, Ginny has a long monologue about the garden she created in her hometown of Philadelphia, in an abandoned lot filled with junk and garbage. The reclaimed garden, which she filled with tropical plants from her native Puerto Rico, serves as a metaphor throughout the trilogy for the reclamation of lives from poverty, addiction, and despair.

> GINNY: When Elliot left for Iraq, I went crazy with planting. Begonias, ferns, trees. A seed is a contract with the future. It's saying I know something better will happen tomorrow . . . You have to plant wild. When your son goes to war, you plant every goddamn seed you can find. It doesn't matter what the seed is. So long as it grows. I plant what I like and to hell with the consequences.[5]

Although Ginny dies at the beginning of *Water by the Spoonful*, another character drawn from Hudes' family, Yazmin, gradually grows into the role of family protector during the second two plays.

In developing her characters, Hudes goes beyond writing from memory or observation. She interviews the family members she wants to write about and also discusses with them how she will use the material and takes into account their feelings about having their private lives revealed publicly. She has found "they really do want to talk about their experience and their point of view and tell me their stories." The next step in her process is to undertake research to expand her understanding of the circumstances she wants to work with. Hudes reads widely and interviews additional sources. For *Water by the Spoonful*, that meant extensive research

Ginny describes the tropical garden she created in an abandoned lot in Philadelphia. In *Water by the Spoonful,* the actor Zabryna Guevara, who plays Ginny here, plays the role of Ginny's niece Yazmin, who ends up inheriting her aunt's garden.

about addiction and recovery. She spoke with counselors at the Institute for Living, a recovery institute in Hartford, Connecticut, as well as with Alan Leshner, President of the National Institute for Drug Abuse. Ultimately she spends months or years sifting and processing the material she has gathered.

> Over that long period of time, it is a very slow stream of conscious process. I do a lot of walking and thinking. I think my process is about 70% walking without writing or reading anything.

When Hudes does sit down to write her plays, she enters a new phase of the work, which involves creating a fiction of the life stories and research materials she has absorbed.

The Dual Worlds of *Water by the Spoonful*

In *Water by the Spoonful,* the story of Elliot's reentry into American society connects to his relationship with his birth mother, Odessa. We learn that Ginny from *Elliot, A Soldier's Fugue* is his aunt, who adopted him when Odessa spiraled down into drug use. Another structural component is introduced as a foundation for this character, still locked in a battle with addiction. The play presents Odessa through her online conversations with other recovering substance abusers. The construction of the play alternates between scenes that take place in actual time and space and scenes that take place online, in virtual space.

Whether they appear in the real world or online, all of the characters are hiding truths about themselves. They have retreated in differing degrees from full participation in life. Through the course of this second play of the trilogy, they all seek to repair the damage to their own lives or the damage they have inflicted on others.

QUIARA HUDES: With the real versus the online, the first act basically alternates between the two worlds. Then they come together at the end of act I. The structure breaks down and the worlds start to bleed into each other. I feel very connected to that structure living in 2013 because we live in multiple worlds now all at the same time. Swiftly shifting from world to world on the stage just feels like the way time works and the way that one's traffic moves through the day right now.

Water by the Spoonful

QUIARA ALEGRÍA HUDES
Second Stage production draft

DEDICATION

For Ray Beauchamp.

ACKNOWLEDGEMENTS

This play, its story, and its characters are works of fiction. However, I owe a debt of gratitude to Othet Sauris and Elliot Ruiz, whom I interviewed before writing. Without their generosity of story and spirit, my imagination would not have landed at this play.

More seeds of inspiration came from interviews with Jeremy Cohen, Sandy Moehle, Rik Albani and Alan Leshner. Roger Zepernick, my dear friend, contributed to Scene Ten by sending me a transcript of a speech he gave in Philadelphia along with his permission to adapt it.

Gratitude to all my family, with a special beam of light shining on my mother, Virginia Sanchez. Linda Hudes, Eugenia Burgos and Liz Morales provide ongoing support and inspiration. My siblings keep me young at heart: Gabriela Sanchez, Ariel Hudes and Forrest Hudes. My stepfather, Mercedes Sanchez, told me a tale of his first cold drink. My father, Henry Hudes, sanded the curly maple of my writing desk.

Gratitude to my collaborators. John Buzzetti, your joy is infectious. Michael Wilson, what a champion you are. Davis McCallum, Armando Riesco and Zabryna Guevara—what shall we call our theater company? Hana Sharif and Darko Tresnjak, for steel-beam support at Hartford Stage. Catherine Rush, for drawing the starting line; and Kent Gash, for grabbing the baton along the way. New Dramatists, for seven lovely years.

Gratitude, ongoing, to Paula Vogel.
Gratitude, endless, to Ray.

CHARACTERS

ODESSA ORTIZ, 39, aka Haikumom, founder of www.recovertogether.com, works odd janitorial jobs, lives one notch above squalor.

ELLIOT ORTIZ, 24, an Iraq vet with a slight limp, works at Subway Hoagies, scores an occasional job as a model or actor, Yazmin's cousin, Odessa's birth son.

YAZMIN ORTIZ, 31, adjunct professor of music, Odessa's niece and Elliot's cousin.

FOUNTAINHEAD, 38, aka John, a computer programmer and entrepreneur, lives on Philadelphia's Main Line, white.

CHUTES&LADDERS, 56, lives in San Diego, has worked a low-level job at the IRS since the Reagan years, African-American, his real name is Clayton "Buddy" Wilkie.

ORANGUTAN, 26, a recent community college graduate, Japanese by birth, her real name is Madeleine Mays and before that Yoshiko Sakai.

A GHOST, also plays Professor Aman, an Arabic professor at Swarthmore; also plays a Policeman in Japan.

SETTING

2009. Six years after Elliot left for Iraq. Philadelphia, San Diego, Japan, and Puerto Rico.

The stage has two worlds. The "real world" is populated with chairs. The chairs are from many locations—living rooms, an office, a seminar room, a church, a diner, internet cafes. They all have the worn-in feel of life. A duct-taped La-Z-Boy. Salvaged trash chairs. A busted up metal folding chair from a rec center. An Aero chair. An Eames chair. A chair/desk from a college classroom. Diner chairs. A chair from an internet café in Japan. Living room chairs. Library chairs. A church pew. Facing in all different directions.

The "online world" is an empty space. A space that connects the chairs.

MUSIC

Jazz: John Coltrane. The sublime stuff (*A Love Supreme*). And the noise (*Ascension*).

NOTE

Unless specifically noted, when characters are online, don't have actors typing on a keyboard. Treat it like regular conversation rather than the act of writing or typing. They can be doing things people do in the comfort of their home like eating potato chips, walking around in jammies, cooking, doing dishes, clipping nails, etc.

Scene 1

(Swarthmore College. Elliot and Yaz eat breakfast. Elliot wears a Subway Hoagies polo shirt.)

ELLIOT: This guy ain't coming. How do you know him?

YAZ: We're on a committee together.

ELLIOT: My shift starts in fifteen.

YAZ: Alright, we'll go.

ELLIOT: Five more minutes. Tonight on the way home, we gotta stop by Whole Foods.

YAZ: Sure, I need toothpaste.

ELLIOT: Yaz, you gotta help me with my mom.

YAZ: You said she had a good morning.

ELLIOT: She cooked breakfast.

YAZ: Progress.

ELLIOT: No. The docs said she can't be eating all that junk, it'll mess with her chemo, so she crawls out of bed for the first time in days and cooks eggs for breakfast. In two inches of pork chop fat. I'm like, mom, recycle glass and plastic, not grease. She thinks putting the egg on top of a paper towel after you cook it makes it healthy. I told her, mom you gotta cook egg whites. In Pam spray. But it has to be her way. Like, "That's how we ate them in Puerto Rico and we turned out fine." You gotta talk to her. I'm trying to teach her about quinoa. Broccoli rabe. Healthy shit. So I get home the other day, she had made quinoa with bacon. She was like, "It's healthy!"

YAZ: That's Ginny. The more stubborn she's being, the better she's feeling.

ELLIOT: I gave those eggs to the dogs when she went to the bathroom.

(She pulls some papers from her purse.)

YAZ: You wanna be my witness?

ELLIOT: To what?

(Yaz signs the papers.)

YAZ: My now-legal failure. I'm divorced.

ELLIOT: Yaz. I don't want to hear that.

YAZ: You've been saying that for months and I've been keeping my mouth closed. I just need a John Hancock.

ELLIOT: What happened to "trial separation"?

YAZ: There was a verdict. William fell out of love with me.

ELLIOT: I've never seen you two argue.

YAZ: We did, we just had smiles on our faces.

ELLIOT: That's bullshit. You don't divorce someone before you even have a fight with them. I'm calling him.

YAZ: Go ahead.

ELLIOT: He was just texting me about going to the Phillies game on Sunday.

YAZ: So, go. He didn't fall out of love with the family, just me.

ELLIOT: I'm going to ask him who he's been screwing behind your back.

YAZ: No one, Elliot.

ELLIOT: You were tappin' some extra on the side?

YAZ: He woke up one day and I was the same as any other person passing by on the street, and life is short, and you can only live in mediocrity so long.

ELLIOT: You two are the dog and the owner that look like each other. Y'all are the *Cosby Show*. Conundrum, Yaz and William make a funny, end of episode. You show all us cousins, maybe we can't ever do it ourselves, but it *is* possible.

YAZ: Did I ever say, "It's possible"?

ELLIOT: By example.

YAZ: Did I ever say those words?

(Professor Aman enters.)

AMAN: Yazmin, forgive me. You must be . . .

ELLIOT: Elliot Ortiz. Nice to meet you, I appreciate it.

AMAN: Professor Aman.

(They shake.)

We'll have to make this short and sweet, my lecture begins . . . began . . . well, talk fast.

ELLIOT: Yaz, give us a second?

YAZ: I'll be in the car. (Exits.)

ELLIOT: I'm late, too, so . . .

AMAN: You need something translated.

ELLIOT: Just a phrase. Thanks, man.

AMAN: Eh, your sister's cute.

ELLIOT: Cousin. I wrote it phonetically. You grow up speaking Arabic?

AMAN: English. What's your native tongue?

ELLIOT: Spanglish. (Hands Aman a piece of paper.)

AMAN: Mom-ken men fad-luck ted-dini ga-waz saf-far-i. Momken men-fadluck ted-dini gawaz saffari. Am I saying that right?

ELLIOT: (Spooked.) Spot on.

AMAN: You must have some familiarity with Arabic to remember it so clearly.

ELLIOT: Maybe I heard it on TV or something.

AMAN: An odd phrase.

ELLIOT: It's like a song I can't get out of my head.

AMAN: Yazmin didn't tell me what this is for.

ELLIOT: It's not for anything.

AMAN: Do you mind me asking, what's around your neck?

ELLIOT: Something my girl gave me.

AMAN: Can I see?

(Elliot pulls dog tags from under his shirt.) Romantic gift. You were in the army.

ELLIOT: Marines.

AMAN: Iraq?

ELLIOT: For a minute.

AMAN: Were you reluctant to tell me that?

ELLIOT: No.

AMAN: Still in the service?

ELLIOT: Honorable discharge. Leg injury.

AMAN: When?

ELLIOT: A few years ago.

AMAN: This is a long time to have a phrase stuck in your head.

ELLIOT: What is this, man?

AMAN: You tell me.

ELLIOT: It's just a phrase. If you don't want to translate, just say so.

AMAN: A college buddy is making a film about Marines in Iraq. Gritty, documentary-style. He's looking for some veterans to interview. Get an authentic point of view. Maybe I could pass your number onto him.

ELLIOT: Nope. No interviews for this guy.

AMAN: You're asking me for a favor. (Pause.) Yazmin told me you're an actor. Every actor needs a break, right?

ELLIOT: I did enough Q&As about the service. People manipulate you with the questions.

AMAN: It's not just to interview. He needs a right-hand man, an expert to help him. How do Marines hold a gun? How do they kick in civilian doors, this sort of thing. How do they say "Ooh rah" in a patriotic manner?

ELLIOT: Are you his headhunter or something?

AMAN: I'm helping with the translations, I have a small stake and I want the movie to be accurate. And you seem not unintelligent. For a maker of sandwiches. (Hands him a business card.) He's in L.A. In case you want a career change. I give you a cup of sugar, you give me a cup of sugar.

ELLIOT: If I have a minute, I'll dial the digits. (Takes the business card.) So what's it mean?

AMAN: Momken men-fadluck ted-dini gawaz saffari. Rough translation, "Can I please have my passport back?"

Scene 2

(Odessa's living room and kitchen. She makes coffee. She goes over to her computer, clicks a button. On a screen we see:)

HAIKUMOM, SITEADMIN
STATUS: ONLINE

HAIKUMOM: Rise and shine, kiddos, the rooster's a-crowin', it's a beautiful day to be sober. (No response.) Your Thursday morning haiku:

if you get restless

buy a hydrangea or rose

water it, wait, bloom

(Odessa continues making coffee. A computer dings and on another screen we see:)

ORANGUTAN
STATUS: ONLINE

ORANGUTAN: Ninety one days. Smiley face.

HAIKUMOM: (Relieved.) Orangutan! Jesus, I thought my primate friend had disappeared back to the jungle.

ORANGUTAN: Disappeared? Yes. Jungle? Happily, no.

HAIKUMOM: I'm trying to put a high-five emoticon but my computer is being a capital B. So, high-five!

(They high-five in the air. Another computer screen lights up:)

CHUTES&LADDERS
STATUS: ONLINE

CHUTES&LADDERS: Orangutan? I was about to send a search party after your rear end. Kid, *log on.* No news is bad news.

ORANGUTAN: Chutes&Ladders, giving me a hard time as usual. I'd expect nothing less.

CHUTES&LADDERS: Your last post says, "Day One. Packing bags, gotta run," and then you don't log on for three months?

ORANGUTAN: I was going to Japan, I had to figure out what shoes to bring.

HAIKUMOM: The country?

CHUTES&LADDERS: What happened to Maine?

ORANGUTAN: And I quote, "Get a hobby, find a new job, an exciting city, go teach English in a foreign country." Did you guys think I wouldn't take your seasoned advice? I was batting 0 for ten, and for the first time, guys, I feel fucking free.

HAIKUMOM: (Nonjudgmental.) Censored.

ORANGUTAN: I wake up and I think, "What's the world got up its sleeve today?" and I look forward to the answer. So, thank you.

CHUTES&LADDERS: We told you so.

ORANGUTAN: (Playful.) Shut up.

HAIKUMOM: You're welcome.

ORANGUTAN: I gave my parents the URL. My username, my password. They logged on and read every post I've ever put on here and for once they said they understood. They had completely cut me off but after reading this site they bought me the plane ticket. One way. I teach English in the mornings. I have a class of children, a class of teens, and a class of adults, most of whom are older than me. I am free in the afternoons. I have a paycheck which I use for legal things like ice cream, noodles, and socks. I walk around feeling like maybe I *am* normal. Maybe, just possibly, I'm not that different. Or maybe it's just home-land delusions.

CHUTES&LADDERS AND HAIKUMOM: Homeland?

HAIKUMOM: You're Japanese?

ORANGUTAN: I *was,* for the first eight days of my life. Yoshiko Sakai. Then on day nine I was adopted and moved to Cape Lewiston, Maine, where I became Ma— M.M., and where in all my days I have witnessed *one* other Asian. In the Superfresh. Deli counter.

CHUTES&LADDERS: Japan . . . Wow, that little white rock sure doesn't discriminate.

HAIKUMOM: Amen.

ORANGUTAN: Mango Internet Café. I'm sitting in an orange plastic chair, a little view of the Hokkaido waterfront.

HAIKUMOM: Japan has a waterfront?

CHUTES&LADDERS: It's an island.

HAIKUMOM: Really? Are there beaches? Can you go swimming?

ORANGUTAN: The ocean reminds me of Maine. Cold water, very quiet, fisherman, boats, the breeze. I wouldn't try swimming. I'm just a looker. I was never one to actually have an experience.

CHUTES&LADDERS: Ah, the ocean . . . There's only one thing on this planet I'm more scared of than that big blue lady.

HAIKUMOM: Let me guess: landing on a sliding board square?

CHUTES&LADDERS: Lol, truer words have never been spoken. You know I was born just a few miles from the Pacific. In the fresh salt air. Back in "those days" I'm at Coronado Beach with a few "friends" doing my "thing" and I get sucked up under this wave. I gasp, I breathe in and my lungs fill with water. I'm like, this is it, I'm going to meet my maker. I had never felt so heavy, not even during my two OD's. I was sinking to the bottom and my head hit the sand like a lead ball. My body just felt like an anvil. The next thing I know there's fingers digging in my ankles. This lifeguard pulls me out, I'm throwing up salt water. I say to him, "Hey blondie, you don't know me from Adam but you are my witness: today's the day I start to *live.*" And this lifeguard, I mean he was young with these muscles, this kid looks at me like, "Who is this big black dude who can't even doggy paddle?" When I stand up and brush the sand off me, people *applaud.* An old lady touches my cheek and says, "I thought you were done for." I get back to San Diego that night, make one phone call, the next day I'm in my first meeting, sitting in a folding chair, saying the serenity prayer.

ORANGUTAN: I hate to inflate your already swollen ego, but that was a lucid, touching story. By the way, did you get the lifeguard's name? He sounds hot.

HAIKUMOM: Hey Chutes&Ladders, it's never too late to learn. Most YMCAs offer adult swimming classes.

CHUTES&LADDERS: I'll do the world a favor and stay out of a speedo.

ORANGUTAN: Sober air toast. To lifeguards.

CHUTES&LADDERS/HAIKUMOM: To lifeguards.

ORANGUTAN/CHUTES&LADDERS/HAIKUMOM: Clink.

HAIKUMOM: Chutes&Ladders, I'm buying you a pair of water wings.

Scene 3

(John Coltrane's *A Love Supreme* plays. A Subway Hoagie shop on Philadelphia's Main Line. Elliot sits behind the counter. The phone rings. He gets up, hobbles to it—he walks with a limp.)

ELLIOT: Subway Main Line. Lar! Laaar, what's it doing for you today? Staying in the shade? I got you, how many you need? Listen, the delivery guy's out and my little sports injury is giving me hell so can you pick up? Cool, sorry for the inconvenience. Let me grab a pen. A'ight, pick a hoagie, any hoagie!

(Elliot begins writing the order.

Lights rise to a seminar room at Swarthmore College. We find Yaz mid-class. She hits a button on a stereo and the Coltrane stops playing.)

YAZ: Coltrane's *A Love Supreme*, 1964. Dissonance is still a gateway to resolution. A B-diminished chord is still resolving to? C-major. A tritone is still resolving up to? The major sixth. Diminished chords, tritones, still didn't have the right to be their own independent thought. In 1965 something changed. The ugliness bore no promise of a happy ending. The ugliness became an end in itself. Coltrane democratized the notes. He said, they're all equal. Freedom. It was called Free Jazz but freedom is a hard thing to express musically without spinning into noise. This is from *Ascension*, 1965.

(She plays *Ascension.* It sounds uglier than the first sample.

In the Subway shop, a figure comes into view. It is The Ghost.)

GHOST: Momken men-fadluck ted-dini gawaz saffari?

(Elliot tries to ignore the Ghost, reading off the order.)

ELLIOT: That's three teriyaki onion with chicken. First with hots and onions. Second with everything. Third with extra bacon. Two spicy Italian with American cheese on whole grain. One BMT on flatbread. Good so far?

GHOST: Momken men-fadluck ted-dini gawaz saffari?

ELLIOT: Five chocolate chip cookies, one oat-meal raisin. Three Baked Lays, three Doritos. Two Sprite Zeros, one Barq's, one Coke, two orange sodas. How'd I do?

GHOST: Momken men-fadluck ted-dini gawaz saffari?

ELLIOT: Alright, that'll be ready in fifteen min-utes. One sec for your total.

(Elliot gets a text message. He reads it, his entire demeanor shifts.)

Lar, I just got a text. There's a family emer-gency, I can't do this order right now.

(Elliot hangs up. He exits, limping away.)

YAZ: Oh come on, don't make that face. I know it feels academic. You're going to leave here and become R&B hit makers and Sondheim clones and never think about this noise again. But this is Coltrane, people, this is not Schoenberg! This is jazz, stuff people listen to *voluntarily.* Shopping period is still on, go sit in one session of "Germans and Noise" down the hall and you'll come running back beg-ging for this muzak.

(Yaz turns off the music.)

In fact, change the syllabus. No listening report next week. Instead, I want you to pinpoint the first time you really noticed dissonance. The composer, the piece, the measures. Two pages analyzing the notes and two pages describing the experience person-ally. This is your creation myth. Before you leave this school you better figure out that story and cling to it for dear life or you'll be a stockbroker within a year.

I was thirteen, I worked in a corrugated box factory all summer, I saved up enough to find my first music teacher—up to that point I was self-taught, playing to the radio. I walked into Don Rappaport's room at Settlement Music School. He was old, he had jowls, he was sitting at the piano and he said, "What do you do?" I said, "I'm a composer, sir." Presumptuous, right? I sat down and played Mr. Rappaport a Yazmin original. He said, "It's pretty, everything goes together. It's like an outfit where your socks are blue and your pants, shirt, hat are all blue." Then he said, "Play an F-sharp major in your left hand." Then he said, "Play a C-major in your right hand." "Now play them together." He asked me, "Does it go together?" I told him, "No sir." He said, "Now go home and write." My first music lesson was seven minutes long. I had never really heard dissonance before.

(Yaz's phone vibrates. She sees the caller with concern.)

Let's take five.

(As students file out, Yaz makes a phone call. Lights up on Elliot outside the Subway Hoagie shop.)

YAZ: ("What's the bad news?") You called three times.

ELLIOT: She's still alive.

YAZ: Okay.

ELLIOT: Jefferson Hospital. They admitted her three hours ago, Pop had the courtesy to text me.

YAZ: Are you still at work?

ELLIOT: Just smashed the bathroom mirror all over the floor. Boss sent me out to the parking lot.

YAZ: Wait there. I'm on my way.

ELLIOT: "Your mom is on breathing machine." Who texts that? Who texts that and then doesn't pick up the phone?

YAZ: I'll be there within twenty.

ELLIOT: Why did I come to work today?

YAZ: She had a good morning. You wanted your thing translated.

ELLIOT: She cooked and I wouldn't eat a bite off the fork. There's a Subway hoagies around the corner and I had to work half an hour away.

YAZ: You didn't want your buddies to see you working a normal job.

ELLIOT: Not normal job. Shit job. I'm a butler. A porter of sandwiches.

YAZ: Ginny's been to Hades and back, stronger each time.

ELLIOT: What is Hades?

YAZ: In Greek mythology, the river through the underworld—

ELLIOT: My mom's on a machine and you're dropping vocab words?!

(A ding.)

YAZ: Text message, don't hang up. (She looks at her phone. A moment, then.) You still there?

ELLIOT: It was my dad wasn't it? Yaz, spit it out.

YAZ: It was your dad.

ELLIOT: And? Yaz, I'm about to start walking down Lancaster Avenue for thirty miles til I get back to Philly and I don't care if I snap every wire out my leg and back—I need to get out of here. I need to see mom, I need to talk to her!

YAZ: He said, "Waiting for Elliot til we turn off the machine."

Scene 4

(The chat room. A screen lights up:)
No Image

FOUNTAINHEAD
STATUS: ONLINE

FOUNTAINHEAD: I've uh, wow, hello there everyone. Delete, delete.

Good afternoon. Evening. Delete.

(Deep breath.)

Things I am taking:

-My life into my own hands.

-My gorgeous, deserving wife out for our seventh anniversary.

Me: Mildly athletic, but work twice as hard. Won state for javelin two years straight. Ran a half-marathon last fall. Animated arguer. Two medals for undergrad debate. MBA from Wharton. Beautiful wife, two sons. Built a programming company from the ground up, featured in the New York Times Circuits section, sold it at its peak, bought a yellow Porsche, got a day job to keep myself honest. Salary was 300 K, company was run by morons, got laid off, handsome severance, which left me swimming in cash and free time.

Me & crack: long story short, I was at a conference with our CFO and two programmers and a not-unattractive lady in HR. They snorted, invited me to join. A few weeks later that little rock waltzed right into my hand. I've been using off-and-on since. One eight ball every Saturday, strict rations, portion control. Though the last three or four weeks, it's less like getting high and more like trying to build a time machine. Anything to get back the romance of that virgin smoke.

Last weekend I let myself buy more than my predetermined allotment—I buy in small quantity, because as with my food, I eat what's on my plate. Anyway, I ran over a curb, damaged the underside of my Porsche. Now it's in the shop and I'm driving a rental Mustang. So, not rock bottom but a rental Ford is as close to rock bottom as I'd like to get. Fast forward to tonight. I'm watching my wife's eyelids fall and telling myself, "You are on punishment, poppa. Daddy's on time out. Do not get out of bed, do not tiptoe down those stairs, do not go down to that basement, do not sit beside that foosball table, do not smoke, and please do not crawl on the carpet looking for one last hit in the fibers."

(Pause.)

In kindergarten my son tested into G&T. Gifted and talented. You meet with the school, they tailor the program to the kid. Math, reading, art, whatever the parent chooses. I said, "Teach my son how to learn." How to use a library. How to find original source material, read a map, track down the experts so he becomes the expert. Which gets me to—

You: the experts. It's the first day of school and I'm knocking at your classroom door. I got my number two pencils, I'll sit in the front row, pay attention, and do my homework. No lesson is too basic. Teach me every technique. Any tip so that Saturday doesn't become every day. Any actions that keep you in the driver seat. Healthy habits and rational thoughts to blot out that voice in the back of my head.

Today, I quit. My wife cannot know, she'd get suspicious if I were at meetings all the time. There can be no medical records, so therapy is out. At least it's not heroin, I'm not facing a physical war. It's a psychological battle and I'm armed with two weapons: willpower and the experts.

I'm taking my wife out tomorrow for our seventh anniversary and little does she know that when we clink glasses, I'll be toasting to Day One.

(Odessa is emotional. Chutes&Ladders and Orangutan seem awestruck.)

ORANGUTAN: (Clapping.) That was brave.

CHUTES&LADDERS: What. The.

HAIKUMOM: Careful.

CHUTES&LADDERS: Fuck.

HAIKUMOM: Censored.

ORANGUTAN: I'm making popcorn. Oh, this is gonna be fun!

CHUTES&LADDERS: Fountainhead, speaking of experts, I've been meaning to become an ass-hole. Can you teach me how?

HAIKUMOM: Censored!

ORANGUTAN: "Tips?" This isn't a cooking website. And what is a half-marathon?

CHUTES&LADDERS: Maybe it's something like a half crack addict. Or a half husband.

ORANGUTAN: Was that an addiction coming out or an online dating profile? "Married Male Dope Fiend. Smokin' hot."

CHUTES&LADDERS: Fountainhead, you sound like the kind of guy who's read *The Seven Habits of Highly Effective People* cover to cover. Was one of those habits crack? Give the essays a rest and type three words. "I'm. A. Crackhead."

ORANGUTAN: You know, adderall is like totes cool. Us crackheads, we're like yucky and stuff. We're like so 90s. Go try the adderall edge!

HAIKUMOM: Hey.

ORANGUTAN: The guy's a hoax. Twenty bucks says he's pranking. Let's start a new thread.

HAIKUMOM: Hi, Fountainhead, welcome. As the site administrator, I want to honestly congratulate you for accomplishing what so many addicts only hope for: one clean day. Any time you feel like using, log on here instead. It's worked for me. When it comes to junkies, I dug lower than the dungeon. Once upon a time I had a beautiful family, too. Now all I have is six years clean. Don't lose what I lost, what Chutes&Ladders lost.

CHUTES&LADDERS: Excuse me.

HAIKUMOM: Orangutan, I just checked and Fountainhead has no aliases and has never logged onto this site before under a different pseudonym, which are the usual markers of a scam.

ORANGUTAN: I'm just saying. Who toasts to their first day of sobriety?

CHUTES&LADDERS: I hope it's seltzer in that there champagne glass.

ORANGUTAN: Ginger ale, shirley temple.

CHUTES&LADDERS: "A toast, honey. I had that seven year itch so I became a crackhead."

CHUTES&LADDER/ORANGUTAN: Clink.

HAIKUMOM: Hey, kiddos. Your smiley administrator doesn't want to start purging messages. For rules of the forums click on this link. No personal attacks.

ORANGUTAN: We don't come to this site for a pat on the back.

HAIKUMOM: I'm just saying. R-e-s-p-e-c-t.

CHUTES&LADDERS: I will always give *crack* the respect it deserves. Some purebred poodle comes pissing on my tree trunk? Damn straight I'll chase his ass out my forest.

HAIKUMOM: This here is my forest. You two think you were all humble pie when you started out? Check your original posts.

ORANGUTAN: Oh, I know mine. "I-am-scared-I-will-kill-myself-talk-me-off-the-ledge."

HAIKUMOM: So unless someone gets that desperate they don't deserve our noble company? "Suffer like me, or you ain't legit?"

ORANGUTAN: Haikumom's growing claws.

HAIKUMOM: Just don't act entitled because you got so low. (To Fountainhead.) Sorry. Fountainhead, forgive us. We get very passionate because—

CHUTES&LADDERS: Fountainhead, your Porsche has a massive engine. You got bulging marathon muscles. I'm sure your penis is as big as that javelin you used to throw.

HAIKUMOM: Censored.

CHUTES&LADDERS: But none of those things come close to the size of your ego. If you can put that aside, you may, *may* stand a chance. Otherwise, you're fucked, my friend.

HAIKUMOM: Message purged.

ORANGUTAN: OH MY GOD, WE'RE DYING HERE, DO WE HAVE TO BE SO POLITE ABOUT IT?

HAIKUMOM: Censored.

ORANGUTAN: Oh my G-zero-D. Democracy or dictatorship?

CHUTES&LADDERS: Hey Fountainhead, why the silence?

(Fountainhead logs off.)

HAIKUMOM: Nice work, guys. Congratulations.

CHUTES&LADDERS: You don't suppose he's . . . crawling on the carpet looking for one last rock??

ORANGUTAN: Lordy lord lord, I'm about to go over his house and start looking for one myself!

HAIKUMOM: That's why you're in Japan, little monkey. For now, I'm closing this thread. Fountainhead, if you want to reopen it, email me directly.

Scene 5

(A flower shop in center city Philadelphia. Yaz looks over some brochures. Elliot enters, his limp looking worse.)

YAZ: I was starting to get worried. How you holding?

ELLIOT: Joe's Gym, perfect remedy.

YAZ: You went boxing? Really?

ELLIOT: I had to blow off steam. Women don't get it.

YAZ: Don't be a pig. You've had four leg surgeries, no more boxing.

ELLIOT: Did Odessa call?

YAZ: You know how she is. Shutting herself out from the world.

ELLIOT: We need help this week.

YAZ: And I got your back.

ELLIOT: I'm just saying, pick up the phone and ask, "Do you need anything, Elliot?"

YAZ: I did speak to your dad. Everyone's gathering at the house. People start arriving from PR in a few hours. The next door neighbor brought over two trays of pigs feet.

ELLIOT: I just threw up in my mouth.

YAZ: Apparently a fight broke out over who gets your mom's pocketbooks.

ELLIOT: Those pleather things from the ten-dollar store?

YAZ: Thank you, it's not like she had Gucci purses!

ELLIOT: People just need to manufacture drama.

YAZ: He said they were tearing through Ginny's closets like it was a shopping spree. "I want this necklace!" "I want the photo album!" "Yo, those chancletas are mine!" I'm like, damn, let Ginny be buried first.

ELLIOT: Yo, let's spend the day here.

YAZ: (Handing him some papers.) Brochures. I was being indecisive so the florist went to work on a wedding bouquet. I ruled out seven, you make the final call. Celebration of Life, Blooming Garden, Eternity Wreath.

ELLIOT: All of those have carnations. I don't want a carnation within a block of the church.

YAZ: You told me to eliminate seven. I eliminated seven. Close your eyes and point.

ELLIOT: Am I a particularly demanding person?

YAZ: Yes. What's so wrong with a carnation?

ELLIOT: You know what a carnation says to the world? That they were out of roses at the 7-Eleven. It should look something like Mom's garden.

YAZ: (In agreement.) Graveside Remembrances? That looks something like it . . . I'm re-nominating Graveside Remembrances. Putting it back on the table.

ELLIOT: You couldn't find anything tropical? Yaz, you could find a needle in a damn haystack and you couldn't find a bird of paradise or something?

YAZ: He just shoved some brochures in my hand.

ELLIOT: (Stares her down.) You have an awful poker face.

YAZ: Now, look here.

ELLIOT: You did find something.

YAZ: No. Not exactly.

ELLIOT: How much does it cost? Yaz, this is my mom we're talking about.

YAZ: Five hundred more. Just for the casket piece.

ELLIOT: You can't lie for shit, you never could.

YAZ: Orchid Paradise.

(Yaz hands him another brochure. They look at it together.)

ELLIOT: Aw damn. Damn. That looks like Mom's garden.

YAZ: Spitting image.

ELLIOT: (Pointing.) I think she grew those.

YAZ: Right next to the tomatoes.

ELLIOT: But hers were yellow. Fuck.

YAZ: It's very odd to order flowers when someone dies. Because the flowers are just gonna die, too. "Would you like some death with your death?"

ELLIOT: (A confession.) I didn't water them.

YAZ: (Getting it.) What, are you supposed to be a gardener all of a sudden?

ELLIOT: It doesn't rain for a month and do I grab the hose and water Mom's garden one time?

YAZ: You were feeding her. Giving her meds. Bathing her. I could've come over and watered a leaf. A single petal.

ELLIOT: The last four days, she'd wake me up in the middle of the night. "Did you water the flowers?" "Yeah, Mom, just like you told me to yesterday." "Carry me out back, I want to see." "Mom, you're too heavy, I can't carry you down those steps one more time today."

YAZ: Little white lies.

ELLIOT: Can you do the sermon?

YAZ: This is becoming a second career.

ELLIOT: Because you're the only one who doesn't cry.

YAZ: Unlike Julia.

ELLIOT: (Imitating.); "¡Ay dios mio! ¡Ay! ¡Ay!"

YAZ: I hate public speaking.

ELLIOT: You're a teacher.

YAZ: It's different when it's ideas. Talking about ideas isn't saying something, it's making syllables with your mouth.

ELLIOT: You love ideas. All you ever wanted to do was have ideas.

YAZ: It was an elaborate bait and switch. The ideas don't fill the void, they just help you articulate it.

ELLIOT: You've spoken at City Hall. On the radio.

412

YAZ: You're the face of Main Line Chevrolet. (Pause.) Can I do it in English?

ELLIOT: You could do it in Russian for all I care. I'll just be in the front row acting like my cheek is itchy so no one sees me crying.

YAZ: The elders want a good Spanish sermon.

ELLIOT: Mami Ginny was it. You're the elder now.

YAZ: I'm thirty-one.

ELLIOT: But you don't look a day over fifty.

YAZ: You gotta do me a favor in return. I know this is your tragedy but . . . Call William. Ask him not to come to the funeral.

ELLIOT: Oh shit.

YAZ: He saw the obit in the *Daily News*.

ELLIOT: They were close. Mami Ginny loved that blonde hair. She was the madrina of your wedding.

YAZ: William relinquished mourning privileges. You fall out of love with me, you lose certain rights. He calls talking about, "I want the condo." That I decorated, that I painted. "Oh, and where's the funeral, by the way?" You know, he's been to four funerals in the Ortiz clan and I could feel it, there was a part of him, under it all, that was disgusted. The open casket. The prayers.

ELLIOT: It is disgusting.

YAZ: Sitting in the pew knowing what freaks we are.

ELLIOT: He's good people.

YAZ: Truth is I was at his side doing the same thing, acting like I'm removed, that I'm somehow different.

ELLIOT: Hey, hey, done.

YAZ: One more condition. I go to Puerto Rico with you. We scatter her ashes together.

ELLIOT: Mami Ginny couldn't be buried in Philly. She had to have her ashes thrown at a waterfall in El Yunque, just to be the most Puerto Rican motherfucker around.

YAZ: I saw your Colgate ad.

ELLIOT: Dang, cousin Yaz watches Spanish TV?

YAZ: Shut up.

ELLIOT: I walked into the casting office, flashed my pearly whites, showed them my military ID and I charmed them.

YAZ: Do it.

ELLIOT: Give me a dollar.

YAZ: For that big cheeseburger smile?

(She gives him a dollar.)

ELLIOT: (Smiling.) "Sonrisa, baby!"

(Yaz cracks up laughing, which devolves into tears.)

How we gonna pay for Orchid Paradise?

YAZ: They should have a frequent flower card. They punch a hole. Buy nine funeral bouquets, get the tenth free. We'd be living in a house full of lilies. Look at that guy. Arranging his daisies like little treasures. What do you think it's like to be him? To be normal?

ELLIOT: Normal? A hundred bucks says that dude has a closet full of animal porno at home.

YAZ: I bet in his family funerals are rare occasions. I bet he's never seen a cousin get arrested. Let alone one under the age of eighteen. I bet he never saw his eight-year-old cousin sipping rum through a twisty straw or . . . I just remembered this time cousin Maria was babysitting me . . .

ELLIOT: Fat Maria or buck tooth Maria?

YAZ: Pig. I was dyeing her hair. I had never dyed hair before so I asked her to read me the next step and she handed me the box and said, "You read it." And I said, "My rubber gloves are covered in toxic goop, I can't really hold that right now." And so she held it in front of my eyes and said, "You gonna have to read it because I sure as hell can't."

ELLIOT: I been knowed that.

YAZ: I said, "But you graduated from high school." She said "They just pass you, I just stood in the back." I was in fourth grade. I could read! (Pause.) I have a degree written in Latin that I don't even understand. I paid seventeen thousand dollars for my piano.

ELLIOT: Oh shit.

413

YAZ: I have a mortgage on my piano. Drive two miles north? William told me every time I went to North Philly, I'd come back different. His family has Quaker Oats for DNA. They play Pictionary on New Years. I'd sit there wishing I could scoop the blood out my veins like you scoop the seeds out a pumpkin and he'd be like, "Whatchu thinking about, honey?" and I'd be like, "Nothing. Let's play some Pictionary."

ELLIOT: Yo, being the scholarship case at an all-white prep school really fucked with your head, didn't it?

YAZ: I should've gone to Edison.

ELLIOT: Public school in el barrio. You wouldn't have survived there for a day.

YAZ: Half our cousins didn't survive there.

ELLIOT: True. But you would've pissed your pants. At least their pants was dry when they went down.

YAZ: I thought abuela dying, that would be the end of us. But Ginny grabbed the torch. Christmas, Easter. Now what? Our family may be fucked-up but we had somewhere to go. A kitchen that connected us. Plastic-covered sofas where we could park our communal asses.

ELLIOT: Pop's selling the house. And the plastic-covered sofas. He's moving back to the Bronx, be with his sisters.

YAZ: You going with him? (Elliot shrugs.) Wow. I mean, once that living room is gone, I may never step foot in North Philly again.

ELLIOT: I could go out to L.A. and be a movie star.

YAZ: You need a manager? Shoot I'm coming witchu. Forget Philly.

ELLIOT: Change of scene, baby. Dream team.

YAZ: Probably we should order some flowers first, though. Don'tcha think?

ELLIOT: Orchid Paradise? (Yaz hands him the brochure. To the florist:) Sir?

Scene 6

(The chat room. Orangutan is online, seems upset.)

ORANGUTAN: 2:38 A.M. Tuesday. The witching hour.

(Chutes&Ladders logs on.)

CHUTES&LADDERS: 1:38 P.M. Monday. The lunch hour.

ORANGUTAN: I'm in a gay bar slash internet café in the city of Sapporo. Deafening dance music.

CHUTES&LADDERS: Sure you should be in a bar, little monkey?

ORANGUTAN: (Disappointed.) I flew halfway around the world and guess what? It was still me who got off the plane. (Taking comfort.) Sapporo is always open. The world turns upside down at night.

CHUTES&LADDERS: You're in a city named after a beer sitting in a bar. Go home.

ORANGUTAN: Everything in this country makes sense but me. The noodles in soup make sense. The woodpecker outside my window every evening? Completely logical. The girls getting out of school in their miniskirts and shy smiles? Perfectly natural. I'm floating. I'm a cloud. My existence is one sustained out-of-body experience. It doesn't matter if I change my shoes, there's not a pair I've ever been able to fill. I'm a baby in a basket on an endless river. Wherever I go I don't make sense there.

CHUTES&LADDERS: Hey little monkey. How many days you got?

ORANGUTAN: I think day ninety-six is when the demons really come out to play.

CHUTES&LADDERS: Ninety-six? Girl, hang your hat on that.

ORANGUTAN: I really really really want to smoke crack.

CHUTES&LADDERS: Yeah, well *don't.*

ORANGUTAN: Distract me from myself. What do you really really really want, Chutes&Ladders?

CHUTES&LADDERS: I wouldn't say no to a new car— my Tercel is one sorry sight.

ORANGUTAN: What else?

CHUTES&LADDERS: Tuesday's crossword. On Monday I'm done by the time I sit at my desk. I wish every day could be a Tuesday.

ORANGUTAN: What about your son? Don't you really really really want to call him?

CHUTES&LADDERS: By all accounts, having me be a stranger these ten years has given him the best decade of his life.

ORANGUTAN: I've known you for how long?

CHUTES&LADDERS: Three Christmas Eves. When you logged on you were a stone-cold user. We sang Christmas carols online all night. Now you've got ninety days.

ORANGUTAN: Can I ask you a personal question? What's your day job?

CHUTES&LADDERS: IRS. GS4 paper pusher.

ORANGUTAN: Got any vacation days?

CHUTES&LADDERS: A solid collection. I haven't taken a vacation in ten years.

ORANGUTAN: Do you have money?

CHUTES&LADDERS: Enough to eat steak on Friday nights. Enough to buy pay-per-view boxing.

ORANGUTAN: Yeah, I bet that's all the pay-per-view you buy. (Pause.) Enough money to fly to Japan?

(Pause.)

CHUTES&LADDERS: You should know I'm fifty years old on a good day, I eat three and a half donuts for breakfast and save the remaining half for brunch, I have small hands, six toes on my left foot, and my face resembles a corgi.

ORANGUTAN: If I was looking for a hot screw I wouldn't be logging onto this site.

CHUTES&LADDERS: Damn, was it something I said?

ORANGUTAN: (With honest admiration.) I've been on this planet for twenty six years and you're the only person I've ever met who's more sarcastic than I am yet still believes in god.

CHUTES&LADDERS: (Taking the compliment.) Says the agnostic.

ORANGUTAN: The atheist. Who is very envious of believers. My brain is my biggest enemy—always arguing my soul into a corner. (Pause.) I like you. Come to Japan. We can go get an ice cream. I can show you the countryside.

CHUTES&LADDERS: I don't have a passport. If my Tercel can't drive there, I generally don't go.

ORANGUTAN: Come save me in Japan. Be my knight in shining armor.

CHUTES&LADDERS: I'll admit, I'm a dashing concept. If you saw my flesh and blood, you'd be disappointed.

ORANGUTAN: I see my flesh and blood every day and I've learned to live with the disappointment.

CHUTES&LADDERS: I'm the squarest of the square. I live in a square house on a square block watching a square box eating square-cut fries.

ORANGUTAN: I get it. You were the kid who colored inside the lines.

CHUTES&LADDERS: No, I was the kid who ate the crayons. Was. I went clean and all personality left my life. Flew right out the window. I had to take life on life's terms. Messy, disappointing, bad shit happens to good people, coffee stains on my necktie, boring life.

ORANGUTAN: Maybe we could hang out and have a relationship that has very little to do with crack or addiction or history. We could watch DVDs and microwave popcorn and take walks on the waterfront while we gossip about celebrities. It could be the land of the living.

CHUTES&LADDERS: Stay in the box. Keep things in their place. It's a simple, effective recipe for ten clean years.

ORANGUTAN: Forget simple. I want a goddamn challenge.

CHUTES&LADDERS: You're in recovery and work in a foreign country. That's a challenge.

ORANGUTAN: No. No it's fucking not. Not if I just stay anonymous and alone. Like every day of my shit life so far. A friend, the kind that is nice to you and you are nice to in return. *That* would push the comfort zone. The invitation is open. Come tear my shyness open.

CHUTES&LADDERS: Alright, now you're being weird. Can we change the subject?

(Haikumom appears. She's reading the newspaper.)

HAIKUMOM: Orangutan, cover your ears.

ORANGUTAN: Big Brother, always watching.

HAIKUMOM: Cover your ears, kiddo.

ORANGUTAN: That doesn't really work online.

HAIKUMOM: Okay, Chutes&Ladders, can we g-chat? One on one?

ORANGUTAN: Come on! No talking behind backs.

HAIKUMOM: Fine. Chutes&Ladders, you listening?

CHUTES&LADDERS: Lord have mercy spit it out.

HAIKUMOM: Orangutan may be immature . . .

ORANGUTAN: Hey.

HAIKUMOM: She may be annoying at times . . .

ORANGUTAN: What the f?

HAIKUMOM: She may be overbearing and self-obsessed and a little bit of a concern troll and she can type faster than she can think which often leads to diarrhea of the keyboard—

CHUTES&LADDERS: Your point?

HAIKUMOM: But she's telling you, "Be my friend." When's the last time someone opened your closet door, saw all them skeletons, and said, "Wassup?! Can I join the party?"

CHUTES&LADDERS: Alright, my wrist is officially slapped. Thank you, oh nagging wives.

HAIKUMOM: Internal Revenue Service, 300 North Los Angeles Street 90012? Is that you?

CHUTES&LADDERS: Need my name, too? It's Wilkie. I'll leave it at that.

HAIKUMOM: I'm sending you a care package. Orangutan, you can uncover your ears now. I love you.

ORANGUTAN: Middle finger.

(Fountainhead's logon appears.)

FOUNTAINHEAD: Hey all, thanks for the warm two by four to my head.

HAIKUMOM: Alright, look who's back.

FOUNTAINHEAD: Knives sharpened? Last night we ran out of butter while my wife was cooking and she sent me to the store and it took every bit of strength I could summon not to make a "wrong turn" to that parking lot I know so well. I got the butter and on the car ride home, I couldn't help it, I drove by the lot, and there was my dealer in the shadows. My brain went on attack. "Use one more time just to prove you won't need another hit tomorrow." I managed to keep on driving and bring the butter home. Major victory. And my wife pulls it out of the plastic bag and says, "This is unsalted. I said salted." Then she feels guilty so she says never mind, never mind, she'll just add a little extra salt to the pie crust but I insist. "No, no, no, my wife deserves the right kind of butter and she's gonna get it!" I mean, I bark it, I'm already halfway out the door, my heart was racing all the way to the parking lot and raced even harder when I sat in the car and smoked. So, Michael Jordan is benched with a broken foot. But he'll come back in the finals.

HAIKUMOM: Thanks for the update, Fountainhead. You may not believe this, but we were missing you and worried about you. Don't beat yourself up about the slip. You had three days clean. This time you'll make it to day four.

FOUNTAINHEAD: Be ambitious. Why not reach for a whopping five?

ORANGUTAN: Maybe you'll make it to day thirty if you tell your wife.

FOUNTAINHEAD: I told you, I have my reasons, I cannot do that. My wife has some emotional issues.

ORANGUTAN: (Sarcastic.) No!

FOUNTAINHEAD: Listen? Please? Are you capable of that? She's in therapy twice a week. Depression, manic. I don't want to be the reason she goes down a tailspin. I actually have her best interest in mind.

CHUTES&LADDERS: Yawn.

FOUNTAINHEAD: Ah, Chutes&Ladders. I could feel you circling like a vulture. Weigh in, by all means.

CHUTES&LADDERS: And I repeat. Yawn.

FOUNTAINHEAD: Chutes&Ladders, why do I get the feeling you'd be the first in line for tickets to watch me smoke again? That you'd be in the bleachers cheering if I relapse?

CHUTES&LADDERS: How can you relapse when you don't even think you're addicted?

FOUNTAINHEAD: If you read my original post clearly, I wrote that it's a psychological addiction, not like heroin.

CHUTES&LADDERS: Well see then, you're not a junkie after all.

FOUNTAINHEAD: What is this, first grade recess?

CHUTES&LADDERS: No, this is a site for crackheads trying not to be crackheads anymore. If you're not a crackhead, leave, we don't want you, you are irrelevant, get off my lawn, go.

HAIKUMOM: Chutes&Ladders, please.

CHUTES&LADDERS: I got this.

ORANGUTAN: He's still logged on.

CHUTES&LADDERS: Hey Fountainhead, why did you come to this website?

FOUNTAINHEAD: Because I thoroughly enjoy getting shit on.

HAIKUMOM: Censored.

CHUTES&LADDERS: Why do you want to be here?

FOUNTAINHEAD: Want? The two times I've logged on here I've *wanted* to vomit.

CHUTES&LADDERS: Well? Did you receive some sort of invitation? Did one of us ask you here?

FOUNTAINHEAD: Look, I'm the first to say it. I have a problem.

CHUTES&LADDERS: Adam had problems. Eve had problems. Why are *you here?*

FOUNTAINHEAD: To get information.

CHUTES&LADDERS: Go to Wikipedia. Why are you *here?*

FOUNTAINHEAD: Because I smoke crack.

CHUTES&LADDERS: Go to a dealer. Why are you here?

FOUNTAINHEAD: Because I plan to stop smoking crack.

CHUTES&LADDERS: Fine, when your son has a tummy-ache in the middle of the night and walks in on you tweaking and geeking just tell him, "Don't worry, Junior, daddy's sucking on a glass dick—"

HAIKUMOM (overlaps): Hey!

CHUTES&LADDERS: "—but daddy makes 300K and this is all a part of Daddy's Plan!"

FOUNTAINHEAD: I'M A FUCKING CRACKHEAD.

HAIKUMOM: (Apologetic.) Censored.

FOUNTAINHEAD: Fuck you, Chutes&Ladders.

HAIKUMOM: Bleep.

FOUNTAINHEAD: Fuck you . . . Don't talk about my sons. Don't fucking talk about my boys.

HAIKUMOM: Bleep again.

FOUNTAINHEAD: Are you happy, Chutes&Ladders?

CHUTES&LADDERS: Absolutely not, my friend. I'm a crackhead too and I wouldn't wish it on my worst enemy.

FOUNTAINHEAD: And I *made* 300K, I'm currently unemployed. An unemployed crackhead. At least I still have all my teeth. (They laugh.) Better than I can say for my dealer.

CHUTES&LADDERS: (Being a friend.) Ex-dealer, man.

FOUNTAINHEAD: Ex-dealer. Thank you.

HAIKUMOM: Fountainhead, welcome to the dinner party. Granted, it's a party we never wanted to be invited to, but pull up a chair and pass the salt. Some people here may pour it in your wounds. Just like you, we've all crawled on the floor with a flashlight. We've thrown out the brillo and bought some more. But guess what? You had three days. For three days straight, you didn't try to kill yourself on an hourly basis. Please. Talk to your wife about your addiction. You need every supporting resource. You are in for the fight of your life. You mentioned Wharton. I live in Philly. If you're still in the area and you have an emergency or even a craving, email me directly. Any time of night. Don't take it lightly when I say a sober day for you is a sober day for me. I know you can do this but I know you can't do it alone. So stop being a highly functioning isolator and start being a highly dysfunctional *person*. The only way out it is through it.

ORANGUTAN: (Nostalgic.) Slogans . . .

HAIKUMOM: Y'all know I know em all.

CHUTES&LADDERS: They saved my life.

ORANGUTAN: Your personal favorite. Go.

HAIKUMOM: "Nothing changes if nothing changes."

(Elliot appears at the boxing gym, punching a bag. The Ghost watches him.)

GHOST: Momken men-fadluck ted-dini gawaz saffari?

ORANGUTAN: "It came to pass, it didn't come to stay."

FOUNTAINHEAD: "I obsessively pursue feeling good, no matter how bad it makes me feel."

CHUTES&LADDERS: Okay, now!

ORANGUTAN: Nice!

HAIKUMOM: Rookie don't play!

GHOST: Momken men-fadluck ted-dini gawaz saffari?

(Yaz appears with a pen and notepad, writing.)

YAZ: "We are gathered here in remembrance."

ORANGUTAN: "One hit is too many, one thousand never enough."

HAIKUMOM: "Have an at-ti-tude of gra-ti-tude."

CHUTES&LADDERS: "If you are eating a shit sandwich, chances are you ordered it."

ORANGUTAN: Ding ding ding. We have a winner!

HAIKUMOM: Censored. But good one.

YAZ: (Crossing out, scribbling) "Today we send off our beloved, Ginny P. Ortiz."

GHOST: Momken men-fadluck ted-dini gawaz saffari?

HAIKUMOM: (Turning a page in the paper.) Oh shit!

ORANGUTAN: CENSORED!!!!!! YES!!!!!! Whoooooo!

HAIKUMOM: You got me.

ORANGUTAN: (Victorious.) You know how long I've been waiting to do that?!

HAIKUMOM: My sister Ginny's in the *Daily News!* A nice big picture!

GHOST: Momken men-fadluck ted-dini gawaz saffari?

YAZ: (Scribbling, erasing) "Ginny P. Ortiz was known to many as Mami Ginny."

HAIKUMOM: "Ginny P. Ortiz, A Force For Good In Philadelphia!" That's my sister alright! Page 46 . . .

(Haikumom looks for the page. Elliot punches harder. His leg is starting to bother him.)

ELLIOT: Your leg feels great. Your leg feels like a million bucks. No pain. No pain.

HAIKUMOM: (Finding the page) Obituaries? "In lieu of flowers contributions may be made to . . ."

(Haikumom drops the newspaper.
The Ghost blows on Elliot, knocking him to the floor.)

Intermission

Scene 7

(A diner. Odessa and John, aka Fountainhead, sit in a booth.)

ODESSA: To lapsed Catholics. (They clink coffee mugs.) And you thought we had nothing in common.

JOHN: When did you become interested in Buddhism?

ODESSA: My older brother used to terrorize me during mass. He would point to a statue, tell me about the evil spirit hiding behind it. Fangs, claws. I thought Saint Lazarus was gonna come to life and suck my eyes out. Buddhism? Not scary. If there's spirits, they're hiding inside you.

JOHN: Aren't those the scariest kind?

ODESSA: So, how many days do you have? It should be two now.

JOHN: I put my son's picture on my cell phone so if I get the urge, I can just look at him instead.

ODESSA: How many days?

JOHN: (Small talk.) I love Puerto Rico. On my honeymoon we stayed at that hotel in Old San Juan, the old convent. (Odessa shrugs.) And that Spanish fort at the top of the city? El Morro?

ODESSA: I've always been meaning to make it there.

JOHN: There are these keyholes where the cannons used to fit, and the view of the waves through them, you can practically see the Spanish armada approaching.

ODESSA: I mean, one of these days I've gotta make it to PR.

JOHN: Oh. I just figured . . .

ODESSA: The Jersey shore. Atlantic City. The Philadelphia airport. Oh, I've been places.

JOHN: On an actual plane?

ODESSA: I only fly first class, and I'm still saving for that ticket.

(Odessa's cell phone rings.)

JOHN: You're a popular lady.

ODESSA: (Into her phone, her demeanor completely changing.) What? I told you, the diner on Spring Garden and Third. I'm busy, come in an hour. One hour. Now stop calling me and asking fucking directions. (She hangs up.)

JOHN: Says the one who censors.

ODESSA: My sister died.

JOHN: Right. You sure you're okay?

ODESSA: She's dead, ain't nothing left to do. People act like the world is going to fall apart.

JOHN: You write very Zen messages. And yet.

ODESSA: My family knows every button to push.

JOHN: My condolences. (Pause.) You don't strike me as a computer nerd. I used to employ an entire floor of them.

ODESSA: You should've seen me at first, pecking with two fingers. Now I'm like an octopus with ten little tentacles. In my neck of the woods staying clean is like trying to tap dance on a minefield. The website fills the hours. So how are we gonna fill yours, huh? When was the last time you picked up a javelin?

JOHN: Senior year of high school.

ODESSA: (Hands him a sheet of paper.) There's a sober softball league. Fairmount Park, games on Sundays. Sober bowling on Thursdays.

JOHN: I lied in my first post. I've been smoking crack for two years. I've tried quitting hundreds of times. Day two? Please, I'm in the seven hundredth day of hell.

ODESSA: You got it out of your system. Most people lie at one time or another on the site. The good news is, two years in, there's still time. (Hands him another sheet of paper.) Talbot Recovery Center in Atlanta. It's designed for professionals with addictions. Paradise Recovery in Hawaii. They actually check your income before admitting you. Just for the wealthy. This place in Jersey, it's right over the bridge, they have an outpatient program for professionals like you.

JOHN: I'm tenacious. I'm driven. I love my parents.

ODESSA: Pitchforks against tanks.

JOHN: I relish in paying my taxes.

ODESSA: And you could be dead tomorrow. (Pause.) Is your dealer male or female?

JOHN: I had a few. Flushed their numbers down the toilet like you suggested.

ODESSA: Your original connection. The one who got you hooked.

JOHN: Female.

ODESSA: Did you have sex with her?

JOHN: You don't beat around the bush do you?

ODESSA: I'll take that as a yes. (No answer.) Do you prefer sex when you're high to sex when you're sober?

JOHN: I've never really analyzed it.

ODESSA: It can be a dangerous cocktail. Some men get off on smoking and fucking.

JOHN: All men get off on fucking.

ODESSA: Are you scared your wife will find out you're addicted to crack? Or are you scared she'll find out what came of your wedding vows?

JOHN: I should go.

ODESSA: We just ordered.

JOHN: I promised my son. There's a science fair tomorrow. Something about dioramas and crazy glue.

419

ODESSA: Don't talk about them. Get sober for them.

JOHN: Fuck you.

ODESSA: Leave me three bucks for your coffee.

(He pulls out three dollars. She throws the money back at him.)

You picked up the phone and called me.

JOHN: (He sits down again.) I don't know how to do this. I've never done this before.

ODESSA: I have and it usually doesn't end up so good. One in twenty, maybe, hang around. Most people just don't write one day and then thirty days and then you're wondering . . . And sometimes you get the answer. Cuz their wife looks on their computer and sees the website and logs on and writes, "I found him face down in the snow."

JOHN: How many day ones did you have?

ODESSA: Seven years' worth.

JOHN: Do you still crave?

ODESSA: On the good days, only every hour. Would you rather be honest with your wife, or would you rather end up like me? (Pause.) That wasn't rhetorical.

JOHN: You're not exactly what I wanted to be when I grew up.

ODESSA: Truth. Now we're talking.

(Elliot and Yaz enter.)

YAZ: There she is.

(Elliot and Yaz sit down in the booth.)

ELLIOT: You were supposed to meet us at the flower place.

YAZ: The deposit was due at nine.

ODESSA: My alarm clock didn't go off.

ELLIOT: Were you up on that chat room all night?

ODESSA: (Ignoring him.) Can I get a refill, please?

ELLIOT: Where's the money?

ODESSA: I told you I don't have any money.

ELLIOT: And you think I do? I been paying for Mami Ginny's meds for six months straight—

ODESSA: Well get it from Yaz's mom.

YAZ: My mom put in for the headstone. She got an expensive one.

ODESSA: Headstone? She's getting cremated.

YAZ: She still needs a proper Catholic piece of granite. Right beside abuela, right beside your dad and sister and brother.

ELLIOT: And daughter.

YAZ: Everyone agreed.

ODESSA: No one asked my opinion.

ELLIOT: Everyone who showed up to the family meeting.

ODESSA: I wasn't invited.

YAZ: I texted you twice.

ODESSA: I was out of minutes.

ELLIOT: We just spoke on the phone.

ODESSA: Whatchu want me to do, Elliot, if I say I ain't got no fucking money, I ain't got no money.

JOHN: Hi, I'm John, nice to meet you.

YAZ: Yazmin.

ELLIOT: You one of mom's rehab buddies?

JOHN: We know each other from work.

ELLIOT: You scrub toilets?

ODESSA: (To John.) I'm a practitioner of the custodial arts.

ELLIOT: Is she your sponsor?

JOHN: (To Odessa.) I thought this was going to be a private meeting.

ELLIOT: I'm her son.

JOHN: (To Odessa.) You must have been young.

ELLIOT: But I was raised by my aunt Ginny and that particular aunt just died. (To Odessa.) So now, you got three hours to find some money to pay for one basket of flowers in her funeral.

YAZ: We're all supposed to be helping out.

ODESSA: You both know I run out of minutes all the time. No one could be bothered to drive by and tell me face to face?

ELLIOT: Because you always bothered to drive by and say hello to Mami Ginny when you knew

420

she was sick? Because you bothered to hit me up one time this week and say, "Elliot, I'm sorry your mom died."

ODESSA: You still got one mom alive.

ELLIOT: Really? You want to go there?

YAZ: The flower place needs the money today.

ODESSA: She was my sister and you are my son, too.

YAZ: Guys. Two hundred dollars by end of business day.

ODESSA: That's my rent.

ELLIOT: Then fifty.

ODESSA: I just spent fifty getting my phone back on.

ELLIOT: Ten dollars. For the woman who raised your son! Do we hear ten dollars? Going once!

ODESSA: I spent my last ten at the post office.

ELLIOT: Going twice!

(John goes into his wallet.)

JOHN: Here's fifty.

(They all look at him like he's crazy. He pulls out some more money.)

JOHN: Two hundred?

(Elliot pushes the money back to John with one pointer finger, like the bills might be contaminated.)

ELLIOT: No offense, I don't take money from users.

JOHN: I'm not . . . I think that was my cue.

ODESSA: Sit down. My son was just going.

ELLIOT: Did World's Best Mom here tell you about her daughter?

ODESSA: I'm about to throw this coffee in your fucking face.

YAZ: Come on, Elliot, I'll pay for the flowers.

(Elliot doesn't get up.)

ELLIOT: I looked at that chat room once. The woman I saw there? She's literally not the same person I know. (To John.) Did she tell you how she became such a saint?

JOHN: We all have skeletons.

ELLIOT: Yeah well she's an archaeological dig. Did she tell you about her daughter?

ODESSA: (Suddenly resigned.) Go ahead, I ain't got no secrets.

YAZ: (Getting up.) Excuse me.

ELLIOT: Sit here and listen, Yaz. You were born with a silver spoon and you can't stand how it was for me.

YAZ: I said I'd pay for the goddamn flowers so LET'S GO. NOW!

ELLIOT: My sister and I had the stomach flu, right? For a whole day we couldn't keep nothing down.

ODESSA: Three days . . . You were vomiting three days straight.

ELLIOT: Medicine, juice, anything we ate, it would come right back up. Your co-worker here took us to Children's Hospital.

ODESSA: Jefferson.

ELLIOT: It was wall-to-wall packed. Every kid in Philly had this bug. ERs were turning kids away. They gave us a flier about stomach flu and sent us home. Bright blue paper. Little cartoon diagrams. It said give your kids a spoonful of water every five minutes.

ODESSA: A teaspoon.

ELLIOT: A small enough amount that they can keep it down. Five minutes. Spoon. Five minutes. Spoon. I remember thinking, wow, this is it. Family time. Quality time. Just the three of us. Because it was gentle, the way you said, "Open up." I opened my mouth, you put that little spoon of water into my mouth. That little bit of relief. And then I watched you do the same thing with my little sister. And I remember being like, "Wow, I love you, mom. My moms is alright." Five minutes. Spoon. Five minutes. Spoon. But you couldn't stick to something simple like that. You couldn't sit still like that. You had to have your thing. That's where I stop remembering.

ODESSA: I left.

ELLIOT: A Department of Human Services report. That's my memory. Six hours later a neighbor kicks in the door. Me and my sister are lying in a pile of laundry. My shorts was all messed up. And what I really don't remember is my sister. Quote. "Female infant, approximately two years, pamper and tear ducts dry, likely cause of death, dehydration." Cuz when you dehydrate you can't form a single tear.

JOHN: (To Elliot.) I'm very sorry . . . (He puts some money on the table.) For the coffee. (Exits.)

ELLIOT: That's some friend you got there.

(Pause.)

YAZ: Mary Lou. We never say her name out loud. Mary Lou. Mary Lou. (To Odessa.) One time you came to babysit me, you brought Elliot and Mary Lou—she had just learned to use a straw and she had this soda from 7-Eleven. She didn't want to give me a sip. You yelled at her so bad, you totally cursed her out and I said, "You're not supposed to yell at people like that!" And you said, "No, Yaz, she's gotta learn that y'all are cousins, y'all are flesh and blood, and we share everything. In this family we share everything." You walked out of the room, came back from the kitchen with four straws, sat us down on the floor in a circle, pointed to me and said, "You first." I took a sip. "Elliot's turn." He sipped. "Mary Lou's turn." She sipped. Then you sipped. You made us do like that, taking turns, going around the circle, til that cup was empty.

(Odessa hands Elliot a key.)

ODESSA: The pawn shop closes at five. Go into my house. Take my computer. Pawn it. However much you get, put towards a few flowers, okay?

(Odessa exits.)

Scene 8

(Split scene. Odessa's living room and the chat room. Chutes&Ladders holds a phone.)

ORANGUTAN: Did you hit the call button yet?

CHUTES&LADDERS: I'm working on it.

ORANGUTAN: Where are you? Are you at home?

CHUTES&LADDERS: *Jeopardy!*'s on mute.

ORANGUTAN: Dude, turn off the tube. This is serious. Did you even dial?

CHUTES&LADDERS: Yeah, yeah. (He does.) Alright, it's ringing. What am I going to say?

ORANGUTAN: "Hi, Son, it's Dad."

CHUTES&LADDERS: Wendell. That's his name. (Hangs up.) No answer.

ORANGUTAN: As in, you hung up?

CHUTES&LADDERS: Yes. I hung up.

ORANGUTAN: Dude, way too quick!

CHUTES&LADDERS: What do you have, a stop watch? Do you know the average time before someone answers a telephone?

ORANGUTAN: 3.2 rings.

CHUTES&LADDERS: According to . . .

ORANGUTAN: I don't reveal my sources.

CHUTES&LADDERS: Look, my son's a grown man with a good life.

ORANGUTAN: Quit moping and dial Wendell's number.

CHUTES&LADDERS: This Japan thing is cramping my style. Different networks, different time zones. No concurrent *Jeopardy!* watching.

ORANGUTAN: Deflection: nostalgia.

CHUTES&LADDERS: Humor me.

ORANGUTAN: (Humoring him.) How's my little Trebeky doing?

CHUTES&LADDERS: He's had work done. Man looks younger than he did twenty years ago.

ORANGUTAN: Needle or knife?

CHUTES&LADDERS: Needle. His eyes are still in the right place.

ORANGUTAN: Well, it's working. Meow. Purrrrr. Any good categories?

CHUTES&LADDERS: Before and After.

ORANGUTAN: I love Before and After! But I'll go with . . . Quit Stalling for two hundred. (She hums the *Jeopardy!* theme.)

CHUTES&LADDERS: It's ringing.

ORANGUTAN: My stopwatch is running.

CHUTES&LADDERS: Still ringing.

ORANGUTAN: You're going to be great.

CHUTES&LADDERS: It rang again.

ORANGUTAN: You're a brave soul.

(We hear a man's voice at the other end of the line say, "Hello?" Chutes&Ladders hangs up.)

CHUTES&LADDERS: He must not be around.

ORANGUTAN: Leave a voice mail.

CHUTES&LADDERS: Maybe next time.

(Chutes&Ladders logs off.)

ORANGUTAN: Hey! Don't log off, come on. Chutes&Ladders. Whatever happened to tough love? Log back on, we'll do a crossword. You can't fly before "Final Jeopardy!" Sigh. Anyone else online? Haikumom? I'm still waiting for that daily poem . . . Bueller? Bueller?

(In Odessa's living room, Elliot and Yaz enter.)

YAZ: Wow, look at that computer. Stone age.

ELLIOT: Fred Flinstone shit.

YAZ: Positively Dr. Who.

ELLIOT: Dr. Who?

YAZ: That computer is actually worse than what they give the adjuncts at Swarthmore.

ELLIOT: What does "adjunct" even mean?

YAZ: Exactly. It's the nicest thing she owns.

ELLIOT: Let's not act like this is some heroic sacrifice. Like this makes her the world's martyr.

YAZ: We're not going to get more than fifteen bucks for it.

ELLIOT: Symbols matter, Yaz. This isn't about the money. This is shaking hands. This is tipping your hat. This is holding the door open. This is the bare minimum, the least effort possible to earn the label "person." (Looks at the screen.) What do you think her password is? (Types.) "Odessa." Nope. "Odessaortiz." Nope.

YAZ: It's probably Elliot.

(He types. Haikumom's log-on appears.)

ELLIOT: The irony.

YAZ: I think legally that might be like breaking and entering.

ELLIOT: (Typing.) Hello? Oh shit it posted.

ORANGUTAN: Haikumom! Hit me with those seventeen syllables, baby!

YAZ: Haikumom? What the hell is that?

ELLIOT: Her username. She has the whole world thinking she's some Chinese prophet.

YAZ: Haiku are Japanese.

ELLIOT: "Haiku are Japanese." (Typing.) Hello, Orangutan. How are you?

ORANGUTAN: (Formal.) I am fine. How are you?

ELLIOT: (Typing.) So, I guess you like monkeys, huh?

ORANGUTAN: An orangutan is a primate.

YAZ: Elliot.

ELLIOT: Chill.

ORANGUTAN: And this primate has ninety-eight days. That deserves a poem, don't you think?

ELLIOT: (Typing.) I don't have a poem, but I have a question. What does crack feel like?

ORANGUTAN: What?

YAZ: Elliot, cut it out.

ELLIOT: (Typing.) Sometimes I'm amazed I don't know firsthand.

ORANGUTAN: Who is this?

ELLIOT: (Typing.) How does it make your brain feel?

ORANGUTAN: Like it's flooded with dopamine. Listen, cyberstalker, if you came here for shits and giggles, we are a sadly unfunny bunch.

ELLIOT: (Typing.) Are you just a smoker or do you inject it right into your eyeballs?

ORANGUTAN: Who the fuck is this?

ELLIOT: (Typing.) Haikumom.

ORANGUTAN: Bullshit, you didn't censor me. Quit screwing around, hacker, who are you?

YAZ: You think Ginny would want you acting this way?

ELLIOT: I think Mami Ginny would want Mami Odessa to pay for a single flower on her fucking casket.

YAZ: (Types.) This is not Haikumom. It's her son.

ORANGUTAN: Well, if you're looking for the friends and family thread, you have to go to the home page and create a new logon. This particular forum is for people actually in recovery. Wait, her son the actor? From the Crest ad?

ELLIOT: (Typing.) Colgate.

ORANGUTAN: "Sonrisa baby!" I saw that on YouTube! Your teeth are insanely white. Ever worked in Hollywood?

ELLIOT: (Typing.) Psh. I just had this guy begging me to do a feature film. Gritty, documentary-style, about Marines in Iraq. I just don't want to do anything cheesy.

ORANGUTAN: So you're the war hero . . .

ELLIOT: (Typing.) Haikumom brags.

ORANGUTAN: How's your recovery going? (No answer.) This is the crack forum, but there's a really good pain-meds forum on this site, too. Link here.

YAZ: What is she talking about?

ORANGUTAN: There's a few war vets on that forum, just like you. You'd be in good company.

YAZ: Pain meds? Elliot? (He doesn't respond. Yaz types.) What are you talking about?

ORANGUTAN: Haikumom told us about your history.

YAZ: (Typing.) What history?

ORANGUTAN: Sorry. Maybe she told us in confidence.

ELLIOT: Confidence? They call this shit "world wide" for a reason.

YAZ: (Typing.) I can search all the threads right now.

ORANGUTAN: That you had a bunch of leg surgeries in Iraq. That if a soldier said they hurt, the docs practically threw pills at them. That you OD'd three times and were in the hospital for it. She was real messed up about it. I guess she had hoped the fruit would fall a little farther from the tree.

YAZ: (To Elliot.) Is this true?

ELLIOT: I wasn't a soldier. I was a Marine. Soldiers is the army.

YAZ: Oh my god.

ELLIOT: (Takes the keyboard, types.) What I am: sober. What I am not and never will be: a pathetic junkie like you.

(He unplugs the computer. He throws the keyboard on the ground. He starts unplugging cables violently.)

YAZ: Hold on. Just stop it, Elliot! Stop it!

424

ELLIOT: The one time I ever reached out to her for anything and she made me a story on a website.

YAZ: Why wouldn't you ask me for help? Why would you deal with that alone?

ELLIOT: The opposite of alone. I seen barracks that looked like dope houses. It was four months in my life, it's over. We've chopped up a lot of shit together, Yaz, but we ain't gonna chop this up. This shit stays in the vault. You got me?

YAZ: No!

ELLIOT: Yaz. (He looks her straight in the eye.) Please. Please.

YAZ: I want to grab the sky and smash it into pieces. Are you clean?

ELLIOT: The only thing I got left from those days is the nightmares. That's when he came, and some days I swear he ain't never gonna leave.

YAZ: Who?

(Elliot tries to walk away from the conversation, but the Ghost is there, blocking his path.)

Who?!

ELLIOT: (Almost like a child.) Please, Yaz. Please end this conversation. Don't make me beg, Yaz.

YAZ: The pawn shop closes in fifteen minutes. I'll get the monitor, you grab the computer.

Scene 9

(Chutes&Ladders is at work, on his desk phone. A bundled pile of mail is on his desk. He takes off the rubber band, browses. Junk, mostly.)

CHUTES&LADDERS: (Into the work phone.) That's right. Three W's. Dot. Not the word, the punctuation mark. I-R-S. Not F like flamingo, S like Sam. Dot. Yup, another one. Gov. Grover orange victor.

(Orangutan appears, online.)

ORANGUTAN: I'm doing it. I'm almost there. *And* I can chat! Japan is so advanced. Internet cafés are like parking meters here.

CHUTES&LADDERS: Where are you and what are you doing?

ORANGUTAN: Sapporo train station. Just did some research. Get this: in the early 80's, they straightened all the rivers in Hokkaido.

CHUTES&LADDERS: Why?

ORANGUTAN: To create jobs the government straightened the rivers! Huge bodies of water, manual laborers, scientists, engineers, bulldozers, and the rivers became straight! How nuts is that?

CHUTES&LADDERS: People can't leave good enough alone. Why are humans so damn restless?

ORANGUTAN: It's not restlessness. It's ego. Massive, bizarre ego.

CHUTES&LADDERS: Can't let a river be a river. (Into the phone.) The forms link is on the left.

ORANGUTAN: Now it's the aughts, people keep being born, jobs still need creating, but there's no curves left to straighten, so, drum roll, the government is beginning a new program to put all the original turns back in the rivers! Ever heard of Kushiro?

CHUTES&LADDERS: Is that your new boyfriend's name?

ORANGUTAN: Ha. Ha ha ha. It's home of the hundred-mile-long Kushiro River, which is the pilot project, the first river they're trying to re-curve.

CHUTES&LADDERS: Kushiro River. Got it. Burned in the brain. One day I'll win a Trivial Pursuits wedge with that. (Into the phone.) You, too, ma'am. (He hangs up.)

ORANGUTAN: My train to Kushiro leaves in twenty minutes. My heart is pounding.

CHUTES&LADDERS: I don't follow.

ORANGUTAN: Kushiro is the town where I was born. I'm going. I'm doing it.

CHUTES&LADDERS: Hold on, now you're throwing curve balls.

ORANGUTAN: In my hand is a sheet of paper. On the paper is the address of the house where my birth parents once lived. I'm going to knock on their door.

(Chutes&Ladder's desk phone rings.)

CHUTES&LADDERS: (Into the phone.) Help desk, please hold. (To Orangutan.) How long have you had that address for?

ORANGUTAN: It's been burning a hole in my pocket for two days. I hounded my mom before I left Maine. She finally wrote down the name of the adoption agency. The first clue, the first evidence of who I was I ever had. I made a vow to myself, if I could stay sober for three months, I would track my parents down. So a few days ago class ended early, I went to the agency, showed my passport, and thirty minutes later I had an address on a piece of paper. Ask me anything about Kushiro. All I've done the last two days is research it. I'm an expert. Population, 190,000. There's a tech school, there's an airport.

CHUTES&LADDERS: Why are you telling me this? To get my blessing?

ORANGUTAN: I tell you about the things I do.

CHUTES&LADDERS: You don't want my opinion, you want my approval.

ORANGUTAN: Hand it over.

CHUTES&LADDERS: No.

ORANGUTAN: Don't get monosyllabic.

CHUTES&LADDERS: Take that piece of paper and use it as kindling for a warm winter fire.

ORANGUTAN: Jeez, what did they slip into your Wheaties this morning?

CHUTES&LADDERS: Do a ritual burning and never look back. You have three months. Do you know the worth in gold of three months? Don't give yourself a reason to go back to the shadows.

ORANGUTAN: I'm in recovery. I have no illusions about catharsis. I realize what will most likely happen is nothing. Maybe something tiny. A microscopic butterfly flapping her microscopic wings.

CHUTES&LADDERS: Live in the past, follow your ass.

ORANGUTAN: Don't you have the slightest ambition?

CHUTES&LADDERS: Yes, and I achieve it every day. Don't use and don't hurt anyone. Two things

I used to do on a daily basis. I don't do them anymore. Done. Dream realized. No more dreaming.

(His phone rings again.)

(Into the phone.) Continue holding, please.

ORANGUTAN: When was the last time you went out on a limb?

CHUTES&LADDERS: Three odd weeks ago.

ORANGUTAN: Did you try Hazelnut instead of French Roast?

CHUTES&LADDERS: There's a new secretary down the hall, she's got a nice smile. I decided to go say hello. We had a little back and forth, I said, let's have lunch, she said maybe but meant no, I turned away, looked down and my tie was floating in my coffee cup.

ORANGUTAN: I waited three months to tell you this, every step of the way, the train ride, what the river looks like. What their front door looks like. (Pause.) I'm quitting this site. I hate this site. I fucking hate this site.

CHUTES&LADDERS: You're already losing it and you haven't even gotten on the train.

ORANGUTAN: Three days ago I suggested you and I meet face to face and you blew a fucking gasket.

CHUTES&LADDERS: That's what this is about?

ORANGUTAN: Don't flatter yourself. This is about me wanting relationships. With humans, not ones and zeroes. So we were once junkies. It's superficial. It's not real friendship.

CHUTES&LADDERS: I beg to differ.

ORANGUTAN: Prove me wrong.

CHUTES&LADDERS: Search down that address and a hundred bucks says your heart comes back a shattered light bulb.

ORANGUTAN: You mean, gasp, I'll actually FEEL something?

CHUTES&LADDERS: What are you going to do if the address is wrong? What if the building's been bulldozed? What if some new tenant lives there? What if the woman who gave you birth then gave you away answers the door?

ORANGUTAN: I DON'T KNOW! A concept you clearly avoid at all costs. Learn how to live, that's all I'm goddamn trying to do!

(His phone rings. He picks up the receiver and hangs it up.)

CHUTES&LADDERS: I have three grandsons. You know how I know that? Because I rang my son's doorbell one day. Step 9, make amends. And his wife answered, and I don't blame her for hating me. But I saw three little boys in that living room and one of those boys said, "Daddy, who's that man at the door?" And my son said to *my grandson,* "I don't know. He must be lost." My son came outside, closed the door behind him, exchanged a few cordial words and then asked me to go.

ORANGUTAN: So I shouldn't even try.

CHUTES&LADDERS: I had five years sober until that day.

ORANGUTAN: You really believe in your heart of hearts I should not even try. (Pause.) Coward.

(His phone rings. He unplugs the phone line.)

CHUTES&LADDERS: You think it's easy being your friend?

ORANGUTAN: Sissy. You walk the goddamn earth scared of your own shadow, getting smaller and smaller, until you disappear.

CHUTES&LADDERS: You tease me. You insult me. It's like breathing to you.

ORANGUTAN: You fucking idiot. Why do little girls tease little boys on the playground at recess? Why the fuck were cooties invented? You fucking imbecile!

CHUTES&LADDERS: You disappeared for three months. I couldn't sleep for three months!

ORANGUTAN: I wanted to impress you. I wanted to log on and show you I could be better. And I was an idiot because you're just looking for cowards like you. I'm logging off. This is it. It's over.

CHUTES&LADDERS: Orangutan.

ORANGUTAN: Into the abyss I climb, looking for a flesh and blood hand to grasp onto.

CHUTES&LADDERS: Little monkey, stop it.

ORANGUTAN: I'm in the station. My train is in five minutes, you gave me all the motivational speech I need, I'm going to the platform, I'm getting on the train, I'm going to see the house where I was born.

(She logs off. Chutes&Ladders grabs his phone and hurls it into his wastebasket. He throws his calculator, his mail pile, his pen cup to the ground. Left on his desk is one padded envelope.)

CHUTES&LADDERS: "To Chutes&Ladders Wilkie." "From Haikumom Ortiz."

(He rips it open, pulls out a deflated orange water wing, puts it over his hand.)

Scene 10

(Split scene. Lights rise on a church. Elliot and Yaz stand at the lectern.)

YAZ: It is time to honor a woman.*

ELLIOT: A woman who built her community with a hammer and nails.

YAZ: A woman who knew her nation's history. Its African roots. European roots. Indigenous roots. A woman who refused to be enslaved but lived to serve.

ELLIOT: A carpenter, a nurse, a comedian, a cook.

YAZ: Eugenia Ortiz.

ELLIOT: Mami Ginny.

(Lights rise on Odessa's house. She sits on her floor. She scoops a spoonful of water from a mug, pours it onto the floor in a slow ribbon.)

YAZ: She grew vegetables in her garden lot and left the gate open so anyone could walk in and pick dinner off the vine.

ELLIOT: She drank beer and told dirty jokes and even the never-crack-a-smile church ladies would be rolling laughing.

YAZ: She told me every time I visited, "Yaz, you're going to Juilliard."

_____
*This eulogy is inspired by and owes much debt to Roger Zepernick's eulogy for Eugenia Burgos.

ELLIOT: Every morning when I left for school, "Elliot, nobody can make you invisible but you."

(Lights rise on the Sapporo train station. Orangutan is on the platform. We hear a loudspeaker boarding announcement in Japanese.)

YAZ: Zero.

ELLIOT: Birth children.

YAZ: One.

ELLIOT: Adopted son.

(Odessa pours another spoonful of water on the floor. Again, it creates a slow ribbon.)

YAZ: Three.

ELLIOT: Years in the army nurse corps.

YAZ: Three.

ELLIOT: Arrests for civil disobedience. I was in Iraq and she was demonstrating for peace.

YAZ: Forty seven.

ELLIOT: Wheelchair ramps she installed in homes with disabled children or elderly.

(Odessa pours another spoonful of water to the floor. A small pool is forming.)

YAZ: Twelve.

ELLIOT: Abandoned lots she turned into city-recognized public gardens.

(Another spoonful.)

YAZ: Twenty-two.

ELLIOT: Godchildren recognized by this church.

(Another spoonful.)

YAZ: One hundred and thirty.

ELLIOT: Abandoned homes she refurbished and sold to young families.

(In the Sapporo station we hear a final loud-speaker boarding announcement. Orangutan is still on the platform. She seems frozen, like she cannot move.)

YAZ: All while having a fresh pot of rice and beans on the stove every night. For any hungry stranger. And the pilgrims stopped. And they planted roots, because she was here. We are the living, breathing proof.

427

ELLIOT: I am the standing . . . Excuse me.

(He exits.)

YAZ: Elliot is the standing, walking testimony to a life. She. Was. Here.

(Odessa turns the cup upside down. It is empty.)

Scene 11

(Chutes&Ladders at his desk. In front of him: an inflated orange water wing.)

CHUTES&LADDERS: (On the phone.) Yeah, it's a 1995 Tercel. Midnight blue. It's got a few miles. A hundred and twenty thousand. But like I said, I'll give it to you for three hundred below Kelley Blue Book. Yup, automatic. Just got new brake pads. Cassette deck, mint condition. I'll even throw in a few tapes. Tina Turner and Lionel Richie. Oh, hold on, call waiting.

(He presses mute. Sings to himself.)

A tisket, a tasket.

A green and yellow basket.

I bought a basket for my mommy.

On the way I dropped it.

Was it red? No no no no!
Was it brown? No no no no!

(Back into the phone.) Sorry about that. I got someone else interested. No, it's alright, I have them on hold. You need to see this thing tonight if you're serious. I put this listing up thirty minutes ago, my phone is ringing off the hook. 6:30? Hey I didn't mention. Little lady has racing stripes.

Scene 12

(Split scene. Lights rise in the Sapporo train station, same as before. Orangutan has laid down on the platform and fallen asleep, her backpack like a pillow.

Lights rise on Odessa's house, that night. Her phone rings. We hear loud knocking.)

ELLIOT: (Offstage.) Mami Odessa! Open the door!

(More ringing.)

ELLIOT: (Offstage.) Yo, mom!

YAZ: (Offstage.) She's not there.

ELLIOT: (Offstage.) Can't you hear her phone ringing? Move out the way.

YAZ: (Offstage.) Be careful, your leg!

(A few kicks and the door bursts open. Yaz and Elliot enter, switch on the lights. Odessa is in a heap, motionless, on the floor. Yaz runs and holds Odessa in her arms.)

YAZ: Oh shit. Odessa! Odessa! Wake up.

(She slaps her face a few times.)

YAZ: Her pulse is racing. (Yaz opens her cell phone, dials.)

(Elliot finds a spoon on the floor.)

ELLIOT: Oh no. Oh no you fucking didn't! MOM!!! Get up!

YAZ: (Into the phone.) Hi, I need an ambulance. I have someone unconscious here. I think it's an overdose, crack cocaine. Yes, she has a pulse. 33 Ontario Street. No, no seizures, she's just a lump. Well what should we do while we wait? Okay. Yes. (She hangs up.) They're on their way. Elevate her feet.

ELLIOT: Help me get her to the sofa. One, two, three.

(Elliot lifts her with Yaz's help. They struggle under her weight. In fact they lift the air. Odessa stands up, lucid, and watches the action: Elliot and Yaz struggling under her invisible weight.)

YAZ: Watch her head.

ELLIOT: Aw, fuck, my leg.

YAZ: Careful.

(They set "Odessa" on the sofa, while Odessa watches, unseen, calm.)

ODESSA: I must be in the terminal. Between flights. The layover.

YAZ: Oh god, not two in one day, please.

ELLIOT: She's been through this shit a million times. She's a survivor! WAKE UP! Call your mom. She'll get here before the ambulance.

(Yaz dials.)

ODESSA: I've been to the airport, one time. My dad flew here from Puerto Rico. First time

I was gonna meet him. We stood by the baggage claim, his flight was late, we waited forever. There was one single, lone suitcase, spinning around a carousel.

YAZ: (To Elliot.) Voice mail. (Into the phone.) Mom? Call me back immediately, it's an emergency.

ELLIOT: Give me that. (Grabs the phone.) Titi, Odessa fucking OD'd and she's dying in her living room and I can't take this anymore! COME GET US before I walk off and leave her on the sofa! (He hangs up.)

YAZ: If you need to, go. No guilt. I got this.

ELLIOT: She's my *mom.* Can I be angry? Can you let me be angry?

YAZ: Why is this family plagued? (Elliot gets up.) Where are you going?

ELLIOT: To find something fragile.

(He exits. We hear something shatter.)

ODESSA: Everyone had cleared away from the carousel. Everyone had their bags. But this one was unclaimed. It could still be there for all I know. Spiraling. Spinning. Looking for an owner. Abandoned.

(In the Sapporo station, a policeman enters with a bright, beaming flashlight and points it at Orangutan.

In Odessa's house, a radiant white light suddenly pours in from above. Odessa looks up, is overwhelmed. It is beautiful. Yaz sees it.)

YAZ: Dear god, do you see that?

ELLIOT: (Enters, looks up, not seeing it.) What?

YAZ: (To Odessa.) It's okay Odessa, go, go, we love you, I love you Titi, you are good, you *are* good. Oh my god, she's beautiful.

ELLIOT: What are you talking about?

YAZ: It's okay, it's okay. We love you Odessa.

POLICEMAN: (In Japanese.) Miss, miss, are you okay?

ORANGUTAN: (Waking.) English, please.

POLICEMAN: No sleeping on the floor.

ORANGUTAN: (Getting up slowly.) Sorry.

POLICEMAN: Are you sick?

ORANGUTAN: No.

POLICEMAN: Are you intoxicated?

ORANGUTAN: No. I'm very sorry. I just got tired. I'll go. I'm going.

POLICEMAN: Please, can I give you a hand?

ORANGUTAN: No. I got it.

(Orangutan exits. The policeman turns off his flashlight, exits.

The sound of an ambulance siren and suddenly the white light disappears. Odessa crawls onto the couch and slips into Yaz's arms, where she's been all along.)

YAZ: Holy shit . . .

ELLIOT: What's happening, Yaz? What the fuck was that?

YAZ: You've got to forgive her, Elliot. You have to.

Scene 13

(The chat room.)

CHUTES&LADDERS: Oh nagging wives? Orangutan? Hello? Earth to Orangutan. Come on, three days straight I been worrying about you. I have time-sensitive information. Ground control to major Orangutan.

ORANGUTAN: Ta da.

CHUTES&LADDERS: Where you been?

ORANGUTAN: Here. There. Morrisey and Nine Inch Nails on loop.

CHUTES&LADDERS: Is that what the kids like these days?

ORANGUTAN: (Rolls eyes.) That was me rolling my eyes.

CHUTES&LADDERS: Guess what I did.

ORANGUTAN: (She shrugs.) That was me shrugging.

CHUTES&LADDERS: Guess.

ORANGUTAN: Guess what I didn't do?

CHUTES&LADDERS: Meet your birth parents?

ORANGUTAN: Board the train.

CHUTES&LADDERS: Sorry.

ORANGUTAN: Don't apologize. You had my number.

CHUTES&LADDERS: Guess what I did.

ORANGUTAN: Told me so. Had my shit pegged.

CHUTES&LADDERS: I sold my Tercel. My plane lands in Narita Airport on Wednesday.

ORANGUTAN: What?

CHUTES&LADDERS: American Airlines flight 3312. Arriving 10:01 A.M.

ORANGUTAN: You're a dumb ass. Tokyo? Do you have any idea how far that is from Hokkaido? And how much a ticket on the train costs? Oy, and how the hell am I going to get out of teaching that day? Oh, you doll-face, you duckie!

CHUTES&LADDERS: I'll be wearing a jean jacket and a Padres cap. That's how you'll know me.

ORANGUTAN: Oh Chutes&Ladders. You old bag of bones, you! You old so-and-so, you mensch, you human being! Why the hell didn't you tell me?

CHUTES&LADDERS: I'm just hoping I have the guts to get on the plane.

ORANGUTAN: Of course you're getting on that damn plane! For me you did this?

(Fountainhead logs on.)

FOUNTAINHEAD: Hey everyone. I managed to find one computer here at the hospital that works. Odessa asked me to post a message on her behalf. She landed on "Go." Hit reset on the timer. Back to day one.

ORANGUTAN: Who's Odessa?

FOUNTAINHEAD: Sorry. Haikumom.

ORANGUTAN: What? Do you log on here just to mock us?

CHUTES&LADDERS: Hold on, is she okay?

FOUNTAINHEAD: Cardiac arrest. They said she was one hair from a coma. She hadn't used in six years and her system went nuts.

CHUTES&LADDERS: So she's alive?

FOUNTAINHEAD: And just barely ticking. Tubes in and out of her nose. She's responsive, she mumbled a few words.

ORANGUTAN: You can't be serious.

CHUTES&LADDERS: Why are you there? Were you using with her?

FOUNTAINHEAD: No.

CHUTES&LADDERS: Did you sell her the stuff?

FOUNTAINHEAD: No, Jesus, of course not. She gave them my number, I'm her emergency contact. Why, I have no idea, we're practically strangers. Getting here to the hospital, seeing her like that . . . I don't mean this as an insult, but she looked not human. Bones with skin covering. Mummy-like.

ORANGUTAN: Fuck. You.

FOUNTAINHEAD: I'm being descriptive. I'm being honest. The thought of my boys walking in on me like that. My wife finding me . . .

ORANGUTAN: That woman is the reason I'm. Oh god, you get complacent for one second! One second! You get comfortable for one minute!

CHUTES&LADDERS: Fountainhead, does she have family there? Has anyone come through her room?

FOUNTAINHEAD: Apparently a son and a niece but they had to catch a flight to San Juan.

CHUTES&LADDERS: No parents? No other children? A friend? A neighbor?

FOUNTAINHEAD: None showed up.

CHUTES&LADDERS: Fountainhead. You have a family, I absolutely understand that, and I mean zero disrespect when I say, when I beg of you this: your job on this earth has just changed. It's not to be a husband or a father or a CEO. It's to stay by that woman's side. Make sure she gets home safe. Bathe her. Feed her. Get her checked into a rehab, inpatient. Do not leave her side for a second. Can you do this?

FOUNTAINHEAD: I have one day clean. I'm not meant to be a saint.

CHUTES&LADDERS: Tell me now, swear on your mother's name, otherwise I'm on the first flight to Philadelphia.

FOUNTAINHEAD: I don't know.

CHUTES&LADDERS: Look man, do you believe in God?

FOUNTAINHEAD: Sure, along with unicorns and the boogeyman.

CHUTES&LADDERS: How about miracles?

FOUNTAINHEAD: When the Phils are winning.

CHUTES&LADDERS: How about actions? I bet you believe in those.

FOUNTAINHEAD: Yeah.

CHUTES&LADDERS: Your lifeboat has just arrived. Get on board or get out of the way.

FOUNTAINHEAD: I'll take care of Odessa. You have my word. My solemn word. (Pause.) She did manage to say one thing. Someone has to take over site admin. She doesn't want the chatroom full of curse words.

(Fountainhead's phone rings.)

I gotta go.

CHUTES&LADDERS: You gave us your word. Don't be a stranger.

(He logs off. Into the phone.)

FOUNTAINHEAD: Hi, honey, sorry I haven't called sooner. Listen, I'm not coming home tonight, just order in. I have a friend who got sick, she's having an emergency. No, it's not a romantic friend but she needs my help. Honey? Honey . . .

(The call is over.)

Scene 14

(Puerto Rico. A hotel room. Yaz works on her laptop as a screen lights up:)

FREEDOM&NOISE
STATUS: ONLINE

FREEDOM&NOISE: Hello, I am Freedom&Noise. Current location: Rainforest B&B, Puerto Rico. This is my job app for interim site admin. Experience with chat rooms: zero. Experience with drugs: one doobie in high school. But Fountainhead said it was up to you guys if you would have me so please hear me out. Haikumom is my aunt. For a few years she was my crazy babysitter. The baddest hide-and-seek player north of Girard Avenue. Dress up, booby traps, forts. Until I was eight and, poof, she disappeared. New babysitter, zero explanation. So my first Thanksgiving home from college I walk in and there's Haikumom, stuffing pasteles in the kitchen. Hadn't seen her in ten years. "What up, little niece? Congratulations on college." She planted a big wet one on my cheek and pulled a necklace from her shirt and said, "You know what these gold letters mean? The N is for Narcotics, the A is for Anonymous, and today is my two-year anniversary of being clean." (Pause) I remember sitting next to her at that Thanksgiving table, this question first rooting itself deep in my gut. "What did I do to earn all that I have? Have I done anything difficult in my whole life?" So if you'll have me while Haikumom recovers, I'll be paying a babysitter back for all the times she let me win at Uno. Five-seven-five right? (Counting syllables on her fingers) Box full of ashes . . .

(Elliot enters from the bathroom, freshly showered, pulling on a shirt.)

ELLIOT: Whatchu looking at, Willis?

YAZ: Sh. I'm counting syllables.

(Elliot looks over her shoulders at the computer.)

ELLIOT: Hold up. Don't read that shit, Yaz.

YAZ: You know how Odessa got into haiku in the first place?

ELLIOT: For real, close the computer.

YAZ: I went through this Japanese minimalist phase freshman year. Rock Gardens, Zen Buddhism, the works. I gave her a haiku collection for Christmas.

ELLIOT: Yeah, and you gave me a midget tree that died by New Year's.

YAZ: Bonsai. You didn't water it.

ELLIOT: (Closing her laptop.) For the two days I'm away from Philly, let me be away from Philly?

YAZ: You know where I was gonna be by thirty? Two kids. Equal-housework marriage. Tenure, no question. Waaaay tenured, like by the age of twenty-four. Carnegie Hall debuts Yazmin Ortiz's "Oratorio for Electric Guitar and Children's Choir." I wrote a list on a piece of paper and dug a hole in Fairmount Park and put it in the ground and said, "When I turn thirty, I'll dig it up and cross it all off." And I promise you I'll never have the courage to go to that spot with a shovel and face my list full of crumbs, decoys, and bandaids.

ELLIOT: Married with kids, what an awful goal.

YAZ: Odessa's done things.

ELLIOT: Well, when you throw her a parade, don't expect me to come.

YAZ: You've done things.

ELLIOT: I wouldn't come to my own parade either.

YAZ: Ginny did things. What have I done?

ELLIOT: Second-grade Language Arts. You glued my book report.

YAZ: I couldn't stop your leg from getting chewed up.

ELLIOT: Fairmount little league basketball. You kept score, you brought our equipment.

YAZ: I didn't hold your hand when you were in the desert popping pills trying to make yourself disappear. I didn't keep Odessa away from that needle. I didn't water a single plant in Ginny's garden. We're in PR and I'm gonna dig a new hole and I'm not putting a wish or a list in there, I'm putting a scream in there. And I'm gonna sow it like the ugliest foulest and most necessary seed in the world and it's going to bloom! This time it's going to fucking bloom!

ELLIOT: My eyes just did this weird thing. For a second, it was Mom standing in front of me.

YAZ: Odessa?

ELLIOT: Ginny.

YAZ: Elliot, your birth mother saved your life by giving you away. You think she's the one holding you back? Nobody can make you invisible but you.

(Elliot doesn't respond. Yaz begins gathering her stuff hastily.)

Now we got some ashes to throw. El Yunque closes in an hour and a half.

ELLIOT: Maybe we should do this tomorrow.

YAZ: I gotta make a call. I'll be in the lobby!

(She exits.)

ELLIOT: Yaz?

(The Ghost appears. He's probably been there the whole time.)

Yaz!

GHOST: Momken men-fadluck ted-dini gawaz saffari?

(The Ghost reaches out his hand to touch Elliot.)

Momken men-fadluck ted-dini gawaz saffari?

(The second they make contact, Elliot spins on his heels and grabs the Ghost. The Ghost defends himself, pulling away. They start pushing, grabbing, fighting. The Ghost is looking for something—is it Elliot's wallet?)

Momken men-fadluck ted-dini gawaz saffari?

(The Ghost finds Elliot's wallet and tears through it, hurling its contents onto the floor. Elliot attacks again, but this time the Ghost reaches out his hand and touches Elliot's face. Elliot freezes, unable to move, as the Ghost's hands glide across his features, considering each one with authority, taking inventory.)

Momken men-fadluck ted-dini gawaz saffari?

(The Ghost is gone. Elliot catches his breath, shaken. He reaches into his pocket and pulls out a bottle of pills. He puts one pill in his hand. Then he empties the entire bottle of pills into his hand. He stares at the pills, wanting to throw them away.)

432

Scene 15

(Split scene. Odessa's bathroom. The bathtub is filled with water. John enters, carrying a very weak Odessa. Odessa is wearing shorts and a bra, a modest outfit for bathing. John lowers her gently into the bathtub.)

JOHN: Does that feel okay?

(Odessa barely nods.)

It's not too hot or cold?

(Odessa shakes her head.)

I don't know how to do this. These are things women do. Take care of sick people. Make the wounds go away.

(He takes a sponge and starts to bathe her.)

Is this okay?

(He lifts her arms and washes her armpits. Embarrassed at first, but quickly gets the swing of it.)

We check you in at 4:30 so we have plenty of time to clean you up and get you in good clothes, okay? You'll go in there looking like a decent woman.

(He stops.)

I spoke to my wife while you were sleeping. I told her to go under my bookmarks, find the website. I gave her my logon, my password. She's probably reading it right now. So, uh, thank you.

(Odessa whispers something inaudible.)

What was that?

(She gestures for him to lean in. She whispers into his ear.)

One more time.

(She whispers a little louder.)

Did someone take swimming lessons?

(She whispers again.)

Did someone put on water wings?

(She nods. He continues to bathe her, gently, in silence as:

Lights rise on Tokyo. Narita Airport. Orangutan sits on the floor by the luggage carousel. At her feet is a sign that says CHUTES&LADDERS. She throws the sign like a Frisbee across the floor and gets up to leave. Chutes&Ladders enters, rolling a suitcase behind him. He waves to Orangutan.)

CHUTES&LADDERS: Orangutan?

ORANGUTAN: What the holy hell?

CHUTES&LADDERS: Sorry. Sorry. I tried calling but my cell doesn't work here. I told you I'm no good at this fancy kind of living.

ORANGUTAN: You were supposed to land yesterday, you were too scared to get on the plane. You rebook, you were supposed to land today, three hours ago. Everyone got their luggage already. The last person pulled the last suitcase from the carousel half an hour ago. I thought, wow, this one sure knows how to play a joke on the ladies. I thought you had left me at the fucking altar.

CHUTES&LADDERS: I got sick on the flight. Totally embarrassing. I had a panic attack as the plane landed and I started tossing into the doggy bag right next to this nice old lady. I've been sitting on the bathroom floor emptying my stomach. Then I had to find a toothbrush and toothpaste and mouthwash because I didn't want to greet you with bad breath and all.

(She looks skeptical. She sniffs his mouth quickly.)

ORANGUTAN: Minty. (Pause.) Oh, you dummy, you big old dummy. Put her here, you San Diego Padre.

(She extends her hand, he takes it. A long handshake. Their first physical contact.)

ORANGUTAN: What's your name?

CHUTES&LADDERS: Clay. Clayton Buddy Wilkie.

ORANGUTAN: I'm Madeleine Mays.

CHUTES&LADDERS: It's weird, huh?

ORANGUTAN: Totally weird. The land of the living.

(They hug. They melt into each other's arms. A hug of basic survival and necessary friendship. Then they exit, rolling his suitcase off as lights rise in:

Puerto Rico. A rock outcropping looking out over a waterfall. Elliot is there, looking down at the water.)

ELLIOT: (Looking down.) Oh shit! Yaz, you gotta see this! Yaz? Fucking Johnny Appleseed of El Yunque.

(Yaz enters holding a soil-covered flower bulb. She compares the root against a field book.)

YAZ: I found my spiral ginger! This is going right next to the aloe by the kitchen door, baby!

ELLIOT: Yo, this science experiment ain't getting past security.

YAZ: Experiment my ass. I'm planting these in Ginny's garden.

ELLIOT: Customs gonna sniff that shit from a mile away.

YAZ: (Putting the bulb in a Ziploc baggie full of dirt and bulbs.) China rose . . . Seagrape . . . Some kind of fern . . .

ELLIOT: When they cuff those wrists, I don't know you.

YAZ: I'll hide them in my tampon box.

ELLIOT: That don't work. My first trip to PR, Mami Ginny smuggled a coquí back with her Kotex and got arrested. Front page of the *Daily News*.

YAZ: Good shit. (A dirty little secret.) You know what grandma did?

ELLIOT: Do I want to?

YAZ: She used to smuggle stuff back, too. She'd tuck it below her boobs. She had storage space under there!

ELLIOT: Yo you think if I jumped off this rock right now and dove into that water, I'd survive?

YAZ: Just watch out for the huge boulders and the footbridge.

ELLIOT: It's tempting. That spray. (His phone beeps.) Reception in the rainforest.

YAZ: Kind of ruins the romance.

ELLIOT: (Reads a text message.) Damn, that was fast.

YAZ: What?

ELLIOT: Pop sold the house. Did he even put out a listing?

YAZ: Not that I know of.

ELLIOT: That's like a VW bus going from zero to sixty in three seconds. Don't make no sense.

YAZ: Must have been an inside job.

ELLIOT: I guess so.

YAZ: A way way inside job . . .

ELLIOT: Yaz . . .

YAZ: (Conspiratorially.) Yeeeees?

ELLIOT: What did you do?

YAZ: (Very conspiratorially.) Nothing . . .

ELLIOT: Holy shit!

YAZ: Put my Steinway on craigslist. Got four responses before you made it down to the lobby. My eighty-eight keys are worth more than Ginny's whole house. Sadly. I'll buy an upright.

ELLIOT: You are one crazy motherfucking adjunct! Yo, I don't know if el barrio is ready for you. I don't know if they can handle you!

YAZ: Oh, they gonna handle me. It'll be the Cousins House. We'll renovate the kitchen. You redo the plumbing, I'll hook up a little tile backsplash.

ELLIOT: I watched Bob Villa with Pop, but I ain't no handyman.

YAZ: Just wait, Mr. Home Depot. You're gonna be like, "Fuacata, fuacata, fuacata" with your power drill and nail gun and vice grips.

ELLIOT: Something like that.

YAZ: Well? Get to it. Toss 'em.

ELLIOT: Me? Why the hell do you think I let you come along?

(He hands Yaz the box.)

YAZ: Well then say something. Pray.

ELLIOT: I'm all out of prayers.

YAZ: Me, too. Make a toast.

ELLIOT: To LAX. I'm not flying back with you.

YAZ: What do you mean?

ELLIOT: I called from the hotel and changed my flight. One way ticket. Watch out, Hollywood. (Pause.) You know how you had to shake me awake last night?

YAZ: (Demeanor shifting.) You were literally sobbing in your sleep.

ELLIOT: This dream was different than usual. I'm fixing a Subway hoagie, I feel eyes on the back of my neck, I turn around and expect to see him, the first guy I shot down in Iraq. But instead it's Mami Ginny. Standing next to the bread oven, smiling. You know how her eyes smile?

YAZ: Best smile in the world.

ELLIOT: Looking at me, her son. Coming to say goodbye.

YAZ: That's beautiful.

ELLIOT: She puts on her glasses to see my face even better. She squints and something changes. The moment I come into focus, she starts trembling. Then she starts to cry. Then she starts to scream loud, like, "Ahhh! Ahhh!" She won't stop looking at me, but she's terrified, horrified by what she sees. And I'm touching my face like, is my lip bleeding, is there a gash on my forehead? Or is she looking through my eyes and seeing straight into my fucking soul?

YAZ: Jesus.

ELLIOT: I wanted Mami Odessa to relapse, Yaz. I wanted her to pick up that needle. I knew precisely what to do, what buttons to push, I engineered that shit, I might as well have pushed the thing into her vein. Because I thought, why would God take the good one? Yo, take the bad mom instead! I was like, why wouldn't you take the bad fucking mom? If I stay in Philly, I'm gonna turn into it. I'm gonna become one of them. I'm already halfway there. You've got armor, you've got ideas, but I don't.

YAZ: Go. Go and don't you ever, ever look back.

(She takes his hand.)

But if you do, there will be a plastic-covered sofa waiting for you.

(Below them, in Philadelphia, John is done bathing Odessa. He lifts her and holds her like an angel above the bathtub. She is dripping wet and seems almost radiant, and yet deeply, deeply sick.)

I'm the elder now. I stay home. I hold down the fort.

ELLIOT: I'm walking.

YAZ: On three?

YAZ/ELLIOT:

One.

Two.

Three.

(They toss the ashes. Blackout.)

Producing *Water by the Spoonful*

Second Stage

Second Stage is an Off-Broadway, New York theatre organization founded in 1979, dedicated to the development and presentation of contemporary plays. Until recently they produced plays by both emerging and established playwrights in two spaces: a 108-seat theatre on the Upper West Side and a 296-seat theatre on West 43rd Street. In 2013 they were in the process of expanding to include a Broadway presence as well by starting to produce plays at the Helen Hayes Theatre. With these three different venues, the Second Stage mission remains the same: to focus on the presentation of new works for the theatre and to provide an opportunity for the growth of young theatre artists. The newly acquired Helen Hayes Theatre will be one of only four not-for-profit theatres on Broadway.

In January 2013, Second Stage produced the New York premiere of *Water by the Spoonful* at its midsize theatre on West 43rd Street. Although this theatre is only a few blocks from Times Square and the elaborate theatres on Broadway, it offers a much simpler, stripped down theatre environment to producers and audiences. This was New York's first opportunity to see the play that had won the Pulitzer Prize for 2012 and had received its world premiere at Hartford Stage, Connecticut, in 2011.

In accordance with its mission, Second Stage provided a "second" opportunity for the artists who had produced *Water by the Spoonful* in Hartford to continue their work on the play. The playwright Quiara Hudes made major revisions to the script based on the earlier production as well as through considering input from the creative staff and some of the actors who had become close collaborators in the process. Those revisions are part of the script of the play presented in this book. The director and

designers made adjustments to the staging to bring greater clarity to the complex storytelling and in response to the new theatre space, an end stage instead of the thrust at Hartford Stage (see page 166). And the actors deepened their understanding of the characters.

Dramatic Structure and Spectacle

Design

The structure of *Water by the Spoonful* with its scenes that alternate between the real world and the online world presents particular challenges for the production team. The director and the scene designer must create a spatial arrangement that will clearly and quickly guide the audience between the two kinds of scenes. All of the designers must determine how much visual information is necessary to the telling of this story and the kind of detail that provides the appropriate background to help define the characters' lives. And since the play moves between several actual geographic locations, as well as into virtual space, the creative staff must decide what will bring unity to the many different elements of the play. For the production of *Eurydice* discussed in Chapter 6, we saw an abstract, lyrical approach to solving similar kinds of problems. For *Water by the Spoonful*, an entirely different approach was taken. *Eurydice* is a poetic play that explores relationships through a mythical, even fantastic, form of play making. *Water by the Spoonful* comes from a gritty, urban environment that gives us harshly realistic details of social breakdown.

If we were to list the actual geographic locations in the play we would see Philadelphia, San Diego, Japan, and the El Yunque Rain Forest of Puerto Rico. Within Philadelphia we would need to add the Swarthmore College campus, the Subway shop, Odessa's house, the diner, and the flower shop. And prominently placed would be the chat room with its links to the lives and

In 1999 renowned Dutch architect Rem Koolhass and New York architect Richard Gluckman were commissioned by Second Stage to create a theatre in a historic bank building. This became Second Stage's intermediate size theatre on West 43rd Street. The box office is in what was once the bank's vault; the second floor was converted to an end stage theatre space. Usually theatres are built without windows to create as dark a space as possible. But here the windows remain to allow a view of the city when it is appropriate. As Koolhass observed, "Second Stage Theatre will be the only theatre that can claim Manhattan itself as its décor." This is the theatre space where *Water by the Spoonful* was staged. All of the audience members share the same view of the stage.

locations of the group of characters who connect with each other online. The first challenge for the scene designer Neil Patel is "to keep the play moving and flowing from scene to scene, which is critical." But the spectacle needs to go beyond simply accounting for many different locations. Underlying the jump cuts between scenes and the movement from real space to virtual space and back is a state of mind. The spectacle needs to support the progression of this particular plot, which involves the characters moving toward each other across physical and mental distances and breaking free of their old limitations and old spaces to enter each others' spaces. There is a psychological environment that the characters share that unifies the action of the play.

Neil Patel tracks the movement of a play by storyboarding the scenes with rough models that he creates scene by scene. He spent three months developing storyboards for *Water by the Spoonful* in collaboration with the director, Davis McCallum, well before the beginning of rehearsals. Each scene is constructed in model form, which is then photographed. Lights and projections are also tested on the models. The models were essential to working out the speed and ease of transitions to allow the play to "flow as seamlessly as possible from scene to scene." In all, he made seventeen scene models for the Second Stage production. This first model shows the stage at the beginning of the play, with the walls closed and the bench set for the opening scene between Elliot and Yazmin on the Swarthmore campus. The white cardboard figure is used to establish scale.

This model shows the walls slid apart with furniture placed to allow Odessa, Orangutan, and Chutes&Ladders to be onstage together in Scene 2, each communicating online from their own private locations. Stage right is Odessa's kitchen, which was given more detail than the spaces of the other online characters. Stage left is the Chutes&Ladders desk from which he doesn't move until the end of the play. In the center is simply a chair for Orangutan, which indicates an Internet cafe in Japan. The gray walls, with greenery growing through the cracks, are used as the background for all of the scenes. The walls can be transformed with lights and can also be transparent.

Neil Patel describes two essential visual components of that psychological environment as an "urban, oppressive look and the hopeful life represented through gardens." Both were to be found in the Philadelphia of Quiara Hudes' childhood now inhabited by her principle trio of characters: Elliot, Odessa, and Yazmin. For Patel the starting point for his work on the play was "pictures of abandoned lots with overgrown plants."

> The images we were looking at were abandoned lots with plants growing through cracked concrete and broken walls, life breaking through as it does. And in the same way the characters in this play do. Through all kinds of hardship and suffering, there's this kind of vibrant and undefeatable life popping through. And because everything is vertical,

This third model shows the scenic arrangement for the end of the play: upstage Elliot and Yazmin prepare to scatter Ginny's ashes at the waterfall in the El Yunque Rain Forest; downstage is the bathtub where Fountainhead will bathe Odessa before she checks into a rehabilitation facility. A functional scaffold is used to make a cliff for Elliot and Yazmin to stand on.

we were also looking at vertical gardens, something you see on buildings now, mostly in Europe. And it was sort of interesting to imagine a garden growing out of the side of a building. So it was really the actual urban lots in Philadelphia and the urban gardens that were our inspiration. And I think you get it, as an audience, that it ties into the tropical scenery at the end. And then we added flowers so it's related to the idea of the flowers and the flower shops, but they aren't tropical flowers. They are flowers that would grow in a back lot in Philadelphia, or an urban vertical garden.

The director, Davis McCallum, saw Ginny's garden, first described in *Elliot, A Soldier's Fugue*, as the "deep metaphor for the play."

Ginny's garden began in an abandoned lot, which she turned into city-recognized public gardens. Flowers and planting seeds, things that come to bloom is one of the big poetic images of the play. And I feel there is a certain amount of isolation—something inhospitable about the world of the play, but it's not that the play is cold or forbidding. Even in difficult circumstances, life is always growing. So that central idea, which was a starting place for the play, came from these pictures of Philadelphia.

It also incidentally came from a children's book that Quiara has written called *El Barrio ABC*, which I read to my children at night. It's one of those alphabet books for kids. And it's all about barrio. It feels a lot like Washington Heights, but it's also based on the neighborhood in North Philadelphia where Elliot grew up. And for "Q"—which is always a hard thing in an alphabet book— Q is for the word *quemar*, which is Spanish for "to burn." In the book, the image shows a row of houses where a house has burned to the ground and it becomes this empty space where a house just was, like a row of teeth, missing one tooth. That triggered the thought, "Oh, between two buildings, there is this no man's land that could be turned into a place of fecundity and life and growth."

Vertical walls looming over small abandoned lots provided a structural framework for the stage and continued the metaphoric ideas in the set. And as a functional device, the walls slid into different configurations, allowing the stage to be transformed quickly from one location to another to indicate the change of scenes. Designed as grids, the walls could look like they were made up of concrete blocks or metallic squares. They could be part of a decaying urban landscape or suggest a representation of separate locations on the Internet.

NEIL PATEL: We wanted to have a complex, abstract environment with gray, industrial materials. We tried to avoid the slick, high tech manifestation of Internet which seemed antithetical to the play. The text did not seem like it belonged on a slick, clean surface.

The grungy, hard-edged appearance of the gridded walls was continued in the selection of the stage furniture. Odessa's house was sparsely furnished with small, rectangular, rundown, thrift store appliances. Chutes&Ladders's IRS office was indicated with a grubby, metal desk. The lighting was done with squares and rectangles on the floor, creating an impression of characters who were separated from each other and isolated in boxes. Even if they were close together on stage, the audience understood the psychic distances that would need to be bridged for the characters to achieve sustaining connections.

Acting

The online sequences and multiple narratives contained in the rapidly shifting scenes also presented technical challenges for the director and the actors. The director was guided by a statement from the playwright in choosing how to stage the Internet conversations. "It's a play about a family, except they're online." He therefore chose to stage these conversations to suggest that there is a domestic intimacy among the online characters. They are regular visitors in one another's lives.

In the chat room scenes all of the actors behave as if they are continuing with their lives in their own private spaces. They do not type their thoughts into their computers but perform mundane tasks of daily life or speak as if they are talking to friends. When these three characters first appear in the chat room it is clear that they have already been communicating with each other for a long period of time. A major convention of the staging is that the characters in the chat room do not look at any of the other actors. They look out into the audience as if they are connecting to the other characters in a separate dimension. From left to right the actors are Liza Colón-Zayas (Odessa), Sue Jean Kim (Orangutan), and Frankie Faison (Chutes&Ladders).

DAVIS McCALLUM: We see Odessa in her apartment, and she goes over to the kitchen and putters around and then comes to the computer, which is a desk with a keyboard but not a monitor. She punches in the code and we see projections of icons for all the online people. But now, her friends from the chat room come into her apartment and they use her apartment *as if* they are in their own real spaces. So that's a vocabulary that we set up in the first part of the play. Then whoever starts the next chat room scene, we use that as a kind of anchor.

However, in order to maintain the illusion of Internet conversations, in spite of the implied familiarity, the online characters do not look at each other. Instead they deliver their lines looking out into the auditorium. In fact, the director had headshots taken of the actors and placed strategically in the auditorium to guide the actors among focal points. Liza Colón-Zayas, who played Odessa, identifies one of the problems in observing this convention. "I always have to be on guard not to look in the wrong direction. It's hard, facing straight out, with bright lights in my eyes." But beyond the concentration issues is the very important need to build connections and emotional energy between the characters.

In most traditional theatre scene work, the tension in a scene is built through the give and take between actors playing off of each other, making eye contact, responding to all of the shifts in another actor's body language, facial expression, and vocal tone. So the early rehearsals for the online scenes were done with the actors facing each other to develop that crucial rapport before they made the change to the outward focus that would be used in performance.

Furthermore, the actors were directed to be very physical in their individual performances, moving actively through the stage space and sometimes standing or sitting close to the other characters even though they are not looking at each other. Their blocking was determined by character issues. For example, Chutes&Ladders protects himself by staying in one place. Davis McCallum says, "his rootedness offers him a kind of stability, but then it becomes a prison." On the other hand, Orangutan's "hunger" to find herself drives her into continuous, restless motion.

Orangutan and Chutes&Ladders begin the play on different continents, but gradually are able to take the steps to help each other overcome their paralysis and cement a deep friendship. A lighting effect is used to reinforce the distance encompassed by the Internet and the number of other people who may also be online. Lines across the back wall indicate the many connections being made; specific icons represent the characters Orangutan, the monkey, and Chutes&Ladders, the game board. The lighting design is by Russell H. Champa; the projection design is by Aaron Rhyne.

The staging sets up an internal tension shared by the online characters. As long as they communicate via their computers, they can be open, direct, warm or scathingly honest in their responses to each other. But each character uses the Internet to keep from taking the steps that would expose them to greater risks.

> **LIZA COLÓN-ZAYAS** (speaking of her character, Odessa): She maintains sobriety by isolating from her triggers. But she has relied too heavily on the online world because there

you can remake yourself and you're not disappointing people. Whereas going to therapy and going to actual meetings with real people, you don't get to hide behind that.

Because a number of storylines are maintained throughout the play, the actors also face the challenge of connecting the pieces of their narratives that are interrupted or not shown onstage. For example, scenes involving Elliot and Yazmin alternate with scenes that take place in the chat room, involving other characters. The actors

The play opens on the downstage bench that indicates the Swarthmore College campus where Elliot is waiting to meet the professor whom he hopes will translate the phrase that haunts him from his tour of duty in Iraq, "please give me back my passport." The vitality of the actors is evident in the warmth and ease of their relationship as cousins. This relationship will become the foundation for a renewal of their family, after the death of their Aunt Ginny. Following this scene, the scenes involving Elliot and Yazmin alternate with scenes for the online characters until Act II. The actors must maintain their throughlines as well as imagine parts of the story that are taking place offstage. Yazmin is played by Zabryna Guevara and Elliot is played by Armando Riesco. Riesco, who originated the role of Elliot in the first play of the trilogy, also played Elliot in the premiere production of the third play, *The Happiest Song Plays Last,* at the Goodman Theatre in Chicago in 2013.

must stay connected to the evolution of their own part of the story and return to the stage for each new scene as if the events being described just happened. Armando Riesco says, "You've got to stay in it between scenes, which is the hardest part of playing this."

> **ZABRYNA GUEVARA:** It doesn't stop. I'm onstage every other scene. There are no two scenes that happen without us showing up on the other end of it. For instance, Ginny dies in between scenes 3 and 5. All that has to happen offstage. Between my finding out Elliot overdosed while he was in the service and the eulogy, a lot happens. The whole funeral has been prepared. And after the eulogy, there's the tracking of how Odessa's absence has affected us. We come down the stairs from the eulogy, take off mic pacs, put on a coat, get a phone, Elliot takes off his military top half, and all that is happening while we're mentally thinking about the events that have transpired to get us to the door knocking and Elliot's line, "Odessa, open the door, open the door." The play is still happening offstage.

Defining the Characters

By assembling scenes that take place in the real world and online, Quiara Hudes is able to draw together a surprisingly disparate group of characters. Through this gathering of individuals we see that the struggles of her characters take place in multiple American communities, not just one. In *Elliot, A Soldier's Fugue*, the playwright uses a structure of repetition to focus on circumstances that recur from generation to generation within the same family. In *Water by the Spoonful*, she uses a structure that ripples out from the family to connect people across a broader spectrum. The traumatic experiences that lead people into isolation and destructive behavior occur in a variety of social environments. But Hudes' characters are not **types** who simply represent categories of behavior or social background. They have their own highly individual personal histories and obstacles that the actors must fill out to

bring the play fully to life. Davis McCallum says, "You believe the people are real and you feel you could walk up on stage and introduce yourself to them."

Researching the Social Environment

To create authentic characters, the actors did extensive research into the social issues that define the world of the play as well as psychological exploration of their characters' given circumstances and interior journeys. When Armando Riesco prepared to play Elliot in the first play of the trilogy, his research focused on combat, through conversations with marines about their tours of duty and watching documentaries about troops deployed to Afghanistan such as *Restrepo* and *Armadillo*. For *Water by the Spoonful*, he turned to the experiences of young veterans returning from the Iraq War and the way those experiences fall disproportionately on certain communities. He looked at the difficulty vets have finding work and the way that erodes self-esteem.

> **ARMANDO RIESCO:** Many returning vets are unemployed or underemployed, a much higher rate than the regular civilian population. A great number of them struggle daily with anger issues and such. It's the really mundane stuff they come back to and they can't deal with. It's no coincidence that Elliot is working at Subway when the Ghost first visits him.

He studied the web site of IAVA, Iraq and Afghanistan Veterans of America, and found a documentary of a young man like his character, Elliot, with a similar injury.

> **ARMANDO RIESCO:** The very first story I found in my research was a 24 year old who did not know what to do with his anger. He regularly drove at 90 miles an hour through his town, got into fights at bars for no reason. He was constantly tempting fate.

He read accounts of veterans who are addicted to pain medications and examined statistics on suicide.

> **ARMANDO RIESCO:** How many veterans are killing themselves? The figures from 2012 detail the numbers: 22 per day. Suicides outnumbered soldier combat deaths in the Iraq conflict.

He found the state of mind of a returning veteran in a short story by Phil Klay entitled "Deployment" to be influential in understanding the disorientation of young men unable to reconcile their lives in Iraq with their lives in the United States.

Liza Colón-Zayas worked in a variety of social service settings while she was building her career as an actor. For this play she drew on what she learned working in support groups with high-risk women and men in lock down facilities and as a teaching artist in homeless shelters and in jails. In addition to her personal experiences, she watched videos and documentaries, confronting the painful realities of behavior related to addiction and overdose. Colón-Zayas explains her understanding of her character, drawing on her analysis of the text and her awareness of circumstances surrounding substance abuse.

> Odessa is a recovering addict. She's had six years clean. She's had over twenty years of struggling with a crack-cocaine addiction. She had an episode which got her locked up which I think was the thing to help her get on the road to recovery. But because of this tragedy in her life, she's been an outcast. So she created an online recovery web site. She's created this community of relationships that are as real to her as family. And they check in regularly on the web site, focusing on retaining their sobriety and sharing their stories, supporting each other. And on this particular day, she get's the rug pulled out. The thing that she's been trying to escape comes back and she ends up back in the life, at least momentarily. I grew up in the South Bronx when it was on fire. So I've seen a lot of this first hand and I've seen people, from one moment to the next,

become Jekyll and Hyde. So, I wanted to be truthful about that, and not judge that, because it's real. You can be sober and still not have worked out your issues. And so, I wanted to show that dichotomy. I wanted to show the extreme mood changes that can take place and still give her heart, and empathy, and humanity and focus on how fragile sobriety is. Because I can easily play someone who is rough around the edges, but I was resisting that in this play because I didn't want people to judge her unfairly. I didn't want her to just be a stereotype.

The Interior Journey

Like the process described by Liza Colón-Zayas, each of the actors was faced with imaginatively constructing his or her character's autobiography and then building a progression of attempts to take control of situations made increasingly difficult by new reversals or setbacks. Much of the rehearsal process involved lengthy conversations with the director, the playwright Quiara Hudes (who was frequently in rehearsals), and the other actors about key points in each character's development. Given the painful nature of these characters' lives, this is a process that requires a deep emotional investment on the part of the actors in order to be genuinely open to the truth of the characters' circumstances. As Armando Riesco says, "I think when you don't open yourself 110% you are doing a disservice to the play. Your job is to try every single time to open yourself completely and to be in the moment and to feel all these terrible things." However, he also makes clear that the focus of each actor's work cannot be on the enormity of the character's hardships but rather on what the character is doing to overcome those obstacles.

> The baggage is evident. You read the play and the given circumstances are there. The trick to making this play fly is that you have to have those given circumstances deeply weighing you down. But then your action is not to show how you're weighted down. It's the

The Sapporo train station is created through lights and projections at the same time that Odessa's house exists on another part of the stage. Orangutan has fallen into a confused sleep in the train station at the same time that Odessa has overdosed. The lines from the two different scenes overlap and each connects to the meaning in the other scene. The lowest points in the progressions of Odessa's and Orangutan's characters coincide in this scene.

opposite of that. And in between that weight that's pulling you down and you trying to stay above water, now we have a play.

The Language of Resilience

One of the coping mechanisms written into the play is the characters' earthy language that is laced with humor. Sarcasm and jokes, some self-deprecating, some aimed at other characters, are a way of negotiating painful subjects without giving in to self-pity. The characters use humor as a form of self-protection, a kind of armor to defend against showing their true feelings. It is one of the ways to try to prove that they are not "weighted down,"

that they are surviving. Although the humor is noteworthy in four of the characters' language: Yazmin, Elliot, Madeleine Mays (Orangutan), and Clayton Wilkie (Chutes&Ladders), it is not generic, but comes out of each character's particular circumstances, some of which are cultural. In performance, the effective use of humor by the actors makes an important contribution to building the energy of the production.

> ZABRYNA GUEVARA (speaking from the viewpoint of her character, Yazmin): I think that the sarcasm you see comes from a real sense of heartbreak and a need for love, a *real* need to be understood and for me to love *me*. Elliot and I love each other unconditionally.

But up until now, I have love from my family in the form of admiration for my achievements. I went to school. I play music. I'm a composer. Nobody knows me. I don't know them. There's a mutual disconnect. And then my husband divorces me and I don't even have that. He fell *out* of love with me. Maybe he loved me at some point, but it was probably admiration. I didn't even have what I thought I had. But we're not self-indulgent sentimental people, so there's bite behind it, because otherwise you'll just lay down and cry. So if you're not going to let that overtake you, then there's bite behind the comment to lay a spine in the pain. It doesn't just double you over and kill you. There's got to be strength in it. I have anger through the pain and it keeps you up, it keeps you going, it gets you to the eulogy, it gets you past the eulogy, it gets you past the OD. It's a coping mechanism. I think it is in the language and it's definitely cultural. Just to get through really hard times, in my family, you make light, you make jokes, throw this anger, just to make you feel better.

The Musical Environment

We began our discussion of Quiara Hudes' work as a playwright by considering the importance of music in the structure of her plays, particularly for the Elliot trilogy. The musical idea behind *Water by the Spoonful* is first introduced into the play in Yazmin's speech when she is giving a lecture to her students about the music of the great jazz composer John Coltrane. She challenges them to think about dissonance in their lives and introduces them to the idea of "free jazz." In free jazz, the compositional structure lacks the harmony and resolution of other musical forms, but instead offers continuing sequences of notes that clash, producing a discordant sound. Improvisation is an essential component of free jazz and the form depends on the improvisational contributions of all the performing participants rather than a single composer.

The jazz of John Coltrane and the concept of free jazz had implications for the production in a number of ways. Davis McCallum believes that the entire text of the play is like a jazz score, but also that instrumental music is "invited" into the text in important places. It became clear to him that John Coltrane should be considered the play's "composer," and he asked Josh Schmidt to be the production's sound designer because of his expertise in jazz and composition as well as sound design. Together they listened to many hours of Coltrane pieces and then carefully chose selections from *Ascension*, *Love Supreme*, and other works that emphasized drum rhythms rather than saxophone. During the first act there was some reggaeton to suggest the barrio, Puerto Rican music for the scene in the flower shop, and club music for the scene in the Japanese nightclub. But there was no jazz other than Coltrane, and Coltrane was played increasingly in act 2 as the play moved to conclusion. For example, loops from *Ascension*, which is the dissonant piece that Yazmin's character says spins toward "noise," was heard each time the Ghost appeared. And in fact, the first entrance of the Ghost occurs immediately after the "dissonance" speech. *Love Supreme*, with its more focused, pure, haunting notes, was heard at the beginning of act 2.

McCallum also encouraged the actors to find "the jazz in the language."

> The language was coming out clearly and honestly, but rather straight, almost square. I wanted them to feel the freedom, to rediscover some of their own idiosyncrasies; their individuality in the way they approached the language; to linger on one word, to vary their speed, tempo, rhythm, and pitch, so we could regain a more varied color.

In terms of a musical analogy, McCallum sees the jazz inspiration for *Water by the Spoonful* leading to a "wilder" form of staging than the tightly choreographed staging of *Elliot, A Soldier's Fugue*. The "collision" between the needs of the different characters and the turmoil of their emotional lives brings an undercurrent of chaos to the intersecting narrative strands.

DAVIS MCCALLUM: People are fighting for their lives, not just in the chat room, in the

All four characters in this scene participate in healing rituals that are part of their path of recovery. Fountainhead is played by Bill Heck.

real world. They're battling with addiction; they're battling with each other; they're battling with themselves. That fight needs to be a brawl. There's blood on the floor.

These battles uncover enough vulnerability to allow the characters to approach connections with each other that will make recovery possible. Through these connections, they gain the courage to face the most painful knowledge about themselves. Liza Colón-Zayas says the play is "not just about recovery. It's about redemption. It's about forgiveness. People of all colors, from all stations of life. Every single person on that stage needs some sort of forgiveness."

Because of these mutually supportive relationships, all of the characters are able to change the directions of their lives. The chat room characters move beyond their online dialogues to accept each other in real space. They give up their identities as Internet icons with symbolic names. The actors stop facing out and turn to each other in intimate ways. John gently bathes Odessa, a form of touch that allows them both a moment of peace. Clayton Wilkie and Madeleine Mays embrace joyfully in the Tokyo airport. And as Elliot and Yazmin scatter Ginny's ashes, they are able to let go of parts of the past that have kept them from beginning a new journey into the future.

 # Summary

Quiara Alegría Hudes has written a new American trilogy consisting of three plays: *Elliot, A Soldier's Fugue, Water by the Spoonful,* and *The Happiest Song Plays Last.* Together the three plays examine the experiences of a young marine who is injured during combat in the Iraq War and his struggles to find a place for himself when he returns to the United States. The first play also includes the experiences of Elliot's father and grandfather who served in two previous wars in

Vietnam and Korea. The second play introduces additional characters from Elliot's family, his mother Odessa and his cousin Yazmin, but also expands the frame of reference to present characters who enter the lives of this family via the Internet. In writing her plays, Hudes draws on the stories of actual members of her own family, which she uses as the foundation for some of the characters. Many of the characters in *Water by the Spoonful* are struggling with substance abuse and the play focuses on the interactions among the characters that lead them toward recovery.

Hudes is an accomplished musician and musical structures were an important factor in writing these plays. In *Elliot, A Soldier's Fugue*, the repeating war experiences of the three generations are expressed through language and action that are tightly woven together in a pattern of themes that echo each other. *Water by the Spoonful* is influenced by the jazz compositions of John Coltrane. The structure of this play is expansive with a number of different character narratives and speeches that suggest jazz improvisation. The structure of *Water by the Spoonful* is also distinguished by scenes that alternate between characters who meet face-to-face and characters who interact online. The play is written as duets for three sets of characters, who come from very different walks of life.

The last play, *The Happiest Song Plays Last*, opens up the frame of reference further yet to include international characters. The musical background is provided through Puerto Rican traditional songs. Other notable trilogies in dramatic history include *The Oresteia* by the Greek playwright Aeschylus and *Mourning Becomes Electra* by the American playwright Eugene O'Neill.

Topics for Discussion and Writing

1. Read the scene from *Elliot, A Soldier's Fugue*, beginning on page 394, aloud. How do you think the scene should be staged to bring out the differences between the active characters, Elliot and Pop, and the characters who serve as narrators in this scene, Ginny and Grandpop? How would you describe the different kinds of language spoken by the characters in the scene, and what is the effect of the differing styles?

2. The line spoken by the Ghost of a dead Iraqi in *Water by the Spoonful* repeats a number of times, first in Arabic and then in English: "Please, give me back my passport." How do you interpret the meaning of this line for the character of the Ghost? What is the significance of the passport and the appearances of the Ghost for Elliot? How does this line apply to the other characters?

3. The playwright Quiara Alegría Hudes sees online language being distinct from the language that we use in face-to-face conversations. She says, "I think online language is more formal than conversational language, which is more casual and fumbling. You get language that is being used in a more thoughtful way. It is heightened and uninhibited." Do you agree with her statement? What do you think distinguishes the way people communicate online? How would you stage the scenes that take place in the chat room?

● For suggested readings and interviews with the playwright, director, scenic designer, and actors, please visit
  www.mhhe.com/creativespirit6e

CHAPTER 14

Genre

In the preceding chapters we looked at the playwright's artistic vision and the development of that vision through style and dramatic construction. In this chapter we consider another dimension of playwriting: the way the drama views human existence or divides human experience. In simple terms, we divide drama into the serious and the comic, into tragedy and comedy. To these divisions we can add tragicomedy, a form of drama that moves between serious and comic views. The term **genre** refers to a specific division, or classification, of drama. The most frequently used clas-

sifications, or genres, of drama are tragedy, comedy, melodrama, tragicomedy, and farce. Following our consideration of genre, we turn our attention to writers whose work involves analyzing plays and performances. These writers, the dramaturg and the critic, must understand the nature of theatrical communication on the stage and the elements of dramatic construction and classification, which are the subjects of Chapters 12, 13, and 14.

Introduction to Genre

In thinking about genres, we must remember that categorization is a tool for exploration, not an end itself. Furthermore, genres frequently merge or overlap rather than stay within neat and tidy boundaries. The organization of the drama into genres offers a way to examine the shifting viewpoint on human experience and a comparable shift in the audience's response to the drama.

What makes the study of genre worthwhile is the insight that each particular form of drama contributes to our understanding of the relationship between human beings and the world or the universe. Studying genre leads us to consider some of the most troublesome questions about human existence. How much control do we have over our own lives? Are human beings responsible for their own actions? Are we merely victims of circumstance? Are human beings capable of heroic action, or do we often blunder at the critical moment or fail to recognize the significant issues? How high or low is our aim? Are we free, or is there an external force, either divine or random, that ultimately controls, contradicts, or renders meaningless all of our actions?

ARTISTIC FOUNDATIONS

Characteristics of Comedy

- Comedy celebrates the continuation of life, the success of generations through love and rebirth.

- The plot of comedy usually involves an outrageous idea or fantastic scheme that disrupts the normal workings of the community and leads to chaos.

- Comedy usually looks at characters as part of a social group.

- Comic characters tend to reflect human weakness.

- Comedy often takes place in the realm of the ludicrous.

- The world of comedy is a protected world where there is no pain.

- Comedy ends with a reconciliation or happy resolution, frequently including an engagement or marriage.

- Comedy exists to make us laugh, but its underlying subject matter is often serious and involves some kind of social critique.

- The performance of comedy depends on broad physicality, timing, and rapport between actor and audience.

Tragedy and Comedy

Genre begins with tragedy and comedy, the most basic—though not necessarily opposite—parts of the dramatic experience. Tragedy and comedy are two different ways of understanding the fundamental rhythms of the human life cycle. Tragedy frequently ends in disaster. Although violence and death are central to most tragedies, it is the awareness of our mortality that seems most relevant to the tragic understanding of life. Tragedy explores the notion that no matter how great our human achievement, life is finite. We cannot overcome our mortality, nor can we overcome the hostilities or inconsistencies in the universe. The limitations of human mortality are addressed in the following passage from the Greek poet Pindar:

> One is the race of gods and of men; from one mother we both draw our breath. Yet are our powers poles apart; for we are nothing, but for them the brazen Heaven endures forever, their secure abode.[1]

Pindar suggests that human beings are godlike in their aspirations. But the gods, however we interpret them or whatever forces they represent, are constant. They do not die. Human beings, for all their intelligence, courage, and will, can never achieve the immortality of the gods or the constant forces of the universe.

Molière (1622–1673) is a beloved playwright of comedies whose works are widely produced and translated into many languages. In *A Doctor In Spite of Himself* a woodcutter masquerades as a doctor in a satire of pretense and hypocrisy. One of Molière's broader escapades, this piece invites theatrical invention such as the puppets, silent film costumes, rap music and opera, slapstick and sight gags featured in the 2012 production at Berkeley Repertory Theatre, directed by Christopher Bayes. The actors are Liam Craig, Renata Friedman, Steven Epp, and Julie Briskman.

In contrast to tragedy, comedy looks to the continuation of life rather than to its finality. In spite of all the pitfalls and the setbacks, in spite of the pettiness of human behavior and our foolish self-importance, life goes on. Comedy focuses on the success of generations rather than on the mortality of the individual. Through love and rebirth, there is continuance.

The plot of comedy usually begins with an outrageous idea or a fantastic scheme that disrupts the normal workings of the community. Incongruous events are frequently complicated by mistaken identity and misunderstandings. Gullibility, greed, egotism, and hypocrisy appear to rule the day. Lovers are separated, fortunes are lost, and chaos seems to reign supreme. But common sense prevails, the misunderstandings are resolved, and the reconciliation of all the separated factions leads to the affirmation of true love. Comedies frequently end in marriage or engagements.

Comedy exists to make us laugh. But the brilliance of comedy lies in its ability to take on the most serious subjects while evoking the deepest laughter. Perhaps we laugh hardest at the exposure of things that concern us the most or, as Bill Irwin has observed, that frighten us the most. War, religion, politics, generational conflict, and sexual relationships are common subjects of comedy.

Origins in Greek Drama

The original designations of tragedy and comedy in the theatre were arrived at simply. In the early Greek theatre, all plays that dealt with lofty and serious subjects were called tragedies. The word *tragedy* is derived from the Greek word that means "goat song"—a song that was sung in honor of Dionysus. Plays that dealt with human weakness and folly were called comedies.

The Greeks were certainly aware of the proximity of tragedy and comedy in describing human experience. Originally, comedies were performed as companion pieces to tragedies to complete the picture of human endeavor. The tragic side looked to the human actor engaged in noble causes. The comic side revealed that underneath the heroic guise, humans are terrified and capable of the most ridiculous posturing and mistakes. In the Greek theatre the genres were maintained as separate but complementary entities. In contrast, contemporary playwrights frequently mix comic and tragic elements in the same play because that approach seems to most effectively reflect their understanding of life's rhythms in today's world.

Aristotle on Tragedy and Comedy

In his series of lectures that were collected under the title *The Poetics* (see Chapter 12), Aristotle described the nature of tragedy. In defining tragedy, he included a few asides on the nature of comedy. Aristotle summarized the distinction between tragedy and comedy in two statements. In the first he wrote:

> Comedy aims at representing men as worse,
> Tragedy as better than in actual life.[2]

We may interpret "better than in actual life" to mean that the characters in tragedy come from noble houses. And Aristotle in fact writes later in *The Poetics* that a tragic character must be "highly renowned and prosperous."[3] Tragic characters, by their royal birth, are distinguished from ordinary citizens. But Aristotle's "better" refers more significantly to character, behavior, and choices. In tragic characters, nobility of conduct corresponds to nobility of position.

In his second statement on comedy Aristotle wrote:

> Comedy is, as we have said, an imitation of characters of a lower type—not, however, in the full sense of the word bad, the Ludicrous being merely a subdivision of the ugly. It consists in some defect or ugliness which is not painful or destructive. To take an obvious example, the comic mask is ugly and distorted, but does not imply pain.[4]

Comedy's "imitation of characters of a lower type" suggests conduct that may make audience members feel superior—or that may make them recognize themselves at their worst. Aristotle uses the word *ludicrous* to further delineate the particular area of behavior comedy addresses. *Ludicrous* implies the contradictions in life that make our efforts ridiculous. When Harpo Marx uses huge scissors to cut off pieces of a formal dinner jacket worn by a pompous diplomat while he is conducting serious business, we are in the realm of the ludicrous. Ludicrous has to do with the loss of control, with the incongruous, with the undermining of whatever we take too seriously.

Comedy: A World Without Pain   In his second statement, Aristotle made another simple observation about comedy that has far greater significance than the words communicate at first reading: "It consists in some defect or ugliness which is not painful or destructive. To take an obvious example, the comic mask is ugly and distorted, but does not imply pain." The implication here is that comic characters may do all kinds of ridiculous things and may suffer temporary losses, but they are not in pain. And most particularly, the audience does not respond to them as if they were suffering. When we laugh in the theatre, we laugh at the incongruous, we laugh at the foolish, we laugh at ourselves, but we do not laugh if we believe that people are genuinely in pain.

Tragedy: Catharsis and Awareness

The audience's experience in tragedy is quite different from that in comedy. In tragedy we feel

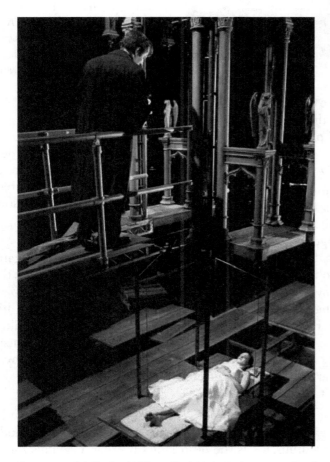

Romeo and Juliet by William Shakespeare is a tragedy of young lovers separated by their feuding families. While trying to escape together, misunderstandings bring about both of their deaths. Here a family member, Paris, played by Lee Mark Nelson, comes upon the apparently dead body of Juliet, played by Christine Marie Brown, in a 2004 production at the Guthrie Theater in Minneapolis directed by Ethan McSweeney.

the pain and suffering of the characters intensely. The audience empathizes with the tragic characters and shares in their inner journeys. The identification with the suffering in tragedy brings about an emotional release or cleansing of the spirit that is referred to as catharsis. Catharsis is one of the most discussed and debated concepts in the study of drama. To understand catharsis, imagine that you have witnessed an ordeal and have been caught up in the terrible tensions of the situation. When those conflicts and tensions are finally resolved, you feel both relief and heightened awareness. The same emotional experience occurs in tragedy: the tragic character comes to a new understanding or a greater wisdom through his or her suffering, and we in the audience come to a new awareness of life's meaning. This experience that combines emotional sensitivity with insight into life's most difficult questions brings us a degree of exhilaration at the same time that we are deeply moved by the struggle we have witnessed.

Plot Summaries of Selected Tragedies

Today we are surrounded by comedies—on the stage, on television, and in the movies. We have abundant material to draw on in our attempt to identify the distinguishing qualities of comedy. But we have only a generalized sense of the "tragic," which we tend to think of in terms of painful incidents that end in loss, disaster, or death. We do not have a large, well-known body of contemporary theatre works to create a frame of reference for identifying that part of human experience explored by tragedy.

To provide a partial foundation for our discussion of tragedy, we include here brief plot summaries of the plays most frequently cited in discussions of tragedy. To the tragedies listed, written in either the fifth century B.C.E. or Elizabethan England, could be added more plays from either of these periods as well as the tragedies of Racine, written in seventeenth-century

Another famous tragic drama of generational conflict is Sophocles' *Electra,* which tells the story of Electra's determination to revenge herself on her mother, Clytaemnestra, for the death of her father, Agamemnon. The plot of Electra is drawn from the same material as the plot of *The Oresteia* described in this chapter. The contemporary playwright Luis Alfaro has adapted *Electra* in a new version he has titled *Electricidad* and set in the middle of gang warfare in Southern California. In this photograph, the brother of Electricidad, Orestes, played by Maximino Arciniega Jr., considers the murder that his sister is asking him to commit in a 2006 production at the Goodman Theatre in Chicago. Nino is played by Edward Torres.

France. But even with these additions, we quickly see that a huge area of literary and dramatic study is based on a very small sample of plays.

Oedipus Rex (Sophocles) When Oedipus is a young man, he is told by an oracle that he is fated to kill his father and marry his mother and have children with her. Horrified at such a future, he leaves the home and kingdom of his parents, not knowing that he is, in fact, an adopted child. Unwittingly, he travels to the city of his actual parents, where the prophecy comes true. Oedipus murders his father King Laius and marries his mother Queen Jocasta. Because Laius is dead, the people of Thebes choose Oedipus to be their new king. The play focuses on the day, many years after Oedipus's arrival in Thebes, the true city of his birth, that Oedipus comes to know who he really is.

Antigone (Sophocles) The sons of Oedipus, Eteocles and Polyneices, have both been killed battling each other for the throne. Their uncle, Creon, declares that one is a hero and will be buried appropriately and that the other is a traitor and will be left unburied with his remains to be destroyed by the elements. Creon, who has become the king on the death of Oedipus's sons, further decrees that anyone attempting to bury the abandoned body will be stoned to death. The young men's sister, Antigone, refuses to obey her uncle's decree and performs burial rites for her brother. Creon has Antigone imprisoned in a cave, where she commits suicide.

The Oresteia (Aeschylus) Agamemnon, the Greek king and general who leads the Greek army against Troy in the ten-year Trojan war, is killed by his wife, Clytaemnestra, on his return from the war. Clytaemnestra is then killed by her son, Orestes, as revenge for his father's death. Orestes is tried for murder in a trial by jury and acquitted.

Hamlet (Shakespeare) Hamlet's father, King Hamlet, is murdered by his uncle Claudius, who is the dead king's brother. Claudius then marries Hamlet's mother, Gertrude, and takes the throne of Denmark. Young Prince Hamlet fears that his uncle has murdered his father but lacks conclusive proof. In the course of Hamlet's attempt to prove his uncle a murderer and avenge his father's death, violence claims eight lives, including those of Hamlet, Claudius, and Gertrude.

Macbeth (Shakespeare) Macbeth is presented with visions of future power by three witches whom he meets on the heath. The witches' mysterious prophecies fire his own ambitions. He and his wife Lady Macbeth embark on a course of murder, beginning with the reigning king, that ultimately leads to their downfall.

King Lear (Shakespeare) Seeking to bind his three daughters more closely to him, King Lear divides up his kingdom and bestows what would be his children's inheritance in advance of his death. He announces the division of his kingdom in a public ceremony, in which he expects his daughters to declare their love for him above all else. His treacherous older daughters easily proclaim the adulation they know he awaits. However, Cordelia, his youngest daughter (for whom the ceremony is probably staged), refuses to compromise herself with false flattery to surpass her sisters. Lear banishes Cordelia, opening the way for a vicious power struggle that results in the deaths of both Lear and Cordelia.

Common Themes of Tragedy

A Struggle Over Succession As these six plot summaries show, the major tragedies all deal with power struggles over succession. Oedipus unknowingly kills the legitimate king, his father, and then taints his own children and heirs through incest. Creon imprisons his rebellious niece, Antigone, to consolidate his own power as king following the deaths of the two legitimate heirs to the throne. Clytaemnestra kills her husband to avenge the death of their daughter and then assumes the leadership of the state; Orestes, Clytaemnestra's son, kills his mother to reclaim the throne he believes by right should be his. Claudius and Macbeth both scheme for power and murder the legitimate king. By giving up his power prematurely, King Lear unleashes a bloody struggle for control of the kingdom. And in *Medea*, Jason leaves his wife to form a new marital alliance that will make him successor to the throne of the aging king of Corinth.

Although succession is not necessarily the primary focus of tragedy, it is integral to many of the works of the past that we categorize as tragedy. A crisis over succession exposes a society at its most vulnerable. Tragedy explores a breakdown or challenge to a society's system of values. And it is during these times of vulnerability that the moral choices of the characters are the most difficult and significant.

A Rupturing of Family and Societal Bonds Classical tragedies test the moral foundations of human civilization. Tragedies take place when the bonds that tie human society together are ruptured. The family is almost always at the center of tragedy, and it is a royal family that represents both the larger society and the essential relationships between family members. Tragic characters become engaged in

ARTISTIC FOUNDATIONS

Characteristics of Tragedy

- Tragedy deals with serious subjects and characters who are confronted with their own mortality.
- Many tragic plots revolve around a crisis over succession to a throne, representing a rupture in the bonds that tie families and society together.
- Murder and death occur frequently in tragedy and usually as a result of the transgression of sacred principles.
- Tragic characters come from aristocratic or royal families and usually exhibit admirable behavior.
- Tragic characters act alone and take responsibility for their choices and actions.
- The audience empathizes with tragic characters, identifies with their suffering, and often experiences catharsis.

conflict leading to or in response to the transgression of principles deemed sacred by the community. All the major tragedies involve royal or aristocratic characters who kill members of their own families. The health or disruption in the royal family is intricately tied to the social and political health of the community.

The relationship of the tragic characters to this wrenching of fundamental values changes from play to play and playwright to playwright. Some characters—such as Oedipus, unknowingly; and King Lear, knowingly—initiate all the events that lead to catastrophe. Others, such as Hamlet and Antigone, must respond to situations initiated by others. What the characters share is an unwillingness to let other characters or circumstances shape their individual destinies. They are determined, even at the cost of their own lives and sometimes the lives of others, to find a course of action that is true to their own natures and true to a value system as they understand it. Some of them, such as King Lear, Creon, and Macbeth, make enormous errors of judgment or miscalculations. Some, such as Oedipus, are caught in such a tangled web that extrication is impossible. Some, such as Hamlet and Antigone, give their lives to restore justice. For all these tragic characters, great suffering results from the actions they choose, and through that suffering comes not only wisdom but also self-determination. They have defined themselves.

Isolation of the Tragic Character   Whereas comedies look at characters as part of a social unit, tragedies examine characters who stand alone. Hamlet was part of the court of Denmark before the play opens; he had family, friends, a woman who loved him, and the highest regard of the people of Denmark. Part of his tragedy is that he becomes increasingly isolated as he pursues his course of action. His father is dead. He is betrayed by his friends Rosencrantz and Guildenstern, attacked by his uncle Claudius, rejected by Ophelia, and abandoned by his mother. In *Medea* the central character is viewed as an outsider who should be banished.

Isolated, the tragic hero or character struggles with a hideous situation: Hamlet's father has been murdered, and the apparent murderer now wears the crown and has married Hamlet's mother; the body of Antigone's brother lies unburied, to be torn apart by wild dogs and vultures, and the king has decreed that anyone burying the body will be stoned to death; Oedipus's people are dying of plague because an old murder goes unpunished; Medea's husband has left her for another woman and she has become a social outcast. The tragic character determines to follow his or her own conscience in addressing these situations rather than accept the solutions of others or the supposed decrees of fate.

The Acceptance of Responsibility   Although the circumstances with which they are presented are not always of their own making, tragic characters take full responsibility for their actions. Tragedy is about human potential and our ability to choose for ourselves and take responsibility for the consequences of those choices. It is no coincidence that the great tragedies were written in periods of optimism about the ability of human beings to control their own destinies. The fifth century B.C.E. saw the rise of both Athenian democracy and the Athenian empire. In Shakespeare's time, the English navy defeated the Spanish armada and then pursued Queen Elizabeth's goals of building an empire.

Can Tragedy Exist Today?

Because the drama has changed and our philosophical perspective has changed, we might question whether tragedy can exist today. Certainly, the tragedies that we use as our reference points were written during times when dramatists saw royal characters rather than common characters as the best personages to convey their meaning. These characters were seen as larger than life as they undertook epic struggles with the universe.

Medea is so obsessed with revenging herself on Jason for his lack of fidelity that she kills their children. At the end of the play, Medea (Fiona Shaw) cradles the body of one of her dead sons while Jason (Jonathan Cake) denounces her actions. But he is too late to stop the course of events that his duplicity set in motion. The tragedy, *Medea,* was produced by the Abbey Theatre in 2002 and directed by Deborah Warner.

They spoke a poetic, highly charged language that also lifted them out of the realm of ordinary existence. And they were further enlarged by their relationship to myths or legends. They were characters ready to fight the gods or fate.

Today, much of our drama frames human action in realistic terms and examines the struggles of average people to overcome economic and social problems. Our sense of the universe and our place in it has changed. The vastness of the universe defies comprehension; human beings have become no more than flecks barely registering on the surface of endless space and time. Because so much of our lives seems out of our control, much of today's nonrealistic drama

has focused on the absurd, on our inability to give meaning to our brief passage on the planet. The idea of taking responsibility for our actions, which is at the heart of tragedy, may seem impossible or irrelevant.

If indeed tragedy is possible today, it cannot be produced from the models of Greek or Elizabethan tragedy. It will have to take a different course. The very nature of democracy, for example, precludes a tragedy of the aristocracy. In the mid-twentieth century several playwrights, including Arthur Miller and Eugene O'Neill, contributed to an American idea of tragedy. And, as part of his epic cycle on America, the playwright August Wilson provides tantalizing

Early film made the most of melodramatic plots in which young women were threatened by villains. The scene depicted here comes from a film of 1919: *Chelsea 7750*. Although such damsel-in-distress scenes are the most vivid representations of melodramatic form, melodrama encompasses a range of plots in which good and evil are clearly opposed.

possibilities of a tragic view in *Joe Turner's Come and Gone*. The central figure, Herald Loomis, has a larger-than-life quality that comes from both the intensity of his feelings and the symbolic nature of his character. And he speaks a language that is poetic and charged. His name, Herald Loomis, suggests that he brings redemption; he is the "herald" of the light. He emerges from a background of slavery and the chain gang, a background comparable to the harrowing circumstances of classical tragedy.

Just as the tragic figures of ancient Greece or Elizabethan England represented their communities, so Herald Loomis represents his community—all of the enslaved. He endures terrible suffering, and through that suffering he comes to wisdom. Like Oedipus, he is searching for himself, and he reviews his past and those closest to him as he comes to recognize and take his place in the world. Although, like Hamlet, much of his suffering is not of his own making, the play focuses on his spiritual crisis, for which he *is* responsible. And ultimately he chooses the path of self-determination, acting symbolically when he cuts himself. Freedom is central to classical tragedy, and it is central to Herald Loomis. He is not waiting for someone else to bleed or suffer for him. He will suffer for himself. And in that moment of accepting himself, he discharges the spectral chains of Joe Turner.

In its own way, *Joe Turner's Come and Gone* may also deal with the struggle over succession. Herald Loomis may not be a king, but he is a representative of a people enslaved by another people. By throwing off the oppressor and reclaiming himself, Herald Loomis asserts the rights of black people to participate fully in society. His actions help bring change in succession to the rights of the nation. August Wilson places his characters in a world that has meaning and a moral framework.

Melodrama

We may see very little tragedy in the theatre and films of today, yet we do see a great deal of another genre, **melodrama**. Melodrama has its origins in very simple conflicts of good and evil. Melodrama externalizes the cause of our problems; there is little internal conflict or probing of moral issues. The nature of good and evil is clear at the outset. The hero or heroine may have terrifying obstacles to overcome. But the heroic figures are not their own primary obstacles nor do they set in motion the forces that threaten them.

In traditional melodrama, a helpless young woman would be held hostage in some gruesome way by an obvious villain—only to be rescued at the last possible moment by a courageous and virtuous young man. This was a celebrated formula on the early American stage that has transitioned into many Hollywood movies. For example, a version of the young woman in distress takes place in the third film of George

Kneehigh is a theatre company from Cornwall, England, that is known for its adventurous approaches to theatrical storytelling. *The Wild Bride* is based on a Grimm's fairy tale entitled, "The Handless Maiden." The heroine, played here by Audrey Brisson, is plunged into a nightmare journey when her father makes a careless bargain with the devil. In the photograph the character's hands have been cut off to satisfy the devil's escalating frustration as he finds he is unable to possess the innocent and virtuous young bride. In the spirit of early melodrama, the play relies on music to shape its changing moods, in this case lively bluegrass with dance that also lighten the darker plot episodes. The production was adapted and directed by Emma Rice, the co-artistic director of Kneehigh, and is shown in performance at Berkeley Repertory Theatre in 2013.

Lucas's *Star Wars* trilogy, *Return of the Jedi*. Princess Leia and Han Solo have been taken captive by the evil and disgusting Jabba the Hutt. Solo,

weak and blinded from having been imprisoned in ice, is temporarily unable to defend Leia from the vile Jabba, "the slimy piece of worm-ridden filth." Leia, for all her modern courage and independence, is dressed seductively in a bikini with a metal collar and chain about her neck. Jabba holds the chain and uses it to pull Leia closer to his voluminous flesh. It is a particularly gross version of the villain taking advantage of the heroine, a new way of tying her to the railroad tracks. At this point Luke Skywalker, now a Jedi knight, arrives. But he must face more evil before he can win the release of his friends. First he must outwit the horrible Rancor, and then they must all take on the dreaded Sarlac, the vast, pulsing mouth on the desert floor, filled with hundreds of tusk-like teeth. As the battle builds, the well-known *Star Wars* theme music supports the action. Like the early stage melodramas from which the name of this genre is taken, music is an extraordinarily important part of the action film experience, building a sense of fear or triumph as needed.

Different versions of melodramatic stories involving the good guy who takes on the many incarnations of the forces of evil, all with state-of-the-art special effects, are at the heart of a long list of Hollywood movies, from *Star Wars* to *Indiana Jones* and James Bond to *Spiderman* and *Mission Impossible*. Sometimes there are whole cities of innocent people to be rescued instead of an individual woman, but the basic premise is the same. However, we do see a shift in gender roles as more women characters participate actively in the battle for salvation, such as in *The Hunger Games*.

The popularity of such movies is due to more than simply the rush of the special effects. The world is a difficult place. Contemporary life is stressful. We worry about everything from financial difficulties to crime to international tensions to climate change and its effect on the environment. There is great and simple satisfaction in being clear on the distinction between good and evil and in seeing the triumph of the good and the crushing of the bad. Although we may celebrate such triumph at the moment, we know that life is much more complicated than in the movies and that celluloid villains and heroes are as thin as the film on which their exploits are recorded.

Pure melodrama is most easily identified in action movies and popular drama from the nineteenth century. More serious drama that clearly opposes the forces of good and evil can also be described in part by the term *melodrama*. With Roy Cohn as the obvious villain, *Angels in America* can be seen to have some melodramatic tendencies. And the work of the playwright Lillian Hellman (discussed in Chapter 7) is also sometimes categorized as melodrama because it examines the way evil spreads when good people do not fight it.

Tragicomedy

Tragicomedy is a form of drama that has particular resonance today. The plays that fall into this classification are not merely plays that combine serious and comic elements. *Hamlet*, for example, has a generous amount of comedy and humor, yet we are clear that it is a tragedy. Similarly, there are some tragicomic—as well as melodramatic—tendencies in *Angels in America*; yet because the play focuses on the possibility of social and personal change, it does not fall under the category of tragicomedy.

Tragicomic plays are concerned with human awareness rather than a program of social change. In particular, they tend to explore an existential philosophical position. In simple terms, existentialism has to do with relativity—a belief that no fixed meaning underlies human existence and that the best we can do is to invent a framework for meaning that will be highly personal and individual and will inevitably have to change. What distinguishes tragicomedy is the way one perspective undercuts or changes the other. There is an interplay between the serious and comic sides of a situation that results in an unstable landscape, a kind of shifting terrain where the footing is hard to secure. The truth of the situation becomes elusive or impossible to ascertain, as is the case in Luigi Pirandello's 1922 play, *Six Characters in Search of an Author*.

Six Characters in Search of an Author presents a bizarre situation in which a group of characters arrive at a theatre where actors are rehearsing a play. The characters request and then insist that the actors put on the story of the characters' lives instead of the play that they are rehearsing. The characters claim that their playwright abandoned them partway through the process of making them into a play, and now they are desperate to have the opportunity to play out their drama. The six characters want to perform their play for the actors and then have the actors restage that play with the characters as the audience. Built into this confusing structure of real actors playing stage actors who are then impersonating characters who are actually present are all kinds of questions about the nature of reality. The Father, who is one of the six characters, expresses his fear that human beings cannot understand each other:

We all have a world of things inside ourselves and each one of us has his own private world. How can we understand each other if the words I use have the sense and the value that I expect them to have, but whoever is listening to me inevitably thinks that those same words have a different sense and value, because of the private world he has inside himself too? We think that we understand each other, but we never do.[5]

Later he comments to the director on the slippery, changing nature of reality:

I'm only asking to try to find out if you really see yourself now in the same way that you saw yourself, for instance, once upon a time in the past, with all the illusions you had then, with everything inside and outside yourself as it seemed then—and not only seemed, but really

The tormented family of "characters" reappears mysteriously at the end of *Six Characters in Search of an Author* at the Oregon Shakespeare Festival's second company in Portland, Oregon (now Portland Center Stage). Because each of the characters tells a different version of their tormented family history, it is impossible for either the actors whose rehearsal they interrupt or the actual audience members to determine what is the truth of the characters' situation. Pirandello leaves us with an unsolvable puzzle.

was! Well then, look back on those illusions, those ideas that you don't have anymore, on all those things that no longer seem the same to you. Don't you feel that not only this stage is falling away from your feet but so is the earth itself, and that all these realities of today are going to seem tomorrow as if they had been an illusion?[6]

Pirandello's play challenges the audience members not to be relentless in pursuing the truth about one another, because the truth is impossible to ascertain. In the difficult areas of human relationships, Pirandello suggests that compassion may be the best we can offer.

Plays that communicate the existential, tragicomic perspective embodied by *Six Characters* range from the realistic plays of Anton Chekhov to the absurd plays of Samuel Beckett. Tragicomedy probably offers the least affirmation of any of the theatrical genres. These plays are usually disturbing and present more questions than answers. The mixture of forms as well as the frequently provoking stage images are deliberate challenges to complacency or certainty. Tragicomedy offers neither the catharsis of tragedy, nor the moral satisfaction of melodrama, nor the emotional release through laughter of comedy or farce. The laughter of tragicomedy is laughter that is interrupted when we are reminded once again of how genuinely painful the situation actually is.

In tragicomedy, the characters are cut off from a fixed value system and at the same time are cut off from one another. The condition of loneliness or alienation is at the heart of tragicomedy. We have observed that tragic characters are also alone, but their isolation heightens the grandeur and courage of their actions. The scale of the characters in tragicomedy is greatly reduced. These are small characters beset by anxiety, failure, and emptiness.

American playwrights who write tragicomedy include both Edward Albee and Sam Shepard. Both Albee and Shepard focus on breakdowns in the American family—breakdowns that result from the spiritual isolation of the characters. In *Buried Child* and *True West*, Shepard's distinctly American characters are rough around the edges, restless, and in search of something that can be called home. Humor in Shepard's plays is interrupted by the very real threat of violence that always simmers underneath the surface. By contrast, Albee's characters, in such plays as *Who's Afraid of Virginia Woolf?* and *A Delicate Balance*, are more educated and upper-class than Shepard's, but their education becomes part of the source of their spiritual crisis.

Like the American tragicomic playwrights, the Russian playwright Anton Chekhov focuses on a realistic social group of family, friends, and associates. Of all the tragicomic playwrights, Chekhov seems to be the most gentle with his characters and yet the most unforgiving. As a group, his plays present situations in which the gulf between people cannot be bridged. The isolation and self-focus are complete. For example, in the poignant final moments of his play *The Cherry Orchard*, the characters are making plans to depart. But they are so absorbed with their personal needs that they fail to provide for the care of their aged servant, Firs. Each exits thinking someone else has arranged to take Firs to a nursing home. As they go off, calling out their good-byes, with the house bolted from the outside, it becomes apparent to the audience that Firs has been forgotten. The last image of the play is of Firs, locked alone in the house to die, with the sound first of a breaking string and then of an ax chopping down the cherry trees.

The ending of Beckett's *Waiting for Godot* is widely considered a definitional moment in tragicomedy, when the two tramps repeat for the last time, "Let's go." But once again, they cannot leave the stage and remain sitting, waiting into eternity as the light fades. What sustains these two characters in the end is their companionship, however difficult and contentious. There is genuine affection between the two characters, and they choose to stay together rather than part.

Tragicomic plays involve human desperation, yet they are some of the most eloquent theatrical works of our times. In their arresting and imaginative creation lies the challenge of the playwright to confront our own illusions—about ourselves and the world we inhabit—without any of the protective devices that we usually employ to hold back the truth.

Farce

Whereas comedy generally takes as its subject some kind of social critique, **farce** is concerned with the humorous possibilities of the moment. Farce attacks pretentiousness of all kinds and uses the social situation as a launching pad for the ridiculous. Farce is about anarchy, about breaking all the rules. Taking on authority is one of the trademarks of farce, and frequently the characters are only one step ahead of the law. In the film *Animal House*, the Deltas, a group of low-life fraternity brothers, scheme to destroy the obnoxious dean and his pal the mayor as well as the rich and condescending members of the student elite. This film is a classic example of a farce involving a rowdy assault on authority. Similarly, in the Marx Brothers' films, Groucho, Harpo, and Chico invade various forms of high society and bring them crashing down.

Troublemaker, or The Freaking Kick-A Adventures of Bradley Boatright offers a title that captures the spirit of rebellion permeating this play by Dan LeFranc. A fantasy adventure that shifts between the home shared by a twelve-year-old boy and his mother and the world of comic book superheroes, this production (2013) is part of the new play development program at Berkeley Repertory Theatre. The actors are Ben Mehl, Chad Goodridge, and Matt Bradley, directed by Lila Neugebauer.

Farce almost always highlights actors rather than playwrights. Performances are memorable not because of the playwright's words but because of the comic genius of the actor. Farce has a brilliant history in the United States if we consider as a whole the work of actors on the stage, in film, and on television. It is not surprising that farce would flourish in a nation whose origins are revolutionary and whose goals are democratic. The actors of farce rebel against notions of aristocracy, against the imposition of high culture, against institutions that have lost touch with the people, against all forms of arbitrary rules and hierarchical power structures.

Jim Carrey is an actor known for creating characters who have a wild, anarchic streak. He performs with a highly energized physical abandon that seems to defy the bodily limitations of most humans. In films such as *The Mask* (1994) and *Liar Liar* (1997) he challenges authority with an attitude of defiance well suited to contemporary farce. His film *The Mask* offers another model of a typical plot in farce. Carrey's character, Stanley Ipkiss, is the little man at the bottom of the ladder at the bank where he works. He is taken advantage of by everyone, abused by his landlady, swindled by his auto mechanics. He wears the ultimate in "geek" ties and pajamas.

The Marx Brothers honed their acting skills in vaudeville before turning their special brand of lunacy into films. Animals were frequently featured as part of their performance onstage and in the movies. The French theatre practitioners Antonin Artaud and Samuel Beckett acknowledged the Marx Brothers' influence on their own work well before the comedy team was taken seriously in the United States. Major films of the Marx Brothers include *Duck Soup* and *A Night at the Opera.*

But by placing a mysterious mask on his face, Carrey breaks through all the social restraint of his "Mr. Nice Guy" role, throws caution to the wind, and becomes the embodiment of physical and spiritual anarchy. With a ludicrous green face and an outrageously suave wardrobe, he robs the bank where he works, defeats the town gangsters, and has the police dancing in the streets while he plays the maracas in his persona as "Cuban Pete." With the broadest possible physical humor, sometimes even rendered through cartoon images, he revenges himself on everyone who previously pushed him around. Carrey's character says of the power of the mask, "It brings your innermost desires to life." The same could be said of farce.

Writing about the Theatre

The unique structural elements of the drama discussed in Chapter 12 and the views of human existence that shape dramatic genres are foundational for the work of the playwright. The study of structure and genre is also essential to the

Stanley Ipkiss, played by Jim Carrey, re-creates himself as a bizarre, but romantic, hero dancing with Cameron Diaz in *The Mask*. The masked character fulfills the fantasies of the nice guy who always finishes last.

work of two other theatre writers: the dramaturg and the critic. The dramaturg and the critic are particularly concerned with analyzing the work of the playwright in connection with the production of plays. They seek to understand what distinguishes the ideas in the play and what distinguishes the play as a work of art. Frequently dramaturgs and critics have similar backgrounds and interests. They must both be broadly educated in the theatre and be strong and creative writers. In fact, the same individual may work sometimes as a dramaturg and sometimes as a critic. For example, for many years Michael

Feingold served as the chief critic of *The Village Voice* in New York City and currently writes for *TheaterMania*. He is also a highly regarded dramaturg as well as a translator and adaptor. Each of these roles requires a different perspective.

The dramaturg can be seen as a writer and thinker engaged at the beginning of theatre making, whereas the critic participates at the end. The dramaturg is part of the collaborative process of creating the work; the critic assesses the work when it is performed onstage for an audience. The dramaturg is on the inside, the critic on the outside. But the dramaturg must maintain a certain independence if he or she is to serve the production well. And the critic must be an engaged and respectful member of the larger theatre community in order to be effective, while remaining entirely independent of the production process. Michael Feingold could not review a production for which he was dramaturg. We now consider the contributions of these two important theatre writers who serve both theatre practitioners and theatre audiences.

The Dramaturg

More and more frequently, resident theatre companies—organizations producing a season of plays—employ at least one staff member who works as a dramaturg. The dramaturg is an ongoing member of the company and is involved continuously with the selection of plays and research and writing about those plays. Although the dramaturg is a relatively new position in the American theatre, the idea of the dramaturg is much older; it is usually credited to the German critic G. E. Lessing, who wrote in the late eighteenth century. Stephen Weeks, who is both a dramaturg and a teacher of dramaturgy and playwriting, sees the dramaturg as occupying a unique position in a theatre organization:

> Dramaturgy is a fluid enterprise and dramaturgs wear many hats. Whereas we might think of actors or directors as having specific, well-defined responsibilities, the dramaturg is

Passing Strange (2007) is a new musical by the composer and performer Stew, produced at the Public Theater where one of Oskar Eustis's primary goals as artistic director is the development of new work. "On a piece like *Passing Strange* it started with a singer in Joe's Pub to whom we said, 'Have you ever thought of making a theatre piece out of your songs?' and he said, 'I've never been to a piece of theatre.' Now he's opening on Broadway next month. It takes three and a half years to do that. You invest the time and figure out the way for each particular art form."[7]

a theatrical generalist. The dramaturg makes connections, starts conversations, builds bridges.[8]

In Chapter 10, we discussed the work of Oskar Eustis, who served as the dramaturg at the Eureka Theatre in San Francisco and collaborated with the playwright Tony Kushner on the development of *Angels in America*. Eustis is now the artistic director of the Public Theater in New York City. As dramaturg at the Eureka Theatre, he focused on encouraging the development of new plays and bringing those plays into production. Like Eustis, dramaturgs at other theatre companies provide feedback and assistance to playwrights who are creating new work; and, as Stephen Weeks observes, they must demonstrate great sensitivity to the needs of the play and the needs of the playwright:

> The goal is usually to assist the writer to realize his or her vision for the play. This is a complex task, and the dramaturg might need to serve as a guide, a cheerleader, a surrogate audience member, a critic, or all of these things. A good dramaturg will also know when to leave the playwright to his or her own devices and good judgment.

Tom Bryant, dramaturg for *Apollo*, contrasts the perspective of the dramaturg with that of the director, who is also often concerned with new play development.

> Directors tend to be very pragmatic. They have to focus on immediate production results. Given production demands, directors tend to ask, "What can I do with this text onstage? What kind of actor choices would I make here? What kind of choices would the designers make?" These are all production-oriented choices. The dramaturg looks at the text, beyond the current production choices, and asks, "Does this work as a scene? Does this work as an act? Is there strong momentum here?" They think beyond the current production to the play's future productions. When directors face literary issues in a script they sometimes tend to compensate for the material by production adjustments. They think, "Oh, this isn't working so well. Maybe what I'll do is create a piece of staging that really makes the rhythm faster here." This may solve the problem in the current production but it doesn't necessarily solve the inherent literary problem in terms of the text of the play. So part of what the specialization in dramaturgy becomes is helping the playwright fix those problems on the page.[9]

The dramaturg also works with the artistic director of the theatre to select a provocative and complementary group of plays for the season and must have a wide knowledge of classical as well as recent plays. Another part of the dramaturg's work is to research background materials related to a particular play—first to provide necessary information to the director and the actors, and then to write introductory material for the audience to be presented in the program or possibly in a lobby display. Research that the dramaturg does for the theatre company may be

WORKING IN THE THEATRE

Summary of the Dramaturg's Responsibilities

- To keep up with developments in the drama.
- To assist playwrights in the development of new plays.
- To advise the artistic director on selecting plays.
- To study the play text.
- To research appropriate historical materials for the director, designers, and actors.
- To research production history.
- To provide assistance with textual analysis and meaning of words.
- To assist with cuts or adaptation of the text if appropriate.
- To attend rehearsals and provide the director with feedback.
- To write program notes.
- To prepare lobby displays.
- To contribute to public relations materials.
- To lead discussions before or after the show.

presented through discussion or informally written notes or summaries. Dramaturgs frequently participate in the table work sessions at the beginning of the rehearsal period to explain the historical and philosophical background of the play and to provide resource materials such as photographs, maps, and biographies. They may also be responsible for locating highly specialized information. For example, Nilo Cruz's Pulitzer Prize–winning play *Anna in the Tropics* takes place in a cigar factory, and the actors must learn how to roll cigars. The dramaturg may arrange for a cigar maker to come to one or more rehearsals to demonstrate these skills. The areas of research the dramaturg may be called upon to pursue are limitless.

Once the rehearsal process is under way, the dramaturg must engage in more formal

Necessary Skills and Talents of the Dramaturg

- Love of dramatic literature.
- Fascination with research.
- Wide knowledge of dramatic literature and theatre history.
- Strong analytical skills.
- Strong writing skills.
- Commitment to collaborative work.
- Teaching skills.
- Ability to clearly articulate observations made in rehearsals.

writing for the program and, sometimes, for lobby displays. The lobby display is being used by an increasing number of theatres to expand the amount of contextual information available to audience members. The lobby display also offers the dramaturg an opportunity to use visual materials such as photographs, historical objects, and video clips to support written statements. In the program notes and the lobby display, the dramaturg communicates why the company has chosen to do a particular play and why this play is important for the community that makes up the audience. Background materials are presented to enrich the audience's understanding of the significance of the events in the play. Most of all, the dramaturg shares the excitement that the theatre company feels in undertaking the production, an excitement that should be infectious for the audience.

The Critic

The critic has been in existence almost as long as there has been theatre. Aristotle's writing on drama, which has been part of our discussion of structure and genre, is considered a work of criticism. In *The Poetics*, Aristotle writes about what makes a successful and admirable play. Over the centuries, critics have followed Aristotle with heated arguments about what makes good theatre or art and what place theatre should have in a particular society. Most critics are passionate about their views and recognize something vital and essential in the theatre, although they have strongly divided opinions about what the essence of good theatre is.

Sometimes a critic's ideas are formulated slowly and represent a cumulative process of evaluation. But often criticism is written quickly, particularly when it takes the form of a review composed immediately following a play's opening to be published in a newspaper or online within a day or two. Some writers and theatre practitioners would separate critics and reviewers into different categories, concluding that the role of the critic is to try to answer larger questions about the significance of a work of theatre than a reviewer can tackle in the sprint to the deadline. But with that reservation in mind, we will examine the role of the contemporary critic in relationship to the theatre.

When the dramaturg writes a program note or prepares a lobby display, it is quite clear who the targeted readers are: the people who have chosen to come to see this particular play. And when the dramaturg provides analysis and research early on in the production process, he or she knows the director and the actors for whom that work is intended and how it is to be used. It is less clear for whom the critic is writing, and so it is profitable to explore who the critic's audience is in order to assess the role the critic plays.

The most immediate source in which a critic may publish an article or review in response to a play is a newspaper, a magazine, or an online site. The readers of this publication may or may not become audience members, and many of them will look to a review to provide guidance about whether a production is worth their time and money. In this regard the review functions as advice for the consumer and there is no doubt that commentary published immediately after a play opens is expected to offer judgment about the production's overall merit. But the critic has a larger obligation to the general reader than merely to indicate thumbs-up or thumbs-down.

Julius Novick, a well-known critic who has spent decades writing about the theatre, sees his responsibility as communicating the experience of the performance as fully as possible to the reader who has not yet seen the play:

> But our obligation and our joy as writers is to convey what we have seen and heard and thought and felt at the theatre, as truthfully and vividly, as gracefully and clearly, and with as deep an understanding as we can, and, if possible, to refract the truth about the show we've just seen through our individual selves to a larger truth about the theatre and a still larger truth about the world.[10]

In Novick's judgment the critic must be open and sensitive to the theatre event and then be ready to put that experience into words in order to distill its meaning. There is also a recognition that describing and interpreting one's own experience of an event is not a simple matter. Writing good criticism is itself an art form, requiring creative choices and drawing the significant parts into a coherent whole.

As a way of organizing one's responses to a performance, Novick proposes that the critic answer four questions.

1. What is the work itself trying to do?
2. How well has it done it?
3. Was it worth doing?
4. Why was it or wasn't it worth doing?

WORKING IN THE THEATRE

Summary of the Critic's Responsibilities

- To do appropriate preparation before the performance such as reading the play and researching background on the play, playwright, or performance style.

- To attend the performance in an alert and receptive state of mind.

- To write a review that focuses on the particular production, not the preferences or cleverness of the reviewer.

- To provide readers with a vivid sense of the audience's experience and the style and ideas of the play and the production.

- To provide theatre practitioners with constructive feedback about their work.

- To engage in a public dialogue about the significance of work being done in the theatre.

And he says of the fourth question, "That's where the bones are buried. That can get us into the relation between the work and the world, the subject to which all the great critics are drawn."[11] In these questions, Novick leads the critic away from judging a theatre work according to personal preference and instead asks the critic to consider the terms of the play itself and the production of that play.

Furthermore, when critics ask Novick's four questions, they are setting up an apparatus to address a second set of readers in addition to potential audience members: the theatre practitioners who have produced the play. A productive review, which serves the theatre profession well, gives the practitioners vital feedback about how successfully they communicated their ideas and how their work was received. Directors, actors, and designers work very hard to craft their storytelling and expressive stage metaphors. A thoughtful response from an insightful critic can be very important to the theatre artists in assessing the impact of their work. The actor Billy Crudup says he hopes that critics will engage in a dialogue with the production by answering important questions for him:

> What was successful? What wasn't successful? Why? Is that interpretation an interesting interpretation?[12]

Of course, all theatre practitioners seek approval of their stage efforts. But the responsible critic contributes far more to the health of the theatre by considering the artistic choices made than by merely announcing which actor was a hit and which one wasn't and whether the scenery and costumes were dazzling.

ARTISTIC FOUNDATIONS

The Necessary Skills and Talents of the Critic

- Enthusiasm for the theatre.
- Belief in the importance of the arts in the life of the community.
- Wide knowledge of dramatic literature and theatre history.
- Understanding of the contributions of playwrights, directors, actors, and designers.
- Strong writing skills.
- Ability to communicate the experience of the theatre performance through lively, accessible language.
- Ability to understand symbolic and metaphorical constructs.
- Ability to interpret the meaning of a play in relation to philosophical, cultural, or political concerns of the community.
- Ability to generate interest and excitement about the theatre for readers.

Although critics are writing most obviously for those who are involved with a production as audience members or producers, they are also participating in a larger conversation about art and culture that extends to many people beyond the immediate radius of a particular production. Criticism is read by those interested in the arts and in the relationship between art and society whether they are other critics, appreciators of art, producers of art, or academics and students of all backgrounds. Frank Rich was for many years the head theatre critic of *The New York Times*. He now writes what may be called cultural criticism that is particularly concerned with the direction of our country and the various forces that affect political decision making. He draws heavily on his involvement with the theatre to explain contemporary actions through comparisons with characters of great playwrights and by considering political performances in light of the way actors construct stage identities.

Through their writing, critics also address readers of the future by creating a record of the impact of the theatre performance. One of the defining factors of theatre production is its nature as a live event. As we observed at the beginning of the book, the theatre actually exists only during the performance itself with an audience present. Films are by their very nature preserved for future generations. A theatre performance can be documented through video or film, but that documentation does not re-create the actual event of the performance. By exploring the visual, aural, kinesthetic, emotional, and intellectual experience of being an audience member at a particular performance, the critic leaves a written impression, however imperfect, of the nuances and excitement communicated by the actors' work. This written record of the most eloquent details of the performance offers students of the art of theatre the chance to understand what was meaningful in a given time and place, years after the actors and designers who made the work no longer hold forth on the stage.

Two Reviews of *Medea*

Following are two reviews of contemporary productions of the Greek tragedy *Medea*. The first review considers the production done by the Classical Theatre of Harlem; the second evaluates the production done by the Abbey Theatre of Ireland. Both reviews were published in *The New York Times* in 2002. The reviews of *Medea* are included here because they allow us to continue our discussion of this play begun in Chapter 2 in the section on ancient Greek theatre and

continued in this chapter's examination of genre and tragedy. The reviews also illustrate the manner in which two different critics approach constructing a review. In each case, the critic creates a vivid sense of the performance by describing the work of the actors and the arrangement of the physical space. Both critics also tell us what distinguishes these productions and how the play's conflicts are interpreted for modern audiences. The reviews demonstrate that the critics have studied the play, its history, and other productions in order to be authoritative in assessing the work of the theatre companies involved.

Passions of *Medea*, Brought Up to Date
By D. J. R. Bruckner, *The New York Times*, April 16, 2002

Every performance of "Medea" is an adaptation. Euripides' text is a highly selective commentary on a hugely popular series of legends about this semidivine psychotic, and we can only dimly perceive aspects of what he meant to say about them. We also have far from perfect knowledge of stagecraft in the fifth century B.C. So even those rare performances given in Euripides' own language are adaptations.

That said, the one adapted and directed by Alfred Preisser for the Classical Theatre of Harlem, running until April 28 at the Harlem School of the Arts, is special. Its language is current street talk. Its chorus dances, chants spare lines and occasionally sings to music of striking ingenuity by Kelvyn Fell and David Red Harrington. But this chorus does not carry the burden of the narrative as

in Euripides. Here the whole story is told by the three characters: Medea (April Yvette Thompson), Kreon (Arthur French) and Jason (Lawrence Winslow).

This radical personalizing of the lethal conflicts among men and a woman, between different nations, and between mortals and divinities brings out surprising qualities and instabilities in the characters. I suspect that no matter how many versions I see in the future, my perception of them all will be affected by the revelations here.

It is very clear that Kreon, King of Corinth, is not arrogant or unfeeling when he banishes Medea so that Jason will be free to marry the king's daughter; he simply cannot perceive the justice of this barbarian woman's refusal to lose her husband and her sons. And

Jason really believes he honors Medea by leaving her and marrying a princess so that Medea's sons will become royal heirs.

As for Medea herself, the transformation is haunting. There is no mistaking her outrage and injury when she spits curses of defiance at both men and reminds them of the murderous betrayals of her own people she committed in the past for Jason's glory. But in this version her tenderness toward her children touches Kreon and Jason at times, and her fury at Jason's betrayal makes her murder of those children appear to be an act of passionate satisfaction.

At 70 minutes, Mr. Preisser's "Medea" is considerably shorter than most, but it sends one away with more to think about than most. It also causes more anxiety and excitement in the audience. Viewers sit on opposite sides of a relatively intimate space, and the rising hostility between Jason and Medea seems to spill out into the audience. That a couple of audience members uttered audible replies to a few of the lines at the performance I saw cannot be a rare occurrence. It is very hard to remain silent.

Inevitably, in a revision so extensive, some things are lost. The gritty idiom removes the aura of mystery surrounding the action in Euripides' play. And there are other disjunctures. But do they add up to too great a price? Probably not, for most.

This ambitious undertaking puts 19 actors onstage. But of course the overall effect depends most on the principal three. Mr. French gives Kreon the appearance of stunned dignity that is absolutely demanded by Mr. Preisser's reading of the story. Mr. Winslow makes Jason so honestly ignorant of how mortal is his betrayal of Medea that he elicits more pity than scorn. And Ms. Thompson's Medea is a real hell cat, a bundle of contradictions that are all the more threatening for seeming so natural in someone who is half human but who has power no human can control or even comprehend.

MEDEA By Euripides; adapted and directed by Alfred Preisser; choreography by Tracy Johnson and Angela Hughes; sets by Anne Lomel; lighting by Christopher McElroen; costumes by Kimberly Glennon; sound by Stefan Jacobs; stage manager, Frantz Cayo; fight direction by T. J. Glenn; original music and songs by Kelvyn Bell and David Red Harrington. Presented by the Classical Theatre of Harlem, Mr. McElroen, co-founder and executive director; Mr. Preisser, co-founder and artistic director. At the Harlem School of the Arts Theatre, 645 St. Nicholas Avenue, near 141st Street, Hamilton Heights.

WITH: Arthur French (Kreon), Joan Green (Nurse), Angela Hughes (Fate), Zainab Jah (Choral Leader/Death), April Yvette Thompson (Medea) and Lawrence Winslow (Jason).

Next Wave Review; A *Medea* Fit for the World of Today
By Ben Brantley, *The New York Times*, October 4, 2002

The word has gone out in Corinth that there's a celebrity in pain in the vicinity. And when the groupies who sniff for blood wounds among the incredibly famous arrive at her house, Medea doesn't disappoint.

There she is, as embodied with a harrowing lack of vanity by the brilliant Fiona Shaw, her recognizable features smudged by unhappiness, her eyes hidden by the formal shield of dark glasses, her mismatched wardrobe a thrown-on hash of running shoes, a cardigan and a little print dress. Why, she might have stepped from those pages of The National Enquirer devoted to stars foolish enough to leave home without makeup. The question is: Will she talk to us? Will she let us in on her truly sensational problems?

You bet she will. How satisfying, after all, can revenge be unless you have an audience to reflect it, to magnify it, to turn it into legend? Without their urging, how will you know who you really are?

In the thrilling Abbey Theatre production of Euripides' "Medea," which runs at the Harvey Theatre of the Brooklyn Academy of Music through Oct. 12, Greek tragedy's most spectacularly vengeful woman has rematerialized in the dawning years of the 21st century. And it is, to tell the truth, a little frightening to see how comfortably this volcanically uncomfortable woman fits into the world of today.

What Ms. Shaw and the director, Deborah Warner,

who collaborated so memorably on their staging of T. S. Eliot's "Waste Land," have achieved here seems so obvious, when you think about it, that you're amazed it hasn't been done before. For this "Medea" homes in on the parallels between the very form of Greek tragedy—with its dialogue between uncommon heroes and heroines and the common folk of the chorus—and an age in which private breakdowns, breakups and humiliations have become public rituals.

Of course if this were the only point of Ms. Warner's "Medea," it wouldn't have turned out to be the most essential ticket of this theatre season. This isn't one of those stagings in which a clever concept reduces characters to glossy illustrations.

The miracle of this "Medea" is how completely it integrates its ideas of a latter-day culture of celebrity into a classic text, freshly translated by Kenneth McLeish and Frederic Raphael, without ever seeming to warp the spirit of the original. The anxious perfume that saturates this production is a compound of the passion, terror and existential ambivalence that have plagued humans for as long as they have been able to think.

Ms. Shaw's Medea has little in common with the usual majestically angry sorceress who is guided by one idée fixe: to avenge herself on her husband, Jason, for whom she

betrayed her homeland and who has now left her for the young princess of Corinth. There is scant evidence of the commanding icy intellect so elegantly incarnated by Diana Rigg in Jonathan Kent's production of a proto-feminist "Medea" on Broadway in 1994.

It's not that you doubt the intelligence of Ms. Shaw's Medea. But her lacerating misfortunes have broken the circuits of that intelligence, and her responses are a toxic jumble. She seems to wear her nerves outside her skin. Numbness and excruciating pain, shrill anger and mordant, bizarre humor flit across her raw features in disjunctive parade.

Set in a half-finished courtyard littered with children's toys and cinder blocks (the designer is Tom Pye), suggesting a life interrupted, the entire production seems to occur in that heightened, instinct-addling realm that occurs during times of emergency. The evening begins in a state of breathlessness that never really lets up. And as upsetting as much of it is, the show radiates such high theatrical energy and insight that you can't help grinning through most of it.

The first image is of Medea's Nurse (Siobhan McCarthy), represented here as a student au pair type, rushing onto the stage with a handful of knives. She is also, it turns out, carrying bottles of pills. And she

proceeds to hide these commonplace household objects, which in this context have suddenly turned threatening.

This interpolated scene is inspired in its banal immediacy, translating abstract terror into specific and familiar physical terms. You can't help feeling like a visitor who has showed up at just the wrong moment. Of course, you keep staring. And if you don't, there's the chorus of five townswomen who emerge from the audience and swarm onto the stage as if to act as your proxy.

They have the feverish look of fans addicted to real-life soap operas, like the kind of people who rushed to the site of Nicole Simpson's murder and stood in line for the trial of Michael C. Skakel. Their relentless talk to Medea, shaped by a sooty mix of empathy and prurience, seems perfectly natural. So, more surprisingly, does Medea's willingness to respond to them.

Then again, as a notorious exile now spurned by even the husband who brought her here, who else does she have to talk to? Besides, as Jason (Jonathan Cake) later says nastily, he and Medea have become people who would "rather be sung about than sing."

This production acutely accents the talk of reputation and fame and its rewards. And you can see that Jason and, in her more befuddled way, Medea are quite keen to put forth their respective versions of their lives together. Medea knows very well she is playing to a crowd and, by extension, to history. She accepts as her due the applause that the chorus gives after she has successfully pleaded with Kreon (Struan Rodger), the king of Crete, to postpone her exile.

If it sounds as if Ms. Shaw's Medea is a smooth spinmeister, then I'm misrepresenting her. What's so mesmerizing and truly frightening about her performance is how cogently she evokes a mind that is anything but clear. This Medea is an all too sensitive instrument played upon by overwhelming forces that come from both without and within.

Among these is simple brute lust. The superb Mr. Cake's vanity-driven Jason may not be his wife's match in ingenuity. But he knows exactly where to touch Medea to turn her into jelly. Their most rancorous arguments are punctuated by perverse sexual sparks that threaten to subdue Medea into passivity. And then the spell is broken, and she emerges all the more addled and angry.

The play's grotesque climax (mercilessly rendered here), in which Medea murders her two sons, does not seem a foregone conclusion. Ms. Shaw and Ms. Warner have created a Medea who isn't even sure herself how she will act from one moment to the next. There are stretches, as Medea rants about her diabolical plans for vengeance,

when you think, "Oh, she's just playing," or to use the preferred psychobabble, "acting out."

For this Medea has a wide-ranging mind that, even in abject pain, keeps shifting perspectives on her. Suddenly, without warning, she'll do something like pick up a toy gun and simulate murder with a goofy smile. And she's funny when she's deriding her husband and his bride-to-be, finding the idea of them so unspeakable that she's reduced to making "bleah" and "ick" noises. But the noises also suggest an eloquent woman for whom words are no longer adequate.

When, toward the play's end, a messenger (Derek Hutchinson) arrives to describe the excruciating deaths of Kreon and his daughter, Jason's intended, Ms. Shaw's face goes dead white and still, showing flickers of gratification and just as often of incomprehension that her plan has come to fruition.

And therein lies the real genius of Ms. Shaw's portraiture. Real life seldom affords the tidy motives of murder mysteries or the stark psychological blueprints of novels about serial killers. And the recent spate of reality television serials have confirmed that famous people are never just the cleanly drawn cartoons we would like them to be. Witness the on-camera disintegration of Anna Nicole Smith.

Ms. Shaw and Ms. Warner have created one of the most

human Medeas ever, precisely because they have refused to simplify her. Medea's acts may be monstrous, but the woman who performs them is a mass of confused impulses and thwarted drives that elude easy categorization. It is this very blurriness that makes her so vivid, so haunting and so damningly easy to identify with.

MEDEA By Euripides; directed by Deborah Warner; translated by Kenneth McLeish and Frederic Raphael; set by Tom Pye; costumes by Jacqueline Durran; original lighting by Peter Mumford; associate lighting designer, Michael Gunning; soundscape, Mel Mercier; sound by David Meschter. Produced in association with Max Weitzenhoffer, Roger Berlind, Old Vic Productions, Nica Burns for the Really Useful Theaters and Jedediah Wheeler. The Abbey Theatre presented by the Brooklyn Academy of Music, Alan H. Fishman, chairman; William I. Campbell, vice chairman; Karen Brooks Hopkins, president; Joseph V. Melillo, executive producer. At the Brooklyn Academy of Music, Harvey Theatre, 651 Fulton Street, Fort Greene.

WITH: Fiona Shaw (Medea), Siobhan McCarthy (Nurse), Robin Laing (Tutor), Struan Rodger (Kreon), Jonathan Cake (Jason), Joseph Mydell (Aegeus), Dylan Denton (Son) and Derek Hutchinson (Messenger).

Summary

The division of drama into genres is a way of identifying different perspectives on human existence. Tragedy focuses on human mortality and often ends in death or disaster. But tragedy is not a pessimistic form of drama. Tragic characters assume heroic stature as they struggle to control their own destinies and take responsibility for the consequences of their actions. Tragedy flourished as a form of drama in the Greek and Elizabethan theatres, which produced such masterpieces as *Oedipus Rex* and *Hamlet*.

Comedy is concerned with the human ability to endure. Comedy looks at the way human weakness leads to the ridiculous and the ludicrous. But in spite of all their failures, comic characters find a way to go on. Comedy frequently involves a group of characters separated by misunderstanding who are reconciled in the end.

Tragicomedy reflects the anxiety of life. Plays of this genre shift between serious and comic perspectives, and each view undermines the other. In plays such as *Six Characters in Search of an Author* and *Waiting for Godot*, the nature of reality is uncertain, and no fixed meaning underlies the characters' existence. The plays emphasize the characters' frailty and isolation. Tragicomedy also challenges traditional ideas of dramatic structure by questioning the ability of language to communicate or the ability of characters to act in any purposeful way.

Two other genres, melodrama and farce, have become very popular on television and in film as well as in the theatre. Melodrama builds on clear-cut conflicts between good and evil. Farce is a comic form that attacks pretentiousness and all forms of authority.

The dramaturg is an additional member of a theatre company who is responsible for assisting playwrights to develop new work and helping directors and actors interpret plays they are preparing for production. The dramaturg may provide background research as well as dramatic analysis in the service of both the rehearsal process and publications related to a production. The critic evaluates a theatre production when it is performed for an audience. The critic is responsible for analyzing the production for potential audience members and also for providing constructive feedback to the theatre practitioners.

Topics for Discussion and Writing

1. What are the fundamental differences between tragedy and comedy? How can they be considered as complementary genres rather than as opposites?

2. How does comedy offer social criticism? Where do you see social criticism in comedies in the theatre or in films? Because we laugh, do we take social criticism less seriously in comedy than in other genres?

3. What is the philosophical perspective expressed by tragicomedy? What view of life is expressed by the situation of the characters in *Waiting for Godot*?

For interviews with some of the dramaturgs in this chapter and other resources, please visit www.mhhe.com/creativespirit6e

The World's a Stage: TPS1107 Theatre in Society, 3rd edition
Department of Theatre and Performance Studies
Kennesaw State University

PHOTO CREDITS

Front Cover Photos

Top Left: *Peter and the* Starcatcher, by Dave Barry and Ridley Pearson. Adapted for the stage by Rick Elice. Directed by Karen Robinson with choreography by Nicole Livieratos. Produced by the Department of Theatre and Performance Studies, Kennesaw State University, Spring 2017. Photo credit: Robert Pack, Widescreen Video Productions.

Middle Right: *Ruined,* by Lynn Nottage. Directed by Karen Robinson with choreography by Theresa M. Howard. Produced by the Department of Theatre and Performance Studies, Kennesaw State University, Spring 2014. Photo credit: Robert Pack, Widescreen Video Productions.

Bottom Left: *Three Sisters*
By Anton Chekhov, adapted by Tracy Letts. Directed by Rick Lombardo. Produced by the Department of Theatre and Performance Studies, Kennesaw State University, Spring 2017. Photo credit: Robert Pack, Widescreen Video Productions.

Background: *In the Red and Brown Water*. By Tarell Alvin McCraney. Directed by Angela Farr Schiller. Produced by the Department of Theatre and Performance Studies, Kennesaw State University, Fall 2016. Photo credit: Donald Woodruff.

Back Cover Photos

Top Right: *The Followers: A Retelling of The Bacchae*, by Margaret Baldwin. Directed by Michael Haverty with choreography by Ofir Nahari. Produced by the Department of Theatre and Performance Studies, Kennesaw State University, Fall 2016. Photo credit: Robert Pack, Widescreen Video Productions.

Bottom Right: *Spring Awakening*, by Duncan Sheik and Steven Sater. Directed by Rick Lombardo with choreography by Sonya Tayeh. Produced by the Department of Theatre and Performance Studies, Kennesaw State University, Spring 2016. Photo credit: Robert Pack, Widescreen Video Productions.

Background: *The* Killer, by Eugène Ionesco. Directed by Peter Torpey. Department of Theatre and Performance Studies, Kennesaw State University, Spring 2016.
Photo credit: Robert Pack, Widescreen Video Productions.